P9-BJR-219

Legal Rights,
Local Wrongs

SUNY series, Restructuring and School Change

H. Dickson Corbett and Betty Lou Whitford, Editors

Legal Rights, Local Wrongs

When Community Control Collides with Educational Equity

Kevin G. Welner

with a Foreword by Jeannie Oakes and Martin Lipton

STATE UNIVERSITY OF NEW YORK PRESS

WITHDRAWN

Published by
State University of New York Press, Albany

© 2001 State University of New York

All rights reserved

Printed in the United States of America

No part of this book may be used or reproduced in any manner whatsoever without written permission. No part of this book may be stored in a retrieval system or transmitted in any form or by any means including electronic, electrostatic, magnetic tape, mechanical, photocopying, recording, or otherwise without the prior permission in writing of the publisher.

For information, address State University of New York Press,
90 State Street, Suite 700, Albany, N.Y., 12207

Production by Michael Haggett
Marketing by Michael Campochiaro

Library of Congress Cataloging-in-Publication Data

Welner, Kevin Grant, 1963–
    Legal rights, local wrongs : when community control collides with
educational equity / Kevin G. Welner ; with a foreword by Jeannie Oakes
and Martin Lipton.
        p. cm. — (SUNY series, restructuring and school change)
Includes bibliographical references and index.
ISBN 0-7914-5127-5 (alk. paper) — ISBN 0-7914-5128-3 (pbk. : alk. paper)
    1. Educational equalization — United States — Case studies.   2. Track
system (Education) — United States — Case studies.   3. Ability grouping in
education — United States — Case studies.   4. Educational change — United
States — Case studies.   I. Title.   II. Series.

LC213.2 .W39 2001
379.2'6 — dc21   2001034166

10 9 8 7 6 5 4 3 2 1

Contents

List of Figures

List of Tables

Foreword

Schools are essential battlegrounds on which Americans fight to define and achieve opportunity, equality, and fairness. In and around our schools we witness the broad range of politically powerful forces that maintain social stratification. We see society's powerful arrayed steadfastly against other forces struggling for social justice. These struggles appear in the form of democratic moments, arrayed against power and privilege. And yet, through the lenses provided in this book, we see that even those who appear to be the weakest, when allied with the courts and armed by law, can make a difference. These changes will never bring enough improvement, and the gains will always be years or generations too late. Nevertheless, here, Kevin Welner offers reason for encouragement, revealing important insights into current struggles and proposing theory to guide how we proceed. His research and stories are not happy, but they are hopeful, and they deserve our closest attention.

Welner tells the stories of four mid-sized United States cities struggling under the watchful eye of the judiciary to educate diverse, heterogeneous groups of young people. Too powerless to battle on their own for socially just schooling, citizens in these four cities turned to the courts to support their demand that schools live up to our national rhetoric of access and equity. Welner offers historical, legal, and statistical analyses of these demands and of the courts' actions. Then, with observations and interviews, he reveals how the districts, under the watchful eyes of the judiciary, grappled with court-ordered detracking—a reform designed to remedy the effects of prior racial discrimination. Together, the legal analysis, the statistics, and the voices of educators and citizens add welcome clarity and definition to the larger story of a nation deeply divided by race and profoundly ambivalent about its promise of equitable, common schooling for all.

So much of the history of American education has been shaped by beliefs about children's supposedly different abilities, needs, and interests. These perceived differences often play out along race, social class, and gender lines. By now, we must be familiar with the mounds of undeniable evidence that the educational opportunities for children of color and for the poor are not equal to those afforded to children who are white and wealthy. The nearly universal schooling practices of tracking and ability grouping consign most students to a poorer-quality education than those fortunate enough to be chosen for the highest groups. Too many Americans believe that tracking is warranted because children in high tracks, by virtue of their intelligence and hard work, deserve superior resources: the best-trained teachers, fully equipped classrooms, and the most rigorous course content. This belief rests within a complex and pervasive ideology of merit that sees educational opportunity and resources as rewards for some, rather than as entitlements for all. This ideology is patently flimsy and unfair, and one would expect it to have eroded after a quarter century of evidence that tracking is not necessary for any child to learn, is harmful to most children, and is disproportionately harmful to poor children and children of color.

Of course, for tracking to be fair, the bases on which schools make tracking decisions must be fair, and they are not. The commonly accepted definition of ability rhetorically signifies talent and achievement. However, in practice "high ability" (or greater merit) means little more than prior family and school advantage. Schools disproportionately adjudge African-American and Latino students to have learning deficits and limited potential and place them in low-level classes. Schools attended by African Americans and Latinos provide limited access to critical college "gatekeeping" courses such as advanced mathematics and science. Teachers at these schools tend to place less emphasis on developing inquiry and problem-solving skills, and they offer fewer opportunities for students to become actively engaged in learning. Making matters worse, disadvantaged students have fewer well-qualified teachers than their peers at affluent, white, suburban schools; they suffer from dilapidated facilities and fewer resources.

Within schools, educators sort students in multiple ways, dividing them into "ability-grouped" classes, tracking them into programs that either prepare for college or provide general or vocational courses, and separating them in special programs for "gifted" or "learning disabled" students. Those students who are not "high ability," "college prep," or "gifted" typically have much less exposure to rigorous content, and teachers seldom ask them to grapple with critical thinking or problem solving. Seldom do they experience engaging, hands-on lessons; more often they read texts or fill out worksheets—passive and alone.

These schooling differences play out in all too familiar educational outcomes. From at least the fourth grade on, African-American, Latino, and low-income children lag behind their white and better-off peers. They more often take low-ability and remedial classes, and they drop out of school at higher rates. They consistently score lower on measures of student achievement that schools claim are crucial for measuring future success. Far fewer take college preparatory classes and go on to college; fewer still earn college degrees. Through tracking, then, schools enact their fundamental role of sorting and certifying students for lives in a socially stratified and economically disparate society. Instead of equalizing educational opportunities and life chances, tracked schools prepare students for their "rightful" (often race- and class-based) places in an unequal labor market and society.

Because detracking is fundamentally redistributive—altering how schools allocate their most precious resources, including time, teachers, materials, and high-achieving students—those who seek such reform must challenge traditional ways of thinking about opportunity, merit, and which students "deserve" the best that schools have to offer. Doing so, they become enmeshed with racial and cultural politics in local communities and the larger society.

Welner uses sophisticated case study methods to reveal what happens when courts alter and perhaps tip the balance between the prevailing political culture—the status quo—and reform advocates. He also brings his background as an attorney to an examination of schooling practices that purportedly implement court orders mandating equal educational opportunity. Probing these practices, he finds that they substantially change in response to a court's pressure. Yet these court-supported efforts fail to eradicate or overwhelm the powerful forces underlying the unequal distribution of educational resources. Welner, through his exploration of court mandates and local responses to corrective redistribution, invites substantial rethinking of the body of scholarly literature concerning educational reforms.

Welner's unsettling analysis suggests modifications to influential theories and practices that often leave reformers watching helplessly as communities, courts, and schools sabotage well-intentioned, rational, but politically naive schemes for change. Welner argues for combining a nuanced awareness of local practices, sensitivity to local norms, and the firm hand of the courts. The "third order change" process he envisions sees mandates as often necessary but never sufficient for equity-minded reform. This framework explicitly accounts for local normative and political forces as fundamental to policy development rather than afterthoughts of policy implementation. His recommendation concerning downward mutual adaptation argues for an "equity exception" to accepted reform dogma, as does his rehabilitation of the importance of top-down mandates as tools for equity-minded reform.

While his recommendations frequently contradict conventional school reform wisdom, Welner grounds his unorthodoxy in powerful, first-hand observations and clear explanations, demonstrating that community resistance will almost always contort bottom-up efforts at reforms like detracking. Finally, Kevin Welner has much to teach all of us about the need to redefine "successful" reform. Rather than superficially judging the success of reforms only to the extent to which they "worked" as intended—an overly simplistic approach that condemns most culturally demanding efforts as failures—we need to appraise such efforts by the extent to which they challenge the status quo. To the extent that reforms press against the normative and political forces that consign students to a lesser education than promised by our democratic rhetoric, we must consider even imperfect implementation of these equity-minded reforms to be hopeful moments in the struggle for a more socially just society.

Jeannie Oakes
Martin Lipton
December 2000

Acknowledgments

To the colleagues, friends and family who helped me produce this book, I owe a debt of gratitude. Jeannie Oakes provided everything from my first introduction to the book's issues 8 years ago, to the book's foreword. Truly blessed are those of us who have benefited from her guidance and inspiration. Marty Lipton, who also has done me the honor of co-authoring the foreword, added tremendous insights over this same long period of time. Both Jeannie and Marty, as well as Mike Rose, Amy Stuart Wells, Joel Handler, and Stuart Biegel, read and commented on earlier drafts of this material, helping me enormously with the development of my ideas. I benefited too from the editing and thoughtful feedback of Don Weitzman, the insights of John Puckett, Kathleen Hall, Nick Burbules, and Sandra Esslinger, and the support of Ken Howe and my other colleagues at the University of Colorado. Particular thanks go to four people whom I worked with on analyses and projects that lead up to this book: Haggai Kupermintz, Gilbert FitzGerald, Susan Yonezawa, and Jeannie Oakes.

Perhaps my greatest appreciation should be offered to the teachers, administrators, school board members, students, parents, and community members who volunteered their time, experiences and opinions, only to have their struggles critiqued in a manner that some might find unduly harsh. Their anonymity in this book prevents me from thanking any of them by name, but I sincerely thank them for their generosity. I thank them, too, for engaging in the struggles documented in the following pages—for that, we all owe them our appreciation.

I also want to acknowledge and thank the Ford Foundation, the Edna McConnell Clark Foundation and California Policy Seminars for financially supporting the research presented in this book. Ford's Janice Petrovich and McConnell Clark's Hayes Mizell each deserve high praise for grounding their work in a compassionate vision of American schooling.

Dick Corbett, Betty Lou Whitford, and the reviewers for SUNY Press gave me wonderful advice and guidance, pushing me to refine the book in its later stages. In addition, my editors at SUNY, Priscilla Ross, Jennie Doling, and Michael Haggett, provided great assistance.

I have adapted several previously published articles and book chapters, and these earlier works are cited throughout this book. Chapter Three includes material published as "(Li)Ability grouping: The new susceptibility of school tracking systems to legal challenges," *Harvard Educational Review*, 66(3), 451–470 (with Jeannie Oakes, 1996). Similarly, Chapter Five is based on a piece that I wrote with Jeannie Oakes, entitled "The importance of judicial values." This piece was written as a chapter for a book entitled *Resegregation and its consequences* (G. Orfield (ed.)). Cambridge, MA: Harvard Education Publishing Group (2001).

Chapters Six and Fifteen build on "Norms and politics of equity-minded change: Researching the 'zone of mediation,'" in M. Fullan (Ed.), *International handbook of educational change* (Norwell, MA: Kluwer Academic Publishers, 1998) (with Jeannie Oakes, Susan Yonezawa and Rick Allen).

Most of Chapter Nine was originally published in the *Journal of Negro Education*, 68(2), 200–212 (1999), as "They retard what they cannot repel: Recognizing the role that teachers sometimes play in subverting equity-minded reforms." Some material concerning San Jose, sprinkled throughout this book, was published in 1998 in *Mandating equity: A case study of court-ordered detracking in San Jose schools* (Berkeley, CA: CPS Publications) (with Jeannie Oakes and Susan Yonezawa).

Finally, I close these acknowledgements on a personal note. For their support and love, I thank Alison, Joe, Sadie and Estelle. For this, and for editorial assistance, thanks to Sylvia and Jerry. And, for each of the foregoing, plus so much more, I give Kariane my utmost appreciation and love.

Preface

"Some people need a boot in the butt." I was told this by a middle school principal describing his faculty's aversion to classroom changes. Those teachers, of course, did not welcome a kick to their respective rears any more than they welcomed the changes themselves. But good educational policies are not always popular.

In fact, those good educational policies are often political pariahs when they aim to benefit students and parents who hold less powerful positions in schools and communities (generally Latinos, African Americans, and the poor). That was, indeed, the situation faced by this principal: his school was in the process of implementing detracking—moving from ability-grouped classes to mixed-ability classes—and this reform was not popular among his teachers or among the most vocal parents in his school's community.

This book explores the unique change issues associated with such school reform. Based on an examination of four school districts' experiences with court-ordered detracking, I call into question many of the fundamental assumptions that educational scholars, practitioners, parents, and policy-makers have held about successful educational change. These case studies highlight the heightened political and normative obstacles faced by equity-minded reforms as well as the positive—and sometimes indispensable—role played by top-down mandates, such as court orders or legislation, in driving these reforms forward.

Just as importantly, I stress the need to re-think the manner by which the success of reform efforts is measured. In much the same way that one can only understand school organizations within their larger context, reform processes and their impact on students must be approached broadly and contextually. Too often, reforms are regarded as failures when their only real failings are the size of the obstacles facing them, combined with unrealistic expectations. Such an approach disregards the obvious: no reform operates in isolation. The force of a reform effort is just one among many, some favoring the progress of the reform and some opposing it. Yet policy evaluations, both informal and formal, rarely employ a paradigm that recognizes this crucial fact, thereby dooming many equity-minded policies to erroneous denunciations.

It is my hope that this book is received by educators, researchers, parents, and policy-makers as it is offered—as an explanation of the need and the means to rededicate ourselves to the task of pushing equity-minded policies forward with wisdom and vigor.

Part I

Courting the Courts

1

The Utopian Project:
Detracking and Equity-Minded Reform

On one level, this book can be added to the mountain of publications dedicated to "Why schools don't change." On another level, however, this book offers a hopeful yet pragmatic message stressing the need for school reformers to recognize and confront the obstacles that await them.

Even under the best circumstances, promoting meaningful school change presents a daunting prospect. And this book concerns schools that have undertaken to change a notoriously unyielding policy: tracking. The difficulty of this reform is intensified in these schools because their districts are all racially diverse. As might be expected, this combination of factors introduces a host of normative (e.g., beliefs and values) and political reform obstacles, many revolving around the lowered educational expectations often placed on African-American and Latino students by policy-makers and educators.

Further compounding the difficulty of these detracking reforms was the fact that they were mandated by federal courts. They did not arise from the bottom up; they were not supported by a substantial initial buy-in from parents or faculty.

Such a scenario and the challenges it poses might give pause to even the most stalwart change agent. All fundamental change—even the most straightforward and non-controversial reforms—must confront extensive technical needs as well as routinized school practices, but such demands were dwarfed in these court-supervised districts by daunting political and normative obstacles. Nonetheless, these reform efforts teach many encouraging lessons about how progress can be achieved by people who directly confront these challenges and strive to make their schools more just and excellent places of learning.

   This book presents an in-depth, comparative analysis of change processes
in four school districts struggling with racial equity and school reform. As part
of court-supervised desegregation plans, three of the districts embarked upon
ambitious, mandated detracking reforms (the fourth fought back attempts to
initiate such a reform). These court-mandated reforms present a unique reform dynamic, particularly when compared to reforms initiated from the bottom up—a dynamic that opens up certain options while limiting others. Yet
court mandates as educational policy tools are best understood using a comprehensive theory of school change that emphasizes that such mandates are
simply one powerful force superimposed upon many layers of additional
forces. By placing the analysis of detracking mandates within such a conceptual framework, this book offers insights into broad issues of school change.

THE FOUR CASES

In most ways, the struggles of the four communities discussed in this book represent typical episodes in the history of school desegregation. Each district formerly maintained racially segregated schools, and each operated under federal
court supervision following a determination that it had violated the equal protection clause of the Fourteenth Amendment.
   These four examples are atypical, however, in that the additional issue of
tracking arose as an alleged "second-generation" discriminatory tactic. That is,
the plaintiffs in these cases alleged that tracking systems subverted the goal of
between-school desegregation by resegregating students at the school site. Supporters of tracking generally argue that the practice can structure classrooms to
efficiently target curriculum and instruction to students of designated ability
levels. However, tracking can be (and has been) used by schools to discriminate against African Americans and Latinos by separating them into less challenging classes. Allegations of such discrimination, while common in social
science literature (e.g., Meier, Stewert, & England, 1989), are now made with
increasing frequency in America's courts (Welner & Oakes, 1996).
   The cases discussed in this book run the gamut of results. Two, in San
Jose, California (south of San Francisco) and Woodland Hills, Pennsylvania
(east of Pittsburgh), resulted in consent decrees requiring that the districts detrack and create racially balanced classrooms. Two other cases, in Wilmington, Delaware (southeast of Philadelphia) and Rockford, Illinois (northwest of
Chicago), eluded a voluntary settlement and went to trial. The Wilmington
plaintiffs lost, no detracking order was ever obtained, and the district remained free to track its students.[1] In contrast, the Rockford plaintiffs won, resulting in a strongly-worded order condemning the district's discriminatory
use of tracking.[2]

All four districts are mid-sized and racially diverse, and their demographics have remained fairly stable throughout their desegregation efforts. Unlike many larger cities, where White and middle-class flight have devastated integration efforts, these communities have maintained racially-mixed schools with sizable middle-class participation. Yet their tracking practices threatened to undermine what, in three of the cases, could otherwise be described as successful desegregation endeavors (Rockford being the exception, since it had not yet begun serious desegregation efforts at the time of the tracking litigation).

The opportunity to study these districts arose when one or more parties in each case sought out the tracking expertise of Dr. Jeannie Oakes. She served as an expert for the plaintiffs in the Rockford, San Jose, and Wilmington cases.[3] In addition, Dr. Oakes, Dr. Susan Yonezawa, and I conducted a subsequent study of San Jose, examining the court-ordered detracking reform process. Dr. Oakes, Gilbert FitzGerald, and I conducted a similar post-mandate study in Woodland Hills, at the invitation of the school district, plaintiff, and court. And Dr. Oakes, Dr. Haggai Kupermintz, Dr. Todd Franke, and I conducted a subsequent study in Rockford in connection with Dr. Oakes' second round of testimony in that case.

The Woodland Hills story provides the narrative and analytic backbone for this book. While each district contributed quantitative and qualitative data concerning the attributes of its tracking system, and while I was able to view and study the legal machinations in each district, it was Woodland Hills that afforded me the opportunity to observe most closely the challenges and rewards associated with the post-mandate reform process.

Notwithstanding this focus on Woodland Hills, the themes of this book are best developed through a cross-case analysis that includes all four districts. Together, these projects amassed an enormous amount of statistical, interview, and observational data. Over a period of several years, I considered and reconsidered this information. I lived and worked within these stories. I listened to people in these communities who dedicated themselves to making detracking work for their students, and I also listened to those who fought against the detracking reforms with equal dedication and resolve. That dynamic and its intriguing consequences for the reform process prompted me to write this book.

TRACKING AND EQUITY

Defining Tracking

I have chosen to use the terms "tracking" and "ability grouping" interchangeably throughout this book to identify any and all between-class grouping practices (e.g., arrangements that sort students into different classrooms for either all or part of the day) that have the following characteristics: (a) a process by which educators judge students' intellectual abilities or past achievement, or predict their future accomplishments, and use these judgments as at least part of the basis of class placement; and (b) differentiation of the curriculum and instruction to which students in different classrooms are exposed. Some researchers and educators have drawn distinctions between the two terms, usually labeling as "tracked" those systems that place students at a given level across subject areas and labeling as "ability grouped" those systems that group students subject by subject (see discussion in Slavin, 1993, pp. 535–552). In reality, both terms are misnomers, since some students "jump the tracks" of almost every tracking system and since placements in these systems are, at best, based on perceived ability. More importantly, and as described throughout this book, the day-to-day reality is virtually the same for the vast majority of students in schools approximating either definition.

The *Encyclopedia of Education Research* offers the following synopsis of ability grouping and tracking under the entry "Grouping Students for Instruction:"

Despite the many differences among ability-related grouping practices, they all represent efforts to organize schools so that students who appear to be similar in their educational needs can be taught together and apart from other students, either in specialized schools or in distinct programs, classes, or instructional groups within the same school. Moreover, they are all part of a larger curriculum dynamic that includes not only grouping students, but also,

- Widespread beliefs that students' educational needs and abilities vary widely; that schools should both transmit the knowledge and values that the culture values and prepare students for productive workforce participation; and that by separating students by ability, schools can best accommodate these different needs and purposes.
- The division of knowledge and skills, emphases, or modes of presentation in school subjects into distinct curricula considered appropriate for different groups of students (e.g., courses of study identified as college preparatory or vocational; reading programs divided into levels that vary in quantity and type of content and instruction).
- Policies establishing criteria for entry into particular groups (e.g., ability, prior achievement, student or parent preference, completion of prerequisites) and procedures for sorting individual students into the groups or curricula for which they seem

best suited (e.g., teacher judgment, counselor guidance, survey of grades and test scores, student requests).

- Labels, status differences, and academic and (at the secondary level) occupational expectations that accompany membership in particular groups.

The terms ability-grouping, tracking, curriculum differentiation, and homogeneous grouping are used (sometimes interchangeably) to describe these practices. (Oakes, 1991, p. 562).

Perhaps the most helpful way to think about tracking is as an organizational feature existing on a continuum. Thus, if I characterize the Woodland Hills School District's science department as more severely tracked than its English department (as was the case after the district detracked English), I am offering descriptive information rather than a dichotomous label. The usefulness of that information is enhanced if I also explain the underlying basis for my judgment. In this instance, the science department sorts students into different classes based on perceived academic abilities and expectations. These classes are identifiable in terms of their academic level (e.g., the high-track classes have a more challenging curriculum), and these placements tend to be stable over time (e.g., a student in low-track 10th-grade science is likely to be placed in low-track 11th-grade science).

Defining Equity

I refer to detracking as an "equity-minded" reform. Such reforms aim to benefit those who hold less powerful positions in schools and communities, such as Latinos, African Americans, and the poor. But "equity" means different things to different people. For example, parents with a child in a high-track class may cite equity concerns in arguing that their child should be separated from lower-achieving students. "Equity requires that my child be rewarded for past achievement by being put in a more challenging class," such parents might say. While some may focus on "natural ability" and others may focus on "effort" to justify such claims, their basic idea of equity is that merit deserves reward.

The federal courts discussed in this book, on the other hand, turned to a legal definition of equity, as provided by Fourteenth Amendment jurisprudence. When schools intentionally segregate African-American or Latino children into low-track classes, they unconstitutionally deny these children equal protection of the law. Thus, equity for these federal courts revolves around issues of race[4] and is limited to prevention (or remedy) of intentional discrimination.

Both this constitutional definition and the above parental definition of equity require the *equal treatment of equals* (so-called "horizontal equity" or what
Howe (1997) labels "formal" educational opportunity). However, a third,
needs-based definition calls for the *unequal treatment of unequals* (so-called
"vertical equity" or what Howe (1997) labels "compensatory" educational opportunity). "My child," a parent might assert, "is academically struggling, and
equity requires that the school take action to address this disadvantage."

In contrast to these three options, however, the definition of equity chosen
for this book emphasizes political and societal structures. It hinges on inequalities in schools' and districts' policy-making processes. Recall the above
definition of equity-minded reform: school change efforts aimed at benefiting
those who hold less powerful school and community positions. I define equity,
then, as treatment of less powerful people and groups in ways that confer benefits equal to those obtained by more powerful people and groups.

When I asked principals, superintendents, and school board members
about this aspect of educational opportunity, most candidly admitted that their
policy decisions were influenced by social and power dynamics. One, for example, referred to gifted education as a "third rail," telling me that he had
learned the hard way that touching it risked political electrocution. My definition of equity would require that each student's interests be equally protected
by policy-makers, as if they all merited such third-rail treatment.[5]

But educational practices rarely fall neatly within any single ideal of equity. While I approach detracking as an equity-minded reform because it
attempts to reform school policies to better accommodate under-served populations, it may also be viewed as an attempt to reconcile competing conceptions of equity. That is, school leaders designing detracking reforms invariably
attempt to address a range of legitimate equity concerns. In much the same
way that states reacted to mandated school finance reform by raising the funding for the poorest districts while preserving benefits for the wealthiest districts
(see Evans, Murray and Schwab, 1997), detracking reforms aim to "accelerate" all students—to raise the bar for all. For instance, most schools engaged in
detracking are careful to continue to reward and challenge high achievers
while also supporting and challenging less successful students. They devote
considerable effort to helping teachers avoid the traps of watering down curriculum and targeting the perceived "middle" of mixed-ability classes with
traditional lesson plans. Instead, teachers are encouraged to use flexible, individualized instructional techniques, such as project-based learning, portfolio-
based assessment, and collaborative grouping.

Because these reforms are very difficult, implementation inevitably falls
short of perfection. (Indeed, a healthy portion of this book is dedicated to describing that exasperating process.) But by reforming both the tracking structure and the pedagogical models employed in detracked classes, instructional

leaders hope to reconcile the legitimate equity interests of all parties.[6] Accordingly, while I use the term "equity-minded change" to broadly reference the subgroup of reforms designed to benefit those who hold less powerful school and community positions, the reader should remain mindful that such reform efforts often attempt to accommodate several notions of equity.

Tracking Research

Tracking has been roundly condemned by educational researchers and, as discussed in Chapter Three, periodically attacked by courts. Its history is steeped in racism (see discussion in Oakes, 1985).[7] It was flagrantly used to re-segregate African Americans in the wake of *Brown* (see e.g., *Hobson v. Hansen*, 1967) and notwithstanding any such pernicious intent, has resulted in racially segregated classrooms, subverting gains that might otherwise have been produced by desegregation (see Cohen, 1984; Hallinan & Williams, 1989; Koslin, Koslin, & Pargament, 1972; Schofield & Sagar, 1977). Some inner-city magnet schools-within-schools present a startling example of this phenomenon: the desirable magnet becomes populated almost exclusively by suburban students, with the host school remaining overwhelmingly minority, thus giving neighborhood students an ever-present reminder that their own education is inferior (West, 1994). Since these magnet programs are usually ordered by courts for the express reason of prompting integration, this situation presents within-school resegregation in stark relief.

In its pure theory, tracking has some advocates among educational researchers who generally assert that any discriminatory impact of the practice, while unfortunate, is the result of a misuse or abuse of an otherwise sound policy (see Hallinan, 1994). Tracking, they contend, is not inherently discriminatory nor does it necessarily subject low-track students to an inferior education. However, this speculative theorizing is of little import to tracking's opponents, who point to how it is actually implemented in American schools. They focus their attacks primarily on the tendency of tracking structures to institutionalize lower academic expectations for those students enrolled in lower tracks. Additional concerns include arbitrariness and inconsistency of placements, poor quality of curriculum in low-track classes, affective damage to students, and tracking's use as a means of second-generation segregation. The following paragraphs provide a brief overview of that research. In addition, Chapter Four addresses some of these same research questions, using data from the four districts discussed in this book.

At the basic level of academic outcomes, students in low-ability classes have far lower aspirations and less often take (subsequent) college preparatory classes than do students in higher groups. For instance, Braddock and

Dawkins (1993), show that minority and White eighth graders' plans to enroll in high school college preparatory and non-college preparatory classes differed markedly based on the track level of their current classes, even when researchers controlled for other likely influences on students' aspirations, such as gender, socioeconomic status, middle school grades, achievement test scores, and post-high school plans. Students in high-ability eighth grade math classes were more likely to report that they planned to take college preparatory classes in senior high. Further, track assignments impact students' future schooling opportunities. As 10th graders, students in the NELS:88 national database who were in high-ability groups as 8th graders were the most likely to enroll in college preparatory courses, while those who had been in low-ability 8th grade classes were the least likely to so enroll, independent of such factors as grades, test scores, aspirations, and social background factors. Interestingly, too, students in eighth grade mixed-ability classes were more likely than comparable peers in low-tracks to subsequently enter college prep classes.

Dornbush (1994) similarly found that, for eighth grade students who scored in the middle ranges of achievement, initial high school track placements greatly influenced future high school course selection and enrollment. For example, students scoring in the 5th decile on eighth grade tests and who were placed in biology as ninth graders had a 71% likelihood of subsequently taking physics or chemistry. In stark contrast, similarly scoring students who were placed in low-level science in grade 9 had only a 7% likelihood of enrolling in these advanced courses. In fact, Dornbush found that at every level of the eighth grade achievement hierarchy, students placed in high-level classes far outpaced their peers in later advanced science course-taking. Overall, 85% of high school students remained in the same science and math tracks in which they began. Additionally, even when controlling for levels of achievement, low-track students feel less challenged, put forth less effort, do less homework, and report that teachers are less likely to ask them to demonstrate their understanding (see also Oakes, 1985).

Carefully designed and controlled studies that compare the impact of grouped and ungrouped settings on student achievement find that high-achieving students do equally well in both grouped and non-grouped educational facilities. Professor Robert Slavin of Johns Hopkins University has conducted the most meticulous and respected reviews of these studies (see Slavin, 1987, 1990, 1993).

Even staunch advocates of ability grouping concede that research does not support the claim that high-ability students benefit simply from being in separate classes (see, e.g., Kulik, 1992). Rather, separate classes for high achieving students only benefit participants when schools provide those students with an enriched curriculum that is different from that provided to students in lower groups. Not surprisingly, all students, whether high-ability or not, seem to benefit from the types of special resources, opportunities, and support usually present in high-level classes. Gains come from the far richer curriculum and learning opportunities that these classes provide, rather than from high-achievers being separated from their lower-achieving schoolmates.

Another study found that teachers with classes at more than one ability level varied their instructional goals among those classes (Raudenbush, Rowan & Cheong, 1993). Raudenbush, Rowan, and Cheong performed multi-level analyses of data concerning the instructional goals of English, mathematics, social studies and science teachers in 16 secondary schools. They found that variation in teachers' emphasis on teaching higher-order thinking in all four subjects was a function of hierarchical conceptions of teaching and learning related to teachers' perceptions of students' ability group. As a result, teachers placed much greater emphasis on higher-order thinking and problem solving in high-track classes.

Given these pedagogical shortcomings of tracking, any racial segregation within such a system raises serious questions of discrimination. Moreover, as Jeannie Oakes has repeatedly substantiated, such segregation often takes place in racially-mixed schools that employ tracking (see Oakes, 1985, 1990, 1995; Oakes & Guiton, 1995; Welner & Oakes, 1996). African-American and Latino students are often judged to have learning deficits and limited potential (sometimes, regardless of their prior achievement), and they are placed disproportionately in low-track, remedial programs. Once placed, these students learn less than comparably-skilled students in heterogeneous classes, and they have less access to knowledge, powerful learning environments, and resources. Consequently, tracking practices tend to create racially separate programs that provide minority children with restricted educational opportunities and outcomes. Since low-tracked students are negatively affected by being in ability-grouped classes, the achievement gap invariably widens over time between students in high- and low-ability groups (see, e.g., Weinstein, 1976; Barr & Dreeben, 1983; Gamoran & Berends 1987).

Ultimately, tracking is philosophically premised on the belief that some children are so academically different from other children that these two (or more) groups should not be in the same classroom. Accordingly, the academically inferior children are placed in separate classrooms where, in theory, they catch up (remediate) but where, in practice, they usually fall further behind. Tracking, then, is about the rationing of opportunities. From the perspective of the low-track student, it's about deciding that this student should not be exposed to curriculum and instruction that would prepare him or her for subsequent serious learning. From the perspective of the high-track student, it's about enhancing the schooling environment for some students by shielding (segregating) them from other students. Thus, low-track classes serve schools in a perverse way: they allow schools to warehouse racial minority, lower-achieving, and/or otherwise problematic students—keeping them apart from more valued students.

This book examines the detracking reform process. I offer the book's ideas, information, and insights in hopes of improving the success of that process. I view detracking as an important means of addressing inequities of educational opportunity. As such, this book reflects my personal judgment—grounded in my own investigations and in research such as that discussed above—that detracking benefits students who would otherwise be in low-track classes.

OVERCOMING NORMATIVE AND POLITICAL OBSTACLES

These four communities' reform stories share an important element with other desegregation efforts: they combine educational policy issues with social justice issues. Specifically, these detracking reforms confront a familiar conflation of race with intellectual ability, and they bring to the fore cultural anxieties felt by many White parents and educators. Simply put, many administrators, teachers, parents and policy-makers support tracking *precisely because* it separates White and wealthier students from poor and minority students. Combined with detracking's redistribution within schools of educational resources—such as time, teachers, information, and high-status knowledge—these beliefs and values tend to make the reform highly politically contentious.

The work of Jeannie Oakes, Amy Stuart Wells, and Pauline Lipman, among others, convincingly documents the powerful role of these normative issues in tracking debates (Greene, 2000; Lipman, 1998; Oakes, 1985; Oakes, Wells & Associates, 1996; Sapon-Shevin, 1994; Wells & Oakes, 1998; Wells & Serna, 1996; Wheelock, 1992). These writers describe the role played by values and beliefs in creating and maintaining tracked structures, and they offer insights into the equity-minded change process. However, the overwhelming weight of literature on school change—in particular, literature focused on change theory—emphasizes concerns that are normatively and politically neutral, such as the need for schools to become "learning organizations" where teachers and administrators act as "change agents" skilled at dealing with reform as a normal part of their work (Fullan, 1994; Louis & Miles, 1990). This is certainly worthwhile advice, yet the literature rarely moves beyond a neutral analysis to earnestly confront the political and normative obstacles faced by detracking and similarly contentious reforms. Consequently, when school reformers turn to this literature (as did some of those in the districts discussed in this book), their preparation to meet the reforms' technical needs far exceeds their readiness for normative and political challenges.

In practice, the neglect of these additional obstacles by change agents in districts that are detracking can devastate the reform efforts. Oakes, Wells, & Associates (1996) describe several schools which had confidently embarked upon detracking reforms only to have their considerable efforts derailed by opposition completely unrelated to the technical and structural change issues on which the reformers had been focusing. Similarly, the school change stories discussed in the present book illustrate how powerful political and normative forces, if unchecked, can create a context inimical to an equity-minded reform.

The tracking systems in these districts commanded staunch followings among committed groups of parents, teachers, and other community members. These opponents of detracking typified the "local elites" described by Wells and Serna (1996): they were overwhelmingly drawn from among the White and the wealthier constituencies of the schools and they held disproportionate power in relation to school decision-makers. Naturally, the students favored by the tracking systems being challenged reflected similar demographics. From the outset, these local elites viewed detracking as grounded in values different from their own and they used their sizable influence to create an environment inhospitable to such reform.

Given this unwelcoming context for detracking, its supporters faced a dilemma: submit to the unfavorable balance of power or find an alternative way to advance school change. Before turning to litigation, they first considered and attempted other possible methods of initiating detracking, but the political and normative environment stifled their efforts. In most districts, these barriers would draw the story to a close. However, change agents in these four districts concluded that the reforms were of such importance that they would shepherd a lawsuit through the court system.

Responding to the additional impediments presented by an equity-minded reform does not, of course, necessarily entail court involvement. Community organizing, university partnerships, and extraordinary leadership are among the other tools that may be sufficient to counter these obstacles. However, external mandates such as court orders have, as I argue in this book, an important role to play when local forces deny equal educational opportunities for a democratic minority.

LESSONS AND THEMES

The districts' experiences discussed in this book illuminate a basic truth about mandates: while powerful policy tools, they are not panaceas. Policy-makers frequently expect mandates to supplant pre-existing forces, but the reality is more nuanced. When a mandate arrives at a school site, it is placed on top of layers and layers of history—of competing beliefs, ideas and interests. These other layers, including the influence of local elites, continue to exert their own independent force, often in opposition to the mandate.

Each district's account will, in the following chapters, describe the various forces that shape its context. In doing so, these stories will highlight two interconnected lessons: (1) court orders or other mandates are sometimes necessary to make an environment receptive to detracking, and (2) these mandates, while making change possible, are not sufficient by themselves to push forward long-lasting, successful reform. Detracking is essentially a social change, requiring broad-based transformations in the way schools and communities think about students and instruction.

In short, the mandates discussed in this book are flawed and inadequate, but they are also necessary. Many students suffered discrimination and loss of educational opportunities because of the tracking in these districts. Without court action, this unjust system remained in one district (Wilmington) and would have persisted unchecked in the three others.

Popular school reform movements of the 1980s and 1990s focused considerable attention on capacity-building—particularly as regards the role of more centralized educational authorities. They called on state or district educational offices to lend technical expertise for professional development and curricular reform. I agree that this role is beneficial; nothing in this book should be understood to challenge this wisdom. My dispute is with those who contend that the role of these more centralized educational authorities should stop at technically-oriented organizational capacity-building. My experiences with the school districts discussed in this book have underscored the need for a periodic, strenuous, top-down effort to promote equitable educational opportunities (for a similar perspective, see McDermott, 1999).

Implied in the foregoing are a series of important themes. They shed light on the cases as well as reform in general. Throughout this book, I will use these themes as analytic lenses for understanding the nature of the reform processes. Among these themes are the following:

- Community politics are likely to favor systems such as tracking that provide disproportionate benefits to dominant societal actors.
- Governing norms and politics, particularly in socioeconomically and racially diverse communities, are likely to produce an environment unreceptive to attempts to detrack.
- To be most successful, detracking efforts must recognize and respond to normative and political obstacles.
- Mandates such as court orders can change the school context, making it more receptive to detracking.
- By themselves, mandates are insufficient to initiate and maintain long-lasting, successful reform. Because detracking calls for a trans-

formation in the way schools and communities think about instruction, its success is tied to the ability of reformers to bring about meaningful social change in the school environment.

Also emerging from this study was the manifest need for the scholarly literature about school reform to present a more thorough and helpful explanation of the equity-minded change process. Accordingly, this book uses the survey of reform processes in four school districts to expand upon and refine the school change literature. In doing so, I do not challenge the conventional wisdom that reforms initiated from the bottom up, or with substantial subsequent local buy-in, are generally preferable to reforms initiated from the top down. I do, however, challenge the widespread failure to recognize that, due in large part to considerable resistance from local elites, many important reforms, including detracking, are highly unlikely to be initiated from the bottom up or to acquire sturdy bottom-up support later. I also call into question what is, after all is said and done, a "successful" reform.

Finally, I reconsider the mainstream body of educational change literature in light of the uniqueness of equity-minded reforms, and I offer substantial revisions to this literature. Among the implications of these revisions is a rehabilitation of top-down mandates as policy tools. While often depicted in the change literature as pariahs and dinosaurs, these mandates should, I contend, be viewed as potentially the most effective means available to advance crucial equity reforms in American schools.

CHAPTER OVERVIEWS

I make this argument primarily through the experiences, data and narratives of the four aforementioned school districts, which I introduce in Chapter Two. Chapter Three traces some of the history of tracking and tracking litigation. I describe the legal bases for this litigation and discuss the role of litigation as a policy tool, using as a case study the modern-day special education laws that were prompted by a series of legal cases in the early 1970s. Chapter Four presents some of the statistical analyses upon which the detracking orders discussed in this book were grounded.

I close out Part I of the book, however, with a cautionary note based on an appellate decision in the Rockford litigation. Chapter Five uses that judicial opinion to analyze the role played, in ruling on an equal protection claim, by a judge's foundational values concerning the importance of racial equality in a just society. I consider the crucial role of judges' (and other authorities') values in shaping the context of an equity-minded reform, and I appraise the implications of this unpredictable dynamic for litigation as a policy tool.

Part II begins with a description, in Chapter Six, of the conceptual framework used through the remainder of the book. Called the "zone of mediation," this framework offers a mechanism for thinking carefully about the reform context created by the interaction of political, technical, normative, economic, historical and inertial forces. Chapters Seven through Twelve then use this framework to examine the various forces that shaped the context of tracking and detracking in the four districts. Together, these chapters paint a poignant picture of an intense battle over contextual turf.

Chapter Seven explores the forces that generally restrict the ability of detracking to develop from the bottom up. These forces include universal phenomena such as pressure from college entrance requirements and contentious political and racial dynamics. They also include more localized phenomena such as weak leadership and an older, engrained teaching staff.

Even after the court orders were issued, these pre-existing forces remained in effect. Yet, as set forth in Chapter Eight, mandates, as well as associated funding and supervision, can have a dramatic impact, changing the "zone" (i.e., the context) from one that is highly resistant to detracking to one that is receptive to the reform's initiation. This receptivity, however, is tenuous and susceptible to the range of other forces. Chapter Nine examines the most powerful of these: parental and educator opposition. I break down that opposition by type (frustration versus hostility) and by the underlying values, beliefs and interests expressed in the four districts by these opponents of the reform efforts.

Chapters Ten and Eleven look at some powerful forces through distinct lenses. Choice and the market metaphor are tackled in Chapter Ten, while Chapter Eleven highlights symbolism and normative beliefs. These two chapters discuss some forces originally mentioned in earlier chapters—but in a different light—as well as some that were previously unexamined.

Chapter Twelve closes out Part II with an analysis of some compromises and inducements offered to elite parents by schools and districts. These concessionary policies are a testament to the effectiveness of opposition and resistance to court-ordered detracking in these districts. In Wilmington, this opposition blocked the order completely. In the other three districts, the opposition altered and minimized the extent of change. In Woodland Hills, for example, the district first detracked high school English and then expanded AP English from one 12th-grade class to 10 classes: 5 each for 11th and 12th grades—thus creating a new, more legitimate track to placate the most vocal parents.

Part III challenges the maxim that we cannot mandate what matters. Notwithstanding Chapter Twelve's discussion of the partial re-creation of inequitable structures, the students in the three reforming districts (particularly lower-income students of color) did benefit from the opportunities opened up by the court mandates. Chapter Thirteen presents analyses identifying these benefits. Meaningful classroom desegregation followed in each district, and the limited evidence suggests immediate academic improvement. In addition, some teachers, upon witnessing improved performance from formerly low-tracked students, began to have higher expectations for all students and accordingly changed their instructional methods. Redesigned curricula, assessment, and support programs, in line with nationally-recognized best practices, also accompanied the detracking in these districts.

These positive changes are, I contend in Chapter Fourteen, best understood from the perspective of the educational opportunities available to students in these districts before and after detracking. While some teachers were much more successful with heterogeneous classes than others, the same was true of those same teachers when they taught tracked classes. Under either system, these districts would contain inferior teachers. But those teachers' flaws became much more apparent, in two ways, when highlighted by detracking. First, while such teachers had never taught much in the way of higher-order thinking skills, they had paced the drill-and-memorization lessons at a rate arguably appropriate for a tracked student body. The switch to heterogeneous lessons yanked out that comfortable rug. Second, detracking exposed privileged students—and their parents—to these weaker teachers.

Chapter Fifteen critiques some of the fundamental assumptions commonly found in scholarly literature about the school change process. Because of the heightened political and normative obstacles faced by equity-minded reforms, as well as the positive—and sometimes indispensable—role played by top-down mandates in driving these reforms forward, I call into question some basic beliefs. Together, the conceptual ideas set forth in this Chapter present a comprehensive re-thinking of the educational change literature as applied to equity-minded reforms.

CONCLUDING NOTE

Perhaps the broadest theme of this book is the one highlighted in the appellate opinion of the federal Third Circuit Court of Appeals in the *Rockford* case. In striking down part of the detracking order, the court wrote, "Children, the most innocent of the innocent persons occasionally brushed by draconian decrees, should not be made subjects of utopian projects" (*People Who Care v. Rockford Board of Education School District No. 205*, 1997, at 534). Many Americans would disagree with this court, believing instead in the nation's fundamental rhetoric, including that recited by innocent children in classrooms each morning—"with liberty and justice for all." In that sense, we are all subjects of a utopian project. This book tells how four communities, sometimes with the help of courts, are trying to make this American dream a reality.

2

The Ones that Got Caught

Consider a middle school whose new seventh graders have reading levels ranging from second grade through college. This school may choose to separate these students into three tracks, called remedial, college-preparatory, and honors. In theory, the students in the remedial class would be treated to a year of classes that would challenge them to move quickly up to grade level in their reading (i.e., their classes would "remediate" or "remedy" their reading shortfall). The college-prep and honors students would similarly be exposed to a curriculum designed to push them to excel beyond their present levels. This is the ideal.

In practice, since a student's educational success is so closely tied to the level of expectations that a teacher has for that student (Edmonds and Frederiksen, 1978; Mackler, 1969), tracking creates an internal inconsistency that fatally undermines the ideal. That is, tracking institutionalizes low expectations for a sub-population of students (Oakes, 1985; see also Mehan, Villanueva, Hubbard, & Lintz, 1996). Most teachers assigned to remedial classes are implicitly told by their schools, "The students in this class are low achievers; don't expect too much from them." Although many exceptional teachers overcome this structural barrier, the vast majority do not. Low-track classes at the secondary level are rarely remedial in any true sense of the word (genuinely remedial programs at the primary level, such as *Reading Recovery*, have few counterparts at the secondary level). Instead, these classes are overwhelmingly characterized by practices that some teachers disparagingly call "drill-and-kill," "chalk-and-talk," or "sit-and-git."

These problems are amplified when, as is usually the case, teachers assigned to these low-track classes are disproportionately likely to be teaching a subject outside of their area of expertise (e.g., a teacher with a bachelors degree

19

in history but asked to teach science) or to be otherwise less experienced (see Bryson & Bentley, 1980; Darling-Hammond, 1995; Finley, 1984; Ingersoll, 1999). Even when a tracked school is not ordinarily inclined to staff low-track classes with inferior or mismatched teachers, demands from efficacious parents of high-tracked students may prompt the school to reassign the "best" teachers to those students' classes (see Wells & Serna, 1996).

Additional problematic elements of tracking are discussed below and in the following two chapters in connection with the particular legal claims made in Rockford, San Jose, Wilmington, and Woodland Hills. Subsequent chapters, again discussing these districts, further illustrate how tracking systems in racially or socioeconomically diverse schools can favor wealthy and White community members at the expense of low-income students and students of color.

SORTING AS AMERICANA

I recently had dinner with an old friend who shared with me some of the joys that he and his wife were experiencing as they raised their young child. However, he also voiced frustration and disappointment with a series of questions and comments that they repeatedly heard from other parents. He was amazed that, from the date of birth, these parents took pleasure or comfort in comparing the weights and heights of their children. "My child is in the 95% percentile of height," one might say. Another might respond, "Mine is in the 99% percentile for weight." He explained in an e-mail,

> I think the real struggle for [us] is that we try very hard not to fall into the "when did your kid start jumping?" stuff. Some people say to me that it's natural for parents to want to compare, [but] this "natural" thing worries me. If my kid is developing well (i.e., not shrinking or "failing to thrive"), is happy, has a good appetite, plays well, likes a variety of things, etc. . . . then what does it matter if he does any of those things better, earlier, or whatever else-er than anybody else's kids?

The translation is relatively smooth from these early rankings and competitions into those we see in schools, and Americans rarely question their usefulness.

Advocates of tracking tend to argue that any discriminatory impact of the practice, while unfortunate, is a result of a misuse or abuse of an otherwise sound policy. Tracking, they contend, is not inherently discriminatory (see Hallinan, 1994; Loveless, 1999). They make a rationalistic appeal to Americans' predilection for efficiency through competition and sorting. Tracking, in fact, came of age during the Progressive Era, the high-point of what Raymond Callahan called the "cult of efficiency" (Callahan, 1962). Edward Thorndike and other leaders of the group that Tyack (1974) calls "administrative progressives," combined Frederick Taylor's concept of scientific management with John Dewey's emphasis on the individuality of each student. Sadly, the Deweyan ideal was lost somewhere in the process. The resulting Progressive model purported to meet individual needs by placing each student in a classroom with other students of similar abilities and needs and then targeting a different yet appropriate curriculum at each group.

Over the ensuing decades, tracking evolved and endured. In the 1930s through 1950s, educators overtly placed low-income, female, immigrant and minority (language, racial, and ethnic) students in non-academic tracks. The Progressive mind-set saw this as a caring way to prepare a diverse student body for productive lives in American society (Ravitch, 1983). Later, in the wake of the civil rights and equal rights movements, such discriminatory placements could no longer be openly defended. Nonetheless, the prejudices underlying many of these historical injustices remained strongly ingrained in American society and continued to play themselves out in the track placement process (Oakes, 1985).

In addition to the shift away from overt placement based on such suspect features as class, sex and race, there has also been a shift from reliance on IQ tests toward various tests of achievement and academic skills.[1] Placements are also now more responsive to teacher recommendations and parental requests. Professor Sam Lucas recently described how track placements are now less rigid, yet in practice retain much of their old character (Lucas, 1999). While track placement criteria may be multifaceted and may contain elements of student and parent choice, the macro-structural distribution of educational opportunities mirrors the picture of social reproduction of inequality painted by Bowles and Gintis (1976). The reasons for this maldistribution are many and complex, likely including inequalities in social and cultural capital as well as political power (see Bourdieu, 1985; Fraser, 1992). Parental education and other family resources play out indirectly through cultural characteristics and interests passed along to children and through schools' building upon some cultures while ignoring or denigrating others. These resources also play out directly through parental demands made upon schools. Finally, the continuing role of racism and discrimination, both individualized and societal, provides an additional explanation of these inequalities of educational opportunity.

SITUATING THE FOUR DISTRICTS' DISCRIMINATORY USE OF TRACKING

A successful claim under the Fourteenth Amendment Equal Protection Clause must be grounded in proof of intentional racial discrimination. The inverse, however, is not true: Fourteenth Amendment claims, whether successful or unsuccessful, only rarely follow from demonstrable (i.e., provable in court) racial discrimination, and most racial discrimination is not demonstrable. Accordingly, the distinction of the four districts analyzed in this book lies more in the plaintiffs' readiness to litigate and the districts' histories than in the schools' educational practices.

Of the four districts profiled in this book, two, San Jose and Woodland Hills, voluntarily entered into consent decrees and embarked with some enthusiasm upon reforms designed to address the inequities of tracking. A third district, Rockford, also embarked upon such reforms, albeit pursuant to an adverse court judgment. Meanwhile, schools in neighboring districts continued to track and continued to disadvantage students in low-track classes.

Throughout this book, I identify racism as a force undergirding tracking structures. However, I also contend that the normative and political bases for racial discrimination are societal rather than centered in isolated, aberrant school districts. At times, this racism is actualized; at times it is dormant. However, in racially diverse school districts using tracking, the former is much more likely than the latter. Consider an analogy to the concept of "potential energy," from the field of mechanical physics. Potential energy is energy that an object possesses in a stored form. It is not readily noticeable; it is the energy of position. A book on a table has potential energy because of its position, but that energy will not be realized unless the book falls from the table. At that point, the potential energy is converted into kinetic energy (the energy of the object in motion). Similarly, racist beliefs can be thought of as existing in a "potential" form, which tends to be realized only under certain circumstances. Tracking in multiracial schools, because it sorts students and asymmetrically distributes educational opportunities, is one such circumstance.

For this reason, the evidence of racial discrimination in these four districts is best understood within its larger context. Arguably, the tracking systems in most racially diverse districts in America are no less discriminatory than the tracking systems that existed in these four districts. *Every* tracked school must overcome daunting structural, political, and normative hurdles if it is to provide equitable educational opportunities to low-tracked students, while tracked schools in racially diverse communities must overcome these additional hurdles. The sad fact that many, perhaps most, districts never even make a concerted attempt to clear these hurdles is why this chapter, describing the four districts discussed in the book, is entitled, "The ones that got caught." This is also one reason why I hold in such high esteem the educators discussed in this book who have taken on the task of righting past wrongs. Educators who work in districts operating under desegregation orders tend to feel that they are unduly criticized. I hope that the descriptions in this book strike an appropriate balance of praise and criticism.[2]

WOODLAND HILLS

District and Community Characteristics

The Woodland Hills School District has been under a desegregation order since 1981 and a detracking order since 1988. Over the years, these orders have adjusted in reaction to pressures and needs within the district.

The relatively small size of the district,[3] enrolling approximately 6,000 students in nine schools, allowed me to conduct a fairly comprehensive set of observations (I visited all nine schools and focused on three). At the time of my observations (1996–1997), the district was approximately 27% African American and 70% White. The African-American population lives primarily near the district's center. There exists little racial integration in the surrounding communities. Composition of the small communities making up the school district ranged in 1996 from 20% to 43% low-income families, with a high correlation between poverty and race.[4]

Located 8 miles to the east of Pittsburgh, in Allegheny County, Pennsylvania, the district is in the Monongahela Valley, an area originally home to several nineteenth century coal-mining towns. The mines drew numerous European immigrants, whose descendants still live in the area. The industrial boom peaked in the 1950s, but the economy remained strong until the late 1970s. Population levels steadily declined from 1950–1990, ultimately dropping 37%. The damaged economic base eventually contracted to light industry, service, public sector, and retail businesses.

Other population trends in Woodland Hills centered on race and age. Whites and African Americans were separated by profound residential segregation. Four of the 12 boroughs were home to more than 86% of the African-American population. The area's population was also unusually old. Twenty-three percent of the people in Allegheny County were senior citizens—second nationally only to Dade County, Florida—and the proportion in the 12 boroughs (27%) of Woodland Hills was even higher than in the county as a whole.

In recent years, the area's residents have not prospered economically. Between 1980 and 1990, median household income in the district communities decreased over 9% (adjusted for inflation). Great racial disparities existed among income levels, with African Americans bringing home only 72% of the average 1990 White family income. The African-American unemployment rate (18.0%) was over 3 times that of White residents (5.8%). Large distinctions were also apparent between the 12 boroughs, with 6 boroughs suffering from family poverty rates of 12% or more, while the rate was much less in five others (2.9% or lower). As discussed in later chapters, these distinctions between the subcommunities that constituted the Woodland Hills School District played themselves out in the detracking reform process.

The Litigation and Court Orders

The story of the Woodland Hills School District began in the early 1960s, when the Commonwealth of Pennsylvania embarked upon a policy of mandating mergers of small districts in the interests of efficiency. The state required that all such mergers be accomplished by 1966. Local school boards were to give recommendations to county superintendents, who would then pass along their own recommendations to the state Secretary of Education. Most districts resisted the pressure to merge, but state policy allowed small districts to remain independent only if they possessed sufficient wealth.

None of Woodland Hills' seven predecessor districts merged during this initial phase. However in 1971 the Commonwealth stepped in and mandated a merger between the Braddock, North Braddock and Rankin districts, which were all predominantly African American. The rationale offered for the forced merger was that these districts were not financially sound on their own. The new district was named the "General Braddock Area School District" (GBASD).

The fiscal-efficiency rationale for the merger was under-cut by the fact that the GBASD was in trouble from the start; it was officially classified as "financially distressed" soon after the merger. As one African-American parent explained to me, "our tax base declined. We had nothing. . . . [W]e just didn't have the equipment and things like that to properly teach our kids." Therefore, she explained, the lawsuit and merger were "necessary for our kids to have a chance at a proper education."

Desegregation litigation was commenced within a year of the formation of the GBASD. The plaintiff class, consisting of parents and children who resided in the GBASD, brought suit against the Commonwealth of Pennsylvania, the Pennsylvania State Board of Education, the Allegheny County Board of Education, and various individuals who served as officials at the time. The named plaintiff, Dorothy Hoots, worked as a housekeeper in Churchill, one of the wealthier communities in the area. She compared the types of programs provided for the Churchill students with those offered to her own children, and the contrast prompted her to challenge the fairness of the recent reorganization.

The plaintiffs alleged that the creation of the predominantly African-American GBASD and the simultaneous consolidation of two largely White surrounding school districts, Turtle Creek and East Pittsburgh, were purposefully discriminatory and unconstitutional. The district court agreed and ordered the defendants to prepare and adopt a desegregation plan (*Hoots v. Commonwealth of Pennsylvania*, 1973).

In the years that followed, the district court rejected a series of remedies proposed by the defendants. Eventually, in 1981 (10 years after the formation of the GBASD), the court approved a plaintiff-proposed plan to merge the

GBASD with four adjacent, largely White school districts,[5] forming a new entity, later named the Woodland Hills School District (*Hoots v. Commonwealth of Pennsylvania*, 1981). The court also directed the defendants and the new Woodland Hills school board (now joined as a defendant) to design and implement a comprehensive desegregation plan. The following year, the court ordered the implementation of a student assignment plan to desegregate district schools in the 1981–1982 and 1982–1983 school years[6] (*Hoots v. Commonwealth of Pennsylvania*, 1982).

The reaction of district officials and White parents to these orders was less than enthusiastic. The first Woodland Hills superintendent, Bob Breneman, was described by one observer as "not at all reform-minded," "terrible [in terms of desegregation]," and (sarcastically) "a real district-builder." Breneman publicly took the position at school board meetings that the U.S. Supreme Court would hopefully accept the case for review. He reportedly told those gathered at the meetings that he hoped the Court would reverse the order so that everyone could go back to their separate districts. This attitude filtered down to the principals, one of whom acknowledged, "I think that a lot of people felt very strongly that the merger would be dissolved, so principals used their former districts' style of management" (Miller, 1991, p. 64).

Whatever Breneman did or did not do, it failed to assuage the concerns of his constituents. The board meetings during that period were typified by fractious clashes of people and positions; the meetings were, according to a long-time observer, highly unwieldy:

> There was a lot of emotion from the board of education, a lot of emotion from the communities. [During] the first three or four board meetings, when all five school boards were in the room at the same time, . . . there was a lot of very emotional fighting going on.

"Save our Schools" signs appeared throughout the district's White neighborhoods. White parents marched around the courthouse carrying coffins, symbolizing the death of their smaller, elite districts (Brody, 1995). School board elections focused on the merger, with some candidates running on a platform of "Vote for me; I'll get you out of this merger." In addition to general opposition to the merger, there was specific opposition to the busing. However, as one of the administrators from that period explained, this resistance decreased over time. "[We] just wore them down," he said.

The second superintendent, Fred Hill, did not initially stray far from Breneman's path. Both men had formerly served as a superintendent in a predecessor district, and neither had welcomed the change. Hill, however, did grow while in office, and he helped to negotiate the 1988 consent decree (discussed below). By the early 1990s, during his last years in the position, Hill

seemed committed to real reform. Nevertheless, by most accounts, Hill was
not a particularly adept politician or communicator, and many of his efforts
fell short of their target. As one administrator related, the "mood" under these
superintendents was basically of "non-compliance with the court order," at
least at the central administrative-level. At the site level, she said, the feeling
was that "it was the superintendent's order and the superintendent dealt with
it." A principal explained that people in the schools felt as though central office leaders "really [weren't] trying very hard to make this work."

In 1987, Woodland Hills further reorganized its building utilization,
grade structure, and student assignments. Pursuant to the reorganization plan,
the district adopted the basic configuration that it maintained through the
time of my observations: three K–3 elementary schools, three 4–6 intermediate schools, two junior high schools, and one senior high school. The district's
between-school desegregation plan used a "pairing" between White and
African-American communities. For the primary (K–3) schools, students traveled from predominantly African-American communities to schools located in
predominantly White communities. The reverse was true for the intermediate
(4–6) schools. According to a provision in the 1981 court order, the plan was
"designed to achieve an equal sharing of the burden of desegregation between
African-American and white students, parents and communities." As a result of
the 1987 reorganization and the associated busing, the district achieved and
maintained between-school desegregation.

Racial disparities remained, however, in a variety of other aspects of the
district. These included administration, staff, faculty, students' within-school
student assignment, and student activities. In an attempt to identify and remedy these inequalities, the parties negotiated, drafted, and petitioned the district court for approval of a Consent Decree in June 1988. Although all parties
joined in the filing of the motion, the Commonwealth never formally signed
the Decree. Nonetheless, the district court issued an order on July 12, 1988,
stating that "[t]he terms of the foregoing Consent Decree are hereby approved
and entered as an Order of this Court," thus giving the Decree legal effect.[7]

In the pertinent part, the Consent Decree states the following:

> The current practice of grouping students by perceived ability, the
> methods of identification and selection of students for Gifted and Spe-
> cial Education programs, and the structure and design of curricular of-
> ferings, at all instructional levels of the School District, have resulted in
> racially segregated and racially identifiable classrooms and instruction.
>
> Effective desegregation of the School District, eradication of the
> vestiges of past discrimination, and protection from future discrimi-
> nation requires the elimination of all racial segregation in, and in-
> equality of, student instruction [within] the schools.

Therefore, the classrooms, course offerings, instructional materials and educational placements and programs of the School District shall be completely desegregated at all instructional levels, and specific compensatory educational programs shall be offered to students with particular educational deficits or inequalities appearing to result from past segregation.

Specifically, the Consent Decree required, among other things: (a) elementary schools to have desegregated and heterogeneously grouped classrooms; (b) junior high schools to have desegregated and heterogeneously grouped classrooms in core and non-elective courses; (c) the curriculum and pedagogy in the now-desegregated and heterogeneously grouped classrooms at the elementary and junior high levels to use team learning techniques; (d) the senior high schools to have desegregated classrooms in required, advanced, and elective courses, and to eliminate course prerequisites — except for "recognized sequential course offerings;" and (e) compensatory and remedial instruction to be offered at times other than during regularly scheduled course time.

In January of 1991, the district court entered an order mandating the eradication of the "educational deprivation suffered by minority students" caused by the district's segregated system of ability grouping and tracking. In particular, the court ordered the district to redesign its entire curriculum for grades K–12 in order to eliminate the curriculum's segregative and discriminatory structure and to include heterogeneous (mixed-ability) instruction and multicultural content.

The court's appointed hearing officer (who essentially acts as an extension or representative of the judge) presented the tracking issues in a cogent and compelling opinion which clearly influenced both the district court and, later, the Third Circuit Court of Appeals. The following lengthy quotation from that opinion is worth presenting in full because it provides an important backdrop for the district's detracking reforms:

> The unfortunate result of tracking in the short term is that it creates racially identifiable classrooms as culturally biased tests and teacher perceptions improperly categorize many minority students. In the long term, tracking perpetuates the classification and the label first applied. The fast track students are consistently challenged to push the limits of their knowledge and ability, and thus they progress faster and learn more than their counterparts. At the other extreme, low achievers are limited to basic mechanical instruction, focusing on very basic low level skills with little exposure to problem solving or other higher order skills. Thus once the labels are applied and students grouped accordingly, the gap in their knowledge and skills widens with each year because of the level of instruction provided. As

that gap widens, the chance of a child shaking off the label of low or average achiever becomes increasingly remote. The labels thus become self-fulfilling prophecies regardless of the child's actual ability. Because large numbers of minority children in this District have historically been labeled as low achievers, the impact of tracking on minority students has been dramatic.

> Minority students [are] concentrated in standard courses while being virtually absent from advanced level courses. This stratification is the most critical disparity in the system because it is a direct measure of the educational deprivation suffered by minority students as a direct result of the formerly segregated system (Fatla, 1990a).

In a later supplementary opinion, he added:

> [T]he effects of tracking still pervade the entire system. Teachers at all levels have taught almost exclusively in a tracked system and most lack skills needed to handle a heterogeneous classroom. Thus the need for staff development. Virtually all students in the District have been ability grouped in the past and that system has deprived many minority students of adequate instruction. . . . Thus the need for compensatory and remedial instruction at all levels. We must also be cognizant of efforts to perpetuate tracking in other forms. Some teachers create ability groups within the heterogeneous classroom, and some teachers have sought to departmentalize the later elementary grades. Until these attitudes change, until teachers develop the skills to teach effectively in the new system, and until children can make up the ground they have lost under the former system, the deleterious effects of tracking will continue to inhibit the District to the detriment of minority students (Fatla, 1990b).

Even before the 1990 Fatla Report, the district had begun the process of detracking (discussed later in greater detail). However, changing the beliefs and habits fostered within the formerly tracked system has proven more difficult than implementing the structural changes.

The Focus Schools

I focused the Woodland Hills study on the district's three secondary schools: the two junior high schools and one high school.[8] I studied English classes because district attention (and controversy) centered on a secondary school English detracking effort that began at the beginning of the 1995–1996 school year. To a lesser extent, I studied secondary science classes, which retained the most structured tracking in the district. The following presents a very brief overview of the district's three secondary schools.

West Junior High

The district's planners set West's capacity at 650 students. In the 1996–1997 school year, however, almost 950 were enrolled, and its over-enrollment largely dictated its atmosphere.

During the five-minute breaks separating each of the nine class periods, the narrow halls teemed with loud 11–13 year-olds. Most teachers stood by their doorways like mother ducks keeping an eye on their ducklings. To their credit, the students generally walked to the right, adding some semblance of order to the event. Complicating the process, however, was the placement of the students' lockers along the walls. Add to this the ever-present animated conversations and minor disputes, and the overall environment resembled the crowd heading to the restrooms at the end of the second period of a NY Rangers hockey game.

Not surprisingly, this environment carried over into the classroom. Teachers complained that the overcrowding forced sharing of classrooms and hampered their ability to prepare labs and lessons. When asked about the detracking, the teachers at West spoke with a near-universal voice: detracking was an asinine idea.

East Junior High

In contrast with West, East Junior High is housed in a much smaller building with a much smaller student population (less than 500). It suffers no over-crowding problem. Perhaps because of this, the teachers maintained a more positive attitude. Although they too viewed detracking as somewhat problematic, none I spoke with called for a return to tracking. And although they too had not mastered teaching mixed-ability classes, they appeared more comfortable with their classes than did the West teachers.

More than anything that any of these teachers said, however, what most stood out when comparing the two schools was the overall learning environment. While West had a hectic feel, where educators seemed to be perpetually focusing on damage-control, the pace at East seemed more relaxed and focused on education. "The physical presence of that many kids at West," one educator remarked, "gives you a more frenetic sense." Interestingly, even though the two schools are attended by students the same age, the students at East seemed more like junior high school kids in their dress and their mannerisms—it felt less like a high school and more like a middle school. Racially, the two schools presented another point of difference. West's enrollment included 35% African-American students, while East's included only 27% African Americans.[9]

The study's inclusion of both of the district's junior high schools came with a limitation. Identifying quoted educators as teaching at one or the other of these schools would have, I believe, helped the reader to understand their standpoints. However, my concerns regarding anonymity outweighed the potential benefit, and the only distinction occasionally offered is between educators at the junior high and high school levels.

Woodland Hills High School

The two junior high schools fed into a single high school. Woodland Hills High School enrolled more than 1,400 students, 28% of whom were African American. Its teachers varied greatly in their attitudes toward the reform, but they more closely approximated the positive approach at East than the relatively hostile approach at West. Among the teachers, academic departments provided the most significant organizational structure, although there were also various informal networks.

In many ways, the high school was a center of community activity and pride, even as it was the subject of some targeted criticism. This contradiction exemplifies the community's love-hate relationship toward a school district that was formed by the federal courts' shotgun marriage 15 years earlier.

SAN JOSE

In California, concern over tracking practices was particularly salient. Throughout the 1980s and 1990s, California's policy-makers and politicians became increasingly aware that providing its ever-increasing population of Latino and African-American students only limited access to a high-quality education would place the state's economic future at great risk. The potential loss of human capital, in the form of well-educated workers needed to fill the state's high-tech occupations, prompted state policy-makers to pressure educators to raise educational expectations and schools' outcomes. Detracking was advanced by policy-makers as a reform designed to help California schools become more competitive nationally and internationally (see California Department of Education, 1987, 1992a, and 1992b, all urging school leaders to develop alternatives to track structures).

Yet, tracking has remained common in the state's secondary schools. The San Jose Unified School District (SJUSD) was no exception. The district is mid-sized (approximately 30,000 students) and is located on the South Bay area of Northern California, near the Silicon Valley. It includes both an urban area and a suburban area. Roughly speaking, the district can be thought of as a 16-mile long, rectangular, vertical strip. The northern part of this strip runs through, but is not coterminous with, the city of San Jose. High concentrations of Latino families live in this northern area, while the southern part of the district is more suburban and more White (see Levine, 1972, for a historical treatment of the development of these housing patterns in San Jose). Over the past decade, a substantial Asian-American population has also migrated to the south. In 1995, the district was approximately 46% Hispanic, 34% Anglo, 15% Asian American and 3% African American.

As early as 1962, San Jose school officials acknowledged the presence of district segregation. Three years later, the board of education adopted a resolution pledging to avoid segregating pupils by race or ethnicity and declaring integration essential to quality education. At the same time, the state Board of Education notified the district that 41 of its 50 schools were in violation of the state's standards for racial and ethnic balance and directed the district to remedy this situation. Little action was taken.

In 1971, José Vasquez, along with two other parents, Arnulfo and Socorro Diaz, filed an action in federal district court alleging that the SJUSD segregated Latinos, in violation of the Fourteenth Amendment's Equal Protection Clause. This litigation bounced around the court system for 14 years with few consequences; the courts tread lightly and the district yawned. In response to the courts' toothless admonitions to address the segregation problem, the district offered a limited and voluntary desegregation plan grounded primarily in magnet schools (Watson, 1985b, 1985f; Wiehe, 1985). A desegregation order was finally issued on December 31, 1985 (*Diaz v. San Jose Unified School District*, 1985). The plaintiffs had argued that the court should order mandatory busing to remedy the discrimination, but the court accepted instead the "controlled choice" plan offered by the SJUSD. This plan again relied primarily on magnet schools and voluntary choice, but it was now buttressed by preset proportions for ethnic balance within schools (akin to quotas).

By most accounts, this aspect of the desegregation process met with relative success. In the year prior to the desegregation plan (1985–1986), only 53% of the district's students attended desegregated schools, yet 100% of the students did by the 1989–1990 school year. Notwithstanding this apparent triumph, not everyone was impressed by these statistics. A Latina mother I spoke with raised her concern over the way that the desegregation order defined "majority" and "minority" for purposes of integration. Whites were defined as "majority," and all others were defined as "minority." As a result of these definitions, this parent worried that schools would be defined as "integrated" even when they enrolled only Whites and Asian Americans to the exclusion of Latinos and African Americans. Her concerns were not unfounded: this uneven ethnic distribution was indeed found in many of the district's schools (SJUSD, 1994).

Nonetheless, largely based on its success in meeting the court's desegregation mandate, the district headed back to the court in 1992, seeking to be released from the court's jurisdiction and to regain full control over governance. Through their "unitary status" motion, the district sought a finding from the court that it no longer operated a "dual" set of schools and had eliminated all of the vestiges of its past discriminatory (dual) system.

The plaintiffs responded to this motion with evidence that the district had engaged in so-called "second-generation" discrimination—using tracking to resegregate students along racial lines. After considerable negotiation, the parties agreed, in January of 1994, to modify the original desegregation order. This modification became the consent decree.

This settlement required the district to desegregate and detrack its classrooms and programs. The detracking aspects of the consent decree mandated that (a) in elementary schools, all classes would be desegregated and consist of students of mixed ability by the 1994–1995 school year; (b) in middle schools, within a three-year phase-in period, all regular classes would be mixed-ability (using Henry Levin's accelerated school model or a similar program providing "gifted"-type education to all students), and at least 80% of the regular classes would be desegregated; (c) in the ninth grade, all core instructional courses would be desegregated and mixed-ability by the 1994–1995 school year; and (d) for the remaining high school years, the students could be offered advanced and elective courses; however, the schools would be required to engage in a specified program of monitoring and intervention to ensure that minority students were full participants in these courses. In connection with this detracking, the district undertook to identify and use curricular and instructional materials and methods designed for desegregated and mixed-ability instruction (see Londen, 1995, for a discussion of the litigation and settlement in San Jose).

The tracking aspect of the consent decree was influenced by expert findings that the district's tracking system had the effect of creating racially imbalanced classes, with Whites favored systematically over and above Latino and African-American students in class enrollment decisions. As will be set forth in greater detail in Chapter Four, statistical analyses revealed that this skewed enrollment pattern could not be explained by students' previously measured achievement. Moreover, low-track placement was found to have a negative impact on students' subsequent academic achievement.

ROCKFORD

Rockford, Illinois is a blue-collar city with a population of 350,000, located to the north of Chicago. The Rockford Public School District presently serves over 27,000 students. Rockford is the second-largest city in Illinois and has the inglorious distinction of being ranked dead-last by *Money* magazine—300th out of 300—in its 1996 list of the best places to live in the United States.[10] *Money* does not include "integration" or "racial harmony" when drawing up these lists, but curing this oversight would not have improved Rockford's ranking. The seriousness of Rockford's problems is perhaps most vividly illustrated by particular examples of racism. At one school, the nurse sprayed air freshener and wiped her desktop after dealing with African-American students (Nikolai, 2001). At several others, school authorities routinely held minority transfer students on their bus until the White neighborhood students had left the playground, in order to keep separate the students of different races (*People Who Care*, 1994, p. 1005). Of the four districts profiled in this book, Rockford's recent history demonstrates the deepest racial divide and the least racial progress.

As far back as the 1950s, Rockford has been a divided city. The Rock River, which runs north-south through the city, served as a de facto racial dividing line, with the vast majority of Latino and African-American children living on the older, southwest side and the majority of White children living in the developing northeast. In addition, the schools on the eastern side of the city were maintained as White enclaves through the busing of minority students from the few residentially-integrated areas over to the west.

In 1967, the school district appointed a citizens' committee to address the poor academic performance of the southwest's (minority) schools. The committee recommended, among other things, that the district take certain steps toward racial integration, but the district refused. Meanwhile, pressure from civil rights groups and authorities continued to mount for some movement toward integration, but voters responded in 1970 by electing a conservative, anti-busing board of education.

That same year, a group of pro-integration citizens and organizations formed a committee, which then brought a desegregation lawsuit against the district. Two years later, in September of 1972, the State of Illinois notified the district that it was in violation of state desegregation guidelines. The district took two steps to address the issues raised by the citizen lawsuit and the state complaint: it initiated busing of minority students to White schools, and it began a voluntary plan allowing White students to attend alternative programs within minority schools. These alternative programs existed as segregated White enclaves within those schools.

In 1981, both the state action and the citizens' action disappeared. The state action fell victim to a ruling of the Illinois Supreme Court that the state

Board of Education did not have the statutory authority to issue desegregation regulations. The citizens' action was voluntarily dismissed following promises by the district to continue desegregation efforts. Notwithstanding these promises, however, desegregation efforts were scaled back, and the district experienced a renewed pattern of systemwide segregation throughout the 1980s. In 1989, the district adopted an extensive reorganization plan, trumpeted as saving $7.3 million. It proposed to close 10 schools, 7 of which primarily served minority students on the west side of the city. In response, a new citizens' group, called "People Who Care," was formed. It filed a desegregation action against the district. The district quickly responded, agreeing to reopen four west-side schools and to increase funding for minority schools.

During the next several years, the parties negotiated agreements, but the school board failed to honor important terms. Therefore, in 1993 the case went to trial. The court's decision, holding the district to have violated the equal protection rights of the district's minority students, is discussed throughout Chapters Three, Four, and Five.

WILMINGTON

The schools of Wilmington, Delaware, are not unfamiliar to America's federal courts. Indeed, an action on behalf of African-American children in New Castle County, where Wilmington is located, was one of the four cases decided by the U.S. Supreme Court in *Brown v. Board of Education* (1954, n. 1).[11] Wilmington was also a site of the race-awareness tests conducted by Kenneth and Mamie Clark and cited by the Justices in *Brown*. The Wilmington lawsuit, entitled *Gebhart v. Belton*, sought to enjoin provisions of the Delaware State Constitution and statutory code that mandated the segregation of Negroes and Whites in public schools (Del. Const., Art. X, §2; Del. Rev. Code §2631, 1935).[12] The action was successful, and the defendants applied to the U.S. Supreme Court for *certiorari*. (This was the only one of the four *Brown* cases decided at the lower-court level in favor of the plaintiffs.)

Following the Supreme Court's *Brown* decision, many of Wilmington's Whites reacted to the changed legal landscape by moving to the suburbs, and the state of Delaware assisted them by effectively using redistricting to cordon off the increasingly Black city schools from the White suburbs. The New Castle County area was subdivided into numerous districts, some identifiably White, some identifiably African American. In 1971, African-American parents responded to this renewed segregation by filing a new lawsuit.

Seven years later, in 1978, the district court issued an order declaring the various school districts in Northern New Castle County to be operating a dual system in violation of the Equal Protection Clause of the Fourteenth

Amendment. This 1978 order consolidated the various districts into a single district and put in place a comprehensive desegregation plan, including a mandatory "9–3" student assignment plan, which provided that all students will attend formerly "White" schools for 9 years and formerly "Black" schools for 3 consecutive years. This effectively meant that African-American students were bused for 9 years while White students were bused for 3 years. In practice, the plan also resulted in African-American students generally having longer bus rides.

This court decision was similar to the Woodland Hills decision in that it mandated desegregation across district lines. In both cases, the plaintiffs overcame stringent rules set forth by the U.S. Supreme Court in *Milliken v. Bradley* (1974), overturning a ruling that had required suburban Detroit districts be merged with the city school system. Such drastic measures, the *Milliken* Court explained, were only appropriate where suburban school districts, or the state, had themselves acted in racially discriminatory ways. In accordance with *Milliken*, the 1978 order followed a court finding that the state and suburban districts had redistricted the school districts' boundaries with the intention of fostering racial segregation.

The 1978 order addressed the usual desegregation factors, ranging from student assignments between schools to faculty and staff composition and their assignments between schools to discriminatory expenditures and decision-making concerning facilities. Tracking was not a primary focus of this order, although the court did require the defendants to "prevent resegregation under the guise of curriculum or program choices" (*Evans v. Buchanan*, 1978, p. 1016). Three years later, the court expanded on this charge, stating that "resegregation in classrooms apparently caused by ability grouping and tracking" was one of many "vestige effects of de jure segregation" that "need to be addressed" before unitary status could be reached (*Evans v. Buchanan*, 1981, p. 863).

In Chapter Four, I will present some statistical analyses of tracking and its racial impact on New Castle County schools. These analyses were originally offered to the federal district court in Delaware in 1995, as part of the evidence presented in opposition to the defendants' motion for an order declaring unitary status. As will be detailed later in this book, the defendants' motion was nonetheless granted.

Please note, in the interests of accuracy if not clarity, that the court's 1981 order granted the State Board of Education's motion to divide the consolidated district into four separate districts (Brandywine, Christina, Colonial, and Red Clay). This structure continued to exist at the time of my study in 1994–1995. However, for simplicity's sake I will often refer to these four districts in the singular—as the Wilmington school district.

3

Follow the Bouncing Gavel

The legal precedents predating the four cases presented in this book were few yet highly significant. In isolated instances over the past four decades, aggrieved parents have turned to the courts for help in overcoming the powerful political and normative forces that sustained inequitable tracking systems. The courts' anti-majoritarian role (e.g., forcing change when the political majority demands stability) is a well-established principle of our governmental system (Bickel, 1962; Hamilton, 1788; *Marbury v. Madison*, 1803). Nevertheless, courts are extraordinarily reluctant to exercise this role. This chapter explores that tension in the context of legal claims attacking racial tracking.

It bears repeating at this point that the harmful effects of tracking can extend far beyond the racial segregation of children. For example, by attempting to assess children's potential, predict their futures, and target instruction to a student's "ability," tracking systems can arbitrarily deprive students of valuable learning opportunities. Other common flaws in tracking systems include rigidity, lack of mobility, stigmatization, and unequal distribution of resources (Oakes, Gamoran, & Page, 1992). These non-racial factors may, in the future, provide grounds for legal challenges based on a variety of theories.[1] This book, however, focuses on the types of challenges that have, thus far, been most common: those based on federal authority and on allegations of the segregative and discriminatory effects of tracking.

THREE TYPES OF FEDERAL ACTIONS

As a rule, courts in the United States are very hesitant to interfere with the operation of public schools (Tyack, James, & Benevot, 1991). Beginning in 1954 with *Brown v. Board of Education*, however, many courts have overcome this hesitancy. Following *Brown*, courts may intervene in district policy-making if plaintiffs offer convincing evidence of racial discrimination. The federal government has at least implicitly—through the Equal Protection Clause of the Fourteenth Amendment and the Civil Rights Act of 1964, as well as through a variety of other constitutional provisions, statutes, and regulations—determined that racial discrimination presents a greater danger to our society than discrimination based on class, gender, or any other characteristic. Consequently, a school district's racially segregative tracking system is subject to greater judicial scrutiny.

While various state and local legal authorities have the potential to play important roles in tracking litigation, the weight of such litigation has relied on the federal Equal Protection Clause and (to a lesser extent) on Title VI of the Civil Rights Act of 1964. Focusing on these two legal authorities, there are basically three categories of challenges that can arise out of the discriminatory aspect of public school tracking: (a) Original Equal Protection actions (what I refer to as "Type-I" actions), (b) Equal Protection actions in districts operating under pre-existing desegregation orders (Type-II actions), and (c) Title VI actions (Type-III actions).

Type-I (Original Equal Protection) actions require a showing of intentional discrimination (*Washington v. Davis*, 1976). This means that the plaintiffs must prove to the court both that the governmental action has a discriminatory effect *and* that this effect is intended by the government. Desegregation plaintiffs have successfully proven these elements in numerous districts around the country. However, as discrimination has become less overt, proving intent has become more problematic.

Type-II (Pre-existing Desegregation Order) actions can only be pursued after plaintiffs have won a Type-I action and, consequently, the school district is operating under a desegregation order. These are usually not distinct legal actions but, rather, hearings within a larger Equal Protection action. However, given the long life-span of desegregation actions, and given the fact that these hearings generally involve the testimony of witnesses and the introduction of substantial new evidence, it is helpful to view them as distinct actions. Despite the somewhat unique set of circumstances that give rise to such hearings, these Type-II actions appear (based upon the sheer number of reported decisions) to be the most common forums for legal challenges to tracking.

Type-II actions require a lesser showing than Type-I actions. Once a court has made the initial determination that a district has engaged in intentional discrimination, much of the burden is shifted to the defendant school district to show that subsequent discriminatory outcomes are not a vestige of that original discrimination. Accordingly, the requirement to prove intent still exists, but the plaintiff benefits from a presumption of a connection between the earlier-proven discriminatory intent and the later-proven discriminatory impact.

The third type of action existed for 35 years, but was recently eliminated by the U.S. Supreme Court in *Alexander v. Sandoval* (2001). Based on the Department of Education's implementing regulations for Title VI of the 1964 Civil Rights Act, this action also required a lesser showing; that is, it did not require proof of intent (42 U.S.C. § 2000d, 1982).[2] These lawsuits, which can no longer be brought unless Congress reverses the *Alexander* decision, worked as follows. Once the plaintiff has shown that a tracking system has a disproportionate and negative impact on a racial or ethnic group, the defendant district must respond by establishing that there exists a substantial legitimate justification or a legitimate, nondiscriminatory reason (sometimes called an "educational necessity") for the practice. If the defendant is able to meet its rebuttal burden, the plaintiff must then establish either that the defendant overlooked an equally effective alternative with less discriminatory impact or that the defendant's proffered justification is no more than a pretext for racial discrimination (see *Powell v. Ridge*, 1999).

While the *Alexander* case eliminated actions brought under the Title VI regulations by private citizens, it did not address such actions by the federal Office of Civil Rights, which may seek termination of federal assistance to the offending district. Also, a private citizen can still bring lawsuits directly under the Title VI statute (rather than under the implementing regulations) but can do so only upon demonstrating discriminatory intent. Furthermore, the outcome in *Alexander* may prompt the development of a fourth type of action, using the reconstruction era civil rights statute, 42 U.S.C. § 1983, to enforce these same Title VI regulations. Section 1983 provides express statutory authority for private individuals to bring lawsuits alleging violations of their rights under federal laws, evidently including the Title VI implementing regulations (see *Powell v. Ridge*, 1999, p. 403; Mank, 2001).

Each of these types of legal actions has both strengths and weaknesses. Because proving intentional discrimination is extremely difficult, Type-I actions are quite problematic. Since Type II actions are dependent on prevailing in a previous Type I action, Type-II actions have rather limited long-term applicability.

Type-III actions avoided these problems. However, the effectiveness of these actions was tied largely to the dependence of a district on federal money, since Title VI only bans discrimination by those institutions that receive such funding. If a district is willing to forego federal money, it is free to act in discord with the Act's provisions. Moreover, as will be discussed further below, Title VI actions had suffered from a hesitancy on the part of some federal courts to impose liability without evidence of intentional discrimination. Finally, the existence of Title VI remedies, as the remedies tied to the implementing regulations, was always tenuous (even before the *Alexander* decision), because it was subject to congressional amendment or rescission as well as to modification by the Department of Education and, of course, judicial interpretation.

Type-I Cases

Type-I actions are best represented by such well-known cases as *Brown v. Board of Education* (1954) and *Keyes v. School District No. 1* (1973). Also, to the best of my knowledge, *Hobson v. Hansen* (1967) is one of only two officially published Type-I cases in which the finding of intentional discrimination was grounded in significant part upon the district's use of tracking. (But see Dickens, 1996, for an argument that tracking systems, with their racial undertones, should be subjected to heightened scrutiny in a broader range of cases than courts have thus far ventured.)

The second case—one of the four discussed in this book—was handed down more recently than *Hobson*, by a federal district court in Illinois (*People Who Care v. Rockford Board of Education School District No. 205*, 1994). That court found that tracking was used as a tool to intentionally segregate racial groups and held that this segregation constituted a violation of the Equal Protection Clause.

Type-II Cases

As mentioned above, Type-II actions challenging tracking appear to be much more common than Type-I tracking actions. Courts in successful Type-II cases have typically grounded their decisions upon a finding that ability grouping tends, as a factual matter, to perpetuate segregation. Many courts have also noted that the tracking systems in question sprouted up at the time of (and in apparent reaction to) forced integration of schools. (See *Moses v. Washington Parish School Board*, 1972; *Simmons on Behalf of Simmons v. Hooks*, 1994.) Similarly, many of these courts have denounced the use of testing as a basis for grouping or placement in these recently desegregated schools (*Singleton v. Jackson Municipal Separate School District*, 1970; *United States v. Board of Education of Lincoln County*, 1969; *United States v. Tunica County School Dist.*, 1970; see also *Hobson*, 1967, in which the court questioned the validity and accuracy of tests used for placement).

These Type-II cases can be roughly divided into two categories: (a) motions for unitary status (i.e., a court order releasing a district from court supervision), which are generally brought by the defendant school districts; and (b) motions to modify desegregation orders, which are generally brought by the plaintiffs. (The only case that I am aware of that falls outside these two categories is *United States v. Yonkers Board of Education* (2000). The *Yonkers* court was called upon to determine whether the State of New York would be liable, along with the Yonkers school district, for remedial funding. Foundational to this ruling, the court determined that certain practices, including tracking, were vestiges of the prior discrimination. *United States v. Yonkers Board of Education*, 2000, pp. 716–18).

Motions seeking a court determination that the defendant school district has achieved unitary status are a relatively new phenomenon. Relying on the recent U.S. Supreme Court cases of *Board of Education v. Dowell* (1991), *Freeman v. Pitts* (1992), and *Missouri v. Jenkins* (1995), districts are now flooding the courts with motions seeking to be released from court supervision on the ground that they have achieved unitary status. In order to meet the burden of proof established in *Freeman*, these districts must demonstrate (a) that they no longer operate a dual system and (b) the absence of any vestiges of the former dual system. If such a motion is successful, the school district becomes free to abandon any compensatory educational programs and/or student-assignment systems previously ordered by the court.

In opposing unitary status claims, some plaintiffs have pointed to districts' use of tracking systems as a vestige of earlier discrimination. Specifically, these plaintiffs have argued that the district in question used tracking to undermine the intent of the original desegregation order. Through tracking, African-American or Latino students are often shunted into low-ability classes taught apart from high-tracked White students, even though the various racial and ethnic groups physically share the same school site. Three of the court cases analyzed in this book—San Jose, Woodland Hills, and Wilmington—are Type II cases and contain such allegations.

An older, related type of Type-II case concerns plaintiffs' motions to modify desegregation orders. In such challenges, racially disparate grouping in a previously segregated school system is generally held invalid unless the district can demonstrate that the tracking system (a) was not based on the present results of past segregation (i.e., was not a vestige) or (b) would remedy the present results of past segregation by providing enhanced educational opportunities (*McNeal v. Tate County School District*, 1975).

Despite the result in *McNeal* itself (finding the tracking system unconstitutional), several courts have used this test to conclude that, since the *particular* children now being tracked had never attended segregated schools, the earlier discrimination could not be blamed for the present disparate impact of tracking. (*Georgia State Conference of Branches of NAACP v. Georgia*, 1985; *Montgomery v. Starkville Mun. Separate School Dist.*, 1987; *Quarles v. Oxford Mun. Separate School Dist.*, 1989.) Most recently, however, in *Simmons v. Hooks* (1994), the court applied the *McNeal* test in a much less deferential way.

The *Simmons* action sought monetary damages on behalf of three siblings who had been placed in lower-track courses by a school district in Augusta, Arkansas, operating under a desegregation order. The court, in considering these charges of discrimination, recognized that the district had not yet been

declared unitary and applied the *McNeal* test. The court held that the plaintiff could satisfy the *McNeal* test without having to prove intentional discrimination, although the court also made a finding that there had been intentional
discrimination.

Importantly, while earlier courts applying the *McNeal* test had deferred to
the judgment of local educators, the *Simmons* court refused to do so. Instead, it
relied on expert testimony in finding that the tracking system would not remedy
the results of past discrimination by providing better educational opportunities.
Here, the court cited plaintiff's expert Robert Slavin's testimony that educational researchers had concluded that tracking is not beneficial to students
placed in the low group (p. 1299). The court also noted that even the defendant's expert "could not present a credible educational justification for grouping entire classes of children for all purposes" (pp. 1302–1303). For these
reasons, the court ordered that the district cease its use of tracking.

Thus, the success of these Type-II cases has been mixed. Yet, as the hey-
day of Type-I cases fades into the past, we can expect that successful Type-II
cases will also become fewer in number, since (a) the *McNeal* test will become
more difficult to satisfy (thereby discouraging suits), and (b) more districts will
achieve unitary status (thereby being released from court supervision).

Type-III Cases

In response to the increasingly limited choices afforded through Fourteenth
Amendment jurisprudence, Title VI of the Civil Rights Act of 1964 (Type-III
cases) had offered a correspondingly more attractive option for those wishing
to challenge school tracking systems. Plaintiffs in a Title VI action, brought
pursuant to the Education Department's implementing regulations, were entitled to prevail without proving intentional discrimination (see *Guardians Association v. Civil Service Commission of New York*, 1983, p. 584)). However,
these actions had always met with only limited success. In both *NAACP v.
Georgia* (1985) and *Quarles v. Oxford School District* (1989), for example, the
plaintiffs supplemented their Type-II claims with Type-III claims, but to no
avail. Notwithstanding the disparate legal analyses called for under the two
types of causes of action, the courts dismissed both arguments on similar
grounds. Specifically, the courts seem to have defied precedent and required a
showing of discriminatory intent as an element of the Title VI claims. (See
Note, "Teaching Inequality," 1989, for an excellent discussion of this issue.)
That is, after having found a possible nondiscriminatory rationale for the tracking, the courts in these two cases deferred to the judgment of school officials
who preferred to employ this particular pedagogical practice. (See also *Montgomery v. Starkville Municipal Separate School District*, 1987.)

DEFINING THE GOALS OF DESEGREGATION AND DETRACKING

Plaintiffs bringing any of the above-outlined legal claims must, in addition to considering issues of liability, decide among various possible remedial approaches. Consider the task faced by a plaintiff attempting to convince a court to strike down a district's tracking system on the ground that it segregates children by race. At some point (hopefully rather early in the process), the plaintiff's legal team must decide on its argument to the court concerning why tracking is harmful and detracking is necessary. This claim of denial of equal educational opportunity might stress one or more of the following types of damage: psychological, sociological, educational, and moral.

Proving the damage caused by segregation has important repercussions in at least two areas. First, it is necessary in order to prove liability. Second, such proof provides the basis upon which the remedy is formulated. Rockford, Woodland Hills, and San Jose all felt this latter repercussion (Chapter Five presents an in-depth look at the remedial wranglings in Rockford). The following discussion explores various potential goals of desegregation and detracking litigation.

Desegregation has been generally accepted by courts as the appropriate remedy for intentional segregation.[3] However, there is less agreement about what should constitute the ultimate goal of desegregation. Hawley and Rist (1977) list four general goals of desegregation: (1) improvements in academic achievement; (2) increased access to educational resources and to post-education opportunities; (3) improvements in self-esteem, aspirations and other personality-related dispositions of minority students; and (4) reduction in interracial hostility and the elimination of racial intolerance (pp. 414–15). Each of these goals can easily be traced back to a particular type of provable damage in a desegregation case.

The concern about the type of damage proven to the court and the choice of goals for desegregation is legitimate. Once one or more outcomes are accepted as the goal of desegregation, the value and the success of desegregation efforts become tied to measurement of the progress made toward achieving that goal or goals. This has been problematic, because studies of the progress made towards the various proposed goals have shown mixed results.

Some scholars have argued that the evidence of improved academic achievement resulting from desegregation (Hawley & Rist's Goal #1) is inconclusive (Epps, 1977) or that the improvement is slight (see Coleman et al., 1966; Cook, 1984, concluding that desegregation resulted in an increase in reading levels but no noticeable change in mathematics). Weinberg (1977) concluded that desegregation does indeed have a positive effect on minority achievement levels. He reviewed the literature (much of it unpublished), and he found agreement on several points: (a) the achievement levels of white majorities in desegregated schools do not decline, (b) the net effect of desegregation on the academic achievement levels of nonwhites is seen in most studies as positive and in others as at least neutral, and (c) the instrument for obtaining integration—whether through busing, pairing schools, or altering attendance zones—has no direct bearing on the achievement of the children involved. More recently, several studies have shown increased academic achievement and higher test scores among minority students attending desegregated schools (Bankston & Caldas, 1997; Brown, 1999; Crain & Mahard, 1978, 1982, 1983; Schiff, Firestone, & Young, 1999; Schofield, 1995, 2000).

Somewhat mixed results were presented in a literature review by Epps (1977) concerning the impact of desegregation on certain aspects of personality which are generally considered to be important outcomes of schooling: aspirations, self-concept, sense of control over the environment, and achievement orientation (Hawley & Rist's Goal #3). For the most part, Epps found little convincing or conclusive evidence regarding these outcomes (although he did conclude that desegregation probably decreases anxiety and increases motivation). Subsequent studies, however, have demonstrated that this goal is powerfully advanced by integrated schooling (Dawkins, 1983; Hoelter, 1982; Kurlaender & Yun, 2000; Schofield 1995, 2000). These newer studies show how aspirations are heightened in desegregated environments—or, perhaps more accurately, they show how those aspirations are lowered for minorities in segregated environments.

A literature review by Wells and Crain (1994) produced more convincing data on three categories of possible effects of desegregation: the occupational aspirations of high school students, college choice and educational achievement, and occupational attainment and adult social networks (Hawley & Rist's Goal #2). The studies reviewed examined the long-term effects of desegregation in overcoming perpetual segregation and on earning higher income (see Braddock, 1980, and McPartland & Braddock, 1981, for a discussion of perpetuation theory). The authors suggest that current debates on the merits of desegregation need to re-focus on long-term effects and the life chances of African-American students, rather than overemphasizing test score comparisons.

Wells and Crain concluded that desegregated African-American students set their occupational aspirations higher than do those who are segregated, and desegregated African-American students' occupational aspirations are more realistically related to their educational accomplishments and aspirations than are those of segregated African-American students. This finding suggests that African-American students attending desegregated schools have access to social networks that inform them about the connections between education and occupation. In addition, attendance at desegregated schools appears to lead African American students toward attendance at predominantly White colleges and to show higher college attainment than those who attended segregated schools. Finally, they are more likely to have desegregated social and professional networks later in life, are more likely to find themselves in desegregated employment, and are more likely to be working in white-collar and professional jobs in the private sector than are African Americans from segregated schools.

While Wells and Crain (1994) argue for a "life chances" goal of desegregation, Levin (1977) argues that desegregation is better grounded in "basic fairness" and a "just society." He concludes that it is impossible for social scientists to draw accurate inferences about the effects of schooling on life chances (a term which he apparently uses in a somewhat different way than Wells and Crain; for example, he incorporates academic achievement measures and does not necessarily look at long-term effects). Because of the inadequacy of present analytic tools, he reasons, there is no social science consensus on the appropriate educational strategies for improving the life chances of children from low income and minority backgrounds.

Levin also warns about goal displacement. He fears that social science evidence will be incorporated into legal analyses and will tend to redefine the issues themselves. "[T]he prima facie inequities are ignored as the courts are tortured with the convoluted arguments provided by social scientists" about the effects of the particular policy on "life chances" (Levin, 1977, p. 237). With regard to desegregation policy, Levin states, "[r]ather than considering what kind of educational policy regarding school racial patterns is consistent with our democratic ideals, the issue seems to be whether or not African Americans and other minorities gain a few more points on a vocabulary or reading test" (p. 239). Levin concludes that "if social science findings increasingly are used to create what appear to be technical issues out of moral dilemmas, this presents a potential social danger" (p. 240).

Coons (1977) takes a slightly different approach than Levin. He argues that desegregation judgments *necessarily* boil down to courts' moral judgments about a just society:

> I believe that the courts would never have reached the stage of citing Kenneth Clark or Christopher Jencks, unless they had already made a lusty normative leap unaided by anything more than their non-empirical values. These specimens of research were relevant only because judges had already accepted some notion of human equality as a value to be incorporated in the process of judicial rule selection (p. 52).

As Coons explains, "history discloses how narrowly the equal protection clause guarantee could be constructed by a judiciary unconvinced of the moral claims of human equality" (p. 53). "Equality," he states, "is not an inference from data; it is an act of faith about intrinsic human worth" (p. 53).[4]

The elimination of racial intolerance (Hawley & Rist's Goal #4), while clearly not a short-term product of desegregation, is a reasonable long-term goal. Kevin Brown (1992) argues that, while the Supreme Court's ideological framework has generally contained the assumption that racial isolation retards the intellectual and psychological development of African-American children, the Court *should have* based its desegregation remedies on the well-accepted socializing role of public schools. He asserts that the principal harm of *de jure* segregation is the negative and stigmatizing lesson that schools inculcate in all children that African Americans are inferior. Viewed from this perspective, re-mediation of *de jure* segregation benefits all children, not just African Americans. The recent study of Louisville schools by Kurlaender and Yun (2000) demonstrates that this goal can be accomplished. They reported survey results showing Black children, as well as White children, with strong improvements in their attitudes toward diversity.

The above collection of research findings suggests a variety of possible goals for desegregation.[5] Some goals are psychological, some are sociological, and some are moral. Interestingly, each researcher (with the apparent exception of Hawley & Rist, 1977) seems to accept, either explicitly or implicitly, the idea that the choice of one single goal excludes the validity of the other goals—at least in the context of legal challenges. Levin (1977), for one, de-fends this either/or approach by pointing to the role of the other goals in dis-tracting courts from the real (moral) issue.[6]

However, each court is different. Judges and juries are people, with many of the same backgrounds and perspectives that we find elsewhere in society. Consequently, some courts may be particularly responsive to psychological evidence, others to sociological evidence, and some only to moral arguments. Many courts will respond best to a combination of the three types of argu-ments. A civil rights attorney may argue, "Desegregation (or detracking) is a moral and democratic imperative, and, besides, it is necessary to provide an equal opportunity for academic achievement, psychological health and life chances." Those judges who do not feel that the moral argument is sufficient may be convinced by one of the other arguments.

LITIGATION AS A CHANGE STRATEGY

Throughout the past half-century, litigation has served as a primary strategy for making fundamental changes to the nation's schools. School desegregation in the wake of *Brown v. Board of Education* (1954) is only the most well known example. Widespread bilingual education was promoted by a 1974 Supreme

TABLE 2.2

The Workforce of Chicago's Men's Clothing Shops in 1892,
Classified by Gender, Age, and Working Place

		Coats	Pants	Vests	Total
Total		4,694	2,919	1,656	9,269
Male	Men*	1,312	354	247	1,913
	Boys*	148	40	9	197
Female	Women*	23	1,468	205	1,696
	Girls*	3,211	1,057	1,195	5,463
Place	In shop	4,692	1,472	1,480	7,644
	At home	2	1,447	176	1,625

*Unfortunately, IBLS did not define these terms. Throughout its report, however, "Boys" appeared to be children in their low teens or under, while "Girls" were unmarried women.

Source: IBLS, *Seventh Biennial Report*, 419–432.

TABLE 2.3

The Workforce of Chicago's Men's Clothing Shops in 1892, Classified by Job

Job	Sex	Coats	Pants	Vests	Total
Operator	M	146	9	4	159
	F	1,174	955	577	2,076
Finisher	M	41	3	7	51
	F	2,026	1,525	286	3,837
Trimmer	M	394	32	55	481
	F	16	1	0	17
Presser	M	685	306	141	1,132
	F	0	1	0	1
Miscellaneous	M	194	44	49	287
	F	18	43	539	600
Total no. of	M	1,460	394	256	2,110
employees	F	3,234	2,525	1,400	7,159
No. of shops		338	122	90	550
Average no. of employees per shop		14	24	18.4	

Source: Adapted from IBLS, *Seventh Biennial Report*, 443.

which shortly went up to $7.50 and then dropped to $6.00. Other women were less fortunate. A hand sewer employed almost throughout the year first worked at $5.50 a week, but after an increase of $0.50 her rate went down to $3.75; another hand sewer worked forty-six weeks, beginning at a rate of $3.75 a week, which increased to $4.00 and then declined to $1.50.[45]

In fact, wage rates, especially those of unskilled women workers, could be easily reduced in any season, not just the slack period. Although women were employed as regular shop hands, they were the first victims of the slack season and always lived perilously close to unemployment. Because unemployed women constituted the reserve army of the clothing industry, the sweater was in a position "to dole out work in such small quantities that his employés are all eager to get as much as possible,"[46] forcing them to accept the wage rates he offered. This was particularly true of home finishers, who frequently found it hard to distinguish unemployment from underemployment. Combining housekeeping with their sewing, these women often worked for whatever they could get, and kept the wage levels in the clothing industry low. The IBLS revealed that sweatshop employees complained about the downward tendency in wages. Indeed, a female cloak maker reported that for almost the same work she received "$3 in 1890, $1.25 in 1891, and 95 cents in 1892."[47] This tendency was amply confirmed by the Congressional Committee on Manufactures. In his testimony before the CM, Abraham Bisno, a cloak maker who later became a prominent labor leader in the women's clothing industry, said that in 1891 he produced more than he had in 1885, but that he earned less.[48]

These features of the sweating system wrought a distinctive work culture in the small clothing shops. Work was usually intermittent in the sweatshops because the seasonal nature of the men's clothing industry did not allow sweaters to maintain steady work throughout the year. Even during the busy season work was often irregular at a number of small shops whose owners had failed to develop stable business relationships with manufacturers or large contractors. While the sweatshop employees were idle during the slack season (as well as sometimes in the busy season), they worked incessantly whenever there was work to be done. Their working hours extended from 5 A.M. to 10 P.M., seven days a week. Only in Jewish shops did they take Saturdays off for the Sabbath.[49]

Such a work pattern brought forth a familial atmosphere in the sweatshop. The sweater and his employees worked side by side for long hours, knew each others' families, friends, and personal concerns, and took part in each others' important events, such as weddings and funerals. While the sweater frequently loaned his employees money to tide them over in an economic pinch or to bring their family members over from their home country, they knew whether he was making money or not.[50] Claiming that he was also subject to a manufacturer's reduction in contract prices, the sweater described the manufacturer as exploiting both himself and his workers.[51] Like a family, all the members of a sweatshop shared their private lives as well as their work lives.

The familial atmosphere was possible because the boss and his hands shared common language, religion, and social customs. He recruited workers almost invariably through his network of acquaintances among his own ethnic group, so ethnic conformity between the sweater and his employees was a "rule" in Chicago, as in other clothing centers. The IBLS reported only six exceptions out of the 666 clothing shops investigated: One American and three Irish sweaters made no distinction among ethnic groups, while two Jewish shops were filled with Poles.[52] And the sweater often took in a few employees as his boarders or lodgers. Having left their families in Europe, many immigrant clothing workers made arrangements for living with sweaters, who they often found were connected to themselves either by blood or through acquaintance in the old country. And they occasionally sought a sweater's advice on personal matters, because he had come earlier to the United States and knew more about America.[53] Other sweatshop employees lived within walking distance of the workplace.[54] While the sweater located his shop in their neighborhood in order to get cheap labor, they had to be available on a short notice when he managed to secure work.

The familial environment led sweatshop employees to combine work with leisure. When workers found time to take a rest during the day, they enjoyed various forms of recreation in the workroom. They sang songs, chatted and laughed, played cards and discussed diverse issues, telling errand boys "to fetch beer."[55] Such a mixture of work and leisure in the sweatshop was vividly described in a pants maker's testimony before the CM:

> As I visited one tailor shop three weeks ago [in] the first room I came into there was a press stove; in that same room there was a bench for tailors, and, it looked to me, to lie down on and take a rest when they were too filled up with beer. I saw beer glasses and I saw food scattered around on two benches, and when I went into the next room I saw them ready to cook their meat on a stove which was for the purpose of heating irons on, and that it seemed to me that most of them were taking their meals right in that place. . . .[56]

As indicated by this testimony, there was frequently no spatial separation between work and living quarters, one of the main complaints made by investigators of the sweating system. The workers usually ate their meals at the work table or bench. In general the sweater's wife prepared meals for them, or they brought food and had it cooked on the stove that heated the iron.[57] The workers also discussed their personal concerns, became party to each others' ceremonies, and joined together in the various events that took place in immigrant settlements. In the sweatshop, therefore, fierce and ceaseless toil alternated with idleness that cultivated closeness among the workers. This intermixture of work and living, characteristic of sweatshops located in the ethnic neighborhoods, was natural to immigrant workers; in the Old World they had combined both, either in the rural field or at the village workshop.

The work culture hindered labor organizing among sweatshop workers. It did not necessarily prevent them from resorting to collective action, for it helped them build the sort of intimate personal relations that could be effectively mobilized in a strike. The workers, though they seldom struck a particular sweater, occasionally joined factory employees fighting against the manufacturers, and they helped paralyze the whole men's clothing industry during the 1910–1911 strike in Chicago. But the familial atmosphere and neighborliness that existed between the sweater and his employees not only discouraged confrontation between both sides but also limited the workers' contacts beyond their ethnic neighborhood. Working and living in the narrow boundaries of each sweatshop district and constrained by language, the workers lacked any channel of communication with other ethnic groups. "The differences of race, language and religion," observed IBLS, "prove an obstacle to the growth of organization."[58] The sweatshop employees were isolated from the mainstream of American organized labor. For example, on May 5, 1886, when hundreds of Chicago's Jewish cloak makers protested against their working conditions by marching into the downtown clothing districts, they were not even aware of the Haymarket affair, which had shocked the city the day before. It was not until after the police had forcibly driven them back to their own neighborhood that the cloak makers learned about that tragic event.[59]

Another important obstacle to organization was the fact that many of the sweatshop employees, especially unskilled ones, were not so much men's clothing workers as casual laborers. A significant number of them suffered from irregular and meager work. At the boys' jacket shop studied by IBLS, six employees out of the thirty-three men and women worked fewer than ten weeks in the one-year period and another fifteen no more than forty weeks. Moreover, these twenty-one workers were often the lowest-paid employees at the shop.[60] Such chronic underemployment at low wages drove many sweatshop employees to seek other occupations such as peddling and domestic service, especially in the slack season.

Other sweatshop employees, having learned enough to be independent and dexterous workers, sought better-paying positions in the large inside or contract shops. As the division of labor was rather simple in the small shop, an employee could be trained to do various operations. So a Czech contractor, employing twenty-six workers in his Chicago shop, claimed "that as he does not pay high wages his shop is used by employees as a training school, the employees leaving when they have learned the trade and going to the large inside shops."[61]

TOWARD THE FACTORY SYSTEM

The inside shops, willing to employ experienced hands, began to flourish in the late 1890s. As the sweating system became a dominant type of production organization in New York, Philadelphia, and to a more limited extent in other clothing centers where immigrant labor was less abundant, many manufacturers reduced the inside shop to a cutting room. But others, especially those who because of their location could not rely heavily on immigrant labor, did not. They avoided direct competition with sweaters and focused on different lines of products.

The men's ready-made clothing industry, though generally known for shoddy and ill-fitting garments, tried to produce better clothes after the Civil War. In designing garments, more and more manufacturers introduced standard sizes for men, based on the Union Army's orders for military uniforms.[62] Moreover, some began to make garments according to individual customers' measurements and taste. They established an arrangement with merchant tailors, who agreed to be paid a commission for taking orders from customers. These "special-order" or "made-to-measure" manufacturers, prospering in Chicago, achieved economies of scale by producing in volume. They made cheap clothes largely for the southern and midwestern markets.[63]

On the other hand, some large manufacturers offered fine ready-made clothes. As the country became rapidly urbanized in the late nineteenth century, city dwellers, in particular businessmen, professionals, and white-collar workers, demanded inexpensive quality clothing. To these urbanites ready-made clothing was still unattractive because it had long been identified with cheap clothes for the low-income population. Aiming at such customers, some manufacturers sought to offer quality garments after the late 1880s. When the Congressional Committee on Manufactures held its sessions in Chicago in 1892, Herman Elston, a manufacturer in the city, declared, "We are manufacturing a better class of goods than we used to," and added that the change had been "for the better in the last five years."[64] Testifying before the CM, large Chicago manufacturers repeatedly pointed out that they made a better grade of clothes for higher prices while small establishments, those of New York and Philadelphia in particular, produced a low grade of goods like "the cheapest kind of trash."[65] "[T]he better grades are in general wholly or partly made in the larger shop," the committee reported, "while the poorer grades and the finishing of the better ones are more generally made in the smaller shops or tenement-home work. . . ."[66]

It was at this point that the anti-sweatshop campaign reached its peak. On Sunday, July 29, 1888, the *Chicago Times* surprised dwellers of the city with an announcement that a series of articles planned by the paper would report "[a] dreadful, damnable reality." Under the title "Life Among the Slave Girls of Chicago," the editor declared on the front page that a personal investigation revealed working women suffering from a brutal process "whereby the marrow is ground out of the bones, the virtue out of the souls, and the souls out of the bodies. . . ."[67] Indeed, the heart-wrenching series showed that many women and children were working under wretched conditions. The articles also revealed that they were languishing under unabashed exploitation chiefly by the city's manufacturers of ready-made clothing, furnishings, cigars, boxes, and so forth. The story was written by Nell Nelson, who hid her identity as a reporter, got jobs at several shops, and gathered firsthand information about working women during her one-month study. She drew an immediate and emotional response from her readers. A few accused the working women of showing off "their finery" on weekends, or remarked that they could find a job in the country, but many expressed deep sympathy. One reader wrote a poem titled "The Sewing Girl's Lament," and another proposed to form "a society for the protection of laboring women and girls." And yet another proclaimed "opportunities for missionary work much nearer at home" than imagined.[68]

Sympathy sparked more investigations, which focused on the ready-made clothing industry because it employed women and children in large numbers. In 1891, the Chicago Trade and Labor Assembly, a federated body of local labor unions, published a pamphlet called "The New Slavery. Investigation into the Sweating System as Applied to the Manufacture of Wearing Apparel." Prepared with the help of Elizabeth Morgan, wife of socialist labor leader Thomas J. Morgan, it was not shocking or sensational, but specifically pointed out that clothing was made largely under filthy and infectious conditions in sweatshops. Noting that "[t]he conditions of the Old World are rapidly being transferred to the New" under the sweating system, the pamphlet urged the assembly to "agitate this question until the system is a thing of the past and remembered only because of its infamy."[69] The next year, the IBLS set out to study the conditions of working women in Chicago and quickly encountered the public uproar over the sweating system. In its report the IBLS described the sweating system as "a deliberate preying upon the necessities of the poor."[70]

Shortly afterward, reform-minded Chicagoans, including Florence Kelley, attacked sweatshop conditions. Kelley and her friends denounced exploitation of poverty-stricken working women and at the same time stressed the possible spread of diseases through the garments made in the sweatshop.[71] The campaign eventually resulted in the Illinois Factory Inspection Act of 1893, which was enacted with an overwhelming majority of the state legislature in favor of regulation over working conditions. This campaign was but a part of the national anti-sweatshop agitation that involved Massachusetts, New York, and Pennsylvania in the 1890s. In the midst of the agitation, the U.S. House of Representatives, noting that the sweating system had lately attracted great public attention, authorized its Committee on Manufactures to conduct a nationwide investigation in 1892. Although the committee failed to secure support for federal legislation from the House, it visited major clothing centers and held a number of public hearings, arousing much interest in sweatshop conditions.[72]

In order to cater to new demand in the midst of the campaign, therefore, many manufacturers had to dissociate themselves from the negative image of ready-made clothing. They turned their attention to national advertising. The pioneer was Hart, Schaffner and Marx—which had adopted the name when Joseph Schaffner joined the Hart brothers after their former partner Levi Abt left the firm in 1887. Having worked for seventeen years as a bookkeeper at a wholesale dry goods company, Schaffner took charge of accounting and marketing. Before long he decided to venture into national advertising, for which his partners agreed initially to appropriate $5,000. Appearing in the pages of *Harper's*, *Collier's*, *Munsey's*, and the *Saturday Evening Post*, HSM's advertisements stressed the fine quality and low prices of the company's clothes.[73] One national advertisement in 1899 declared:

> The first thing that attracts your attention about the H. S. & M. clothes is their smart, dressy appearance. You would not know them from the work of the finest merchant tailor. They are cut in the latest style, they have the right expression, they fit and keep their shape. On closer inspection you will see the fine details of workmanship, the careful tailoring, the durable quality of goods and linings. They cost only 1/3 or 1/2 the tailor's price. Thousands of good dressers are wearing them. Most men are glad to buy them when they know how good they are.[74]

After a few years of the advertising experiment, Schaffner noted with pride that it was rewarding. "Advertising increased our volume; volume has enabled us to increase our value-giving," he said, "both by lower prices and by putting more quality into the goods."[75]

Although at first other manufacturers in Chicago thought Schaffner was wasting profits and predicted his failure, they soon found advertising necessary for their own businesses. The anti-sweatshop campaign in the early 1890s focused on ready-made clothing as comprising germ-carrying garments made in disease-stricken tenement houses. In Spring 1894, for instance, when smallpox hit the city, Illinois factory inspectors, with the help of Chicago health authorities, burned up five lots of infected clothes made in the sweatshops and fumigated many others. Then the inspectors called a conference of clothing manufacturers and urged them not to send out their work to sweaters.[76] Some manufacturers saw in national advertising one way to flee this awkward situation. HSM's lead was followed by others, such as B. Kuppenheimer and Co., Alfred Decker and Cohn, Edward V. Price and Co., Scotch Woolen Mills, and Royal Tailors, all of whom strenuously advertised that their garments were manufactured in their own factories, not in the sweatshops.[77]

Many firms improved the quality of their products by substituting better material for cheap fabrics. Up until the early 1890s, low grades of ready-made clothing were made of muslin and satinet, a combination of cotton warp with a shoddy filling, while union cassimere, cassimere, and cheviot were used for the medium grades. Union cassimere was a combination of cotton warp with wool filling, and various grades of cheviot were all wool, either waste or better wool. Enterprising firms chose to use better grades of cheviots and cassimeres for their products.[78] In 1900, the pioneering HSM was again the first to announce the "guaranteed all wool" policy. Now fine garments were made of quality fabrics such as worsted, serge, "clay"—a twill weave—and tweed, in addition to better cheviot.[79]

It proved difficult to enhance such fine materials with superior workmanship, however. Although the bitter competition among contractors allowed manufacturers to enjoy lower contract prices, it frequently led contractors to neglect workmanship. They were more interested in the volume of their output, because their profits grew as volume increased. As long as a manufacturer sent out goods to be made up by a number of different contractors, workmanship was beyond his control; contractors had their own particular methods of making garments, which rendered it almost impossible for the manufacturer to get uniform quality.[80]

To produce fine garments, manufacturers needed to supervise the labor process more closely than before. Closer supervision was possible when a manufacturer brought those contractors whom he had already found reliable into his own establishment to work exclusively for himself. They were called "inside contractors." These contractors were generally independent in running their own shops, although there were variations, as some of them borrowed money, machines, and tools from the manufacturer's firm and became subject to its general shop rules and even its control over wages. In any case, the firm obtained close supervision of the production process, while not taking up the burden of managing the manufacturing end.[81]

Through such arrangements, contract shops were integrated into the inside shops. Illinois factory inspectors reported that in 1894 only five out of Chicago's thirty-five largest men's clothing manufacturers had inside shops in addition to their cutting rooms. These shops were relatively small, with the exception of Kuh, Nathan and Fischer, which employed 182 workers in one inside shop. With a combined total of 334 workers employed in their inside shops, the five manufacturers had to rely upon outside contractors, who city-wide maintained 2,196 people on their payrolls.[82] But as the American economy recovered from the depression of the 1890s and continued to prosper almost uninterrupted until the panic of 1907, the demand for better clothing expanded, accelerating the trend toward integration of outside shops. By 1900, at least seven Chicago manufacturers employed 100 or more workers in their own tailor shops. With 475 people working at HSM's alone, there were 1,651 workers in all in the inside shops.[83] A 1911 Congressional report on the men's ready-made clothing industry noted that the contract shop had been "extensively replaced by the inside shop, or by contract shops supervised by the firm," which had often relied upon more than 100 contractors to complete the work.[84]

In its internal structure, however, the enlarged inside shop was not entirely different from the small contract shop. Scholars assume that the inside shop became a factory when a manufacturer put together a number of small shops at one location and provided power and additional machines.[85] In fact, the inside shop was composed of separate production units, each the responsibility of an inside contractor. In 1916, the U.S. Commerce Department study of the men's clothing industry pointed out: "[E]ven now many large inside houses are run on the plan of the small contract shop, being simply a number of small shops assembled under one roof."[86] Although the inside shop appeared to be an integrated production unit, its managerial authority was not centralized yet, and the division of labor presumably remained almost the same as in the small contract shop. Among the 1,651 workers employed in the inside shops of the seven Chicago manufacturers, the men, supposedly skilled hands, outnumbered by two to one the women, who were almost invariably placed in unskilled jobs.[87]

The integration of small contract shops was accompanied by higher production costs. Labor costs increased in the enlarged inside shops, as skilled or experienced workers were needed more than before in order to secure good workmanship. Chicago manufacturers told the Congressional Committee on Manufactures that they offered higher piece rates to those working on better grades.[88] On the other hand, the work week in large shops was usually sixty hours at the turn of the century, much less than that in small ones, as integration made men's clothing firms bigger and more vulnerable to public scrutiny. The firms tried to get out of this dilemma by speeding up the labor process. They substituted a "bonus foreman" for the inside contractor, providing not only the working space but also all of the machinery and equipment, thus denying the contractor the elements of his independence. The bonus foreman was allowed considerable managerial authority on the shop floor so as to maintain absolute command over his workforce. Manufacturers encouraged him to drive workers by whatever means he believed were appropriate, paying him a bonus in proportion to the number of garments produced. The bonus foreman came to characterize the large inside shop, until the organized men's clothing workers pressed manufacturers to reform labor management after World War I. Because large manufacturers wanted to produce fine clothes, however, they found it difficult to quicken the labor process without depressing the quality of work.[89]

Consequently, manufacturers reorganized the inside shop by introducing the "section system." This system was in essence a form of division of labor in which the labor process was subdivided into minute operations, most of them to be carried out by unskilled but dexterous specialists. It was often called the "Boston system." In 1884, a Boston firm, Macullar, Parker, and Company, had boasted of its ready-made clothing department where the employees, specializing in rather simple tasks, attained high speed:

> In the ready-made department, specialization of labor is carefully studied, and each operative has a particular line of work, in which the greatest possible degree of proficiency is attained. A number of girls are set apart for sewing on buttons, each of them can turn out 400 firmly sewed buttons every day. Another group is devoted from morning till evening to the making of button-holes by hand; another, to linings; another, to pockets; and so on through the list.[90]

In this way, the making of a regular sack coat, which required extensive skill, was divided into 117 operations, while vest making and pants making, both less-skilled jobs, were divided into forty-five and sixty-two operations each.[91] In practice, however, some operations were merged, depending on convenience and necessity, as conceived by the firm. Only in extreme cases did a coat pass through between ninety and 100 shop hands before it was completed, while pants were assembled by about sixty workers and vests by forty to fifty. Even so, the division of labor was sophisticated, especially compared with the task system. In a sectionalized coat shop, for example, pressing was done not by one skilled worker, but by as many as nine specialists, seam and pocket pressers, armhole pressers, edge pressers, off pressers, canvas pressers, lapel and collar seam pressers, tape pressers, sleeve pressers, and under-pressers. Basting was now performed by armhole basters, wigan basters, canvas basters, first basters, second basters, and edge basters.[92] In the cutting room, spreaders laid fabrics and markers marked the top layers before cutters did their job with the cutting machines.

The section system involved reorganization of the labor process. Minutely subdivided, the process was extensively deskilled in order to be performed by poorly paid unskilled workers. Workers specializing in a rather simple operation were able to develop great speed after being trained for several weeks, and their output was higher than those working under the task system. In addition, manufacturers took pains to make goods in production flow smoothly from one section to the next; efficiency, specifically in the speed and volume of production, depended not just on the dexterity of individual workers but on organization of cooperation as well. So manufacturers carefully reorganized the whole production process, by juxtaposing, both in time and space, closely connected sections and reducing the movement of goods, accomplished by errand boys running on the shop floor, to a minimum. Subdivision invited coordination.

With the section system and subsequent reorganization of the labor process, large manufacturers such as Hart, Schaffner and Marx seized a competitive edge over the sweatshops under the task system. A study conducted in 1901 by the U.S. Industrial Commission showed that a shop employing 104 workers produced 1,650 coats in a week, completing a coat of the cheapest kind in three hours and forty-one minutes under the section system, while nineteen workers in a task shop made up three hundred coats in a week, spending fourteen more minutes on the same kind of coat. Moreover, the production cost was reduced: The sectionalized coat shop produced a coat for 55.7 cents, nearly four cents less than the task shop.[93] A New York contractor, an employer of more than one hundred people who worked on coats and overcoats under the section system, claimed, with some exaggeration, that the production cost in his shop was half that of a sweatshop, declaring, "The saving comes in utilizing highly skilled workers on the important work and employing cheaper labor for the rest."[94] In the production of better grades, especially fine clothes, large manufacturers probably enjoyed greater advantages because the work required a higher degree of skill and more time.

Such organizational innovation went hand in hand with technological developments around the turn of the century. Electrical power came into general use in the clothing shops, replacing steam power. It was an important innovation. Sewing machines powered by electricity led the way to increased speed and still higher productivity. Machines for special purposes were invented and introduced to substitute for hand techniques, including the collar pressing machine, the shoulder pressing machine, the serging machine, the collar and lapel padding machine, and the tacking machine. Other devices were developed to increase productivity by saving labor. In cutting, for example, the electric band knife made it possible to cut thirty to forty-five layers of cloth at once, whereas the earlier cutting machines could cut only fourteen to twenty layers.[95]

Technological innovations did not, however, trigger the rise of the factory system in the men's clothing industry. While steam engines had been used mainly in large shops, electric motors, whether fitted into individual machines or installed as the central power source, were available even to sweaters. Various machines for special purposes were introduced only after many men's clothing shops had already been reorganized into factories under the section system. Although the buttonhole-making machine had been in use at some inside shops and at small contract shops that specialized in that operation, other special sewing and pressing machines invented around the turn of the century were frequently ignored by leading manufacturers in the men's clothing industry. Most machines worked neither as neatly nor as reliably as experienced hands. Manufacturers of fine men's clothing preferred hand techniques to machine technology, which was extensively adopted in the production of low and medium grades. Because "the opinion prevailed that good clothes had to be handmade," noted the Commerce Department study in 1916, "many manufacturers have . . . been slow in investigating new labor-saving machines."[96] Even after World War I, this situation changed so little that Martin E. Popkin, an industrial engineer, vehemently advocated the advantages of machine tailoring.[97] The U.S. Commissioner of Labor flatly pointed out in 1904: "That which distinguishes the factory [from the small task shop] is minute division of labor, or 'section work,' as it is called in the trade."[98]

Organizational innovation led autonomous production units within the inside shop to be integrated into the factory and eventually changed the structure of the men's clothing industry. In order to adequately staff each of numerous sections, manufacturers had to maintain a large workforce. Some employed more than 500 workers under one roof, while others operated several factories, with 200 to 300 workers each. As manufacturers offering medium and low grades and even large contractors followed fine-clothing makers in adopting the organizational innovations, men's clothing establishments began to grow in size, starting in the late 1890s.[99]

In the men's clothing industry, Steven Fraser argues, the factory system grew up "especially in the period after 1905."[100] Statistics indeed show that the average size of the men's clothing establishment began to grow from 1905 on (see Table 2.4).

But the statistics do not reveal when modern factories began to be established. In addition, the table does not take into account geographical variances that allowed the growth of large factories to be offset by numerous tiny shops. Suppose that in 1900 a 200-worker factory was established in Rochester, while sixteen shops, each employing ten workers, opened in New York. Creating an average of only about twenty-one employees per establishment, this would have made no change in the average factory size throughout the country.

Contemporary observations, complementing the statistics, suggest that the factory began to develop from the late 1890s, as the American economy recovered from the impact of the 1893 depression. Rochester, Chicago, and Baltimore took the lead, later followed by Philadelphia and New York, where sweatshops mushroomed and prospered well into

TABLE 2.4
The Average Size of Men's Clothing Establishments, 1890–1914*

	No. of establishments	Capital	Wage Earners	Average capital/ est.	Average wage-earners/ est.
1890	4,867	$128,253,547	144,926	$26,352	29.8
1900	5,729	120,547,851	120,927	21,042	21.1
1905	4,504	153,177,500	137,190	34,009	30.5
1909	5,584	203,703,112	191,183	36,479	34.2
1914	4,830	224,050,401	173,747	46,387	36.0

*Except buttonhole shops

Source: U.S. Department of Commerce and Labor, Bureau of the Census, *Manufactures: 1905*, Pt. 1: *United States by Industries*, 1907, 6; U.S. Department of Commerce, Bureau of the Census, *Census of Manufactures: 1914*, vol. 2: *Reports for Selected Industries and Detail Statistics for Industries, By States*, 1919, 173–174.

the first decade of the twentieth century. In her study published in 1902, Mabel H. Willett pointed out: "This [the factory system] gained a foothold in New York six or seven years ago, and is now pushing hard the task system and the small shop."[101] And at about the same time, the U.S. Industrial Commission noted: "Quite recently what may be described as a factory system was introduced in a few establishments in New York."[102]

The industrial structure differed substantially among clothing centers; on the eve of World War I tiny shops still predominated in New York and Philadelphia, while large corporations characterized local business in Chicago, Cincinnati, Cleveland, and Rochester. Throughout the nation, however, factories directly run by manufacturing firms, whether large or small, now dominated the production of men's clothing. Although the firms still needed contractors to do the work that temporarily exceeded their own production capacity during the busy season,[103] the contract system, which had characterized the men's clothing industry a generation before, became only a minor factor. By 1914, contractors throughout the country were responsible for a mere 13.7 percent of the total value added by manufacture, though they employed nearly 29 percent of all the wage earners in the industry.[104]

WORK CULTURE IN THE FACTORY

By World War I workers faced a new environment in the men's clothing factories. The factories tended to be located beyond walking distance of most workers' residences. While many firms managed to keep their tailor shops close to immigrant settlements, others found old buildings inadequate and rented or built new ones. New buildings were usually located within the manufacturing districts so that the downtown management offices, now near the factories, could supervise the production process. In the late 1900s, for example, HSM, employing more than five thousand workers, leased a five-story building next to its thirteen-story factory at the corner of Monroe and Franklin Streets and erected two four-story buildings on the West Side of Chicago.[105] During the last decade of the nineteenth century, many small clothing shops scattered in Philadelphia's ethnic neighborhoods were replaced by large factories converging on the wholesale manufacturing area.[106] Unlike the sweatshop, the factory could be located away from immigrant settlements. Chicago's mass transit system took shape around the turn of the century, when the cable car was replaced by the electric street car and the elevated train. It connected the downtown clothing district with the North and West Sides where many Czechs, Jews, Poles, and Italians had settled. Although many could not afford the carfare, and others hesitated to go to an unfamiliar part of the city, an increasing number of men's clothing workers were forced to travel to a workplace distant and separate from their own ethnic neighborhoods.

Factories, especially those occupying new buildings, usually contained modern facilities. Although many still relied on doors and windows for ventilation, some installed suction fans, airshafts, and skylights. Large factories had washrooms, dressing rooms, and restrooms. But legacies of the sweatshop lingered. Fire escapes were frequently inadequate; wooden stairways were dark and narrow and iron steps old and "of doubtful strength"; access to the escapes was often blocked or obstructed by machines or tables. A separate lunchroom was still rare. Most workers ate their meals in the workroom, bringing lunch with them or buying from a food peddler who offered milk, coffee, fruit, cakes, cookies, and candy.[107]

Women were more conspicuous than men in the modern factory. In New York, and to a certain extent Philadelphia, where thousands of immigrant tailors continued to arrive from eastern and southern Europe until the outbreak of World War I, men had increasingly replaced women in sweatshops. But manufacturers in Chicago and Rochester employed many more women than men although the latter had once constituted the majority in the inside shops. In the two inland cities, according to a Congressional report published in 1911, the number of female employees now approached three-fifths of all the workforce in the tailor shops, with cutting rooms, stock rooms, and offices excluded. In Chicago these women were young, more than one-half of them less than twenty-one years old, while only about one-fourth of their male counterparts had not arrived at adulthood. And the women were predominantly of foreign origin, Czechs, Jews, Poles, and Italians in particular; three-fifths were foreign-born, with another one-third native-born of immigrant parentage. In this regard Chicago was also distinctive; in New York almost nine out of ten female employees were foreign-born; in Rochester more than one-half were native-born Americans.[108]

Now factory workers were placed in the industrial-capitalist context. Unlike in the sweatshop, where the relationship between an employer and his employees was sometimes subtle and frequently undefined, the owner of a large firm was almost invariably someone remote from the workers. Whether his factories were located close to his downtown office or not, the manufacturer was more often than not invisible to his employees. "The personal relation between employer and employee . . . is lost in most large factories," declared the Commerce Department study of this industry in 1916, "where the worker knows only the foreman or superintendent, and where the employer is only a name."[109] As Joseph Schaffner lamented when a small strike that had begun at one of the HSM factories in 1910 developed into a full-scale conflict between all men's clothing workers and their employers in Chicago, large manufacturers were badly informed about conditions at the factories.[110]

Lacking any channel of direct communication with their employer, workers could feel only his authority through petty bosses, foremen or forewomen who exercised comprehensive powers handed down from their predecessors. Like the inside contractor, or even the outside contractor, they held the power to hire and fire workers in their sections and to decide each employee's wage rates, as well as to administer disciplinary measures. Exercising these powers, foremen or forewomen constantly drove workers to accelerate production, and earned bonuses; each section was carefully balanced and continually readjusted to minimize overcrowding or undermanning, so that the work could flow from one section to the next according to the pace set by the management.[111] Unlike the outside contractor running a sweatshop, therefore, the bosses rarely became friendly with their section workers. Instead, they were one of the main targets of workers' protests.

Discipline was strict at the factory. As working hours in large establishments gradually declined from sixty to fifty-six a week during the first decade of the twentieth century, manufacturers exacted more labor from the workforce. The hours of entering and leaving the factory were strictly observed. A worker had to be at his or her machine or workbench at exactly eight o'clock in the morning. If late, pieceworkers were not allowed to work in the morning while those paid by the week were fined. Some manufacturers put employees' hats and coats in the dressing room and locked it to prevent them from ducking out of the factory during working hours.[112] Smoking, snacking, singing, or talking was forbidden in the factory. Pieceworkers, who could control their own output, enjoyed a limited privilege in socializing, which manufacturers later abolished so that it would not affect the work pace of those paid by the week. The foreman or forewoman could suspend unruly workers for a few days. Employees were expected to meet high standards of workmanship. When an employee made a mistake that could not be properly repaired, he or she was forced to buy the garment at its retail price.[113]

Under the section system workers lacked control over their work. In the factory, where work was steady and where the employer decided how it was to be organized, the foreman and the superintendent dominated the labor process. Petty bosses required the workers to specialize at only one fragment of the whole manufacturing process and to work at the pace that was set by management and enforced through discipline. As most of the men's clothing workers had never worked in a factory

TABLE 4.8
Likelihood of Placement in San Jose College Prep Math Courses (10th Grade) (1985–1992)

Achievement Score	Latino	White	Asian-American
50–59	8.7%	3.0%	—
60–69	16.7%	42.9%	68.4%
70–79	60.0%	83.3%	73.7%
80–89	—	93.9%	93.3%

Does not include cells representing less than 15 students.

rolled in the highest track and each slice reflected a preference for Whites over African Americans. Corresponding "preferences" were shown for African Americans' placement in the lower tracks for the same slices.[5]

The tracking systems in each of these three school districts perpetuated second-generation segregation—resegregation of students within school sites. The racial disparities between tracks could be partially "explained" by differences in measured achievement. But racial sorting also occurred among students with comparable achievement. That is, the disproportionate placement of African-American and Latino students in low-track classes, and the corresponding exclusion of these students from high-track classes, went above and beyond any disparate effect attributable to prior achievement. To further examine this phenomenon, the following section presents regression analyses of the data from Woodland Hills.

English Track Placement in Woodland Hills

Using a logistic regression model,[6] I evaluated the following predictors of seventh-grade English track placement in Woodland Hills for the year prior to the district's detracking: sixth-grade English grade-point average ("GPA"), sixth-grade ITBS reading score, sex, race, free/reduced lunch status (a proxy for socio-economic status, or "SES"), exceptional ability (including both gifted and special education), and junior high school attended. The results indicated that the two strongest predictors of track placement are the students' GPA and ITBS score. Three factors (sex, lunch status, and junior high school) have no substantial predictive value. Before discussing the role of race, I consider exceptional ability, which the modeling also points to as a strong predictor.

Exceptional ability was—in this database—fixed for each student (the database contained no students whose exceptional-ability status changed

TABLE 4.9
Participation in Wilmington's Advanced Academic English by Race and ITBS Reading Score (1993)

Normal Curve Equivalent Scores		Non-College Prep and Standard Track				Advanced Track				Total	
		freq.	pct.	col. pct.	row pct.	freq.	pct.	col pct.	row pct.	freq.	pct.
0–9	AA	67	4.08	4.34	100	0	0.00	0.00	0.00	67	4.08
	W	42	0.97	1.23	100	0	0.00	0.00	0.00	42	0.97
10–19	AA	151	9.20	9.79	100	0	0.00	0.00	0.00	151	9.20
	W	93	2.14	2.72	98.94	1	0.02	0.11	1.06	94	2.16
20–29	AA	235	14.32	15.23	99.58	1	0.06	1.02	0.42	236	14.38
	W	162	3.73	4.74	100	0	0.00	0.00	0.00	162	3.73
30–39	AA	312	19.01	20.22	98.42	5	0.30	5.10	1.58	317	19.32
	W	393	9.05	11.49	98.74	5	0.12	0.54	1.26	398	9.16
40–49	AA	391	23.83	25.34	96.07	16	0.98	16.33	3.93	407	24.80
	W	752	17.31	21.98	95.43	36	0.83	3.90	4.57	788	18.14
50–59	AA	211	12.86	13.67	94.62	12	0.73	12.24	5.38	223	13.59
	W	728	16.76	21.28	90.21	79	1.82	8.56	9.79	807	18.58
60–69	AA	116	7.07	7.52	83.45	23	1.40	23.47	16.55	139	8.47
	W	658	15.15	19.23	79.95	165	3.80	17.88	20.05	823	18.95
70–79	AA	42	2.56	2.72	66.67	21	1.28	21.43	33.33	63	3.84
	W	362	8.33	10.58	61.77	224	5.16	24.27	38.23	586	13.49
80–89	AA	13	0.79	0.84	56.52	10	0.61	10.20	43.48	23	1.40
	W	158	3.64	4.62	40.62	231	5.32	25.03	59.38	389	8.95
90–99	AA	5	0.30	0.32	33.33	10	0.61	10.20	66.67	15	0.91
	W	73	1.68	2.13	28.63	182	4.19	19.72	71.37	255	5.87
Total	AA	1543	94.03			98	5.97			1641	100
	W	3421	78.75			923	21.25			4344	100

AA = African American
W = White

from, e.g., sixth to eighth grade). It is, therefore, a static, antecedent variable, determined by the school some time prior to the seventh grade. As used in this analysis, it also aggregates special education status (the records for which were incomplete in this database) and gifted status. That is, a student coded as "exceptional" may be either gifted or in a special education category. Looking specifically at gifted status, both high-track placement (the dependent variable) and identification of a student as gifted (a value of an independent variable) are a result of the school staff having higher expectations for the student. For this reason, the correlation is not surprising. Defenders of "giftedness as a natural phenomenon," however, would argue that the predictive value of the exceptional ability variable demonstrates a unique quality coming through and driving the outcome. While I tend to favor the former explanation (gifted identification and course placement both measuring higher school staff expectations), readers can draw their own conclusions.

Because of the above concerns, and because exceptional ability incorporates (and therefore washes out) other important potential predictors,[7] some of my analyses ultimately omitted exceptional ability. For example, consider a logistic regression model predicting course placement with the following three variables: GPA, ITBS, and race. As in all the models exploring this issue, GPA and ITBS are the strongest predictors. However, as represented in Figure 4.7, race also powerfully drives course placement. Controlling for GPA and ITBS, a White student was 2.3 times more likely than an African-American student to be placed in the high-track English class. (This impact remained basically unchanged with the addition of the lunch status and sex variables, but it decreased substantially when exceptional ability was added.)

Note that, while sex and lunch status were not strong predictors in this logistic regression analysis, GPA and ITBS, like exceptional ability, are baseline predictors that measure academic achievement or potential at the end of the sixth grade (or earlier). They all, therefore, incorporate previous impact resulting from, among other things, SES, sex, and race (see the discussion of exceptional ability in footnote 7). The analysis, therefore, shows only that there is no additional, ongoing effect from SES (lunch status) and sex. Consider, for example, a low-income, African-American girl in kindergarten. For the next 6 years, she may receive benefits or damage due to one of more of these personal characteristics. By the end of the sixth grade, these characteristics may have made her more or less likely to be classified as gifted or in need of special education. Similarly, these characteristics may have driven higher or lower ITBS scores and/or GPA. Therefore, when the analysis shows ITBS, GPA and exceptional ability as strong predictors of course placement, we may be seeing hidden effects of the other three variables.

Of course, these cautions and speculations should not obscure the finding, shown above, that, controlling for GPA and ITBS, a White student was 2.3

times more likely than an African-American student to be placed in the high-track English class. Moreover, as will be discussed in the following subsection, this discriminatory result was even more stark for science placements among those students classified as gifted.

Science Track Placement in Woodland Hills

The examination of Woodland Hills' science track placement (again, studying the classes of 1995, 1996, and 1997) used logistic regression models to consider the following predictors: 8th-grade ITBS science score, 9th- and 10th-grade average (GPA), sex, race, free/reduced lunch status (SES), and exceptional ability. As with English, some analyses excluded exceptional ability, primarily because it incorporates, and thus washes out, other important predictors. Suffice it to say that exceptional ability classification was indeed

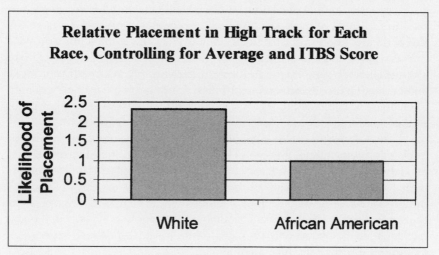

	Value	Std. Error
6th Grade ITBS	0.048	0.014
6th Grade Average	0.235	0.032
Race	−0.837	0.392

African Americans were coded "0," while Whites were coded "1." The product of (−1) and (−0.837), then, is the natural log of 2.31, the odds ratio for Race: exp(−0.837 × −1) = 2.31.

FIGURE 4.7   Predictors of 7th Grade Course Placement in Woodland Hills English Tracks

highly correlated to track placement. I was also forced to exclude lunch status upon discovering that the data for two of the three cohorts were either incorrectly recorded or non-existent. With these modifications in place, the modeling revealed that students' ITBS scores and GPAs were very strong predictors of subsequent placement. In addition, even controlling for these two factors, 9th- and 10th-grade course placement remain as predictors of subsequent placement. Race also continues, year after year, to be a minor predictive force, with being White driving high-track placement and being African-American driving low-track placement.[8]

Among students classified as gifted, race emerged as a particularly powerful predictive factor for course placements. Using cross-tabs, I calculated, for gifted-identified children, the odds of placement for each race in each track for each cohort at each grade level.[9] For ninth-grade placement, gifted-identified African-American students in Cohort 2 were 12 times more likely to be assigned to the low-track course than were gifted-identified White students; for Cohort 3, an African-American student was 10.7 times more likely to be placed in the low-track course. (Cohort 1 did not show a racial disparity.)

This trend continued for 10th-grade placement, with a large racial gap between placement in high- and low-track classes and a smaller racial gap between middle- and low-track classes. For Cohort 1, the gap was a factor of 4.1 between high- and low-track placement and 1.8 between middle- and low-track placement. For Cohort 2, the numbers were 7.5 and 2.8. Incredibly, a gifted-identified African-American student in Cohort 3 was 27.5 times more likely to be assigned to a low-track course than was a gifted-identified White student, and a gifted-identified African-American student in that cohort was 8.7 times as likely to be assigned to a middle-track course, as opposed to a high-track course, as was a gifted-identified White student. Similar numbers emerged for 11th-grade placement. While Cohort 1 showed little racial disparity, for Cohort 2, the gap was a factor of 4.2 between high- and low-track placement and 2.8 between middle- and low-track placement. For Cohort 3, the numbers were 8.6 and 6.9.

This analysis demonstrates that the district provided a much more challenging education to its gifted-identified White students than to its gifted-identified African-American students. The distinction, as well as the distinction between Cohort 1 and Cohorts 2 and 3, can be understood, in part, by referring to a policy change discussed later in this book. The district's gifted program had been dominated by White students since the district's inception. This domination is reflected in the 11th-grade numbers for Cohort 1: 56 gifted-identified White students versus 9 gifted-identified African-American students. In response to such disparities, the district instituted a policy of re-evaluating the African-American student population to bring a greater number into the gifted program. The participants remained disproportionately White, but less overwhelmingly so; e.g., the 11th-grade numbers for Cohort 3 (two years later) show 62 gifted-identified White students and 22 gifted-identified African-American students. Some of the placement disparities found in these analyses may be artifacts of district educators' struggle to view the "new" group of gifted-identified African-American students on equal terms with their "old" colleagues. (Several teachers I interviewed condemned the re-evaluation of students as lowering standards for admission into the gifted program.) This issue of expectations will emerge again later in the book.

THE IMPACT OF TRACKING
ON ACHIEVEMENT

Previous research has demonstrated that placement in a low-track class is likely to have a negative impact on later achievement (see Oakes, Gamoran, & Page, 1992; Slavin, 1990). This section adds several analyses to that body of literature—slice analyses from Wilmington, Rockford, and San Jose, as well as regression analyses from Woodland Hills. Keep in mind that the data from these districts encompass the entire population; they are not random samples drawn from those populations. Therefore, measures of statistical significance, such as confidence intervals and "p-statistics," are unnecessary to discover whether the differences are "real." If one were using samples rather than universal data, however, one would need to use statistical tests to be confident that observed differences would also be found in the larger population.

In San Jose, Jeannie Oakes (1993) used a slice analysis to examine the impact of math placement. Table 4.10 shows the results. As demonstrated by Figure 4.8, tracking allowed high-tracked students to continue improving but stifled the learning of low-tracked students. Differential track placement created an immediate divergence between comparable students, and this divergence continued over subsequent years.

A similar (and more recent) analysis in Rockford produced similar results (see Figures 4.9 and 4.10).[10] The trend shown in these graphs of low-scoring students tending to improve their scores in later years, while high-scoring students' scores tend to fall (regardless of course level), is an example of a statistical phenomenon known as "regression to the mean." This phenomenon, however, cannot account for the separation between students placed in high- and low-ability groups.

The story in Wilmington was no different. Consider, for example, those students with eighth-grade pre-placement math achievement scores between 20 and 29 NCEs in 1991. Students from this slice who were placed in a non-college prep course as ninth graders in 1992 had an average 1993 reading score of 27 NCEs, while those placed in a college prep course had a 1993

TABLE 4.10
Achievement Gains over Time by Initial Achievement Level and Initial Track Placement, San Jose Grades 6–12 (1985–1992)

Initial Achievement Level	Initial Track Placement	Initial Mean	Average Gain After One Year	Average Gain After Two Years	Average Gain After Three Years
0–9	Low	4.3	23.7	—	—
	Standard	3.0	37.5	—	—
10–19	Low	15.2	14.2	7.6	—
	Standard	15.5	18.0	24.9	21.9
20–29	Low	25.4	5.1	7.2	4.7
	Standard	25.1	8.7	16.5	10.5
30–39	Low	34.8	−0.1	0.8	−0.2
	Standard	34.8	3.5	6.7	5.0
40–49	Low	44.5	−1.2	0.8	−1.2
	Standard	44.9	0.2	4.5	5.2
50–59	Low	54.4	−2.2	−1.9	−1.9
	Standard	54.6	0.1	3.7	3.8
	Accelerated	55.4	6.5	11.9	9.6
60–69	Low	64.4	−3.8	0.1	−2.3
	Standard	64.3	−0.7	3.7	3.8
	Accelerated	65.4	5.7	8.4	7.6
70–79	Low	73.4	−2.9	−2.1	—
	Standard	74.2	−2.4	−0.9	−1.0
	Accelerated	74.9	4.4	7.8	7.6
80–89	Low	83.5	−16.0	—	—
	Standard	83.7	−4.2	−5.4	−3.1
	Accelerated	85.0	0.2	2.3	2.6
90–99	Standard	95.7	−11.0	−13.0	−14.0
	Accelerated	95.9	−5.5	−3.6	−3.2

Does not include cells representing less than 15 students.

reading score of 30. Higher-achieving students were comparably affected: among those in the 70–79 "slice," for instance, low-tracked students fell behind their high-tracked counterparts by 8 points. In no slice did the low-track students subsequently outscore those placed in higher tracks.

Repeating this analysis using reading achievement scores and English track placement demonstrated a continuation of this pattern. Among students with eighth-grade pre-placement reading scores between 20 and 29 NCEs in 1991, for instance, those placed in a non-college prep English course as ninth graders in 1992 had an average reading achievement score in 1993 of 23 NCEs. In contrast, students in the same slice who were placed in a college prep class scored an average of 29 NCEs two years later. Among those in the

70–79 slice, there was a 7-point NCE spread in 1993. In only one slice (10-19) did the group of students placed in lower tracks outscore their initially-similar high track peers (by 2 NCEs).

The Impact of Woodland Hills' Science Tracking

To investigate the impact of science tracking in Woodland Hills, I examined the three cohorts (the classes of 1995, 1996, and 1997) using multiple linear regression models predicting students' 9th-, 10th-, and 11th-grade averages (GPAs). The independent variables for the ninth-grade analyses were as fol-

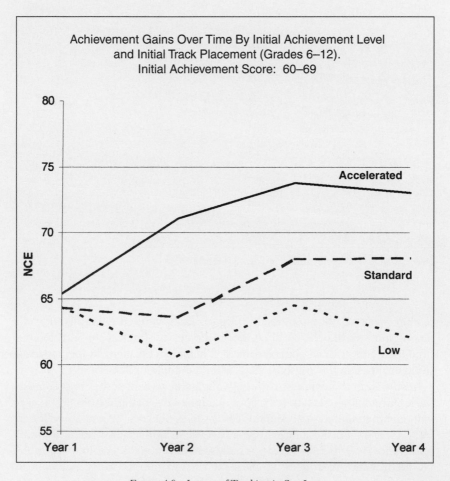

FIGURE 4.8   Impact of Tracking in San Jose

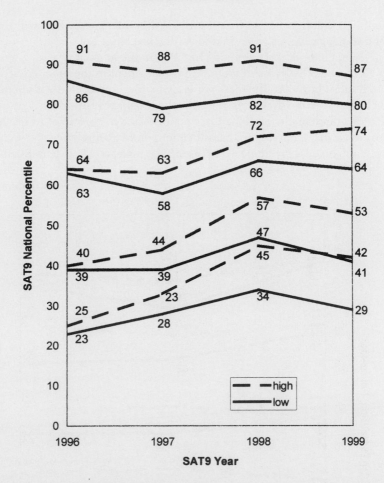

FIGURE 4.9   Impact of 1997 8th Grade Math Placement in Rockford (Series are omitted if high or low contains less than 13 students)

lows: sex, race, course placement (track), gifted status, and the score from the students' eighth-grade ITBS science tests. Since the students did not subsequently take another ITBS or a similar standardized test, the independent variables for the 10th- and 11th-grade analyses were: sex, race, course placement, gifted status, and previous year's GPA.

Because each student's GPA, rather than a standardized test score, is the achievement outcome for all these analyses, one would expect to see two phenomena taking place simultaneously. First, children with similar prior achievement should be getting higher grades in lower-tracked classes, due to an implicit sliding scale. A given level of achievement and effort will likely earn a student a higher grade in a lower-tracked class. Second, track placement should have its largest impact revealed in the following year's achievement. One would expect a student's track placement in the previous year to strongly affect how that student is presently performing. Both these phenomena are overwhelmingly demonstrated by the Woodland Hills data.

At the ninth-grade level, the three cohorts showed consistent results: sex, race, course placement, gifted classification, and ITBS score all powerfully drove ninth-grade GPA. Table 4.11 presents the regression coefficients for Co-

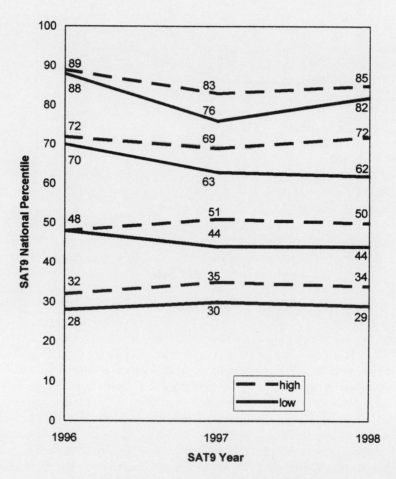

FIGURE 4.10   Impact of 1997 9th Grade English Placement in Rockford (Series are omitted if high or low contains less than 13 students)

TABLE 4.11
Factors Driving Cohort 1 Science Achievement in Woodland Hills (Grade 9)

	Value	Std. Error
Race	5.05	1.43
Track Placement (H to L), 9th Grade	−4.37	1.44
Sex	−4.68	1.17
Gifted Status	6.37	1.80
ITBS Science	0.23	0.04

Multiple R-Squared: 0.350

hort 1.[11] On an achievement scale of 1–100 (with the vast majority of grades falling between 40 and 100), being a female increased one's GPA by 4.7 points; being White increased it by 5.1 points; being placed in high-track science increased it by 4.4 points (this is the single exception to the first expected phenomenon, noted above[12]); and being classified as gifted increased the GPA by 6.4 points. In addition, each single point increase on the eighth-grade ITBS science score drove a 0.2-point increase in GPA. To clarify, consider two hypothetical students with the same ITBS science score. One student is White, female, classified as gifted, and is placed in the high-track course. The other is African American, male, not classified as gifted, and is placed in the low-track course. At the end of one year, and assuming no interactions among the predictors, we can expect the first student's GPA to be 20 points higher than the second's.[13]

With this example in mind, now is a good time to reiterate a caution noted above. Gifted identification and ITBS score are baseline predictors that measure academic achievement or academic potential at the end of the eighth grade (or earlier); they thus incorporate previous impact resulting from, among other things, SES, sex, and race. By the end of the eighth grade, these latter characteristics have likely already made an impact on each student's GPA, her ITBS score, and whether or not she is classified as gifted. Therefore, when an analysis shows ITBS and exceptional ability as strong predictors of GPA, we may also be seeing hidden effects of these other factors.

The 10th-grade analyses yielded results strikingly consistent with the two expected phenomena (see Table 4.12). Not surprisingly, the students' 9th-grade GPA was the most powerful predictor of 10th-grade GPA (GPA and "average" are used synonymously). For Cohort 1, each one-point increase in 9th-grade GPA drove a 0.68-point increase in 10th-grade GPA. In addition, race continued to play a powerful, ongoing role, with being White resulting in an advantage of 5.6 points. Yet it is the effect of course placement that jumps out of this analysis. To illustrate the import of these numbers, consider six students, all of whom have the same eighth-grade ITBS score: Alan, Barbara, Charles, Denise, Ellen, and Frank. Alan, Barbara, and Charles are each placed in low-track ninth-grade science, while Denise, Ellen, and Frank are placed in high-track ninth-grade science. These students' 10th-grade placements are as follows: Alan and Denise are placed in the high track, Barbara and Ellen are placed in the middle track, and Charles and Frank are placed in the low track. Combining the information from Tables 4.11 and 4.12, we know that the three students who were placed in low-track ninth-grade science are disadvantaged by 13.4 points relative to their high-tracked neighbors (4.4 plus 9.0). This is evidence of phenomenon number two, stated above: track placement should have its largest impact evidenced in the following year's achievement.

However, we also see strong evidence of the first phenomenon (children with similar prior achievement getting higher grades in lower-tracked classes). Charles and Frank, the two students placed in low-track 10th grade, have a 15.3-point GPA advantage over their neighbors who were placed in the high track. Barbara and Denise, the two students placed in the middle track, have a 9.8-point GPA advantage over their high-tracked neighbors. In this limited way, low track placement bestows an advantage on the students.

But what happens to these students in the 11th grade? Table 4.13 presumes that all six students are placed in high-track 11th-grade science.[14] Using the regression coefficients set forth in Table 4.14, we see that the students placed in high-track 10th-grade science showed an advantage over those who were placed in low-track 10th-grade science—*even after accounting for the higher 10th-grade GPA obtained by the latter group of students.* For instance, Alan and Charles parted ways in the 10th grade, and Alan suffered an immediate detriment, with his high-track GPA 15.3 points below Charles' low-track grade. In practical terms, Alan was put in a much more challenging situation,

TABLE 4.12
Factors Driving Cohort 1 Science Achievement in Woodland Hills (Grade 10)

	Value	Std. Error
Race	5.58	1.28
Track Placement (H to L), 10th Grade	9.84	2.03
Track Placement (H to M), 10th Grade	15.26	2.80
Sex	−0.28	1.03
Gifted Status	2.23	1.55
Track Placement (H to L), 9th Grade	−9.04	1.91
Average, 9th Grade	0.68	0.05

Multiple R-Squared: 0.403

TABLE 4.13
Longitudinal Impact of Woodland Hills Science Track Placement on GPA

	9th grade placement	9th grade avg	10th grade placement	10th grade avg	11th grade placement	11th grade avg*
Cohort 1						
Alan	low	75.6	high	51.3	high	51.3
Barbara	low	75.6	middle	76.8	high	48.6
Charles	low	75.6	low	66.6	high	50.3
Denise	high	80.0	high	64.7	high	64.7
Ellen	high	80.0	middle	70.2	high	62.0
Frank	high	80.0	low	80.0	high	63.7
Cohort 2						
Alan	low	76.0	high	59.9	high	59.9
Barbara	low	76.0	middle	66.3	high	60.5
Charles	low	76.0	low	69.7	high	51.6
Denise	high	80.0	high	70.2	high	70.2
Ellen	high	80.0	middle	76.6	high	70.8
Frank	high	80.0	low	80.0	high	61.9
Cohort 3						
Alan	low	76.3	high	57.9	high	57.9
Barbara	low	76.3	middle	64.6	high	56.0
Charles	low	76.3	low	70.0	high	50.9
Denise	high	80.0	high	67.9	high	67.9
Ellen	high	80.0	middle	64.6	high	66.0
Frank	high	80.0	low	80.0	high	60.9

*Since all these students are placed in the high track in the 11th grade, these final averages do not include a "contrast." That is, no amounts are subtracted to account for the difficulty of these courses.

TABLE 4.14
Factors Driving Cohort 1 Science Achievement in Woodland Hills (Grade 11)

	Value	Std. Error
Race	2.31	1.13
Track Placement (H to L), 11th Grade	1.22	1.83
Track Placement (H to M), 11th Grade	5.94	2.00
Sex	−1.67	0.88
Gifted Status	−1.21	1.25
Track Placement (H to L), 10th Grade	−8.19	1.63
Track Placement (H to M), 10th Grade	−16.33	1.80
Average, 10th Grade	0.44	0.05

Multiple R-Squared: 0.449

and the more difficult curriculum and higher expectations were reflected in his lower grades. Yet Charles could not maintain his higher GPA when, a year later, he moved up to the high track. In fact, Alan's more challenging curriculum from a year earlier placed him in a slightly better position in 11th grade (1 point). While this small increase is insubstantial in practical terms, the same is not true of Cohorts 2 and 3, where we see much greater benefits for students like Alan (respectively, 8.3 and 7.0 points).

The story told by Table 4.13 is particularly compelling because of its consistency. In each cohort, students' GPAs shot up upon their being placed in low-track classes. Meanwhile, their neighbors who were placed in high-track classes struggled with a more challenging curriculum, and their GPAs plummeted. Yet when these students were reunited in a later high-track class, the struggles paid off for this latter group of students, and they outperformed those who spent the previous year in low-track classes. The strength of these analyses must nonetheless be tempered by the role of students' grades as the dependant variable. Grades introduce a major element of uncertainty since each teacher employs a different standard and since grade distributions are substantially different in each track. This apples-and-oranges problem, while serious, is abated by the consistent (previously-discussed) results from Rockford and San Jose, as well as the below results discussing Woodland Hills' English tracking.

The Impact of Woodland Hills' English Tracking

In order to compare the impact of detracked English classes with the impact of track placement in Woodland Hills, this series of analyses pooled data from two separate cohorts of students, focusing on their experiences in the seventh grade. Cohort A is the entire class of the year 2000; Cohort B is the entire class of the year 2001 (the only students eliminated from the analyses were those who did not remain in the database for all years studied). Students in Cohort A enrolled in either high- or low-track seventh-grade English in the school year 1994–1995. They were then placed in detracked eighth-grade English classes. Cohort B was never tracked in English. (Woodland Hills had, prior to its detracking in the 1995–1996 school year, begun English tracking in the seventh grade.) The pooling of the data from these two cohorts is legitimate in that the two populations have very similar characteristics and backgrounds; however, it should be noted that the findings might nonetheless be biased by unaccounted-for population differences.[15] Controlling for the background (sixth-grade) ITBS reading scores for both Cohorts A and B, I examined the results of a series of linear regression analyses that compared the intervention of track placement in seventh grade (high, low, and mixed). In addition to sixth-grade ITBS, these analyses included the following predictors: course (track), sex, race, free/reduced lunch status, gifted status, and junior high school attended.

Before engaging in the pooled analyses, I focused on the high versus low comparison including just the students in Cohort A. Using seventh-grade ITBS score as the outcome, Table 4.15 shows the regression coefficients for the robustified generalized linear model (glm) including only main effects (multiple r-squared = 0.771).[16] The earlier (sixth-grade) ITBS score was, not surprisingly, the strongest and most consistent predictor of later ITBS score. Each one-point increase in sixth-grade ITBS drove a 0.76-point increase in seventh-grade ITBS. However, three other predictors showed relatively strong effects. Each of these factors is presented as a contrast between two students who are otherwise identical. This can also be thought of as a transition of a hypothetical student from one status to another. For instance, the status of being White, rather than African-American, drove a 3.0-point increase; the status of being identified as gifted drove a 3.7-point increase over those not so identified; and placement in the high-track, rather than the low-track, English class drove a 4.8-point increase.

Because this is population data, each of these results is "real." That is, taking all Woodland Hills students into account, and controlling for these other factors, the difference between low- and high-track really was 4.8 points. In this case, the effect size is also large enough for us to take note. In other cases, such as the 0.2 point impact for both sex and lunch status, the effect size is so small that the difference has no practical value.

Turning to the pooled (Cohort A and Cohort B) data set, I next examined the impact of placement in a high-track versus an untracked class and a low-track versus an untracked class. (The results of both of these analyses are set forth in Appendix 3.) Again, these analyses used seventh-grade ITBS as an outcome. As before, the vast majority of the seventh-grade ITBS score

TABLE 4.15
Factors Driving Achievement in Woodland Hills, Main Effects

	Value	Std. Error
6th Grade ITBS	0.76	0.03
Sex	−0.09	0.41
Race	1.50	0.56
Lunch Status	0.11	0.50
Gifted Status	1.86	0.55
Junior High	−0.63	0.45
Track Placement (L to H)	2.39	0.52

was accounted for by sixth-grade ITBS score. Each one-point increase in sixth-grade score drove a 0.78-point increase in seventh-grade score. But other factors also played a substantial role. For instance, a transition from African-American to White drove a 3.1-point increase on the ITBS test, and a transition from "regular" to gifted-identified drove a 4.1-point increase. A transition from untracked to high-tracked course placement drove a 2.3-point increase; and a transition from low-tracked to untracked course placement drove a 1.1-point increase. Although these results indicate little impact by track placement, even the small (2.3-point) impact of moving from an untracked to a high-track class would merit watching given the concerns held by parents of high-track students.

A more involved analysis, one that includes interaction terms, results in more complex conclusions. Appendix 3 presents two sets of complete regression coefficients for this analysis. Each set includes the three comparisons discussed in this section: high versus low, high versus untracked, and low versus untracked. The first set includes only main effects, while the second includes two-way interactions. Note that the meaning of the course-placement variable changes with each analysis. Note also that any independent variable that includes ITBS (the sixth-grade ITBS reading score), either as a main effect or as part of an interaction term, represents the increase in the seventh-grade score driven by a single-point increase in ITBS. For instance, the figure of 0.04 for the interaction term between ITBS and track placement in the first set of regression coefficients signifies that, for this term of the regression equation, a student who scored 74 on her sixth-grade ITBS test would benefit 5.9 points from being in the untracked class.[17] That is, the main effect of a 5.9-point benefit of being in the high-track class disappears for any student who scores 74 on the sixth-grade ITBS.

In fact, those students scoring greater than 74 would benefit from being placed in the untracked class. Such a finding is consistent with a recent study of detracked "Talent Development" middle schools (a project of the National Center for the Education of Students Placed at Risk), where the students with the strongest academic skills demonstrated the greatest academic benefits from the reform (MacIver, Plank, & Balfanz, 1998). Of course, the Woodland Hills story becomes more complex when one also considers the interaction between course and ethnicity, course and lunch status, course and sex, and course and gifted status. Moreover, the numbers shift considerably for the third set of coefficients.

Clearly, multiple and nuanced conclusions can be drawn from this analysis. But the effect sizes must always be kept in mind. A useful rule of thumb is to think of any conclusion in terms of points scored on the sixth-grade ITBS. For instance, the 5.9-point benefit discussed above is equivalent to approximately seven points on the sixth-grade test. That is, an untracked student would have to have scored seven points higher on the sixth-grade ITBS test to come even with a high-tracked student on the next year's test (ignoring the interaction effects). Similarly, an African-American student would have to have scored about seven points higher on sixth-grade ITBS test to come even with a White student on the next year's test.

The effectiveness of this analysis as well as that of the earlier analyses are limited by all the factors already discussed, including the poor measurement instrument (and the time administered), the small number of students, and the short time of intervention (track placement for only one year). However, the analyses in Woodland Hills, Rockford, and San Jose all strongly indicate that just one year of differential track placement has a strong effect. Students placed in low tracks fall behind their high-track counterparts. In contrast, the Woodland Hills data indicate that placement in an untracked class does not, over the term of a single year, substantially drive later achievement one way or the other. These results, then, point to the need for a better understanding of detracked classes and how to make the detracking reform most successful.

CONCLUSION

A thorough description of the tracking systems in these four districts would take into account the artificial starting point for the above investigations. For instance, consider a standardized test taken near the end of the eighth grade and used in a regression analysis to predict ninth-grade placement. Use of this baseline score from the eighth-grade standardized test as an independent variable (rather than choosing the score of, e.g., the sixth-grade test) is somewhat arbitrary. In fact, this eighth-grade score should be thought of as the dependent variable in some earlier but unmeasured model that pre-dates grade 8.

Nonetheless, the analyses set forth in this chapter paint a compelling and dynamic picture. African-American and Latino students were disproportionately placed in low-track classes that, while they purported to be homogeneous, encompassed a wide range of measured abilities. Once placed in low tracks, these students had to overcome great odds to move up within the tracked structure. Year after year, they fell further and further behind their high-tracked counterparts. These phenomena interacted and existed as a cycle. Using Woodland Hills' science tracking as an example, the students' GPA in the ninth grade was driven by course placement as well as by the students' race and sex. That GPA, in turn, drove 10th-grade placement. This process then repeated itself (with minor variations) in 10th and 11th grades.

The impact of fixed characteristics, particularly race, is thus greater than might be revealed by any given analysis of a static, single moment in time.

Analyses predicting test scores show a minor impact, for any given year, of race (e.g., a 3-point detriment for African Americans). But this impact is cumulative. If this trend continued over a student's K–12 career, this 3-point detriment would snowball into a 39-point detriment. When the racial element of track placement, along with the achievement impact of track placement, is superimposed on this more direct racial impact, we see a double-whammy for African Americans in terms of later achievement. Their race is not only a direct predictor of lower test scores; at the same time, it is also an indirect predictor, through the disparate track placement. Taken as a whole, then, these analyses highlight two harmful elements of tracking. First, the low-track classes have a detrimental impact on students' later academic performance. Second, African-American and Latino students are disproportionately taking these low-track courses, even after controlling for prior achievement.

The analyses of detracked students yield a less clear picture. Superficially, at least, detracking in Woodland Hills appeared to put a halt to the achievement stratification caused by tracking. However, these analyses do not indicate whether all students show achievement gains, and—if all do not benefit—which students might suffer from detracking. The most that can be determined from the Woodland Hills analyses of detracked classes is that the short-term achievement gains or detriments from placement in a detracked class—as opposed to a high- or a low-tracked class—were on a very small scale.

Of course, mechanical, arithmetic modeling is no substitute for systematic observations and interviews. Without the context provided by such qualitative analyses, such as is offered in Chapters Six through Twelve, the results presented here should not be accorded an importance out of proportion to their nonetheless compelling measurement of troubling academic and racial differences.

5

The Importance of Judicial Values

School desegregation is grounded in values that view equality, particularly racial equality, as one cornerstone of a just society. However, desegregation and detracking often conflict with other societal values. While some of these values are expressly racist, others are not. For example, the concept of neighborhood schools, while sometimes invoked to avoid racially mixed schools, also reflects the non-racist value of building and maintaining small-scale communities. Similarly, the argument for local control of schools sometimes masks efforts to avoid racial integration but can also reflect a non-racist aversion to the federal government interfering in local matters (McDermott, 1999).

For many people, including judges, the foundation for a just society lies in a set of values other than that of racial equality. Judges, like other citizens, subscribe somewhat idiosyncratically to various commonly held social values. While we can assume that most judges believe in a just society, if a judge's belief is not solidly grounded in the protection of human equality, then bringing desegregation or detracking litigation in front of him or her is likely to be a futile task.

To illustrate that phenomenon, this chapter compares two judicial opinions written in the Rockford litigation. In a powerfully worded opinion, the trial judge condemned the district for "consistently and massively violat[ing] the dictates of *Brown v. Board of Education*" (*Rockford*, 1994, p. 939). However, when his remedial order was appealed to a three-judge panel of the Seventh Circuit Court of Appeals, that panel saved its condemnations for the lower court—not the school district—accusing that court of overstepping its remedial bounds. The astonishing difference in the approaches taken by these two courts highlights the importance of the personal values of judges.

THE DECISION AND THE APPEAL

The Rockford trial court found a stark pattern of intentional system-wide discrimination against African-American and Latino students in the school district. Although the district filed an appeal from the remedial order that followed, it did not challenge this underlying determination of liability. The Fourteenth Amendment violation was essentially acknowledged. My focus here is only on the challenged provisions of the remedial order concerning the class assignment of students. These provisions limited the use of ability grouping and tracking (eliminating remedial classes while continuing to allow significant course differentiation among the non-remedial, such as gifted and honors, classes) and imposed ranges to control racial segregation in classes. The order required that the racial composition of non-elective classes approximate the racial composition in the given school, plus or minus 5%. Thus, although the district court's remedy required some detracking, it relied most heavily on ensuring integration within ability-grouped classes.

The court presented a long and detailed evidentiary foundation for these remedial provisions.[1] Its opinion begins by stating that the RSD "at times, has committed such open acts of discrimination as to be cruel and committed others with such subtlety as to raise discrimination to an art form" (Rockford, 1994, p. 939). It then offers hundreds of pages of evidence and analysis, discussing the overwhelming proof of discrimination by the school district.[2]

Looking specifically at the conclusions regarding discrimination in the class assignment of students, the court issued two relevant findings:[3] (1) "it was the policy of the [district] to use tracking to intentionally segregate white students" (Rockford, 1994, p. 912); and (2) "the [district] engaged in intentional and purposeful discrimination in the operation of [its] purported desegregation programs, tracking system, bilingual education programs, magnet school programs, and various alternative education programs" (Rockford, 1994, p. 917).[4] Again, please note that the district did not challenge these basic findings of liability.

The following passage from the opinion summarizes some of the evidentiary record supporting the finding of intentional discrimination in the tracking system:

> Groups of higher track students whose scores fell within a range that would qualify them for participation in either a higher or lower track were consistently "whiter" than groups of students whose scores fell within the same range but who were placed in the lower track and in a number of cases, high track classes included exceptionally low-scoring white students, but this was rarely the case for blacks. Con-

versely, quite high-scoring blacks who were often excluded from high track classes were often found instead in low track classes. This was seldom the case for white students. (*Rockford*, 1994, p. 914.)

In addition to these disparities, the plaintiffs proved that school district officials had knowledge of the discriminatory impact of the system and had made "woefully inadequate efforts to correct them" (*Rockford*, 1994, pp. 913–14).[5]

Based on such evidence and findings, the court prepared a comprehensive remedial order that, among other things, limited the use of ability grouping and imposed racial ranges to control racial segregation in classes. It is important to keep these two orders separate; the first (liability) order is the one that contains the extensive and unchallenged findings of discrimination, while the second (remedial) order is the one that was brought before the appellate panel for review. The Court of Appeals reversed the detracking provision and sent the integration provision back to the district court for further examination—holding the plus or minus 5% standard to be overly restrictive. This appellate opinion was authored by Chief Judge Richard A. Posner[6] for a unanimous three-judge panel. The following discussion examines Judge Posner's opinion (in particular, the reversal of the detracking order) in light of the relevant legal standards and of the evidentiary findings of the trial court. Following this examination, I consider the importance and the implications of a judge's own values in such an opinion. (For a separate critique of Judge Posner's appellate opinion, see Tanaka, 1999.)

THE LAW

The structure of the federal judicial system gives appellate courts supremacy over trial courts in matters of law, but it gives trial courts the primary authority over matters of evidence. Thus, for example, an appellate court might be called upon to interpret an unclear law to decide whether a school is legally obliged to maintain a well-lit parking lot, while the trial court's purview would be to decide whether a particular school's lot was, in fact, well-lit.

Federal appellate courts must apply the "clearly erroneous" standard to a trial court's factual findings (*Pullman-Standard v. Swint*, 1982; Federal Rule of Civil Procedure 52). This standard requires the reviewing court in almost all cases to accept the lower court's factual findings, since only the finder of fact at the trial level has an opportunity to assess witnesses' credibility. An appellate court may only refuse to accept such factual findings if left with a definite and firm conviction, based on the entirety of the evidence, that the lower court made a mistake (*Pullman-Standard v. Swint*, 1982). As the Supreme Court explained in *Anderson v. City of Bessemer City* (1985),

[T]his standard plainly does not entitle a reviewing court to reverse the finding of the trier of fact simply because it is convinced that it would have decided the case differently. . . . If the district court's account of the evidence is plausible in light of the record viewed in its entirety, the court of appeals may not reverse it even though convinced that had it been sitting as the trier of fact, it would have weighed the evidence differently. Where there are two permissible views of the evidence, the factfinder's choice between them cannot be clearly erroneous. (*Anderson*, 1985, pp. 573–574, citations omitted).[7]

THE EVIDENCE

With that legal standard in mind, consider the evidentiary findings of the Rockford trial court.

Disparate placement. The court "inescapably" found that "African-American students were enrolled in consistently disproportionate numbers in the slow track, low ability classes [and] consistently over-represented in classes for those students identified as having special educational needs" (*Rockford*, 1994, p. 942). Correspondingly, "the overwhelming evidence finds white students at all grade levels disproportionately assigned to high ability, college preparatory programs" (*Rockford*, 1994, p. 942). The court noted that these disparate course placements were "so striking that one could, simply by walking into a class and looking at the color of the children's skin, determine if the class was a high, middle or low ability class" (*Rockford*, 1994, p. 942).

Remedial tracks served no educational function. The court described the tracks as "different paths that Rockford students followed through the curriculum of the RSD." While it found that "some of the paths led to certifying a student as being prepared for college," others "led to specific occupational preparation and [still] other paths led essentially nowhere" (*Rockford*, 1994, p. 941). This last set of paths, the "low level or basic" classes, was found by the court to "deprive students of the opportunity for various educational experiences" (*Rockford*, 1994, p. 958).

Based on these preliminary findings, the court concluded that the RSD's tracking system—and particularly the remedial classes—"did not remedy differences or ameliorate disparities in achievement among racial groups, nor did it function to move students out of the low level track or move minority children into the high level track" (*Rockford*, 1994, p. 999). For this reason, the court rejected the school district's attempt to justify the lower-tracked classes as a means of targeting minority students in order to advance them to higher achievement levels (*Rockford*, 1994, p. 999).

Track rigidity. Having thus reputdiated the district's rationale for remedial classes, the court found instead that "once a child was ability grouped in the RSD it was very difficult or almost impossible to change ability groups" (*Rockford*, 1994, p. 958). The district's own high school curriculum guide expressly informed parents and students, " 'it is rare that a student is moved from one level to another' " (*Rockford*, 1994, p. 958).

The court noted the testimony of the district's superintendent and one of its principals that they did not expect students in the remedial track to improve and move up to any of the regular tracks. The superintendent testified, " 'It looks to me as an observer that once you get into a particular track, or sometimes I refer to them as tubes, it's very difficult to get out of them' " (*Rockford*, 1994, p. 947).

Poor tests. The court found that the district's standardized placement tests "measured a very narrow range of a child's knowledge and skills [and were] inaccurate [and] culturally biased" (*Rockford*, 1994, p. 948).

Erratic use of tests. While the district claimed that these tests constituted the primary basis for track placement, the court found that the district did not use the tests in a consistent way: "[T]he record is replete with situations where . . . students (usually white) who scored below the national mean . . . were still placed in honors classes and, incredibly, there were students (usually minority) who scored in the ninety-ninth percentile who were placed in basic classes" (*Rockford*, 1994, p. 949). The court noted a principal's testimony that the placement of some African Americans in low tracks arose because of perceived behavioral problems, rather than due to low academic achievement (*Rockford*, 1994, p. 947).

Heterogeneous, but racially identifiable, resulting classes. Based in part on the above findings, the court concluded that the resulting classes contained students with a wide range of abilities (*Rockford*, 1994, p. 958). While part of the sorting of students into these classes could be accounted for by past academic achievement or standardized test scores, the court found that race played a separate and determining role.

THE APPELLATE OPINION

Each of the above findings is factual rather than legal. Moreover, the school district did not appeal these findings to the appellate court. The district challenged only the remedies, successfully arguing that they were too extensive. But the appellate court's reversal of the remedial order used a very broad approach, effectively re-trying the factual issues without the benefit of hearing the evidence that had been before the lower court. Consider the manner in which the Appeals Court addressed (or did not address) each of the above findings.

Disparate placement. The appellate court did not challenge the lower court's finding of disparate placement of African-American students in lower-tracked classes. The appellate court characterized this discrimination as a "misuse" of tracking.

Remedial tracks served no educational function. The appellate court studiously avoided any recognition of the lower court's evidentiary finding that the lower-tracked classes constituted educational dead ends.

Track rigidity. The appellate court also ignored this evidentiary finding.

Poor tests. While the appellate court placed a great deal of faith in "objective" testing (see below), it also ignored this evidentiary finding.

Erratic use of tests. As discussed in greater detail below, this evidentiary finding constituted the appellate court's primary focus. In fact, the Posner opinion creates the impression that the district's only significant problem regarding tracking was its failure to apply the test scores consistently.

Heterogeneous, but racially identifiable, resulting classes. The appellate court implicitly acknowledged this finding, but blamed the problem on the school district's failure to apply objective test criteria consistently.

Thus, the appellate court seized on one evidentiary element of the injury (the segregative track placement) and attributed it entirely to one evidentiary element of causation (the erratic use of tests). The court then characterized the problem as resulting merely from an unfaithful application of an otherwise workable tracking model; it re-categorized the violation so that it could re-categorize the remedy. The lower court had emphatically concluded that the tracking itself must be enjoined because the district used it as a means of intentional racial segregation. The appellate court disagreed, reasoning that the school district did not "adopt" the tracking system in order to discriminate (*Rockford*, 1997, p. 536). Instead, the district only "misused tracking, twisting the criteria to achieve greater segregation than objective tracking alone would have done" (*Rockford*, 1997, p. 536).

To reach this conclusion, the appellate court contorted the lower court's finding concerning the tests' inadequacy as well as the erratic use of those tests. The appellate court reasoned that the plaintiffs had "implicitly" conceded, "by accusing the school district of having placed white kids in higher tracks, and black kids in lower tracks, without always complying rigorously with objective criteria, such as scores on achievement tests," that discrimination in the RSD could be eliminated without abolishing tracking (*Rockford*, 1997, p. 536).

However, the plaintiffs had made no such implicit concession. Rather, they made two inter-related arguments to the trial court. First, they demonstrated that the tests poorly measured "ability." Second, they used a statistical analysis (reproduced in the lower court's opinion and discussed in Chapter Four) to counter the school district's argument that placements were objectively based on these tests. Specifically, the plaintiffs used the test scores to show that so-called "homogeneous" classes in fact contained students with a very diverse set of scores. This second analysis, in addition to responding to the district's claims that the placements were primarily based on these tests, documented a downward placement of African-American students, compared to where they would have been placed if test scores had been the sole determining criterion.

Notwithstanding the role of this evidence in refuting the school district's contentions, the plaintiffs did not offer it to show, nor did the trial court find, that placements based solely on these tests would be pedagogically desirable or even non-discriminatory. In fact, the evidence (and the evidentiary findings) was clear: the tests could not fairly guide these placements. The evidence was offered to demonstrate the arbitrariness of track placements, but substituting another given placement criterion would not be likely to make the process any less arbitrary.

Nevertheless, Judge Posner's opinion concluded that the misuse should be enjoined, but not the tracking. Specifically, he limited the available remedy—based upon the limited evidence on tracking that had been placed before the lower court[8]—to an injunction that would "forbid the district, on pain of contempt if the prohibition is flouted, to track students other than in accordance with criteria that have been validated as objective and nonracist" (*Rockford*, 1997, p. 536).

Of course, this suggested remedy would accomplish little in light of the district court's findings that the remedial tracks served no educational function, that the rigidity of the tracks allowed for no upward mobility, and that the "objective" tests themselves provided no valid basis for track placement.[9]

Interestingly, rather than directly addressing this evidence, the appellate opinion presents a separate set of evidentiary findings. For example, the appellate court did not confront the trial court findings that (a) the Rockford tracking system ensured that low-track students would have no educational future and (b) the rigidity of the Rockford tracking system allowed for no upward mobility. Instead, the appellate court rehabilitated tracking by presenting it as a "controversial educational policy" and arguing that "lawyers and judges are not competent to resolve the controversy." It cited scholarly authority for the proposition that most American students are tracked and reasoned that, "as the consensus of the nation's educational authorities, it [tracking] deserves some consideration by a federal court" (*Rockford*, 1997, p. 536).

Similarly, rather than confront the trial court finding concerning the inadequacy of the "objective" tests, the appellate court simply assumed the existence of "criteria that have been validated as objective and non-racist." What criteria did the appellate judges have in mind? Few if any school districts place students in tracks using only standardized test scores.

LEGAL ANTICS

Clearly, the three-judge panel of the Seventh Circuit Court of Appeals approached this case with a very different set of values than did the trial court. While the trial judge made little effort to hide his sense of outrage at the evidence of discrimination, the judges on the appellate panel substituted an outrage of a different sort: a clear disdain for judicial involvement in desegregation.[10] They approached the question of a remedy as an unpleasant and unnecessary intrusion into the orderly functioning of the district.

Since the appeal had not sought a direct reversal of the finding of liability, the appellate court could only minimize the importance and scope of that finding. Accordingly, it demanded that any remedy be tied very closely to the specific liability finding. But the trial court had set forth extensive evidentiary findings, documenting the overwhelmingly discriminatory nature of the Rockford tracking system as well as the system's pedagogical indefensibility. In light of the *Pullman-Standard v. Swint* (1982) Supreme Court precedent, these findings seemingly stood, or should have stood, as an insurmountable obstacle to the appellate court reversing the detracking order. Yet, the panel never addressed the legal precedent, and it chose to ignore important evidentiary findings.

Such maneuvering allowed the appellate court to set forth its claim that the school district had not adopted the tracking system in order to discriminate, but had "misused tracking, twisting the criteria to achieve greater segregation than objective tracking alone would have done" (*Rockford*, 1997, p. 536). Accordingly, the appellate panel concluded, only the misuse—not the adoption—could be enjoined.[11]

Yet this is a distinction without a difference. After all, why does it matter whether tracking was *initially* adopted with the intent to discriminate? During the years in question, subsequent to its adoption, discrimination was the proven intent of the policy. Consider an analogy. The most common type of injunction in America is the restraining order, generally obtained to prevent threatened incidents of personal violence (e.g., by an ex-boyfriend). Using the Rockford Court of Appeals' reasoning, such an injunction should not mandate that "the offender must stay 500 feet away from the plaintiff." Instead, it should mandate that "the defendant is allowed to come right up to the plaintiff, but he should treat her with the respect she deserves." After all, when the relationship was initially "adopted," the intent was not abuse. Admittedly, the offender misused the opportunity to be within touching distance, but it is the misuse that should be enjoined, not the opportunity.

The legal antics of the three-judge panel are particularly interesting given Judge Posner's often-stated stance of judicial "minimalism." In fact, Posner (1999) fiercely attacks the view advocated by Ronald Dworkin (1977) and others that, when faced with ambiguous laws or cases where no law dictates an outcome, judges invariably rely on broader moral principles to make their decisions. Dworkin contends that judges should therefore abandon the pretense of legal positivism and examine these principles in depth when writing their judgments. Judge Posner (1999) rejects such moral theory, contending that it would invite judges to step beyond the law and impose their own beliefs. Posner's Rockford opinion provides strong support for Dworkin's premise that application of moral principles is indeed inevitable—even among those who most vehemently reject it.[12]

THE IMPORTANCE OF VALUES

The judges on the appellate panel thus reversed the lower court's detracking remedy because, they concluded, it was not related as closely as legally possible to the infraction. "Violations of law," Judge Posner wrote, "must be dealt with firmly, but not used to launch the federal courts on ambitious schemes of social engineering" (Rockford, 1997, p. 534). But one wonders whether any type of interference with the "natural" process of child development wouldn't fall under Posner's "social engineering" rubric. If so, is not the sorting of children into stratified tracks, with hierarchical sets of expectations, pedagogies, and (ultimately) outcomes, also a social-engineering scheme? He selectively applies the social engineering label to actions to ameliorate segregation, but not to the "meritocractic" sorting of students in order to advance different social goals. Perhaps Posner would respond by distinguishing between social engineering mandated through local control of schools and social engineering mandated by a federal court—evoking the value of freedom from federal interference in education.

However, Posner's animus explicitly focused on the content of the mandate—detracking—rather than the source. As noted in Chapter One, Posner cautioned, "Children, the most innocent of the innocent persons occasionally brushed by draconian decrees, should not be made subjects of utopian projects" (Rockford, 1997, p. 534). The trial court issued the "draconian" detracking order in response to overwhelming evidence of discrimination exercised through the tracking system. The "utopian project" of detracking, while based on ideals of social justice, is hardly extreme or unusual; it is supported by such mainstream organizations as the National Governors Association (1993), the Carnegie Council for Adolescent Development (1989), and The College Board (1989). Moreover, Posner mischaracterized the degree of detracking required by the remedial order—it required only limited detracking, so a great deal of stratification would remain in the district's curricular offerings.

Posner's words are hard to reconcile with the utopian ideals explicitly expressed by the nation's founders and implicitly embodied in the concept of universal schooling. But this is the lesson we must learn: forty-seven years after *Brown*, racial justice and racial equality do not rank high among the values of many people, including some judges. Many judges condemn the prolonged and difficult role that courts must play when supervising a desegregating school district; for them, such detailed judicial involvement in the governing of local schools constitutes a greater wrong than does underlying racial discrimination.[13] These are value judgments, grounded in individual visions of what constitutes a just society.[14]

CONCLUSION

Americans look to the courts as bellwethers to assess the seriousness of our problems. *Brown* was, on top of everything else, a signal to the nation that we needed to address the problem of *de jure* segregation. When America's courts backtrack on desegregation decisions, the signal is sent that we as a nation no longer have a serious problem with discrimination. The cautionary tale offered in this chapter warns of some of the limitations of entrusting this bellwether status to courts. If American society is to make real its rhetoric about racial equality, it cannot rely exclusively upon the personal values of judges.

This chapter, however, is not meant to discourage pursuit of equity through the courts—quite the opposite. The judiciary has initiated considerable racial progress. Indeed, Rockford has made progress, and it should be remembered that Judge Posner and his appellate colleagues were not the only judges involved in this case—Rockford's progress is attributable in large part to the judges who heard and decided this matter at the trial level.[15]

Judicial values are thus one more salient force shaping the context surrounding a detracking reform. Later chapters discuss educators and parents, whose values and beliefs concerning the intellect, demeanor, and educability of African-American or Latino students are crucial to any detracking effort. This chapter adds a corollary: a detracking mandate is only as strong as the values of the authority issuing that mandate. If the authority's predominant values are those of local control then we cannot expect a powerful mandate. Even in those cases where the law supports judicial intervention, a mandate will not be a very useful policy tool unless the judge highly values racial equity and equal educational opportunity.

Part II

Romancing the Zone

6

Putting Reform in Context

Whichever organizational level one considers—the classroom, school, district, or broader society—every reform takes place within a specific context, a context that largely determines the reform's path. Shifting forces arising from within as well as outside a given organizational tier continuously shape and reshape that context. These forces are of various types. All reforms confront technical (structural) obstacles as well as inertial forces. Most reforms also face some normative and political obstacles. Moreover, this latter duo—norms and politics—dominates the contextual landscape for equity-minded change and adds enormous complexity to the process of equity-minded reform. Nevertheless, academics and practitioners tend to focus on the technical/structural and inertial, neglecting powerful forces originating from other realms.

To clarify my terms: inertial forces derive from the comfortable and set ways of schooling (e.g., the use of lecturing and worksheets). These are the habits, routines, customs, and practices that are found within most organizations and which, over the years, take on a life of their own. I will also use the term "school ethos" to refer to these forces. Technical forces include the organizational structure and internal functioning of schools, including time and resource allocation, equipment, materials, and curriculum. Normative forces arise from beliefs and values and reflect such matters as conventional conceptions of intelligence and deep-seated racist and classist attitudes and prejudices. Political forces arise out of the demands and concerns of constituents and are subject to political imbalances among states, districts, schools, teachers, and parents.

The reader may note that I have studiously avoided using the terms "culture" and "school culture." These terms are used in much of the literature about school change, but their definition constantly mutates, leaving no clear meaning for general use. Moreover, many anthropologists cringe at terms such as "school culture" because they essentialize a multifaceted and amorphous set of characteristics. Instead, I have broken down the concept of culture, as the term is most often used in the school change literature, into "school ethos" and "normative beliefs." To understand how the two terms differ, imagine that you asked a White southern gentleman in 1960 Mississippi why White and Black children attended different schools. He might respond, "That's the way we do things down here." This is an example of the habits, customs, and procedures that I am calling "school ethos."[1] However, if one probed deeper about why he and his White neighbors maintain the custom of segregation, one would likely uncover a belief system grounded in White supremacy. This is an example of what I am calling normative beliefs. Of course, while I find it conceptually helpful to think about school ethos, normative beliefs, political factors, and technical needs as distinct categories, considerable overlap exists between them. Moreover, other categories can legitimately be included—e.g., historical, demographic, and fiscal factors—which exist within each of the other four.

DEVELOPING THE CONCEPT OF THE ZONE OF MEDIATION

The challenges faced by change agents promoting equity-minded reforms differ from those faced by advocates of other reform efforts in that they invariably provoke highly-charged conflicts, namely (a) a political conflict over resources that are perceived to be scarce, and (b) an ideological conflict over societal values and beliefs as they are acted out in schools. These conflicts take place within reforming schools as well as between schools and resistant communities, and they entangle schools in larger societal patterns related to race, class, language, and gender. The "zone of mediation" is a tool to bring these issues into the dialogue about the change process.

This non-neutral change framework builds on two concepts from existing literature concerning the politics of education. One concept is the "zone of tolerance"; the other is the "mediating institution." The zone of tolerance is the domain within which a local community will allow policy to be changed and developed (Boyd, 1976; McGivney & Moynihan, 1972). A mediating institution is an organized social setting in which people interact (e.g., a school system), that channels macro-political and economic forces into particular "sites" (e.g., individual schools) to mediate (i.e., shape, structure, and constrain) the interactions between individuals within those sites. It is in the context of these mediating institutions that larger social forces actually impact the lives of individuals (Lamphere, 1992).

The zone of mediation is a conceptual tool highlighting the boundaries of debate for a given issue. Such zones do not, of course, exist as natural phenomena. Nor are these zones fixed, but rather are constantly changing. From this perspective, one sees schools as situated within particular local enactments of larger cultural norms, rules, incentives, power relations and values. These forces either promote stability or change, and they accordingly set the parameters of beliefs, behavior, and policy in schools. The intersection of forces around a particular issue shapes the zone of mediation for that issue. Such forces may include such far-reaching items as legislation, judicial decisions, the support of foundations, demographics, housing and nutritional needs, economic and market forces, social/state political climates, educational influence groups (such as teacher unions), district history, individual players within districts, their political ambitions, and the media.

I thus use the term "forces" in a broad sense, encompassing (among other things) people, groups, values, phenomena, and events. The key criterion is that the force must impact the site of mediation by exerting an influence on the way that the issue is addressed at the site. For example, a widespread belief that White students are more likely than others to be intelligent may affect the way that policy-makers and others in a school district perceive and address a detracking reform. Also, a judicial decision in a case in which a given school district is *not* a party may still be a force on the zone of mediation for an issue in that district.

As was mentioned above, I am not the first researcher who has used a "zone" metaphor to help explain school dynamics. To describe the cultural parameters within which schools operate, McGivney and Moynihan (1972) use the concept of a "zone of tolerance." They define this as "the latitude or maneuverability granted (or yielded) to the leadership of the schools by the local community," and they use the concept to explain local resistance to reforms that arise out of conflicting social policy agendas (p. 221). If policy-makers or educators introduce policies that fall outside this zone, the community will object (McGivney & Moynihan, 1972; see also Boyd, 1976).

McGivney and Moynihan recognize that schools must be responsive to both their local communities and their larger societies, and that these two layers may be in conflict. For example, national policy-makers might set a more broad-based agenda (e.g., promoting AIDS education) than a more parochial local community may be willing to accept.

Boyd (1976) uses essentially the same definition of the zone of tolerance in his analysis of who effectively governs schools (e.g., school boards, the public, or professional educators). He suggests that the zone of tolerance is defined through an interaction between the characteristics of a school community and the type of issue or policy question faced. Consequently, each issue produces its own unique zone. Boyd further contends that issues perceived by the community to be redistributive are the most likely to produce conflict and, therefore, to "immobilize" policy-makers. He concludes that professional educators, who tend to dominate local educational policy making, "usually operate within significant, and generally neglected or underestimated, constraints imposed by the *local* community and school board—not to mention those imposed by state and national forces" (p. 572, emphasis in original).

Others have presented variations on this theme. For example, Charters (1953) introduced the "margin of tolerance," which he describes as boundaries composed of values dear to a particular community within which citizens of the community delegate to school personnel the freedom to educate. Similarly, Barnard (1938), Simon (1947), Bridges (1967) and Bolman and Deal (1984) describe a "zone of indifference." Barnard explained that administrator's decisions will be accepted unquestionably by subordinates if they fall within the zone. Bridges specifically applied the Barnard zone to the relationship between teachers and principals. An indistinguishable "zone of acceptance" was described by Kunz and Hoy, within which staff grant an administrator the freedom to make decisions without consulting them (Kunz & Hoy, 1976).[2]

My posited zone of mediation shares many characteristics with these earlier concepts. Like McGivney and Moynihan (1972), I look to the zone to aid my understanding of the change process. Like Boyd (1976) and Bolman and Deal (1984), I believe that a community's level of indifference to an issue helps to determine the strength of the zone. Finally, like each of these authors, I perceive the zone as circumscribing the boundaries of debate. However, my notion of a zone of mediation also differs from these earlier concepts in several important ways.

First, unlike these earlier zones, whose boundaries are defined solely by the community, the boundaries of the zone of mediation are also shaped by forces originating at societal and global levels. I contend that each school exists within a unique context. That context may be defined most directly by the local community, but it is ultimately defined by a myriad of normative, political, technical, and inertial forces at the local, regional, national and global levels. All these forces interact with one another to create a zone of mediation.

Second, while the zone of mediation does define the boundaries of community tolerance, it concomitantly defines the boundaries of the mediation process *within* schools. The zone's boundaries are not simply set by outside forces: they are largely created by people negotiating among themselves and between themselves and those outside forces.[3] If one considers schools as "sites of interaction" (Lamphere, 1992), one can more easily recognize that larger social forces make their impact as they shape the interaction among diverse groups who come together to work, learn, and participate within the sites. For instance, an outside force such as a newspaper article may influence the way that teachers perceive a school reform, the way they discuss that reform among themselves, and the degree of commitment that they ultimately make to the reform. The article may influence opinions both inside and outside the school, joining a myriad of other forces as they shape and reshape the zone.

The mediating activity within sites of interaction explains the difficulty that schools experience when they try to circumnavigate outside forces. It also explains the need for change agents within schools to confront forces inside their institutions and inside themselves, rather than simply to confront the limited and commonly perceived challenges involved in convincing those outside the school. Moreover, individuals' ways of making sense and acting sensibly are influenced by their own positions in, and experiences with, political, economic, and social structures. Therefore, educators—especially those from dominant groups in the community—are as likely to recreate dominant structures and ideologies within schools as are community members to press for them.

Third, while I agree with McGivney and Moynihan (1972) and Boyd (1976), who state that the zone of tolerance is always in flux, I also envision a zone of mediation wherein the boundaries are dependant on the perception or standpoint of individuals. Consequently, this individualized zone changes with time, identity and place.

Nonetheless, while the zone of mediation can be thought of as a unique snapshot for each individual, the concept can also be used to envision a collective zone, encompassing all relevant persons (e.g., all policy-makers or all practitioners). In this book, I primarily discuss such collective zones, as they are more useful in analyzing macro-level policy context. For instance, consider a school board discussing the installation of a metal detector at the district's high school. Each of the board's members would approach his or her vote in a context formed by a variety of forces. The forces influencing board members will sometimes overlap and sometimes be unique to an individual. So too, some mediating institutions will overlap while some will be unique (e.g., the member's family). Consequently, the zone of mediation for this issue will differ for each member. However, the collective zone of mediation for policy-making in the district is created through the interaction of all these forces as mediated by all these institutions. This model prompts an examination of these forces and their mediation in the local context, allowing a reasoned, although not a mathematical, prediction of the likelihood that this district will install a metal detector at its high school.

FORMATION OF THE ZONE

As explained by Cuban (1992) in the context of curricular change, policy-making involves "power, control, coalitions, bargaining, and compromise among and between groups and individuals operating inside and outside a decentralized system of governing schools" (p. 224). Among these external factors, Cuban cites (1) social movements (such as the Progressive movement at the turn of the century and the changes connected with the Cold War); (2) legislative and judicial decisions (such as *Brown v. Board of Education*, 1954); and (3) influential groups (such as publishers, foundations, accrediting and testing agencies, and professional associations). Inside school systems, Cuban notes that groups and individuals such as students, parents, teachers, principals, curriculum specialists, and superintendents can play significant roles in curricular change. In addition, he warns that the "historical curriculum" exerts pressure on schools to maintain curriculum stability.

Expanding on Cuban's list, zones of mediation for school policy options are also sometimes shaped by research literature on educational policies and school change, as well as the staff-development activities that this literature has spawned. Further, the global political economy shapes the role and status of low-income people and people of color within communities (Oakes, Welner, Yonezawa, and Allen, 1998). Similarly, as schools embrace market-oriented solutions to educational problems, the beliefs, values, and norms associated with the "market metaphor" begin to shape schools' zones of mediation (see Wells & Oakes, 1998; see also the discussion of the market metaphor in Chapter Ten). Lipman (1998) offers this synopsis:

> [N]ot only do the values, practices, and beliefs of individual teachers influence the direction of restructuring, but reforms are shaped by social/structural factors such as current and historical patterns of economic, political, and social inequality; racial exploitation; the capitalist economy; relations between schools and communities of color; unequal resources and structures of inequality in schools; and the relative political power of social groups. The ideological influence of dominant constructions of race and the importance of educational ideologies, the framing of public policies, and the national as well as local political climates within which educators work—all shape educational reform (p. 39).

Schools are thus mediating sites for the influence of forces in our daily lives, and these forces may be as local as district policies and as remote as global capitalism. Acknowledging the influence of more remote forces does not entail a devaluation of local forces. School location and context clearly do matter; these factors are simply not separable from their local, regional, national, and global contexts. Identifying and understanding the impact of these (and other) forces is central to understanding the overall fate of a reform as well as the reform's effect on specific populations.

Discussing the importance of context in the formation of teachers' attitudes, Vincent Roscigno (1995) identifies many of these same forces:

> The racial context of a locality along with any corresponding racial cues may influence an individual teacher in a subtle fashion, which would be the case if that individual internalized the racial ideology of that locality. Such influence, however, need not be so subtle. Potentially, it may take the form of direct pressure from groups and individuals within the school setting (i.e., fellow teachers and administrators) as well as those external to the school setting itself (i.e., religious leaders, politicians, and parents). (Roscigno, 1995, p. 148.)

REPRESENTING THE ZONE

One way to visually represent the zone of mediation is as a circle that shifts, in response to the layering of various forces, within two-dimensional space. Consider the following simplified version of the zone as applied to the issue of tracking/detracking in a hypothetical school district, Oakville. Imagine that you arrive in this district, intending to answer the research question, "Might this tracked school district soon embark on a detracking reform?" You interview educators, policy-makers, and community members, and you discover that only four forces are mentioned as influencing the context for this potential reform: (a) the district has existed for 50 years, and it has always been tracked; (b) the state government has just issued a policy in favor of detracking and has offered the district a large financial grant if the district decides to detrack; (c) the local newspaper has editorialized in favor of detracking, arguing that the low-track classes are academic dead-ends; and (d) a group of politically powerful parents of high-track students has formed a community group, "Tracks are Great" (TAG), to lobby against detracking.

This district's collective zone of mediation for the issue of tracking/detracking would be formed by the combined influence of these four forces. To envision how this would look, imagine each of these forces in isolation, represented as overlapping circles. If, for instance, the only force existing in the district was the first (historical) force, then the zone would be highly favorable to retaining the tracked system and highly unreceptive to detracking. Similarly, the other three forces would, in isolation, produce such polarized zones. However, combining or laying these individual zones graphically highlights the determinative factors, allowing for a comprehensive consideration of the potential reform's context. Appendix 4 presents a representation of this visual approach, beginning with a presumption that the foundational zone is neutral. This approach emphasizes the idea that each

new force is layered on top of all pre-existing forces, resulting in a shifting of
the combined zone.

The representation in Appendix 4 assumes that your interviews and observations convinced you that the two factors favoring tracking are more powerful than the two forces favoring detracking, resulting in a combined zone
favoring tracking over detracking. However, since these forces are not quantified, the resulting zone should not be treated as an "answer" to the question
of whether or not detracking will occur in this district. That is, the model is descriptive, not predictive.

To represent more concisely the zone's shifts in response to various forces,
the zone can also be visually represented using arrows to depict the forces. Appendix 5 offers this approach, using the same Oakville scenario and again assuming a neutral starting point for the tracking zone.

In later chapters, I will use the zone model to depict the impact of a wide
array of normative, political, cultural and technical forces on the detracking
reform process. Schools are affected by outside structures, ideologies, and politics—forces that act to limit or expand their normative and political borders.
When one considers which policies and changes are within the realm of the
probable or of the possible in a given school or community, one considers—
explicitly or implicitly, directly or indirectly—these outside forces. The zone
allows a tangible representation of all these factors.

This model confronts the viewer with the reality that a reform's context is
constantly being shaped and reshaped by waves of forces. When a reform idea
first enters an organizational site, it is placed on top of many layers of history—
of competing beliefs, ideas and interests. How that reform proceeds is closely
tied to the recognition of, and response to, this reality. A change agent—
particularly one advancing an equity-minded reform—who is unaware of this
context is setting herself up to be blindsided.

LESSONS FROM THE QUANTITATIVE REALM

Even though the zone model is not easily quantifiable, and indeed is not intended to be quantified, the quantitative paradigm does offer several important
lessons. By highlighting the role played by various *exogenous* forces (forces
other than the intervention force), the layering of component zones helps to
explain the particular role played by the specific intervention. This is analogous to the inclusion, in a linear regression equation, of independent variables
explaining or predicting an outcome of interest, allowing the measurement of
the unique impact of each factor.

That is, a regression equation model should include all the key independent variables that are hypothesized to affect the outcome of interest. The

omission of potentially important variables is referred to as a specification error and can lead to misleading results. Imagine a regression model intended to estimate the impact of various efforts, measured in units of person-hours (P) and financial resources (F), on driving a learning outcome, "L." The simple model reads:

$$b_0 + b_1 P + b_2 F = L.$$

However, the researcher has found that this model fails to take into account at least two exogenous forces: resistant person-hours (R) and opposition financial resources (O). The more complete model therefore reads:

$$b_0 + b_1 P + b_2 F + b_3 R + b_4 O = L.$$

Although quantitative researchers rarely design studies requiring measurement of such subjective independent variables, the modeling dynamic is nonetheless informative. The first, simplified model would not be very useful if it could not account for much of the outcome. Instead, the researcher would explore other potential predictors and test more comprehensive models. This is analogous to the zone model's rejection of a policy-analysis paradigm that judges reform efforts without adequately taking into account hostile context. (In Chapter Fourteen, I will consider the implications of this shift in perspective for the way in which one thinks about the school change process.) Policy analysts too often focus upon their particular intervention to the exclusion of additional forces that may influence the outcome(s) of interest. The zone framework addresses this area of potential oversight by calling upon the researcher to explore the context surrounding the reform, identifying and investigating forces in oft-ignored dimensions.

This becomes particularly important when the reform under observation is equity-minded, because the forces opposed to these reforms can be tremendous. Imagine that you are studying the implementation of two reforms at a middle school: (a) a bell-schedule change designed to accommodate an extra period and (b) a detracking reform, making all English classes heterogeneous. The first change is likely to arouse some resistance among teachers who must now fit each class in a shorter period of time. However, significant resistance or opposition from administrators, counselors, parents, students, media, or the community is unlikely.

Opposition to the second reform might include all these elements. As a result, the implementation process for the bell-schedule change is likely to differ in crucial ways from the detracking reform (and is also likely to proceed much more smoothly). If your outcome of interest is merely the fidelity of each reform's implementation to its original design, then you might have no reason to consider the relative receptivity of each reform's context. However, if you wished to understand the change process surrounding each reform, you might perceive each reform effort as one additional force layered on top of the pre-existing forces. Accordingly, the success of the bell-schedule reform would be judged within its particular context (overcoming the established practices of the school and the pedagogical interest in longer periods), while the success of the detracking reform would be judged within its particular context (overcoming the technical, inertial, normative and political forces identified in the study). By considering reform efforts within these contexts, one moves toward a more realistic evaluation of the efforts.

Another lesson from the quantitative paradigm is the importance of potential interaction terms. That is, the impact of some factors may increase or decrease depending upon the magnitude of other factors. For instance, the impact of class size reduction on achievement may increase with the degree of curricular reform and/or teacher experience. Similarly, the impact of a reform-minded superintendent may "interact" with the support she has from the school board or with the relationship between the administration and the teachers' union.

Such potential interactions should be investigated by the researcher as part of the data-gathering process. These inquiries can add to the understanding of the reform process by allowing for the identification of potential interactions. Pursuing these and other questions, the following chapter begins applying this zone framework to the reform processes in four American school districts.

7

When Bottom-Up Goes Belly-Up

The impressive body of research demonstrating that tracking is pedagogically ineffectual and subject to discriminatory abuse has convinced only a minority of districts to detrack. For public schools in 1990, only 11% of 10th-grade math students and 15% of 10th-grade English students attended heterogeneous classes (Rees, Argys, & Brewer, 1996, using data from the *National Education Longitudinal Study of 1988*). Similarly, in 1990 only 14% of all public secondary schools reported that they offer a variety of undifferentiated courses in their core curriculum and allow students open access to any course provided they have taken the prerequisite(s) (National Center for Education Statistics, 1994, using data from the *Survey of High School Curricular Options*).

A variety of forces have interacted to keep tracking systems firmly in place in the majority of American secondary schools. This was the case in each of the four districts discussed in this book before their respective courts began focusing on tracking as a factor contributing to discrimination. This chapter explores the history of Woodland Hills School District (with a brief discussion of comparable circumstances in San Jose) to illustrate the formation of zones of mediation favorable to tracking. While equity-minded change (and school reform in general) should ideally arise from the bottom up, the context in many school districts is unreceptive to such change initiatives. This chapter explores how such a context is formed.

WOODLAND HILLS

In Woodland Hills, the district's history, the community's political and racial dynamics, certain characteristics of the teaching staff, historically weak district leadership, and pressure from external institutions all acted as powerful forces

103

keeping the zone of mediation quite unreceptive to detracking. Summing up this context, one Woodland Hills leader told me, "Nothing would have bubbled up in this district."

The Community's History

The district's history, recounted in Chapter Two, buttressed the schools' tracking policies. That history shows a pattern of ineffectual leadership, organizational uncertainty, and obstinacy in the face of pressure to change. Prior to the merger that formed the Woodland Hills School District, these patterns were evident in the various communities that came to comprise the district. Even after the merger, the twelve boroughs evinced little willingness to join together, to integrate, or to have mixed-ability classes.

Recall that the Woodland Hills area developed around the coal mining industry, and boroughs arose that were racially and economically segregated. Each community and each school district developed its own identity, even apart from racial issues. One long-time community member[1] commented:

I think there's a lot of parochial problems [in the district] that have nothing to do with race. I think they have to do with [e.g.] people from Swissvale don't like people from Edgewood, don't like people from Churchill. They don't like people from Braddock, whether they're Black [or White.] There's a lot of that going on. It's a great American tradition: hate your neighbor. [I]f he lives just far enough away, you can hate him.[2]

Many of the district's problems were, however, tied to race, and racial segregation increased as a result of—and, in turn, caused further—"white flight." The bulk of this flight followed the 1971 state-mandated merger that created the General Braddock district—described by one administrator as a shotgun marriage.

Most of the schools in the predecessor districts had tracked their students. The old General Braddock schools were among the worst offenders. Steve Larson, an English teacher who had taught in a General Braddock school, outlined the system, using ninth grade as an example. There was, he said, a section called "9A" for the A students and one called "9B" for the B students. This continued all the way to "9K", which none of the teachers wanted. There was only one class per letter of the alphabet. Each track of students spent all day together, having very little interaction with students in a different class/track: "They traveled around for these eight classes or nine classes—all year with the same 27 [students]."

Other teachers explained how their respective predecessor districts, such as Churchill and Swissvale, had been more rigidly tracked than the present setup in Woodland Hills. Swissvale even used a type of tracking in the elementary grades, placing students regardless of age in one of approximately 21 ungraded levels. The students would move through those levels rather than from grade to grade. At the secondary level, Swissvale used a more traditional tracking system, for instance sorting their students into one of six different English tracks per grade level.

Following the 1981 merger, the new district faced, in the words of one principal, the "awesome task" of combining the curricula of the predecessor districts. He mentioned different textbooks for the same subject with correspondingly different classroom curriculum. The various schools essentially horse-traded: "I'll use your English; you use my math; we'll balance out on social studies."

The tracking system also underwent a series of compromises and adjustments. Initially, for the first 4 to 5 years, the new district retained a great deal of the old tracking systems. Basically, reported a long-time teacher, everything that was offered in the old five school districts was offered in the new, merged district.[3] The new assortment of classes must have been mind-boggling.

During the period from 1984 to 1987, this hodgepodge of stratification was, for the most part, reduced to three tracks: remedial, regular, and advanced. By 1988, when the consent decree was being negotiated, the district had begun to rethink the remedial classes. There was concern, as one principal put it, that "minority students were being lumped into" the lower tracks. The district therefore phased out the remaining remedial classes.[4]

Nonetheless, site-level educators during this period of time largely ignored the district's directive to address the problem of racially identifiable classrooms. One elementary principal admitted that he and his colleagues "didn't take this [directive] quite as seriously" until the superintendent "blew his stack." According to this principal, the superintendent told them, "Don't you realize this goes to all the attorneys. This goes to the judge." "That's when it started to hit with us," said the principal. Another elementary principal, however, acknowledged that he still allowed several of his teachers to ability group, even though, "If the main guys would have caught us, it would have been the principal that would catch hell" (Miller, 1991, pp. 66, 97–98).

Notwithstanding these reforms, the two remaining tracks at the secondary level (regular and advanced) allowed for continued segregation. One administrator explained, based on her 1993 observations of one of the junior high schools, that placements were not grounded on any "definable variables." Instead, she said, teacher recommendations were the coin of the realm. She described some resulting classes as "all White" and others as "all Black."

Tracking's Forceful Supporters

This historical, pre-mandate zone was also shaped by a community dynamic favoring the stratified system. The local press and an informal information network catalyzed this anti-reform context.

The local press, particularly the *Progress* and the *Tribune-Review* newspapers, ran many stories skeptical of the detracking reforms. According to one district administrator, 90% of what the *Tribune-Review* writes about the Woodland Hills School District is negative, "and it's always around the court order, or what's not going on because of the court order, or one group of students that's suffering; i.e., the so-called advanced kids are suffering because of the court order." Another district employee ventured that resistant people in the schools and community use the *Progress* and *Tribune-Review* to undermine the general reform process:

> [W]e don't have any different problems, really, than any other school districts regarding discipline or whatever. But we seem to really get off on airing our dirty laundry in the media. [Maybe] people think that if we have 25 bad stories about the district, [then] the merger will be over.

In Woodland Hills, the newspapers influenced teachers' perception of the reform as well as their discourse around the reform. Ultimately, they influenced the degree of the teachers' commitment to the reform. As one teacher observed, "While there are always misstatements in newspapers, they still influence the perception of the public about the schools."

The rumor mill, frequently working in concert with the local press, was exceptionally active. Rumors prompted reporters to write articles, and articles fed rumors. "These are all small communities," one teacher explained, "Everybody knows everybody, and they know very quickly if things are not going well." Another interviewee suggested that the network of information, for him, consisted of "the community club, church, and just within the neighborhood." Also mentioned as nodes on the network were cheerleading squads and sports teams (where parents volunteered) as well as places of employment.

In Chapter Nine, I will explore two examples of this network's power. The first concerns the general collaboration that emerged in opposition to detracking between resistant teachers and resistant parents. This coalition significantly undermined the detracking reform's progress. The second concerns the transfer of an African-American woman, Dr. Judy Taylor, from the principalship of West Junior High School to the principalship of an elementary school. Taylor's transfer was mentioned by many parents, educators, and community members as an example of the type of power wielded in the district by those committed to thwarting equity-minded change.[5] This dynamic in the schools and the community helped to shape a pre-mandate zone of mediation that was quite inhospitable to bottom-up detracking reform.

No Effective Counter-Balance
from the African-American Community

If we can get the African-American community involved, it would change—it would turn this whole district around. [You can have] all the court orders that you want, [and] you could send [the teachers] to all the in-services that you want. If they do not want to comply, they won't. But with parent involvement, demanding [action], they'll turn it around. . . . We have to do it. It's our people. We have to motivate our people.

This African-American parent was not alone in describing her community as uninvolved in school politics. Blacks and Whites agreed that the political voice of the African-American community was quiet and ineffective. While it was true that three or four African Americans had gained wide recognition as community activists or leaders, they did not attract a large or vocal following. One of these activists openly complained that an African-American parent in this community would generally get involved only to advocate for his or her own child: "[O]ne of the problems in our community is that we don't show an interest until it affects us individually."

This latter critique could legitimately be leveled against parents generally—Black and White. However, the concerns expressed by African Americans in Woodland Hills about their ineffectual political voice were grounded in an understanding of the crucial need for united action. White parents began with substantial advantages, including larger numbers, greater wealth, and influential contacts in the schools and the media. The criticisms related in this section should be understood within that context.

The district's school board structure had been designed by the court to ensure African-American board representation. The board has nine members, each elected by a geographic district. Three of these seats represent a substantial African-American population. Yet the board had only one Black member (in 1996–1997). This representational situation was attributed by African-American activists to the low voting rate in their community. How, they wondered, can Black parents overcome their political disadvantages if they vote in such small numbers?

Lack of activism was closely related to a lack of information. One African-American community leader insisted that a randomly selected

African-American parent would likely know nothing about the court order. A principal sympathetically agreed that these "powerless" parents have "no idea" about the court order or its details. She acknowledged that some of the more "empowered" parents did understand that the district was obligated to "make sure that all kids are achieving [and] to meet the needs of all the kids." But, around the detracking issue at least, White parents were most knowledgeable, and they employed this information successfully in lobbying school leadership.

African-American parents' limited involvement was also attributed to a provincialism that continued to reign in the community. When the local NAACP, for instance, tried to call meetings, many failed to participate because the organization was identified with the borough of Braddock; residents living in other boroughs felt little identification with the group. If the NAACP responded to this concern by calling a meeting in another area, then Braddock residents saw themselves as outsiders and failed to participate.

Whatever its reason, this lack of involvement has had the predictable consequence of limiting the political clout of the African-American community in school governance. Thus, a central office administrator, asked to speculate about the future of mandated programs following the lifting of the court order, opined that the programs wouldn't survive because the African-American beneficiaries will not speak up. Evidence of this was already apparent. One African-American parent said that she had been told by a school board member that the board was not responsive to the needs of her community because " 'You people don't do [anything] but fight amongst each other. You people don't have [any issues].' "

The district has, it should be noted, seen some limited examples of an involved African-American community. Once—but only once—Black parents turned out in large numbers when the school board discussed detracking. As described by one White attendee:

> There was one time in the midst of this folderol, . . . where there must have been 25 African-American parents . . . that appeared at a board meeting . . . and simply sat there and listened to what was being said by the Edgewood [White parent] group, and [when the White parents were finished] one of the [African-American] parents got up and said, we just wanted the board to know that the things that these parents—very dramatic—things that these parents want for their children, we want for our children. [I]t was one of those moments where you could hear the cockroaches run around the floor. And that was it. The rest of the people just . . . waived their time at the podium.

This instance, which several interviewees mentioned, points to the potential impact of an involved African-American community on district policies.

The events surrounding the court order took place within this political context. Before the court became involved, the only avenue for African-American influence over school policies was through the political process. Given their limited effectiveness in that forum, African Americans were unlikely to have been able to push the district into a detracking reform. Discussing what will happen after court supervision ends, several people observed that there will be a great deal of pressure from White parents for re-tracking. The success of those efforts will depend, as one White teacher keenly noted, on how vocal the district's White, pro-tracking parents are and whether "other parents, who [presently] aren't vocal—if they could speak up against that." Another observer put it this way: "if the African-American community in the United States could marshal the political clout of the NEA [the nation's largest teachers' union], things would be different than they are."

Weak District Leadership

Reform is unlikely to arise from the local level if local leadership is in disarray. For years, this was the case in Woodland Hills. The era preceding the detracking mandate was marked by considerable disorganization and discord between the school board and district superintendents.

As discussed in Chapter Two, the first two superintendents following the merger experienced little success in bringing together the district's wide array of people, groups, ideas and schools. The environment lacked harmony and cooperation, yielding infertile soil for difficult reforms. In more recent years, under the leadership of superintendent Thomas Young (discussed further in Chapter Eight), the upper-level administration—although not many site-based educators—became more reform-minded.

While some of the district's history of disorganization can be laid at the superintendents' feet, most people in the district singled out the school board for their harshest criticism. Throughout the short history of Woodland Hills, its school boards have suffered from in-fighting, short-sightedness, and even, according to one board member, chair-throwing.

Independent curriculum auditors warned—both in their initial report in 1993 and in their follow-up report in 1997 (AASA, 1993a; ICMAC, 1997)—that board members displayed signs of being combative, disrespectful micromanagers, and lacking in unity and commitment.[6] Some of this divisiveness was evident in my own interviews of board members, who offered unsolicited criticisms (and, it should be noted, praise) of their colleagues.

Explaining these difficulties, a few community members pointed to the court supervision, arguing that this extraneous element has complicated governance. Others disagreed, pointing instead to a flawed political process. An administrator detailed this critique:

> When you look at the school board, you're not talking about educators. [F]ive people on this board don't have children in the district. One of them sent his kids to parochial school—never sent a kid to Woodland Hills. They run for different reasons. They run because their nephew wants to be the basketball coach. They run because they're angry senior citizens and they just want to bring taxes down. Some people run because they use it as a political springboard. Some people use it because [they] have friends and neighbors whose kids are going to school to be teachers, and [they] want to make sure they get a job. I would venture to say little of it has anything to do with, "I give a damn about education; I know [something] about education"—it's all for ulterior motives.

Such condemnations must be kept in perspective. Most community members, teachers, parents, and administrators did not characterize the school board as particularly problematic. And, as one top administrator noted, the school board tends to get blamed when things go wrong, simply because it makes the ultimate policy decisions.

Furthermore, several school board members have demonstrated remarkable insight into issues confronting the district. Arguing that she and her colleagues exert a positive, reformist force, one board member explained,

> The board is very committed to total compliance [with the] court order, although we do not let it drive our goals. The board and the administration [have] always felt we would be doing these programs for kids whether we were under a court order or not; just because they are good for kids. And the school district of Woodland Hills didn't need a court order to drive their activities. The caliber and scope of the administration and professional staff here, I truly believe, would have done it anyway. [W]e do a lot of things that the court doesn't even mandate us to do. They're just good for kids.

The picture she paints of the board may seem excessively rosy, particularly in light of others' criticisms, but perhaps the truth lies in the middle. Whatever the recent status of the board, however, its historical disorganization and discord created a context quite unreceptive to bottom-up, equity-minded reform.

Older Teachers, Unwelcoming of Change

I've been teaching [for about 30 years, and I'm not going to] begin to start something brand new. . . . I've gone through all the different changes and have tried all the changes. You end up doing what you feel is best for you.

Many Woodland Hills teachers, like this one, were nearing retirement age. As of the beginning of 1997, approximately 70 out of 350 teachers were eligible to retire. When the five predecessor school districts merged in 1981, the new district was legally obligated to retain the most senior teachers. Many of those teachers have now put in 25–35 years of teaching, and, as a school board member remarked, are "just not buying into" the reforms.

Many of these more experienced teachers, added a principal, did not welcome feedback or suggestions. When offered such assistance, said this principal, they would respond:

"I've been teaching 25–30 years, and nobody has ever come into my classroom and made any suggestions of what I'm doing." It was like: "I'm the master teacher; how dare you, how dare you make a suggestion?"

Another principal reflected, "Our . . . veteran teachers . . . are somewhat reluctant to change their behaviors in a classroom and how they're interacting with young people." Change, a teacher at the high school explained, "is tough to sell . . . to an older faculty sometimes."

Some of these long-time teachers viewed the detracking reform as a threat, and, according to one district parent, they "sabotage[d] the changes that need to take place." But most teachers saw it only as an annoyance to be evaded. Commented one observer:

My impression is that the majority of the staff have been waiting for the court case to go away. They tend to be veteran educators and they're on the downhill side and they're not inclined to be bothered or worried by some issue that in their opinion they had nothing to do with. [V]eterans are very sharp people, they know how to give you the impression that they they're with you. And then they carry on the next day [with] business as usual. [T]hey are masterful at the game of dodge ball as [it] relates to professional practice.

A secondary teacher cautioned that some of his colleagues "are just determined they're not going to change" because, in his opinion, they lack both the

skills to change and the interest in changing. The curriculum and method-
ologies promoted by the reforms are "very different for a lot of the teachers
from the way they have been trained," suggested an administrator. "[W]hen
you have a staff that's about 90% veteran teachers, that's a concern."

Of course, some of the older teachers did not experience such difficulties.
They believed in the reform effort and they meaningfully changed. After offering the above comment about some teachers being a "concern," the same
administrator added, "some of our best teachers are our veteran teachers, don't
get me wrong."

Many parents, community members, and educators nonetheless agreed
with the administrator who said that it would "be helpful if we had new blood
in here, people to come in and don't have any perceptions of what kids can
do." An African-American educator, for example, voiced his opinion that many
teachers in the district have "a problem with cultural bias." The district includes many veteran teachers, he said, who, "when they started teaching, they
were teaching all White children. And there is a difference in teaching White,
[primarily] middle class children. . . . [A] lot of teachers can't handle the needs
[of African Americans]."

One resistant veteran, however, argued that youth, not experience, was
the greatest danger. He offered his own warning:

> [T]here's going to be a big [faculty] turnover in the district, [and I
> hope it's going to have] a positive effect. But I observe some of the
> younger teachers in the building, and I see the problems that they
> have. [S]ome of the younger teachers who are starting out, I don't
> know how they're going to make it 5 years.

External Institutional Pressures

A variety of external institutional forces pressured the district to maintain ability grouping. The college admissions process provides an excellent example
of such a force. Parents and students repeatedly stated their view that advanced courses provide a way to enhance the appearance of school tran-
scripts. One student even worried that the new science nomenclature
(substituting the name "Science with Lab" for "Advanced Science") might
undermine his admissions chances, since a college might not know that he
took the upper-track class.

District leaders did not seem to share these concerns, but they did strive to
address them. A school board member proposed that the superintendent invite
admissions officers from prestigious colleges to speak to district parents about

admissions criteria. These experts, the board member suggested, could explain that detracking will not damage children's admission chances.

College admission pressures also undergirded the district's gifted programs, which extended through high school. Letters were added to the permanent records of the student participants, noting their level of involvement and accomplishments.

Advanced Placement (AP) tests, administered by The College Board, provided another external pressure on the detracking reforms. According to one of the district's AP teachers, The College Board recommends that students be identified as AP candidates as early as possible and then grouped together and accelerated.[7] Parents and students, according to one school board member, see AP courses as "necessary" for admission "into a good school." In addition to the cachet of the course title, AP courses aid in college admission because they have so-called "weighted grades," meaning that a "B" effectively translates into an "A" when the GPA is calculated for the college admissions process.

Ironically, the college admission process even exerted pressure on the district to discourage some students from considering college. A district administrator related a conversation that he had with a realtor about SAT scores. The realtor complained that the district's average scores were inordinately low because too many district students took the test. In other districts, the realtor explained, only "the bright kids"—the ones clearly headed to college—take the SAT. In contrast, the Woodland Hills policy, according to this administrator, was to "give every kid who wants to go to college an opportunity to take that SAT test." "To me," he continued, "that shouldn't be a negative factor. That should be a positive factor. But people don't see it that way."

The nation's courts—particularly the Supreme Court—exerted an additional external institutional force on the pre-mandate zone. The school district kept a file of newspaper clippings, most of which related directly to Woodland Hills (e.g., "Football Team Wins Championship"). However, the clippings also covered selected matters from outside the district—providing a glimpse into which broader events the district, as well as the press, thought important for Woodland Hills. For instance, the file included articles about a series of U.S. Supreme Court decisions, beginning in 1991. These decisions collectively lowered the standard for unitary status. That is, they allowed school districts to be released from court supervision even without complete remediation of segregation.[8]

Two articles from 1984 concerned a shift in the desegregation stance taken by the United States Justice Department (Associated Press, 1984; Staff, 1984). For the first time in history, the Department had taken a position opposed to busing. One of the articles covered a speech by William Bradford Reynolds, an assistant U.S. attorney general for civil rights in the Reagan administration, at a

Pittsburgh hotel dinner sponsored by the National Association for Neighborhood Schools (NANS). According to the article, Reynolds told the audience of growing evidence that mandatory busing fails to produce sufficient educational gains to offset its purported disruption (Staff, 1984).

Finally, consider an example of court influence that occurred *after* the detracking mandate. When the federal district court in Wilmington, Delaware ruled that the tracking system used by its school districts did not violate the constitutional rights of those districts' students, the local Woodland Hills newspaper ran an article entitled, "Detracking not Backed," speculating that the Delaware case "may provide a look at what the future may hold locally" (Dudiak, 1997a).

Community members and educators within Woodland Hills were affected by these outside forces and changed their perception of their own desegregation case. A parent, for example, called the district superintendent and asked why, given the Delaware case, he "continued to pursue this line of detracking and just didn't simply give in?" Another parent wrote to the local newspaper, asking what "excuse" the superintendent would use "for not fighting for ability grouping and advanced classes" given the Delaware decision (Gaugler, 1997).

Similarly, following the local speech by William Bradford Reynolds, an Edgewood parent (and the Pennsylvania Director of NANS), wrote a letter to a local newspaper describing the district's desegregation plan in the most extreme terms:

> When Americans cease to resent and resist tyranny in any form, our most precious heritage, freedom, is in dire jeopardy. Certainly citizens of the Woodland Hills area should never condone a school merger imposed by the dictatorial edict of an appointed federal judge (Spence, 1984).

As with the impact of college admissions criteria, the impact of outside courts helped form the detracking zone of mediation. The reform did not exist in a void—the surrounding context, shaped in part by judicial institutions, largely defined the perceptions of educators and parents. One can never know whether the zone in Woodland Hills would have ever evolved in the absence of a court order to create a receptive context for *bottom-up* change. However, the reality in Woodland Hills was that the history, community (political and normative) dynamics, the characteristics of the teaching staff, the historically weak district leadership, and pressure from external institutions all acted as powerful forces keeping the zone unreceptive to such reform—and these factors showed little signs of change.

SAN JOSE

As in Woodland Hills, the approach to detracking in San Jose was greatly influenced by previous experience with between-school desegregation. In fact, many people in SJUSD failed to distinguish between the two reforms, conflating the detracking efforts with the district's previous desegregation reform.

By the time of the initial desegregation order, historical factors had already combined with normative and political factors to shape an unreceptive zone of mediation for detracking. The historical forces included the racial division of residential housing patterns as well as governmental housing and transportation policies that effectively encouraged residential segregation. Normative and political forces included college admission pressures and the fear of "white and bright flight" as well as local elites and school administrators who played to their most powerful constituents. This all resulted in a context not conducive to equity-minded reform.

For years, demographic patterns and the district's responsive educational policies defined the context for racial equity issues in San Jose. Political and social forces in San Jose helped to create a district in which the politically dominant White population felt well-served by the public schools, buttressing their belief that their privileged position resulted from individual choice, not racist or discriminatory practices by the community or the district (see Sturges, 1985). White parents, who resided largely in the southern part of the district, were the only parents effectively exerting their political will at this time. These parents often relied on the neutral-sounding concept of neighborhood schools, although their claims of neutrality failed to account for the creation of residential segregation by such non-neutral factors as the prevention of low- and moderate-cost housing in the central and southern sections of the city; the failure of state, federal, and local officials to enforce fair-housing laws; and the absence of a city ordinance prohibiting adults-only rentals (Wilson, 1985).

School policy makers, subject to political pressures exerted by powerful constituents, had little tolerance for the notion that the government should or could interfere on behalf of its less-powerful citizens. As a teacher at one of the northern, downtown high schools explained:

[R]acial bias has existed in this district for years, and anyone who has worked here for 5 or more years knows it. That is how the south side came into being. We all know that. . . . The district, choosing to ignore the obvious facts, created the problem of segregation by building [schools in the south part of the district] so flight from the downtown area could occur (White, 1985).

In the wake of the 1985 desegregation order, the district spent much of its energy maintaining its focus on "quality." By emphasizing issues of excellence, the district was able to make more palatable to the community its court-mandated efforts to promote educational policies aimed at equity. The superintendent at the time announced, for example,

> Integration is not the goal unto itself. Education is the goal. Integration is the environment. They go hand in hand. . . . I think whoever the kid is, regardless of his culture, or ethnicity, he deserves [educational quality] first. Then we can work on desegregation. I want to naturally integrate by improving the quality of schools (Watson, 1985a).

The district's tracked structures thrived within this rhetorical environment.

Yet, notwithstanding the district's stated focus on excellence and the use of tracking to maintain elite enclaves within desegregated schools, White parents in the south of the district continued to voice powerful opposition, framed in terms of their commitment to neighborhood schools: "I would rather see the destruction of the school district than to see one child—whether Hispanic, Anglo, or black—be denied their [sic] right to attend neighborhood schools simply to appease the court while denying the wishes of the people [in the district]" (Watson, 1985d). Another parent explained, "We're not angry because we hate the people across town. We're angry because we've lost control of our own destiny" (Watson, 1985e).

Only a few residents attempted to return the debate explicitly to the issue of equity. One such person wrote in a tongue-in-cheek letter to the editor of the local paper:

> The plaintiffs propose to have counselors help parents decide on the best options for their kids. This will be helpful for parents who aren't used to the luxury of choice. Perhaps some money could be set aside for counselors for the people who are used to getting preference, to help them get over their resentment and get used to equality (Dawson, 1985).

The pre-mandate zone of mediation for San Jose was thus shaped by the combination of all these forces: the focus on neighborhood schools and "quality," the historical and demographic factors, the college admissions pressures and fear of White and bright flight, the discriminatory housing and transportation policies, and the political imbalance of power favoring wealthy, White families. As was the case in Woodland Hills, the San Jose context was very receptive to tracking and very hostile to any attempts at detracking.

The next chapter expands this discussion of the forces shaping detracking zones in these districts. With the introduction of powerful forces connected with detracking orders, the districts' contexts became more reform-friendly. However, the detracking orders did not eliminate the pre-mandate forces discussed above. Those forces were merely joined by an array of additional forces, shaping and reshaping the zone.

8

Initiating Change
through a Mandate

In all four districts, federal desegregation orders propelled policy changes that would otherwise have been inconceivable. This chapter recounts how de-tracking orders in San Jose and Woodland Hills dramatically reshaped the districts' zones of mediation for tracking. Court involvement shifted the policy-making context in these districts, greatly increasing the likelihood of equity-minded reform.

SAN JOSE

When the San Jose desegregation order was issued in 1985, the district's context shifted dramatically. For years, the district had relied exclusively on voluntary desegregation, but now this option had been rejected by a federal court.[1] As the then-superintendent told a mainly White group of parents, "The government has ruled, and we have been found guilty" (Iknoian, 1986). The president of the local teachers' union was similarly resigned to the faculty-desegregation provision of the order: "I think . . . everybody understands that we are under a court order that we have to comply with" (Watson, 1986).

Nonetheless, the zone of mediation still allowed for resegregation within classrooms. Like earlier voluntary efforts at achieving school desegregation in the SJUSD, the new court mandate to integrate schools was disassociated from the goal of integrating classrooms. In fact, given that these two goals were seen by some parents and teachers as incompatible, the desegregation court order

119

arguably shifted the zone, making it even more hospitable to tracking. That is, the pressure to maintain separate facilities shifted from the school level to the classroom level.

When the court-appointed monitor, Dr. Beatriz Arias, released a report detailing the use of tracking to resegregate students, the superintendent denied the charge, saying that "as far as classroom segregation goes, this district has never segregated students ethnically" (Watson, 1988a). Similarly, the *San Jose Mercury News* responded with an editorial defending ability grouping: "We see those problems as the result not of racial or ethnic differences, but of income differences that appear as ethnic differences because more minority students come from poor families" (Staff, 1988). The judge seemed to agree, finding, "The limited classroom segregation that does exist appears to be justified by educationally and demographically valid considerations" (Watson, 1988a).

Yet experiences at the school level belied this argument. The schools had "desegregation, but no integration at all," according to a White woman who had chosen to attend the historically Hispanic northern high school in the late 1980s. She explained to me that she and her fellow White students were segregated into a separate "International Baccalaureate" (I.B.) program that was used as a magnet to lure White students to the school. Interestingly, according to this former student, even the White students themselves complained "that there was an unfair advantage to being White at that school." She then described a discussion she had had recently with a Latina who had been an acquaintance in high school and was now a college honors student. The acquaintance expressed amazement and disappointment that her high school teachers had never told her, "Maybe you could be an honors student. Maybe you could be an I.B. student."

Notwithstanding these students' experiences, tracking did not show up on policy-makers' radar screens. Although the 1985 court order had forced substantial "between-school" desegregation, the resultant zone largely excluded any serious, mainstream debate concerning tracking and its segregative effects within schools.

The Shift Toward Detracking

Not long after the *Mercury* editorialized in defense of the practice of ability grouping, it ran a contradictory news story focusing on the ethnic disparity in gifted classrooms (Hispanic children made up only 12.4% of the gifted students even though they were 35.3% of the total district enrollment). The article quoted the coordinator of the district's gifted programs acknowledging the problems and appeared also to acknowledge some discrimination, albeit unintentional: "It's interesting that the teachers mean well. . . . They'll refer the [Hispanic] kids for special education, but not for GATE programs, mainly because of the language, I think" (Watson, 1988b).

As more time passed, the *Mercury* increased its coverage of the segregative effect of the district's tracking, noting, for example, that more than half of the White students at one middle school attended accelerated classes containing few minority students. Those White students, the article asserted, only mixed with the rest of the school during physical education and elective classes (Watson, 1989).

The increased awareness of tracking's harmful impact in San Jose, as represented by these newspaper articles, set the stage for the court monitor's second tracking report, released in 1990. The district's response differed from its reaction to the first one: instead of trying to minimize the disparities, the district tried to minimize the *significance* of the disparities.[2] The report's release coincided with the district's announcement that it had accomplished full desegregation of its schools. District leaders were beginning to prepare a motion for unitary status. The recently hired superintendent defended the alleged classroom disparities by arguing that any assessment must take into account students' "educational desires." The district's school assignment director seemed to think that the monitor simply wasn't playing fair: "She [the monitor] is applying another standard. We have a different definition of what a desegregated school is" (Torriero, 1990).

The *Mercury* then conducted its own study, and its conclusions supported those of the monitor: "Once inside their new schools Hispanics are subtly resegregated, enrolled far more in remedial than honors courses" (Watson, 1991a). The superintendent, faced with an increasingly strong opposition, conceded that in the beginning the district had concentrated merely on mixing students, but asserted that it was now focusing more on achievement. He further claimed that he had personally encouraged schools to give up tracking[3] and pointed to the district's recent grant from The College Board as a participant in "Equity 2000."[4] Interestingly, he also noted that he was frustrated by his own staff's resistance to the idea of detracking, and by their prediction of its failure (Watson, 1991a).

By 1991, therefore, the district's detracking zone of mediation showed signs of a significant shift: policy solutions could now be debated seriously. The complaints raised about tracking were no longer viewed as unacceptable interference with the main goal of between-school desegregation, and several key actors, including the local newspaper, the superintendent, and at least one principal, joined the court-appointed monitor and the plaintiffs in identifying tracking as a problem to be addressed. Of course, the new forces favoring detracking did not, and could not, supplant the pre-existing forces; they could only be added to those other forces, resulting in a modest reshaping of the zone.

The Consent Decree: Its Acceptance and Its Aftermath

On June 19, 1992, the district filed a motion for unitary status, focusing on its accomplishments in "racially balancing" the schools and arguing that its job had been completed. The plaintiffs countered by highlighting several areas—including tracking—that they claimed were "vestiges" of the original discrimination. Given the relatively hospitable reform context that had developed since 1988, this was an ideal time for the plaintiffs to advance their detracking argument. Moreover, the Latino parents (the plaintiffs) were telling their attorneys that they wanted provisions in the court order to promote academic achievement directly.

By the time the district and the plaintiffs approved a consent decree in early 1994 (a compromise in lieu of the motion for unitary status), the attorneys and their respective expert consultants had examined the tracking issue in great detail. The district, looking at the evidence of second-generation discrimination, had apparently concluded that it was sufficiently compelling to force the compromise formalized in the consent decree. In fact, district leaders seemed genuinely convinced by the pedagogical and equity arguments underlying the legal claims. The district's zone of mediation had clearly shifted. At the time of the settlement the superintendent said, "Within every school, we are going to work very hard to make sure that every student is having equal access to all programs" (Guido, 1994). In September 1994, less than nine months after the parties entered into the consent decree, the school superintendent said she viewed the decree as "a driving force and guiding principle for systemic reform" that would raise "the level of expectation for all students." She added that as a result of the decree the district would have "to start changing the expectations of children, teachers, parents and the community about the potential for these children."[5]

Thus, the legal process had itself produced a rethinking and a reshaping of attitudes. The district, which had begun to recognize the need to detrack even before filing its unitary status motion, seemed now to endorse the detracking goal as one of the "driving force[s]" and "guiding principle[s]" for systemic reform. The zone shifted substantially in the direction of receptivity to detracking efforts. That is, reformers in the district could now work within a policy context in which detracking was a potential school change.

WOODLAND HILLS

In Woodland Hills, involvement by the federal court, including court supervision and mandated state funding, made change imperative, made it easier, and prompted the hiring of a reform-minded superintendent. This new superintendent, Dr. Thomas Young, joined with other reformers to move forward with a change agenda that included detracking.

Funding through the Court Order

Through the budget of the Court-Ordered Implementation Plan (COIP), the annual order specifying the budgetary allocations necessary to implement the court-mandated remedies, the Commonwealth of Pennsylvania funded approximately $4.2 million of the district's activities and personnel in 1996–1997. Some people in the district saw this money as a boon, allowing the district to better care for its most under-served students. Others viewed the money as being tied to costly obligations that the district should jettison at the first opportunity. Even for this latter group, however, the state money provided a spoonful of sugar, helping them to swallow the reform's bitter medicine.

Pennsylvania school funding is governed by an arcane system based on property taxes and state subsidies. In Woodland Hills, for example, the non-COIP revenue breakdown for 1996–1997 was as follows: 55% from local real estate taxes, 32% from state subsidies (including a basic subsidy and one for special education), 6% from an earned income tax,[6] and the remaining amount from federal subsidies (4%) and other assorted sources (3%). The basic subsidy supposedly ensures that poor and rural districts receive ample funding. However, the system's heavy reliance on each district's local property-tax base has produced a substantial disparity between poor and rich districts.[7]

A majority vote of the governing body of a local school district can raise property taxes. These taxes are measured in mills, with each mill amounting to a $1 tax on each $4,000 of market value. Near the end of my study, in 1997, Woodland Hills increased its millage rate by 3, to 106.5 mills (or an increase of $2.50 for each $10,000 of property value) (Dudiak, 1997b). This means that the owner of a house valued at $80,000 would pay an annual property tax of $2,130. While not the highest in Western Pennsylvania, this tax rate was higher than that of many adjoining communities, and some district residents voiced their displeasure. According to school board members and others, a large and vocal constituency of retired persons had blocked or reduced property-tax increase proposals in the past, resulting in a greatly reduced budgetary reserve as well as cutbacks in some programs.

The area's recent economic history, recounted in Chapter Two, provides part of the background for this tax picture. "We're living in a whole bunch of communities where the property values are falling," explained a school board member. "[W]e lose businesses. We lost all the steel mills 10 to 15 years ago. It just seems like one hit after another." The state funding coming into the district through the COIP budget, therefore, was not icing on an already rich cake. In many ways, the COIP funding provided necessities. Many educators accordingly wondered how the district would survive without it. As one administrator observed, "[T]he concern is, what's going to happen [to the programs and the students] when the funds are no longer available. [T]here's a big concern about increasing taxes here."

Pennsylvania's Role

Certain state policies contributed to the district's financial exigencies. Recall that Pennsylvania was the primary defendant in the desegregation case. The court found Pennsylvania to be in violation of the constitutional rights of the plaintiffs. Largely for this reason, the court in 1991 ordered that Pennsylvania reimburse the district for 90% of the remedial costs (Morrissey, 1991).

As district administrators were quick to point out, this order did not come until 10 years after the merger. During that decade, a contentious debate surrounded state reimbursements (see Gaynor, 1985). However, even after the 90% contribution was ordered, the district, the plaintiffs and the Commonwealth faced a great deal of uncertainty over appropriate remedial expenses. The plaintiffs continued to push for extensive remedial programs and spending. The district agreed to some, the Commonwealth to far fewer. Because of this disagreement, the school board passed its budget and began spending money long before the Commonwealth and district reached any agreement.

"[T]he state," charged a district administrator, "was able to delay the audits to where it got to the point where [the district was required] to, by state law, pass a balanced budget." Only later would the court consider whether or not the district had spent this money on appropriate remedial activities. If not, the bill would have remained with the district. For example, for the period from 1991 through 1994, the state contested $3.44 million of the district's remedial spending; the court held the state liable for only $650,000 (Means, 1995c).

In the merger's early years, the budgetary process proved particularly adversarial. "[T]here was animosity between the state and the district and the plaintiffs. [E]veryone was fighting everyone else," explained a top district administrator. In recent years, under the leadership of superintendent Young, the district has made a point of working with the plaintiffs[8] to finish the budgetary process before the start of the school year. If the Commonwealth refused to provide funding, Young suggested that the board should simply not pass the COIP budget and let the issue come before the court: "We are not going to sweat it. If the judge orders [the state] to pay, [they will] pay, whether [they] budgeted for it or not" (Means, 1995b). Pursuant to this new approach, explained one observer, the school board focused on the monetary issues as opposed to the educational concerns underlying the remedial requirements, saying essentially, "I don't give a damn about the court order. We're gonna shut it down right now until we get the money from the state." The Commonwealth, he contended, prompted this approach by taking the position, "If it's not [explicitly] in the court order, we're not paying for it."

A simple rationale explained Pennsylvania's resistant position: it opposed desegregation in general[9] and, more specifically, did not want to pay the money. Superintendent Young reached this conclusion back in 1995: "I've given up on the idea that the state is interested in what is best for the students of Woodland Hills. Clearly, their mission is to spend the least amount of money possible" (Means, 1995a). Another district policy-maker observed, "the state's back there, twisting their mustache and figuring, we're spending too much money [in Woodland Hills]." A top district administrator, looking back on the evolution of this process, observed:

> [I]t was weird the way things were happening. If the district did something the plaintiffs wanted done, then it was the district and the plaintiffs against the state. If the district did something that the plaintiffs didn't want to get done, then it was the plaintiffs fighting the district and then the state and maybe even the district fighting the state. I mean, the state was trying to not do what they should have done.

As a result of the Commonwealth's resistance, specifically its refusal to include COIP expenses in its annual budget, the school district had to include huge proposed real estate tax increases in its own budget. This fed the local perception that the court order placed a financial burden on the community (see Hosek, 1987). A second result of this resistance was more direct: it reduced remedial effort. The superintendent acknowledged in June of 1995 that the district did not go forward with some remedial programs for the simple reason that there was no guarantee that the Commonwealth would provide reimbursement (Means, 1995d). Such restrictions on the remedial effort occurred regularly since the 1981 merger. A 1984 statement by the court documents this foot-dragging, chastising the Commonwealth for "dodging its job" (Rouvalis, 1984). This statement was mirrored in a 1990 conclusion by the federal hearing officer that the Commonwealth's "passive approach" contributed to the continued racial imbalances in the district's educational programs (Solow, 1990).

Financially Burdensome Special Education

Special education allocations, as provided by the Commonwealth, also contributed to Woodland Hills' financial difficulties. The Commonwealth formerly used a method called "excess cost" to calculate special education disbursement to school districts. If, for example, a school district spent $6,000 per year educating a non-special-education child and $9,000 on a special education child, then the state provided the additional $3,000 per child. "So what happened," according to a long-time administrator, "is districts were screening kids, loading up their special ed. [The state was] rewarding people for putting kids in special ed., so the school districts were dumping kids in special ed."

For this reason, the Commonwealth changed its special education funding formula to one providing a set amount based on average daily attendance in the district.[10] Woodland Hills had approximately thirty-two percent of its students in special education—more than twice the predicted number of special education students (Estadt, 1997a). District officials complained bitterly about this formula, describing it as an underfunded mandate, draining district coffers. For the 1995–1996 school year, the district spent $6.7 million on special education and received $1.9 million in reimbursements from the state (Estadt, 1997b; Means, 1996).[11] As several administrators and board members anxiously pointed out, the $4.8 million difference between those two numbers equaled the amount of state money infused into the district through the COIP budget. The financial burden caused by inadequate special education funding had an indirect but strong effect on the detracking zone of mediation, contributing to budgetary limitations as well as to a general concern in the district about higher property taxes (discussed in the following subsection).[12]

The superintendent and board president wrote to the Commonwealth about the special education funding problem, and the district tried to join with other affected districts to lobby for a more equitable formula. Several people, including a board member, stated their belief that the Commonwealth revised the formula as a way to keep Woodland Hills from getting a larger share of the state budget. The board member said:

> [T]he biggest hit was when the state reformulated their special ed formula. . . . I think they reformulated it when that court order was done, . . . when the state was told they had to pay 90% of the court order. [I]f you look at the dollar amounts—if you research it, the dollar amounts we lost on special ed is what the state has to pay out on the court order. . . . And everybody says that it's just a coincidence. It's possible it is. I just think it's an awful strange coincidence.

It is doubtful, of course, that the Commonwealth intentionally manipulated the special education formula for all districts in the state in order to offset exactly the COIP funding for Woodland Hills. But it probably was not a coincidence, either. The politics of Pennsylvania school funding favors wealthier districts with fewer special education students. The financial hit produced by the funding formula was thus felt by other districts serving low-income students of color, such as Pittsburgh and Philadelphia, in addition to Woodland Hills.

Older Community and Taxpayer Resistance

In Woodland Hills, taxpayer resistance and senior citizens were strongly associated. Allegheny County had an extremely large percentage of taxpayers living on retirement income (second nationally only to Dade County, Florida), and the percentage in Woodland Hills was even higher. Furthermore, while real estate taxes fund Pennsylvania schools, few of the district's direct beneficiaries—parents with school age children—owned their homes. While parents rented, senior citizens owned. As a result, explained one of the district administrators, the schools suffered:

> [Y]ou got old folk, [and] where are they going to spend their taxes? For an extra cop or improving their trash pick-up or getting a new reading program for the schools? [The] track record indicates that those people are going to support services that support their standard of living, rather than having some allegiance to kids.

And, of course, they voted. A school board member recounted how, prior to 1997, the district had not raised taxes for 2 years, following a "big, big battle with older people" in 1993 that resulted in "a bunch of board members elected who basically [saw] themselves as a guardian of the millage [property taxes]." These older voters had only one concern, according to this board member: "money."

Other district and community leaders offered similar descriptions of taxpayers in general. "The only thing [voters] are aware of is when their taxes go up," opined a board member. A long-time teacher cited the area's history as one of the industrial towns along the Monongahela River. Education, he explained, did not historically constitute "a top priority" in these communities: "There were good paying jobs [in the mills] as soon as they left school, whether they quit or graduated."

Another observer blamed the turmoil arising out of the court order. While acknowledging that nobody really wants to have their taxes raised, he insisted, "there are other places where there is some greater leeway—where people have [a] somewhat freer hand." He continued:

> [T]he economics of public school administration impinges on the politics of the community, and in places where the community is less uproarious about things, the professionals involved at all levels can focus a little better on the academic tasks.

Thus, the highly polarized district politics created an environment where parochial jealousies and struggles over money replaced communitarianism and overshadowed educational concerns. Taxpayers at a recent board meeting shouted, "[W]e don't care what it does to the schools, don't raise our taxes," according to a district official.

Recognizing this attitude as an impediment to continued district improvement, an administrator outlined a district effort to "sell the value of programs to people that no longer have children in school." The district's plans included bringing senior citizens into the schools as mentors and linking them up with students. She concluded that these efforts presented "a real challenge" and had not reached "the magnitude yet that I think that it's going to make a huge impact. And that's a real concern."

Notwithstanding these obstacles, the district did see some progress. At some board meetings residents have vocally advocated tax increases to fund the schools, declaring, "our children are being shortchanged in [deference] to taxpayer groups" (Dudiak, 1995). More recently, the school board voted 6–3 to raise taxes to support its 1997–1998 budget (Dudiak, 1997b).[13]

The context surrounding the district's detracking efforts was further shaped by a concern lurking at the back of some taxpayers' minds: when court supervision ends, and when the related state funding disappears, the district will be unable to continue all the COIP benefits unless it raises real estate taxes by about thirteen mills ($13 per $4,000 in property value). "The public's gonna go through the roof," predicted a community member.

COIP Filled the Financial Void

Because many people in the district realized the importance of the COIP money, this part of the court order helped to make the zone of mediation more hospitable to the detracking reform. That is, some actors in the district viewed the funding as necessary and as tied to the rest of the court order, including the detracking. A board member, discussing the overall order (as opposed to just the detracking aspect) explained that, because of the associated loss of funding, she no longer wanted to end court involvement. An African-American parent activist expressed a similar position, but he stressed the inequitable state funding mechanism for education, without which, he suggested, the COIP money might prove unnecessary:

> The need for the desegregation [case] comes in the passing out of the tax dollar and the equipment and things like that. [T]he state funds the school district based on the amount of property taxes. Well, that's, to me, inherently unequal. I mean, it's just unequal. You're not going to get the same quality education in every situation. That's the only reason I see a need for desegregation [litigation].

This same parent pointed out the broad nature of the benefits derived from COIP funding. In fact, he took the position that the money benefited White students more than African-American students, the primary intended beneficiaries. District administrators, pointing to otherwise unavailable workshops and programs, offered support for this position. One such administrator noted that Woodland Hills now has better course offerings than surrounding districts, which she attributed to efforts connected with COIP activities. A principal agreed, noting that while the court order focused on African-American achievement, "if we're looking at the African-American kids to improve their scores, all kids' scores are going to increase." All students, she insisted, receive the benefits of these programs.

This general nature of COIP benefits should not be over-stressed, however. The COIP budget ceaselessly and effectively tugged the district's attention in the direction of its African-American students. COIP money coming into the district thus played multiple roles. It assisted the district's most needy students while also funding training and programs that benefited all students in the district. And, by furnishing these otherwise unavailable services, it acted as a force on the zone of mediation for the issue of detracking—sweetening the reform's political context.

Court Involvement

Aside from this COIP funding, the court order exerted both a positive and a negative force on the detracking zone of mediation. It shaped a more receptive zone by exerting direct pressure on the parties, by mandating data collection as well as a curriculum audit and subsequent curriculum revision, and by providing political cover for board members and administrators. It shaped a less receptive zone by engendering resentment, primarily from teachers and parents. Observed a top district official, "there's very little that the district does that isn't in [some] way affected by the court order."

Direct court oversight, resented by many educators, served to keep the district focused on equity issues. Yet the level of court involvement varied at different stages of the litigation. In a reversal of the pattern in San Jose, the judicial transition of the Woodland Hills case (following the death in 1990 of the first judge) resulted in an increase in court involvement. Judge Weber, who initially handled the case, was less hands-on than his successor, Judge Cohill.[14] A board member illustrated this distinction as follows:

> I always felt that the philosophical thinking of these two gentlemen couldn't have been further apart. [Judge Weber] more or less let you do what you wanted to do. [He didn't interfere or] give a lot of direction, he just kind of like gave the order down and says, you're on your own. [W]hen Judge Cohill [took over], things really started to move and they started to move rather quickly.

A top administrator agreed, noting that the district "did virtually nothing" in response to the various court orders until the court "came down hard" in about 1992–1993.

The court's indirect force was felt through its requirements that the district hire an outside consultant to conduct a curriculum audit and that it then rewrite district curriculum according to the auditor's recommendations. The audit, by focusing attention on the district's need to change classroom curriculum and by identifying tracking as a significant problem, elevated the importance of these issues and tied detracking to changes in classroom instruction (AASA, 1993a,b).

The court's indirect force was also felt through requirements that the district collect data. A large chunk of this data—perhaps more than half—related to discipline issues. But the district also kept comprehensive data regarding academic issues such as course placement, grades, and test scores. Educators often cited the mandated collection and reporting of statistics as the worst part of the court involvement. For them, such requirements symbolized the blunt and heavy-handed interference of non-educators from outside their community. Valuable time, they felt, was wasted on unproductive paperwork. Counselors, for example, voiced anger at the burden of having to keep a detailed record of their time. They identified this task as particularly "thankless" because the plaintiffs and the court then "twist" and "distort" the data, taking "what's a good thing and what's an honorable attempt" and causing it to seem unreasonable.

Two principals, however, took issue with this attitude. "It is a lot of paper work," confirmed one, but "it's just something you have to do." She figured that she would have paperwork with or without the court order. "Somewhere else," she ventured, "maybe your superintendent would say you have to keep a daily log." Besides, she concluded,

> it gives you a lot of data, and . . . when you're trying to move a build-ing, you really need data to say to people, "we feel we're doing well, but if we look at it maybe we're not. What do we need to do?" Or, "we are really doing well and maybe you don't realize that." So I like data. I like to be able to use it.

One secondary principal remarked that the data also helped in dealing with parents, who can be told, "'Look, this is what we have—this is showing us that these children are doing A, B, and C, and they are excelling.' I think that is very important."

However, such positive attitudes toward the court order were rare. Many educators and community members expressed resentment at the court in-volvement. Some, as will be discussed later in this book, felt that the reforms promoted by the court order were simply not good policies. Others argued that the courts had unjustly usurped governance power from local citizens. Still others attacked court involvement on the ground that lawyers and judges lack the necessary skills and knowledge to make wise educational policy decisions.

Those whose objections rested on the loss of local control emphasized that people in the community knew what was best for their own children. "We want to do the right thing," said one White parent; "nobody wants to do any-thing that would harm anybody." This stance often translated into complaints that the court had unfairly singled out Woodland Hills for supervision, placing the district "under a microscope" and highlighting problems that exist, but get no publicity, in other districts. In addition to arousing such feelings of oppres-sion, court involvement inspired a bit of cynicism. Said one teacher, "When-ever one of our numerous full-time, on-site overseers wants the newest computer or new office furniture, all they have to say is 'Do you want to ever get out of the decree?,' and it is approved."

Perhaps the most widely-held complaint argued that lawyers and judges simply do not have the expertise or authority to be making educational policy. This contention was particularly popular among principals and school-board members. A principal, for example, protested the court's purported question-ing of district decisions and its assumptions concerning the unfairness of dis-trict actions. He experienced "a problem . . . having to constantly explain [and] having to do that in-depth reporting, presentation, explanation." Another educator expressed the feelings of many when she said, "I think the resent-ment . . . that people feel comes from the fact that there's someone in some blankety-blank courtroom telling us how we should spend our day." Similarly, a board member asserted that the federal court could not understand the real needs and desires of the African-American community members, which she argued were not faithfully represented by the plaintiffs. What these people wanted, this White board member professed, "was a fair education, and they had a right to a fair education." The pre-merger African-American school districts were "falling apart," she said, but "all they wanted was better books, better schools, [and] better teachers. They never wanted their kids shipped up to [another borough]."

A long-time observer of the litigation, while acknowledging that schools should try to remedy the various social ills addressed through the COIP budget, argued that these goals should not be pursued through the courts. Otherwise he foresaw an unfortunate result: people "making decisions about schools who . . . think they know what they're doing because they went to law school." "Eurocentrism, Afrocentrism, all this is all good shit to debate," he continued, "but we shouldn't be doing it down in the federal courtroom, for crying out loud." Taking the English detracking as an example, he maintained, "that's the kind of stuff that needs to be debated by educators and by constituents. That doesn't need to be debated by the lawyers and judges."

In Chapter Fourteen, I will examine the importance of the reality that, had lawyers and judges never become involved in this debate, the detracking reform would not have taken place. For now I will focus on the related issue of the continued shifting of the zone of mediation. Shifts were prompted by the mandate itself and also by the court order's provision of funding, mandatory data collection, and political cover for administrators and board members. Echoing sentiments voiced in San Jose, a principal noted this latter effect when he said that Woodland Hills has an "advantage" that other districts attempting detracking do not have: "When the court tells you, 'You will,' you will. And that's taken a lot of the sting out of it." Another principal mentioned that the court order helped him out with parents of children identified as gifted. In Pennsylvania, gifted children must be offered an Individualized Education Plan (IEP) similar to that provided for special education children in other states. This principal said:

> I'm fairly safe with the gifted parents when I go to an IEP because the court order says it [the child's classroom] has to be heterogeneously grouped. That's off my back. I don't have to discuss . . . that they don't want their son or daughter with individuals that are on a lower level—that's just a fact of life.

This same principal explained that the court order helped him by providing a patent answer to questions about detracking: "it's been ordered by the courts." That "shuts 'em up," he said; "When someone says to me, 'I want my kid with higher kids,' I just say, 'I'm sorry. The court says we can't do it.'" A school board member noted a similar phenomenon among her colleagues. "[R]egardless of how [the board members] feel personally" about the issue, she observed, "detracking is ordered by the courts. You must support it, and you must find a way to work towards making it work."

The court order also effectively subdued opposition to the policy among parents, teachers, and community members. There was, according to a top administrator, "a realization that the court order's here, it's going to [remain] here, and unless we begin to act in a positive fashion, there's nothing to do. There are no more appeals; this is it." When asked how the situation would be different without the court order, one principal responded that he "would have to dig into the literature and substantiate [detracking's merit's] statistically." But, he added, that would not produce the same effect as the court order: "You got a mandate from the court, what can you do? There's nothing you can do."

On balance, then, the court order—even discounting the funding and the direct mandate to detrack—acted as a positive force in making the detracking zone more receptive to the reform. It served as a political bogeyman, and it furnished important oversight, data collection, and curriculum revision.

All this discussion of the mandate, however, should not obscure the fact that most educators in the district simply went about their business, paying little attention to the ultimate source of macro-policies. For these educators, the court order worked in the background. They experienced its effects indirectly but did not link it in their minds with specific programs or policies. As one teacher remarked, "to me, this is just a nice school to come to and a lot of nice kids and a busy day. . . . I never, ever think about court order."

A Reform-Friendly Superintendent

Tom Young, the consolidated district's third superintendent, was generally credited—by teachers, board members, fellow administrators, and community members—with being significantly more reform-minded than his predecessors. Along with his assistant superintendents, he did a great deal to build on the opportunity created by the court order.

In interactions with his staff, Young spoke of both educational research and his own personal experiences. When you hear Young talk, said one district administrator, "you can't help but be impressed with him. I mean, he's just so honest. He's so educationally sound." A board member echoed this sentiment: "I can't imagine a more qualified, competent leader for this school district." A school principal cited the superintendent as crucial to continuing reform. The district, he said, will succeed in moving to heterogeneous grouping "for two reasons. Number one, the courts. Number two, Tom Young is committed to it. And he's a strong enough administrator not to buckle [under]."

Dr. Young offered firm support for the reform as well as improved communications with staff and parents.[15] When I began my study at the outset of the 1996–1997 school year, Young's stated position (to me and others) was that the district's detracking policy did not depend upon (and was, in fact, unconnected to) the court order. He decided not to advertise the court's detracking mandate and instead presented the reform as having a policy-driven rationale because, he explained, "every evil that's come down the pike has been blamed on the courts." Young knew the riskiness of his approach: "[T]here's no question," he reflected, "this [detracking reform] is going to be my Waterloo."

One of the high school teachers commented that Young "could have very easily gone out and said, 'Hey, look the courts have mandated that we get rid of tracking.' " Similarly, a parent supported Young's approach of trying to sell teachers and parents on the policy goals, noting the frustration people feel because "courts are . . . calling the shots." People, she said, "might be glad to know that it was a local decision and not a court-ordered decision, because generally people seem to trust [the superintendent and his] decisions."

Neither the superintendent nor his policies, however, enjoyed universal support. In fact, the detracking reform was subject to widespread and increasing criticism. Consequently, by the middle of the 1996–1997 school year, Young decided to change his approach. This change followed a particularly contentious school board meeting, during which a group of White parents (called the "Citizens for Quality Education" or "CQE") pressured board members to abandon detracking. Young prepared a scathing memorandum to the board members, concluding with a clear statement that "grouping students by ability in Woodland Hills School District is *against the law*" (emphasis in original).[16] He cited the various court orders addressing tracking, and he then told the board members: "I would not be upset, and suggest that when parents pressure you to reconsider tracking, that your response be to simply say, 'It is against the law!' If you believe in your heart that tracking is preferable, say so, but end by saying that it is illegal."

Young explained that he had earlier told people that he personally advocated detracking because he believed in it. "I still believe in it," he affirmed, "but I felt that by [school board members] continuing to ask questions of the parental group and encouraging them, [the CQE] continually set up meetings, [and] that this was just prolonging the situation." Telling the board that the court order mandated the detracking, he explained, "gives them an out, because I think for the most part the public understands violation of the court order and contempt of court and things like that." Thus, Young ended up with a hybrid approach. He continued to take a strong public stand in favor of de-tracking, but he also joined with other district leaders in using the mandate as a cover under which to argue for the inevitability of the reform.

As a general matter, Young also made an effort to improve communications about the district's reforms. Prior to his tenure, the district office had done a poor job communicating with teachers and site-level administrators about court-related issues. Many teachers continued to complain about a lack of information coming from the central office, but they generally agreed that the situation had improved. Remarked one principal:

> Before, it was a closed cycle in the central administration, giving in-formation to principals, who may or may not take that information on down to staff. . . . When Dr. Young came on board there was a much clearer flow of information from the superintendent's office and the district office to buildings, and there was more time taken to delin-eate the rationale behind the decisions that were being made. [We] had a much better understanding of why decisions were made, the di-rection that it was going, and what the expected outcomes are going to be from those decisions.

Young also increased the central office's communications with parents. He made a point of visiting all parent meetings to which he was invited.

A dissenting view of Young, however, questioned his commitment to school reform. Those expressing this perspective argued that Young saw school reform primarily as an avenue leading to a court ruling releasing the district from supervision. One critic contended that Young "sees desegregation as ir-relevant, largely. I mean, it's not really on his screen. He'll talk about school re-form. He'll talk about improving . . . the performance of African-American kids and so forth, [but does not really mean it]."

Indeed, Young did strongly wish to attain unitary status. When hired, he promised that he would achieve that goal. In 1995, he was quoted as saying, "The state can take their money and go fly a kite. I want autonomy. Working under the court order is like running with buckets of sand in each hand" (Brody, 1995). Putting a positive spin on Young's position, one observer sug-gested, "he wants very much to have a quality school district, and he wants to be successful in putting this court case to bed." But a high school teacher of-fered a more cynical perspective:

> Dr. Young has publicly stated on many occasions that he will be the superintendent who history will note for ending the [court supervi-sion in] Woodland Hills. To this end, he has done everything in his power (to the point of paranoia) to please every whim of the plaintiffs.

[Whatever the plaintiffs' attorney] suggests—Woodland Hills does! When he says jump, Dr. Young asks, "How high?" on his way up.

Whatever Young's motivation, his leadership shifted the zone of mediation, making it more receptive to detracking. He stabilized funding, publicly endorsed the reform (even to the point of taking ownership over it), and made earnest efforts to communicate the rationale behind the reform to the district's educators and parents.[17]

CONCLUSION

If the forces forming Woodland Hills' and San Jose's zones of mediation were limited to those discussed thus far, then both districts would have remained solidly receptive to detracking. Such is the powerful impact of a court order. But the districts also contained many other forces, pushing their respective zones in the opposite direction. Resistance from teachers, counselors, and parents dominated this second set of forces. Other powerful forces, such as the local press, taxpayer interests, realtors, racism, and market pressures combined with this resistance to shape zones of mediation which were ultimately only marginally receptive to the detracking efforts. Chapter Nine begins a discussion of these oppositional forces.

9

They Retard What They Cannot Repel: Parental and Educator Opposition

If we lived in a magical land where the process of school reform matched the ideal presented in educational-change literature, then every reform effort would enjoy broad, strong support from parents and teachers. These crucial people would believe in each reform's goals and would wholeheartedly commit themselves to making the changes necessary in their own practices. Occasionally, an auspicious reform garners support approximating this ideal. Such support, however, is not likely to materialize when a reform challenges dominant political and normative beliefs (see Wells & Oakes, 1998). This is particularly true of reforms designed to benefit low-income students and students of color (see, e.g., Lipman, 1998). Moreover, when these reforms are initiated by top-down mandates, they are even less apt to garner substantial commitment by local parents and teachers (Tyack & Cuban, 1995).

Focusing on Woodland Hills' detracking of secondary English classrooms, this chapter examines the meager support—indeed, the potent resistance—that teachers and parents wielded in response to this mandated, equity-minded reform. Woodland Hills' experience demonstrates how parents and educators can exert tremendous adverse force on an otherwise receptive zone of mediation, severely hindering the reform's progress. The intensity and resourcefulness these individuals exercised in opposing the reform far surpassed that generally contemplated by the school change literature.

The following discussion is divided into four main parts, which together describe the chilly reception that Woodland Hills' detracking reform found in schools and in some homes. The first two sections describe opposition from teachers, first presenting some teachers' frustration with the detracking reform and then describing the outright defiance of a core group of teachers. To contextualize this description, both sections include a short discussion of supportive teachers. The third section parallels these first two in discussing opposition from parents. The final section describes how a group of teachers and parents collaborated in resisting the reform.

TEACHER FRUSTRATION

While some teachers expressed unequivocal resistance to the English detracking, most responded with a lesser degree of dissent. The dominant theme was one of frustration: teachers felt they had insufficient time, resources, skills, support, and voice. These teachers wanted to do well by their students but felt unable to reach that goal.

The objects of teachers' frustrations generally fell into two categories: discipline and learning ability. Many of their discipline concerns can best be understood in light of the district's racial issues. Complex matters of discipline played a major role in the ongoing desegregation litigation, with the plaintiffs arguing that discipline was being discriminatorily meted out against African-American students. One Black parent insisted that "a lot of the teachers are afraid of the African-American students. . . . It's their body size. It's the way they dress. It's their demeanor. [The teachers are] afraid. A lot of them can't teach the classes."

Further concerns involved issues related to learning. Teachers complained that it was "humanly impossible" and "ludicrous" to expect them to teach less-skilled students within a heterogeneous classroom. "[H]ow do I do that within a 45-minute period? . . . I'm confused. It's frustrating."

For some teachers, the disruption issues were minor, causing them a bit of frustration when the students became "a little too noisy or rambunctious," but for others disruption completely undermined their ability to teach: "there are teachers who can't—they get so upset—they can have two or three kids who are disruptive, and they just lose it," commented one parent. A secondary teacher related that difficult conditions have caused other teachers to say that they "hate" the students.

The district's past assignment of certain teachers to teach either advanced or basic classes proved another obstacle. Interestingly, people disagreed about which group of these teachers struggled the most with the transition to mixed-ability classrooms and the corresponding need to provide individualized instruction. Teachers who had formerly taught low-track classes, argued one interviewee, had a more difficult time since they now had to move beyond worksheets and prepare material for "students who are used to being challenged." In contrast, this person continued, "the teachers who have always taught the—what they consider the brighter students, [have] gotten a little frustrated, but they're still teaching at that level."

One principal suggested that an opposite dynamic was at work. He pointed to the difficulties encountered by the former teachers of high-track classes. He described "elitist" teachers who felt that a student "who had been in basic English wouldn't be able to deal with the level [at which they'd] like to teach." A supporter of the reforms also noted this attitude: "What we're doing is so good for all the kids and [yet so] many still think that we should just be teaching to the top."

Many English teachers in Woodland Hills voiced deep frustration with students' learning abilities. One complained, "I go over some things so many times I feel like, 'Oh, my God, am I that stupid, or are they that stupid?' It's awful." In the old system, she reminisced, "everyone in the room was on the same playing field," and the teacher "knew what to expect." For such teachers, the new system of mixed-ability classes caused trepidation and confusion.

Teacher frustration in Woodland Hills was attributable in part to the acknowledged difficulty of making the transition to a mixed-ability classroom. To be most successful, these classes should be taught using up-to-date and challenging curricular and instructional methods, but the old, tracked classes— both high- and low-tracked—frequently relied on out-dated, traditional teaching. The changes in Woodland Hills required time, effort, and new forms of pedagogy and curriculum. Most teachers felt that the district had given them insufficient resources in all of these categories. In addition, teacher frustration can be tied to normative issues, such as beliefs that African-American children are dangerous, less able, and inordinately difficult to teach. Finally, as some interviewees contended, frustration also resulted from teacher pride and the unwillingness of some teachers who had formerly taught advanced classes to relinquish their privileged positions.

The Perceived Need to Water Down the Curriculum

When confronted with a mixed-ability classroom and feeling unable to challenge a diverse group of students, most of these frustrated teachers simply targeted their instruction to the perceived middle or lower end of the class. As one explained, "what happens is you lower the standards. Okay, now they say, 'Well, you shouldn't. You should have high standards, and if you have high expectations they'll reach it.' . . . I can't understand that. I really can't." Another teacher related that he simply excised the more difficult questions from his old advanced-level tests.

These teachers either explicitly or implicitly classified students as low-, middle-, and high-track, and they frequently conflated those classifications with the students' race, evidencing the types of normative views that often undermine equity-minded reform efforts such as detracking. Detracking asks teachers to have high expectations for students who were formerly in low-track classes, but these teachers rejected such aspirations.

Some such teachers expressed shockingly low expectations for their mixed-ability classes. One teacher allowed her students to copy test answers from one another because, she said, "I know they can't do it by themselves." While acknowledging the substandard state of her detracked class, this teacher attributed the problems to the students rather than herself. As proof, she explained that she had been able to teach the old, tracked classes effectively, getting through four novels during the year. Now, she grumbled, the class does not even get through half of a single book.

For other teachers, the problems were not as stark but they were still significant. Although many of the district's teachers saw a problem with teaching heterogeneous classes using old teaching methods, they had difficulty envisioning a workable solution. At least one of the district's principals sympathized with these concerns, noting that each class would likely have a couple of mainstreamed special-needs students along with a couple of "super-gifted students." Many teachers, he said, could reasonably be expected to have problems reaching students with such a wide range of needs and abilities.

Like teacher frustration with detracking, this watering-down of curriculum took place on a continuum. Some teachers did not engage in this practice, others did so only to a small degree, and still others made no effort to disguise their lowered standards.

Lack of District Support and Time

In the years prior to the English detracking, the district had required teachers to teach only five academic classes per day plus a "study hall" or "hall duty" that the teacher generally used for grading papers and preparatory activities. However, at the same time that the district asked teachers to adapt to the new, detracked classes, it increased those teachers' academic course-load from five to six, citing financial pressures. Para-professionals took over the hall duty and study halls, and the teachers were given an additional academic class.

Teachers reacted with righteous indignation: "[Y]ou piled more students on us and you gave us more classes, and you expect us to do more things." The district, they complained, had taken away time, increased their responsibili-

ties, and provided little support.[1] "[I]f they expect this from us then they have
to give a little bit," said one. Another declared, "Teaching six classes a day and
three preps a day, I feel like we're those old jugglers on the old Ed Sullivan
show with the plates: I get this one going, and then I come back to this one.
[T]here's just not enough time."

Putting the problem in stark relief, a secondary English teacher explained that while detracking gets blamed for many of the present difficulties,
that focus may be unwarranted. Her problems, she said, were with "an over-
crowded schedule and being asked to cover this many kids." Similarly, a colleague remarked,

> There's a part of me that says that is wrong—we should have track-
> ing; we should have those top courses for those students. And then
> there's a part of me that says if, given the right tools and materials to
> work with, yes, you can make this work. But this school district hasn't
> done that.

Even in the best of circumstances, detracking reforms raise a host of technical,
normative, and political challenges. As these teachers pointed out, linking
these reform efforts with an increased teacher course load places an additional
burden on an already precarious undertaking.[2]

Resentment over Unfair Blame

Due in part to the stigma attached to the desegregation order, a few teachers
were very defensive about the quality of their teaching. "[I]f something doesn't
work," one told me, "they never come out and say it's the teacher's fault, but
there's just always that feeling that it's the teacher's fault." These teachers felt
victimized, that they unfairly bore the brunt of high expectations gone awry.
One asserted, "we're not miracle workers." Teachers try their best, she continued, but "we're blamed for everything. If a kid fails, . . . the question asked in
Woodland Hills [is], 'what did you [as a teacher] do so this child would not
fail?' " Her colleague angrily declared, "We resent when people come in and
say, 'if you can't figure this out, you're no good.'" Agreed another, "if you can't
do a good job of teaching this incredible spectrum, then inherently you're a
poor teacher."

Some of these same teachers also saw the court order's reporting requirements as implicitly blaming them for student failure. Since a teacher must
provide a justification for disciplining or failing a student, many teachers perceived a presumption that their decisions were not appropriate. "You have to

understand that in the context," one administrator explained, "[T]hey're bugs under a 'scope. I mean, you take a look at the amount of documentation that they do. If a kid burps in class, they've got to write up forms in triplicate and send them all over the place, and what amazes me is how they tolerate that stuff." Another observer tied these issues to the detracking:

> [Y]ou've got Johnny-smart-kid sitting next to Johnny-ordinary-kid who's sitting next to Johnny-who-hardly-ever-shows-up, and you are responsible for all three, and if Johnny-who-never-shows-up fails, then you have to give a long list of reasons why that child fails.

In sum, many teachers in Woodland Hills felt that, largely because of the court supervision, they were unfairly scrutinized and unjustly blamed for students' shortcomings.

Perceived Lack of Family Support

Several teachers complained that lack of support from students' families made their job much more difficult. One asserted, "I don't see much success with my slower kids. [W]hat happens when they go home is they don't do anything. . . . [T]here is no family support or any family structure at all when they go home, and that's what's hurting them." The concerns voiced by this teacher were representative of those of many of her colleagues, who attributed much of their frustration to the purported failure of families to reinforce school lessons.

Insufficient academic support at home was mentioned by both Black and White interviewees. However, as will be discussed later in greater detail, Whites tended to offer the students' home life as an excuse whereas African Americans treated it as an issue needing attention. Moreover, references to home and family often carried troublesome racial overtones. One observer put it this way:

> [I]f you were able to probe [teachers' feelings of frustration], they may have told you, "the reason that I can't [teach a mixed-ability group] is because I have 'certain people' in this class." . . . I feel sure that a lot of teachers have that attitude, and while they are not likely to say that, it's awfully easy to observe what's really going on. And kids know when adults don't like them or [when they] disrespect them or have low expectations for them.

This observer insisted that while Woodland Hills teachers will not come right out and say that their frustration is because of the African Americans in the class, it has been strongly implied in his conversations with them.

Feelings of Disempowerment

For many Woodland Hills educators, the desegregation litigation was not only a source of blame but also a source of disempowerment. They felt that they lacked an effective voice with regard to policies that directly affected them. As a school counselor put it:

[F]or some lawyer to come and tell these people, who are compassionate, dedicated, educated, committed and, in most cases, very veteran employees—to tell this category of professional what that person must do to be effective in his or her job, I think is demoralizing. It's frustrating. It's demeaning.

For some faculty, the frustration had become cynicism—questioning the actual goals of the reformers: "If they designed the absolute perfect educational system and implemented it, they'd have to change it or they'd be out of a job, right?" These teachers argued that people pushed the reforms because they made a living off of court involvement:

To keep their jobs under this decree—we have all these people who are evaluating us. If they say, 'you're okay,' they're all out of a job. It's that simple. Follow the money. . . . They do not want an honest evaluation, [and] most of the faculty has come to resent being portrayed in a negative light to intentionally make the district look bad.

Such extreme cynicism was not common in the district, but the few teachers who held this attitude added a great deal of fuel to the resistance.[3]

Reinforcement of Frustration by Colleagues

While some teachers looked to their colleagues for assistance and support in dealing with the detracking, others saw their colleagues as part of the problem. "I don't go in the teachers' room," one told me, "it's one of the most negative places I've ever been." Another teacher, who had a refreshingly positive overall attitude about teaching, said that he "refrain[s] from speaking to too many colleagues because all they do is talk about their discipline problems." He added that his department (language arts) lacked "cohesion" and collegiality. The department meetings, he reported, often disintegrated into a bunch of "petty" disagreements about, for example, cafeteria duty. "How can we have a productive meeting when they are all coming in with this excess baggage from

25 years or 35 years of teaching together? . . . They all hate each other. It's sad." Thus, instead of assisting colleagues with the reform, interaction between faculty sometimes reinforced teachers' frustrations.

Frustration Overcome

To present a complete picture, it is important to note that some teachers overcame initial frustration and began to appreciate the detracking reform. Expressing hope for the reform's future, a teacher told me about one of his colleagues who came to the school mid-year and struggled for a couple months. "[S]he forced them to her standards," he explained. "[S]he was very discouraged for about two months, and then . . . she began to relate some success stories. . . . And by the end of the year she had her kids doing top-level work."

He described another colleague as "a person I might have chalked up on the failure side last year," but he noted that she had recently approached him "saying these kids can really understand Macbeth, and [she] started showing me some things that the kids had done." Such encouraging stories, however, did not prevent this interviewee, as well as other district educators who viewed the detracking as a positive change, from recognizing the need for hard work, perseverance, and time. Noting particularly the importance of time, several district educators opined that the reform's second year was going more smoothly than the first.

In sum, many teachers viewed the detracking reform as a thankless task that was difficult, if not impossible, to accomplish—particularly given the perceived lack of sufficient time and other resources provided by the district. Other teachers had a much more positive experience. The next section examines teachers whose feelings went beyond frustration, to anger and resentment, and who engaged in outright resistance to detracking.

"REBEL TO THE END": TEACHER RESISTANCE TO THE REFORM

Although most Woodland Hills school leaders firmly supported the reform, many classroom teachers simply did not accept the value of and rationale for detracking. Consider the following statement by one of the district's secondary-school language arts teachers:

> [The plaintiffs' attorneys] feel that we should bring every kid up to this [high] level. [E]ven though this child may be brain damaged,

we still have to bring him up to this level. [T]hey should know . . .
that everybody does not have the same ability. But they believe if
you're in [this district] — and it must be the only place in the whole
wide United States, or the . . . whole world, that we have to educate
everybody — everybody has to come out of [our] high school with a
college education. And it's so wrong because not everybody is capa-
ble of that.

This teacher opposed detracking for the basic reason that she did not
have high expectations for all her students. She later insisted, "we're trying
to right something that isn't rightfully our right to right." Such teachers argued that the problems lie elsewhere — in the individual student's home, culture, or genetics.

Opposition to Detracking

The previous section presented many teachers who expressed frustration
with the detracking reform but genuinely wanted to see it succeed. Others,
however, expressed direct opposition to the reform. "[S]ome of these teachers just will not change, will not budge, will not see kids as individuals . . .
or can't look past the color of a kid's skin," asserted a district administrator.
Such resistant teachers, estimated at anywhere from 10% to 30% of the workforce by various observers, were blamed by an African-American parent as responsible for "most of the . . . discipline, suspensions, incidents and
[failures]."

Said a principal, "there's a number of instructors that will grab hold and
run with [the reform], and there's a percentage who will rebel to the end."
These resisters, one educator warned, "are just not going to do what they are
expected to do as it regards desegregating the school district." This statement
was mirrored by a parent: "There's too many [teachers] that feel like, 'I've
been teaching a certain way for a number of years. Why should I change
now?' That's their attitude, and they basically sabotage the changes that need
to take place."

Another parent placed the role of the teacher in a larger context, explaining that, in order for the district to achieve the goals of the desegregation order, three "levels" of tasks must be performed. The first level involved
"the lawyers talking to each other and coming into . . . an agreement as to
what should happen." The second level was the school administration and
school board, who determine how the court order is implemented. "And
then," the parent pointedly noted, "you have the teachers who, to me,

[couldn't] care less. . . . I don't feel that [those] teachers have made any effort to make this work." This parent saw the process as falling apart at the final, implementation stage.

Teacher resistance to detracking exasperated many pro-reform educators in the district. One complained, "I kind of think that teachers are just like children. They don't do anything until they want to do it."

Three African Americans—a site-level administrator, a parent, and a community member—reflected on the distinction between attitudinal and behavioral changes among teachers. The administrator contended that one generally cannot change teachers' attitudes. "You just change the behavior," she said. "It would be good if the attitudes changed. Then the behavior would follow all right. But as an administrator, I know I'm not going to be able to change the attitudes." The parent expressed a like view through an analogy, saying that he strongly believes "that you can force someone to allow you in their house, but you can't make someone take care of you once you get in that house."

The community member spoke of the limitations to in-service training. He stated his belief that such training cannot change teachers' basic values and beliefs. "Over the years," he recalled, the district has

tried new efforts and new ways of reaching them, but . . . when you're dealing with an issue as controversial as parity, equality, desegregation, you're dealing with something that has expectations beyond the realm of the goodwill of the participants. You can only go so far [by] pleading to the conscience and the professional ethics of a veteran people.

Another rationale offered for teacher resistance was the fear of failure. A principal observed that his staff tends to meet "any type of change . . . with initial resistance." "It's my sense," he continued, "that some of our staff feel, 'What if I try this change and I'm not successful? Will I look stupid?' " Teacher pride and self-image clearly affect attitudes towards change.

One observer criticized the staff as lacking professionalism. She said that too many teachers possessed a rigid mind-set focused on their working conditions rather than a professional ethic focused on "what kids are learning."

Perhaps the most biting critique came from a teacher who lamented that "no one trusts anyone, and if you do not trust the change makers, nothing will change." Lack of trust was a very powerful theme in the district, and this teacher was no doubt correct in concluding that such a negative attitude had influenced the reform process.

Resistance to All Change

Like Lipsky's (1980) "street-level bureaucrat" who has ultimate control over what happens at the point of implementation, some teachers used the sanctuary provided by the classroom door to shut out the forces of change. These teachers, an administrator explained, "were used to one kind of a classroom [and] weren't willing to make the change." One such teacher acknowledged that he "shouldn't be this way, [but] I really don't care what they [central office administrators] tell me." "In this room," he asserted, "I'm going to do what's right for [the students], and that's all I'm concerned with."

Support for Change

Several teachers, even while faithfully reciting the party line on the evils of detracking, insisted that mixed-ability education was going well in their own classrooms. Their neighbors and colleagues were the ones suffering.

As in most districts, in Woodland Hills there has always been "a chunk of the faculty [that has] been interested in . . . growing and adjusting and learning new ways to do things," noted one observer. For the most part, it was these teachers who embraced detracking and who provided a challenging education for the range of students in their classes. However, these teachers were subject to substantial peer pressure to adopt a negative stance toward change—and toward detracking in particular. Consequently, with few exceptions, they were not vocal (in the political arena at least) in their support for detracking.

A similar pattern was evident among the district's parents. Some parents supported the detracking reforms, but the most vocal opposed them. As explained by a central office administrator, the most dissatisfied are the ones who tend to be heard:

> Those people who support something typically are not the ones out yelling and screaming. They're the ones who are quiet, and they keep sending their kids, and they go to the schools, and they try to make sure it's running smoothly. [If they] have a problem they'll come to you and say, "I have this problem." They don't run to the newspaper. They don't scream and holler.

Those who do scream and holler are the subject of the following section.

PARENTAL RESISTANCE TO THE REFORM

Many parents strenuously argued that English detracking lowered the high standards that had prevailed in the old Advanced English (high track) class. These parents contended that the mixed-ability classes held back their children due to increased discipline problems. They also opposed the renewed emphasis on cooperative learning, arguing that their children ended up playing "teacher" to the less advanced students. And they contended that not enough homework was given in the detracked class.

Vocal, White Parents' Opposition to the Changes

The district housed a very vocal contingent of pro-tracking parents. Although these parents were few—one frequent observer of board meetings noted that "each time they [tracking supporters] have come to . . . give testimony before the board, it seems to be the same nucleus of parents"—their voice was very loud. They formed an activist group called Citizens for Quality Education, they met with teachers and school leaders, they wrote letters to the local newspaper, they spoke at board meetings, and they were frequently quoted in the media. As described by a central office administrator, these parents reacted strongly to the detracking proposal:

> [W]hen we chose to detrack our English course at the secondary level, the gifted moms came out of the woodwork. [It was like the] old, classic Frankenstein movie where Frankenstein's up in the tower and these people [show up] with torches and scythes and pitchforks and all that. We've been accused of everything—immoral, unethical, illegal.

The children of these parents were perceived to be among the districts' highest achievers. (For this reason, some interviewees, such as the one quoted above, referred to these parents as "gifted moms.") Again, the general perception in the district was that these parents believed that whatever policies the district or the courts determined to be good for all children were somehow not good for *their* children. From them, it was a zero-sum game.

Similar criticisms were based on the belief that schools denied the more skilled students the resources and attention that they deserved. "[T]here's a feeling," said a school administrator, that the district tends "to just sort of shrug off kids who are . . . for lack of a better word, brighter, top-level, whatever you want to call them—that they will do fine no matter what." One parent telephoned an administrator and engaged him in an extended argument about English detracking. The administrator related the story as follows:

> Finally, out of frustration, he says, "Dammit, . . . you know as well as I know that only about 3% of the kids in the high school are going to amount to anything and furthermore they're going to be burdened by having to carry the load for the rest of them. So why are we spending money on the rest of these kids rather than putting it all toward [gifted education for] the kids who are going to amount to something?" . . . And what I wanted to say is that, from my reading of history, this is the kind of things that were discussed in the beer halls in Germany circa '29 and '30 and—only then they weren't talking about African Americans, they were talking about Jews. For me to tell you that racism is not alive and well in the minds of the parents here would be ridiculous. I'd never say that.

Concern about Lowered Standards

A vocal contingent among the district's parents—particularly among the White parents—felt strongly that the detracked English system did not meet the needs of academically-advanced children. More to the point, they felt that detracking denied their own children the opportunity to move ahead at their own, accelerated pace. One teacher explained, "The belief in the community was very strongly that the teachers would not teach to the top level—they would not demand the same performance levels from students as they did when they were in Advanced English class." Her colleague told me of being approached by parents who were "extremely concerned" that if their children were not placed in a class at the "very top," then they would fall to the bottom. These parents, she said, "had this concept of [the detracked class] as not being a college prep course, which it is, and they had this concept of that course not being challenging enough."

Many teachers and administrators felt that these parents' reactions were often unfair and ungrounded. One illustrated this feeling with a story about a student who was identified as gifted and who complained, along with his mother, that he was being under-challenged. The teacher, however, contested this assertion, explaining that she had gone out of her way to provide the student with a diversified and challenging curriculum, but the student simply did not do the work, nor did the mother respond to the student's neglect of his studies.

Notwithstanding such objections, I certainly observed detracked classrooms taught in ways that did not challenge high achievers, as well as classes that failed to engage less-advanced students (and some that failed both groups). On the surface, my observation supports the view of parents opposed to the detracking reform. However, as discussed in Chapter Fourteen, this poor teaching—now redistributed to reach the more advanced students—almost surely existed in the old tracked system as well. The problems of watered-down curriculum and other instructional difficulties are thus rooted in both teaching resources and resources available to teachers.

Concerns about Discipline, Cooperative Learning, and Homework

A frequently mentioned justification for parental opposition to detracking was the claim that mixed-ability classes have more disciplinary disruptions than did the old high-track classes. As noted by a secondary-level principal, the parents "brought discipline up most of the time first. I mean, parent after parent after parent after parent. And in the same breath many of them talked also about their disagreement with cooperative learning." These parents believed that teachers could not maintain a productive learning environment in a diverse classroom.

Many of the same parents opposed cooperative learning because they saw it as using their more-skilled children as tutors for other parents' less-accomplished children. Parents and students complained that the district's practice of cooperative learning forced more skilled students to contribute the important work while other students simply copied. In addition, many parents felt that their children were not bringing home enough homework, which they attributed to detracking.

These three criticisms of detracking, as well as the contention that the teachers watered down the curriculum, were the explanations most frequently offered by the pro-tracking forces for their position. However, as discussed in the following section, some educators and community members suspected that opposition to the reform was animated by more sinister motives.

Excellence as a Finite Resource

Woodland Hills parents are of course not alone in focusing primarily on their own children's well-being. However, I spoke with teachers, administrators, and others who felt that the district was cursed with several outspoken parents who carried this idea to a self-interested and racist extreme. A central-office administrator expressed this sentiment as follows:

> [P]eople will not come out and tell you that they [are hesitant to attend schools in] Woodland Hills because there's Black [students]. But what they'll do is . . . they will find some other excuse, like you're watering down standards . . . or the bright kids aren't advancing or you're dumbing down the curriculum or whatever. But, see, they won't come out and tell you it's because they don't want their children in school with Black kids.

If you have Blacks in your school district, noted an administrator in the district office, you are perceived by some parents as somehow inferior. He reported that parents actually telephone the district office and ask: " 'I'm thinking about moving in . . . what's your percentage of Black and White? Will my child be in a room with Black children? How will this impact my child's learning?' " "It's difficult here," he explained, "and sometimes I feel very discouraged because I know that I'm fighting something that's older than the Civil War."

Another observer described the opposition to detracking as "a group of parents that just don't want to have classes with African-American youngsters in the same class." Talking about these parents, a third observer said, "they're so afraid that their child will be held back because this teacher will be spending so much time handling Black kids." This connection between racial beliefs and attitude toward detracking was recognized by a Woodland Hills educator who described some parents' attitude that, if the district gave African Americans something that they "hadn't had before, then there's less to go around for my kids." He accused these parents of believing that "excellence is finite."

Finally, some informants accused parents who resisted detracking of associational elitism—wanting their "children in with like and same children" for the sake of elite status. The occasional cases of student resistance to detracking were also attributed by some interviewees to this elitist stance: "They want to be with the people that were in their advanced classes from 2 years ago. . . . No matter what you would do, bend over backwards or whatever, give them all the creative things in the world to do, they are looking at it that 'I'm being held back.' "

No one in the district issued a blanket accusation against all parents who opposed detracking. Rather, the interviewees identified racism, elitism, and self-interest as important factors contributing to the opposition. Similarly, I made no attempt, as part of this study, to determine the degree to which such motivations underlay any given person's opposition. My concerns and conclusions focused on the broad array and impact of forces—including these negative normative beliefs.

Satisfaction with the Reform

While some interviewees wondered aloud whether most parents were happy with the detracking reform, making such a determination was beyond the scope of this study in Woodland Hills. Parents were not randomly surveyed for their opinions. Rather, most of the parents interviewed were selected based on their activity in, and knowledge about, school affairs. Yet, some patterns did emerge. For example, involved White parents were more likely to be opposed to the reforms than involved African-American parents.

Describing other general trends, observers said that much of the oppositional sentiment had moved from a tone of "I'm pulling my kids out; you can't do this to us" to "The proof will be in the pudding, and we will wait and see." Some parents' views were in flux: "[a] strong contingency out there that was real apprehensive at the beginning, now [feels] that this is a wonderful place to be," according to a district administrator. Direct evidence, such as rising district attendance, supported this conclusion that parents were gaining confidence in the schools.

Not surprisingly, the quality of individual English classes was a key to the level of parental opposition. A school administrator explained that, when a student's teacher "was doing a good job demanding high standards, treating all kids fairly and the like, there was no outcry from the parent. Where that was not occurring, I got phone calls."

The Last One Standing: Opposition Effectiveness

Policy-makers in the district felt powerful parental pressure. "In Woodland Hills, if you are the last one standing and you are shouting the loudest," one educator told me, "whether you are right or whether you are wrong, you will get your way." "The district," another interviewee noted, "moves in the direction of the most support and consensus." A critic of the reforms agreed, but he contended that "the volume or character of public input" should legitimately have an impact on board decisions: "I have no doubt of that. I mean, it's supposed to [in a democracy]." Another reform critic pointed to this opposition and complained that it was not more effective: "it's obvious that [the reform is] not working if there are people unhappy, and they [still] won't change it."

However, several observers warned that the loudest voices came from those dissatisfied with the policies—and that wealthy and White parents were disproportionately listened to. Therefore, policies implemented in response to these voices do not necessarily respond to the wishes of the majority of parents.

The impact of parental pressure fell not just on policy-makers, but also on teachers and students. Teachers complained that they felt themselves unfairly placed "under the magnifying glass" and "threatened" by the parents opposed to detracking. Perhaps most importantly, students learned a lamentable lesson from their parents, as stated by a school board member:

> These kids see the example that the grownups are putting forward. . . . [I]t's my worst nightmare that the cycle is going to continue. It's going to be generation after generation because . . . until somebody says, "now, wait a minute mom, or dad, I think I'm getting a good education; look, my grades are good, and I think I'm getting what I need," I don't think it's going to stop. . . . We're going to have these generations after generations after generations of malcontents with the curriculum because the parents are too stupid to get out of the way and let the kids do some critical thinking and analyzing for themselves.

Yet the school board itself bent to this parental pressure. In this district, as in others, parental pressure is a political reality. While parental involvement can produce clear benefits, the pressure from parents is often inequitable, driving unfair and unwise policies. One administrator exasperatedly wished that he could say to some of these parents, " 'you're just a bunch of horse's asses.' " "But," he added, "I couldn't do it. . . . I have to deal with them because they're in the papers. They're making my life miserable. They're way too vocal. I just can't dismiss them."

TEACHERS' COLLABORATION WITH PARENTS IN OPPOSING DETRACKING

In part because teachers feared retribution for expressing any overt opposition to the reform efforts, and in part because teachers and parents recognized that they wielded more power when acting together, disgruntled teachers and parents formed an informal alliance—described by one principal as a "strong collaboration"—intended to undermine the detracking reforms. As one district administrator remarked,

> The problem is we just got way too many [teachers] that don't want to . . . do any more than what they're already doing. And, rather than trying to modify their styles, what they're doing is they're poisoning parents. [The parents then] come to meetings and say, "teachers tell us that this can't be done" or . . . "my child is being held back."

Parents acted as the voice—the active political force—while teachers supplied information and educational authority. Some teachers also served as recruiters, reportedly telling parents, "your kids aren't going to get into good colleges if you don't go to the board and get this changed." The teachers, one administrator explained, "know if they tell it to the right parents, they don't have to say a word [publicly], that these parents will do their battles for them, will go to the school board, will call up [the district office, and] will call the media."

For the most part, teachers imparted their message to parents through the students. According to the students themselves, teachers told them how detracking "really makes it harder for them." " 'If it [weren't] for the court order,' " the students were told, " 'I would be able to teach [much more].' " Initially, teachers said these things in the open classroom. Later the statements were reserved for private sessions with higher-achieving students with involved parents. One teacher described what she called the "hang in there" speech that she gave to her "bright" students and their parents—she told them that she sympathized and that at least they were learning a skill: "how to deal with life's problems."

At least two of the district's high school teachers approached students (according to the students) and said, "if you need some information on this I'll give it to you, but . . . you can't use my name." Even more distressing were reports that some teachers were actually "bad-mouthing and stereotyping" the disfavored students to these "bright" students.

In a local newspaper column, a student attacked the detracking reform and thanked "the teachers who have given me their 'off-the-record' support." "I appreciate the encouragement," she concluded (Cowie, 1995). From a different perspective, another student in another local newspaper column reported being "unsettled by many of my teachers' attitudes toward these changes. I have overheard a few say that they 'hate' these alterations. Some unfairly criticize the new curriculum and even the superintendent, himself, out loud and occasionally directly to students" (English, 1995).

In the classroom, acknowledged an administrator, "when [students] hear the teachers talk about the court order, it's [discussed only as] a reason that they can't get a good education." One teacher blamed a class's limited accomplishments on a combination of students and detracking, telling her mixed-ability class, "normally we would be reading five novels in this class, but because some of you haven't done this much before we'll only read three." This is the dysfunctional side of detracking. Resistance, incompetence, scheming, and even hatred combined to undermine students' education as well as the reform's progress.

The following two sub-sections detail specific examples of teacher-parent political collaboration in the district.

Opposition to Principal Taylor

One example of teacher-parent collaboration took place during the 1995–1996 school year at West Junior High. The school principal of 2 years, Judy Taylor, was an African-American woman who, by all accounts, approached the post differently from her predecessors. She tried to make the school more student-centered, and she supported district reform initiatives. Some teachers—overwhelmingly White, senior teachers—recruited parents who, in turn, recruited board members and administrators, until ultimately Taylor was transferred from West to the principalship of a district elementary school.

This much of the story was relatively consistent among all interviewees, but these general points of agreement branched off into different versions of her tenure and ultimate transfer. Some of the opposition, according to a White district employee who had an insider's view, was tied to racist, and perhaps sexist, sentiment: "Those parents wanted her out, [and] these teachers wanted her out. They wanted a White man." Other interviewees mentioned power issues:

> You've got a group of teachers over there who have the power to hire and fire principals. [T]here was a group of teachers that are very proud of themselves that they did that. . . . They've got the ears of the right school board members.

Even one supporter of the transfer admitted that "some of the teachers might have been a little bit racist over there. . . . [T]here were probably a number of teachers there that did not welcome her from day one." The fact that Taylor "came from an outside school [and] wasn't part of the clique" provided another rationale.

In any case, the school experienced a great deal of dissension. I was told that the teaching staff was "burned out and turned off" and "just didn't give a damn." Twenty-six teachers, in fact, sought transfers out of West. The school board and administration recited these reasons in concluding that, although she was "an excellent educational leader," the district was "misusing Taylor's talent" at West—so they transferred her to the elementary school. Describing West's teachers' attitudes, one involved African-American parent said:

> They never wanted to go with Dr. Taylor. They never wanted to deal with her. I would hear comments from teachers that "she makes me feel stupid." She would ask questions that they didn't know [the answers to] about procedures and policies and laws. So they just had a real hard time with her, [and] eventually enough teachers raised

enough noise to get a school board member involved. There was a five-teacher panel [appointed to consider the matter and give the board a recommendation]. Of the five teachers, none of them [was] African American. They got together with this one board meeting, and then the recommendation came down that she be transferred.

It is worth noting that the West teachers most active in Taylor's removal were identified by administrators, others teachers, and community members as the same teachers who later became actively opposed to detracking. As one administrator cautioned: "they're really jumping on [the detracking issue] because they've gotten victories in other areas now."

Opposition to TAI Math

In the 1992–1993 school year, the district introduced "Team Assisted Instruction" (TAI) math as the regular math program for students in grades 4–6. The program involved individualized instruction built around cooperative, team-based learning (see Slavin, 1986). That January, nearly one hundred angry parents crowded into the school board meeting room to complain about the curriculum (Staff, 1993).

District leaders admitted that TAI was "a very difficult program for a teacher to implement, [particularly] under many of the conditions that they had to do it." Still, those leaders did not anticipate the high level of resistance. This resistance was described to me by an outside observer as follows: "[A] couple of math teachers . . . just decided they weren't going to do it. They talked to the parents, got the parents all upset, and it became this big political thing at the board."

Some of the teacher resistance to TAI can be attributed to a generalized opposition to change. As one administrator theorized, "no matter what you do, 25% of the people aren't going to like it; out of that 25%, there [was] probably a subset of teachers who were adamantly opposed to it." These teachers allegedly told their parental allies that administrators had threatened sanctions if they did not implement the program (Staff, 1993).

As with parental opposition to Taylor, I was offered various explanations for the parental resistance to TAI. Some parents felt that it over-emphasized computation; some resisted the individualized-instructional model, which allowed students to move at their own pace; and some rebelled against the assisted-instruction, cooperative-learning aspects. A supporter of these resistant parents said they objected to the "cooperative cheating." The students, she said, found out that "the answers were in the back of the book, and any smart kid's gonna say, why should I work when the answers are there?" The TAI op-position, one interviewee claimed, also found support in the district office. One of the top administrators was purportedly "playing both sides of the fence and gave some encouragement . . . to the insurrection."

In hindsight, the TAI incident was remembered by both its supporters and opponents as a watershed event. Teachers and parents successfully rallied to-gether in opposition to district policy. Individuals emerged as spokespersons, and they learned how to work the system. When recalling the episode, inter-viewees said it was a "nightmare," and "manufactured an enormous amount of hostility." Yet it changed district dynamics. In 1994, the present superintendent came in and, as one of his first actions, replaced TAI with a program from Har-court Brace (Means, 1994).

As all these examples make clear, school reforms are extremely difficult to implement without the support of teachers and parents — even in the face of a direct mandate. However, as I discuss further in Part III of this book, the challenges presented by parent and teacher opposition are not determina-tive — the Woodland Hills zone still offered limited, albeit tentative, support for detracking.

THE POWER OF TEACHER EXPECTATIONS

Two Woodland Hills school board members declared during my conversations with them that their support for detracking was grounded in their commitment to the ideal that all children can learn. The first tied his belief to his religion: "I believe in God. Some people don't. But that's my choice. But I believe . . . that He has endowed every child with gifts, talents, something. Nobody's cut short. And it's our job to bring them out of the kids." The similar view of the second was rooted in basic educational philosophy:

> You don't tell a child in first grade, "You can't achieve [and] we're gonna keep you at this [lower] level," because then the child believes he can not achieve. You don't label a child in first or second, or any grade, and put them in a certain track of learning. [B]ig people do terrible things to little children that follows [them for their] whole academic life.

This perspective was echoed by an administrator who discussed the need for teachers to start "taking a look at themselves and examining their value systems." She asserted that teachers need to ask themselves if they really be-lieve that all students could learn. She acknowledged the difficulty of such a self-examination, "But yet at the same time it's something that I think has to be taken head-on." She continued,

> I don't have the answers, . . . I don't have the magic solution for getting there. But I think first of all, people have to recognize where they are coming from as individuals. And to be real honest, I'm not totally convinced that people are really willing to look themselves in the mirror and say, you know what, I don't believe [that] all kids can learn. And how do we move from that to helping people move in the other direction—to say, hey all these kids really can learn? That to me is a critical piece. I [as a teacher] can tell you, "I believe it." [B]ut once I close my classroom doors I may just still teach to the top or whatever.

To teach a diverse class successfully, asserted a parent, teachers need to show their students greater respect. Over the years, he said, teachers have shown "a negative attitude simply because of the dress, simply because of the way [the students] wear their hair—immediately they're pegged." He also noted the problem of teachers "talking to their buddies" from the student's previous school and being told, "this student is a trouble-maker." This, he declared, denied students "a fair chance when they walk in." The African-American students would not have such a negative response, he insisted, if they felt "somebody's coming at them legit, caringly, sympathetically, as opposed to with an attitude."

A teacher, addressing the same issue from an opposite perspective, arrived at similar conclusions. "[W]hen school starts the first day," he said, "and I have these students, I don't want to hear what they did last year. I want to judge each student myself. I don't want to have any preconceived notions about them." Other English teachers, he continued,

> worried about, "Well, what was this student like last year, what did they do? Oh, he doesn't belong in my class, or she—they'll never make it in AP. Why did this person get in there?" They're worried about all this craziness around them instead of just, the way I look at it, I only have 42 minutes [with each class]. I'm crazy enough.

A district administrator described the wide range of teachers in the district. Some, he said, have made the necessary adjustments to changes in student behavior and demographics. He observed that these teachers recognized that the situation now differed from that which purportedly existed 20 years ago, when everyone came in, sat down, and quietly folded their hands. These teachers, he asserted, understand if a kid doesn't come to class with a book, that's not [a] discipline problem—you give them a damn book. [If] they come [in] chewing gum, you don't put them out of the classroom, you ask them not to chew the chewing gum. If they're talking out in class, you don't put them out, you try to find out what their problem is, and if they become disruptive then you put them out.

He distinguished these "evolved" teachers from others who, he said, "want to teach to a monolithic classroom [pretending that] everybody's the same."

Critical Inquiry

As a method to prompt teachers to re-evaluate debilitating beliefs, Ken Sirotnik and Jeannie Oakes have urged schools to consider the benefits of a "critical inquiry" process (Sirotnik & Oakes, 1986, 1990). Such an inquiry would directly target expectation-based barriers to successful detracking by providing the opportunity for open and serious discussions around these issues. For example, teachers participating in a critical inquiry about detracking would explicitly and openly question whether they believe that all children can learn.

Further, they would question whether they believe that White children have greater intelligence or better behavior than African-American and/or Latino children. If so, they would question the bases of these beliefs. All these questions, explain Sirotnik and Oakes, should be measured against an accepted ideal, such as social justice. Accordingly, teachers would question their beliefs about the nature of a just society and would contemplate how their own norms and behavior conform to that ideal. Critical inquiry's goal would go beyond a superficial understanding of the culture and environment of the schools' students; the goal would instead be to explore and confront individual educators' barriers to understanding their students and having high expectations for them.

Critical inquiry, however, is no panacea. In many ways, it is highly problematic. For instance, the teacher culture of most districts would be hostile to this idea. Many teachers of mixed-ability classes will readily acknowledge their classrooms' imperfections, but will often blame those problems on a variety of external factors: the students' parents, culture and race; the socio-economic differences among the students; and the decision to detrack. Consequently, only a few teachers may be open to such an inquiry. Many educators would likely opt out.

Nonetheless, each district typically contains a group of insightful teachers and administrators who have already begun confronting some of the enormous expectations-based barriers to successful detracking, and Woodland Hills is no exception. This group could be expanded by infusing such issues into staff-development activities. For these reasons, critical inquiry remains very worthwhile as a direct means of honestly confronting the beliefs and values that stand in the way of high expectations.

PARALLELS IN SAN JOSE

As was the case in Woodland Hills, parents in San Jose complained that heterogeneous grouping would result in the "dumbing down" of classes. A mother of two gifted-identified students at a school in the district's White, southern area explained, "You can't have all these levels together and expect to keep the high level. You don't want to sound like an elitist, but you also want to do right by your kids" (Lubman, 1995). And, again as in Woodland Hills, parents repeatedly grounded their opposition in disturbing, prejudicial attitudes against the "foreign" or the different.

The latter attitudes were well captured by a local community activist's anecdote concerning some parents and teachers at one of the district elementary schools. This activist recounted how various educators and parents protested a multicultural training session, by showing up wearing red, white, and blue clothing, and, in some cases, army fatigues. Consider also the case of a White mother who, during our interview, repeatedly associated integration with the introduction of gang activities. She described busing almost in terms of an infestation:

> We have more gang problems—groups—that I really don't appreciate being bused in here. And it is disgusting. And I don't want to sound like a bigot, but I've had it. And we have seen them every day out at the campus. . . . They're in the parks. Everywhere. We have people— lowriders . . . imbeciles that shouldn't even be on the road. They shouldn't even be in school.

Similarly, another parent passionately insisted that her friend's daughter should not be forced to attend a particular middle school which, she said, was 85% Latino and African-American. "Her daughter is this little fair little blond thing that—it's—no, she will not fit in."

These parents perceived the desegregation reforms as benefiting only Latinos—as a special benefit given at the expense of White people. "Why am I being punished because those schools are not being kept up?" one White mother asked. She explained her belief that the goal of desegregation was essentially to rescue the Latino children from their environment: "My idea is that they brought all these kids in to change them, but when they go back home, their lives have not changed there."

As one politically active parent remarked, the San Jose court mandate had been transformed from a guiding document into a powerful symbol promoting fear among White parents who "are really afraid of all these Browns infiltrating their schools and pulling down the standards at their schools."

SUMMARY

"[Get the students] away from their parents and get all new teachers out of the faculty room for 3 years, and you could have a helluva system." This facetious comment by a Woodland Hills central-office administrator is surprisingly representative of those given by many district educators and others when asked to come up with solutions to the problem of resistance by parents and teachers to the detracking reforms. Implicit in such statements is a recognition that resistance is a by-product of a pernicious culture found in many of the district's schools and homes.

These comments also recognize an unpleasant reality: Teachers and parents are likely to resist reform efforts designed to expand educational opportunity, and that resistance can be powerful (see Anyon, 1997; Lipman, 1998). This reality—so far removed from American ideals—should give us pause, but it also offers hope. Notwithstanding such resistance, these districts have experienced meaningful equity-minded change.

The next chapter shifts the focus from the "who"—the particular sources of resistance to detracking—to the "how." I explore the power of the "market metaphor" in undermining attempts to detrack. In these districts, as has been the case throughout the nation, modification of rigidly tracked systems to allow varying degrees of course choices within a stratified structure has provided the supporters of tracking with a philosophically potent argument against the need for any further change.

10

Tracking, Choice, and Inequity

Choice carries powerful meaning in American society. In the sphere of education, choice underlies policies and proposals as varied as vouchers, open enrollment, charter schools, and home-schooling. Many districts around the nation have adopted, as one such choice mechanism, open course enrollment within tracked systems (see NCES, 1994).[1] These open enrollment systems, which have been used at one time or another in each of the four school districts I studied, allow parents and/or students to "overrule" any course placements made by school officials. While tracking is often attacked as denying educational opportunities, the use of open course enrollment allows the supporters of tracking to shift responsibility for those reduced opportunities from the school to the students and families who opt for the lesser education.

In operation, these choice mechanisms do little if anything to alleviate the harmful impact of tracking on students enrolled in lower-track classes. Moreover, as demonstrated in Chapter Four, racial discrimination in course enrollment continues unabated. In numerous ways, then, tracking under a choice regime resembles tracking under the more rigid tracking regimes of the past (see generally Lucas, 1999). But the market metaphor—equating choice with freedom and fairness—has nonetheless provided a sturdy rhetorical foundation of support for tracking structures.

SAN JOSE, WILMINGTON, AND ROCKFORD

School officials in both San Jose and Wilmington touted the choices offered to students and parents. In San Jose, the schools themselves were all part of a controlled choice plan, richly stocked with magnet and themed schools and presented each year to the district's households in a glossy publication entitled "Choices." In Wilmington, the course selection options provided an important element of the districts' successful legal defense against charges stemming from the disparate racial impact of tracking. The district court noted that school course placement systems ostensibly treated all children the same, no matter which racial or ethnic group they belonged to: "The parents and student have the ultimate say in the level to which the student is assigned" (*Coalition to Save our Children v. State Board of Education*, 1995, p. 800). The court was not troubled by the fact that schools played a significant role in the placement process by, among other things, officially recommending a course and requiring parents to sign a waiver in order to move students away from that recommended level.

In Rockford, the historical tracking system could not be similarly redeemed by the limited choice mechanisms then in place. However, choice elements became a crucial part of Rockford's system after the initial court order. In the wake of the 1994 order condemning the district's discriminatory use of tracking, the school district began inserting greater choice and flexibility into the placement system. With considerable success, attorneys for the school district then argued that this new system constituted acceptable "ability grouping," as opposed to the old "tracking" practices denounced by the court.

"Tracking," the school district asserted, "describes the practice of assigning a student to a specific sequence of courses, from which placement there is no provision for change or review. Ability grouping is the assignment of a student to a level of instruction deemed most appropriate to his/her level of performance and capability as determined by a review of test scores, grades, staff recommendations and student interest" (*Rockford*, Case no. 89 C 20168 (W.D. Ill.), RSD's Response to Court Order, February 17, 1998, p. 3). Making use of this distinction, the district justified its continued stratification of courses:

> From a purely educational standpoint, RSD believes that tracking, in its educational context, is harmful to all students and has been eliminated in RSD. RSD also believes that from an educational standpoint, that in order to provide the best educational opportunities for all students in RSD and to allow all students to achieve their full potential, it is an educationally sound practice to provide opportunities for all of the students, including those at an accelerated level and those students who may require supplementary service to complete the regular curriculum (*Rockford*, Case no. 89 C 20168 (W.D. Ill.), Supplementary Response of RSD, March 20, 1998, pp. 2–3).

For these reasons, the district stated, it maintains ability grouping in its secondary schools.

In its response, the court began by rejecting the school district's distinction between ability grouping and tracking: "Ability grouping is considered by the court to be a subset of tracking but, hopefully, not as permanent and not as potentially segregative" (*Rockford*, Case no. 89 C 20168 (W.D. Ill.), Order of Magistrate, May 7, 1998, p. 2). Nonetheless, the court allowed the practice to continue. The only explicit limitation placed on the tracking system was a range of racial tolerance levels (plus or minus 12%) for the course assignments. Perhaps this was the greatest degree of "detracking" that could be ordered by a trial court acting under the skeptical watch of the Seventh Circuit Court panel (see discussion in Chapter Five). However, it demonstrates the persuasive power of a shift from a rigid structure to one purportedly responsive to "student interest" and with "provisions for change."

WOODLAND HILLS

As in the other districts, parents and students in Woodland Hills could opt to accept school placement recommendations or to select a different course level. Although prerequisites did prevent some selections, the same court mandates that targeted tracking also placed limitations on the schools' use of such prerequisites. The resulting system allowed district educators to draw a distinction between their "voluntary" tracking and the rigid tracking that is generally most condemned.

When administrators, teachers, and parents in Woodland Hills defended their stratified structure, they generally argued that choice provided it with a non-discriminatory foundation. A principal asserted that "tracking never existed [in Woodland Hills]. I always felt the kids tracked themselves, which meant they chose what happened." Agreed a White parent, "One thing about this school district, every program's open to everyone." Several other teachers and administrators offered similar comments. For example, notwithstanding the sorting of students between Physical Science, regular Biology, and Biology with Lab, a science teacher insisted that the district did not track these students: "[A]nybody who wants to take [Biology with Lab] can, based on their previous science background." A principal agreed, declaring that no tracking existed in science. Rather, the school gave students "options to take a style or type of science." Another principal contended that only AP courses did not have open enrollment, so "anyone can take anything." Even for AP, a teacher explained, "the option was open for anybody after a conference with their parents and guidance [counselors]—they could be placed in there for the first six weeks on probation."

For many of those sharing this perspective, the element of choice in the placement of students freed the schools and community from responsibility for any resulting segregation or other harm. Via the cleansing power of choice, all associated concerns disappeared. However, for many district students choice was more apparent than real. Scheduling conflicts constrained some students' choices in ways that perpetuated tracking (e.g., taking a lower-level math class prevented scheduling of a higher-level English class). For other students, as discussed in greater detail below, the course selection process amounted to little more than accepting the schools' recommendations. Racial discrimination experienced in prior schooling also played a role in undermining real choice.

On this latter point, consider the analysis offered by one African-American parent: "[T]racking in Woodland Hills had to be the worst scenario [because of] the status of the African-American student over the years — that they were consistently [directed] to the lower track. [Therefore], when they get to the junior high level and the high school level, when the advanced courses are offered, they're not prepared. They see White students in there, [and] they think, that's a White thing." Students could overcome this past discrimination, he ventured, but only with the active help of parents and teachers: "If the parent's not involved in that respect, and if the teacher's not encouraging the student to excel, then [the students] are not going to have the consciousness, they're not going to have the incentive, to make choices about advanced courses when they get in the higher grades. . . . They're not even going to consider it." An African-American administrator provided a similar perspective, stressing the need for all children to receive a challenging education in the early grades. "[I]f you don't have the skills," she observed, "you really don't have a choice, whether I say you have a choice or not."

Layered on top of this cumulative impact of racial tracking was the tendency of many parents to accept school course recommendations unquestioningly (see Yonezawa, 1997). An African-American parent explained how this worked for English courses before they were detracked:

When they send [the course selection material] home, the teacher will highlight what they recommend your child to take, whether it's advanced English or regular English. [M]ost parents will choose what the professional has highlighted on that paper. [If they say] my kid should take advanced English, then I [will enroll her in] advanced English. If you highlighted that my child was only geared for regular English, I'm telling my child, well you [must] take regular English. [T]he majority of the African-American [parents] trust the professionals' opinion.

"Very few" such parents, this mother added, challenged the professionals. And, when they did, it was sometimes in order to move their children downward. For instance, an African-American tenth-grader described how she and her mother decided that she would take a lower-track science class (regular Biology), even though her previous year's science teacher had recommended that she take the advanced class: "I changed it because—not because I couldn't [do it], but [because] it had a lot of writing, and I don't like to write. My mom . . . thought it'd be better for me to take regular Biology because I wouldn't have to write as much." As it turned out, this student found the regular Biology class insufficiently interesting and challenging, so she planned to take the upper-level Chemistry class the following year. She hoped that she had not fallen too far behind.

While this student's decision to move downward in the tracked structure was internally motivated, other students, counselors, teachers, and administrators all cited external pressure from peers as the primary reason why African-American students opted for less challenging classes. One instance of this phenomenon was related by a junior high counselor who said she had recommended giftedness testing for a "real creative" African-American girl with a 4.0 GPA. The girl refused the testing for an entire year "because she didn't want to be singled out from her friends." Others explained that the stigma attached to participating in the gifted program fell more heavily on Woodland Hills' African-American males than on its African-American females. "[M]any African-American males were embarrassed [even] to walk through the halls carrying their books, because they were afraid that they would look like nerds," a counselor explained.

A teacher of one of the high-track science courses explained that very few African-American males enrolled in his course. Even when they did, he said, they felt negative pressure from their friends:

> The bottom line is they have the brains, these kids are intelligent, but they don't want it. And their peers, they are affected by their peers, they don't want to take this course because it's not cool in the eyes of their friends. I know that for a fact because a kid told me. He said I don't want to be in here, I want to be with my friends in [the lower-track course].

After another teacher commented that very few African-American students enrolled in one of the science AP classes, I asked him what might work to increase that number. "To be honest," he said, "I think if they had friends who they knew were going to be taking it." An administrator agreed, commenting that most African Americans at West Junior High School selected General Math (a lower-tracked class) based on their friends' recommendations.

The work of Fordham and Ogbu (1986), among others, suggests that behaviors associated with high educational achievement, such as studying, trying to get good grades, and speaking middle-class English are often viewed as attempts to "act White" and are looked down upon within Black student peer cultures. "[T]hroughout the educational environment," a Black parent told me, students have "the attitude — African American towards African American — [that] if you're striving to get in advanced courses or you're in advanced courses, you're trying to act White." If one accepts this analysis, as did these teachers and administrators in Woodland Hills, then one would expect choice mechanisms to exacerbate, rather than alleviate, racial segregation within a tracked system. Yet many of these same Woodland Hills educators continued to argue that their choice mechanism eliminated the need to detrack. The continued promulgation of this claim did actual educational damage. It created lofty expectations that the educational system could not fulfill and thereby undermined the goal of raising the level of instruction for African-American students. And it concurrently shifted the blame for these failures from the schools to the students themselves.

Nonetheless, educators and policy-makers continued to look to "choice" as a guidepost for their actions. For example, a teacher relied on the choice rationale to explain why he did not counsel students to take more challenging courses: "I think it's a matter of choice for the student[s] to take whatever they'd like to take." In this way, the pursuit of greater choice subverted the court order, including the mandate to push students into more challenging courses. The libertarian ideal was never within reach. As Howe (1997) points out in his discussion of the broader issues of school choice, the real, non-theoretical world places constraints on unfettered options: "Lack of information, lack of time, lack of transportation, lack of childcare, and lack of trust are among the reasons to worry that the poor have a compromised context of choice in comparison to the nonpoor" (p. 119). Within this "compromised context of choice," newer, less rigid tracking systems reproduced the results of the districts' earlier, rigid systems.

I have come to view choice elements within course placement as a safety valve, on both the symbolic and practical levels. Symbolically, they relieve school officials of responsibility. Practically, they channel the energies of efficacious parents away from contesting the tracking system and into contesting their own children's placements. The language of choice reverberated throughout these districts, shaping a detracking zone less receptive to reform.

11

Equating Black with Bad:
Normative Opposition Revisited

The forces discussed in this chapter, which presents an in-depth look at normative issues in Woodland Hills, overlap with the forces discussed in the previous three chapters. Through this separate and additional treatment, I hope to highlight the often-overlooked normative dimension to the context surrounding equity-minded reform. This chapter, then, explores how educators and others conflated race with intelligence and behavior. I discuss the reminiscences of teachers about the good old days, when their district had fewer African Americans, the students academically excelled, and the classes were better behaved. I present teachers' complaints about their African-American students' lack of academic and behavioral reinforcement in their homes. I offer the words of White residents for whom race—along with race-related issues such as desegregation and detracked courses—bore negative symbolic meaning, and I examine how this racial symbolism strongly affected community attitudes toward detracking. Such beliefs greatly undermined detracking reforms grounded in a philosophy that all students should be pushed to achieve academically at the highest levels.

CONFLATION OF ABILITY WITH BEHAVIOR

In the ongoing Woodland Hills desegregation case, as well as in discussions with many district educators and parents, discipline issues dwarfed detracking as an item of contention. The plaintiffs alleged in the strongest terms that the district disciplined African-American students discriminatorily, and the district responded just as strongly that it made every possible effort to treat all students fairly. Said one influential district representative, "In [this district], teachers get

169

hit, they get pushed. And it's far more likely that a Black kid did it. Nineteen out of 20 times, if someone tells a teacher to fuck off or calls a teacher a mother-fucker, it's a Black kid. I'm not saying that that's the way Black kids are, but it is the Black kids that are doing it." My study did not attempt to evaluate these claims; the district, when it invited the study, asked (and I agreed) that discipline issues be addressed only as they related to detracking.

This relationship between discipline and detracking was visible in the easily-witnessed contrast between tracked and detracked classes. Many teachers recognized a decrease in overall disruptions after the detracking. (Even critics of detracking have acknowledged this phenomenon. See Loveless, 1999, p. 144.) Yet most teachers went no further than simply observing the phenomenon. "[T]he one thing that I have noticed is behavior in a regular English class now is much, much better," said one, "It's [a] much more controllable situation." She noted the "terrible" disruptions in the old low-track classes. "[I]t was a constant battle, a constant war," attested another, "But now it seems it's like evened out, instead of having one class with fifteen characters in [it], I have four classes with two in each one. And they're easier to control."

A third teacher agreed that the old low-track classes had "constant discipline problems." However, he also pointed out that the old advanced classes had few, if any, discipline problems. This teacher, along with most other teachers interviewed, contended that there were now somewhat worse disruptions in the mixed-ability classes than there had been in the old advanced classes.[1] Yet two African-American students I spoke with, who had attended the old advanced classes as well as the new heterogeneous classes, disagreed with these teachers' assessments. They reported that the detracked classes had no more interruptions than had the advanced classes. They acknowledged that the new classes contained some difficult students, but they pointed out that the advanced classes also had such students.

Only one interviewee questioned the improvement in classroom-management of heterogeneous classes compared to the old low-track classes. This teacher, who was extremely resistant to the reform effort, argued that mixed-ability grouping in fact made the discipline problems worse. She reasoned that this occurred because the struggling students gave up: "you have that child who's sitting back there that can't do it no matter how low you go into doing it, so as a result he's just going to . . . cause a problem, because the first thing out of their mouth is, 'I can't do it.' So they just cause a disturbance."

Placement Based on Behavior

Teachers typically equate high academic achievement with good behavior, according to a top district administrator. In the past, this resulted in stories such as the following related by an African-American mother:

The teacher told me to take my son out of advanced English . . . because he was talking. [A]nd I asked her, did she feel that he needed to be taken out, or did she feel that he could do the work. And she told me, "Oh no, I know he can do the work, but nobody wants to put up with him talking."

In this particular case, the mother did not allow the school to place her son in the low-track class: "I told her I wasn't taking him out. I said if he talks in your class, you handle it. You're the teacher." However, as this woman herself pointed out, most parents—Black or White—are not so efficacious. Because of this experience, she said, "I know that a lot of kids were put in basic English . . . not because of their lack of ability, but mainly because the teacher felt they talked too much."

Interestingly, the detracking process prompted some teachers to engage in a limited critical inquiry of their own former practices. One such teacher wondered aloud why there seemed to be such a "correlation between [students'] behavior and their ability." He and a few of his colleagues, he commented, had begun to question whether placements in the old tracked system were based on behavior rather than ability:

Why are they there? Are they there because they're discipline problems, or are they there because they can't read? And there were some kids that [would improve] if you would take them out of that class and get [them] in a smaller class situation, work with them one on one or [in] a small group. They do fine. And they had the ability, they could show that they could read. It's just that once they [get] around some other kids that are goofing around, they get sucked right in there.

While many district teachers appeared to conflate ability and behavior, very few recognized doing so. And even those, like the above teacher, who recognized this lapse, failed to take the next step: recognizing the association between perceptions of behavior, perceptions of ability, and racial stereotypes. Because this association went unchecked by teachers and parents, their normative beliefs about discipline bolstered their resistance to the axiom that all students can learn—and their resistance to detracking.

LACK OF COMMITMENT TO PLACING AFRICAN AMERICANS IN CHALLENGING CLASSES

Notwithstanding general movement by the district toward detracking, Woodland Hills retained some ability-grouped courses. In fact, it took a firm policy position against the complete elimination of stratification within its course offerings. For example, the superintendent strongly advocated proliferating the district's AP classes. Also, as noted earlier, the district had not yet phased out a layered system in science. Where such tracks remained, the district (with the court's prompting) decided to remedy their discriminatory impact by counseling African-American students to take more challenging courses. A guidance counselor explained this new policy in glowing terms: "Students who were fearful that they could not be successful in a more challenging class and who've been actually pushed into taking it—almost coerced into taking it— [have been] finding success and finding, 'I really can do this.' "

Notwithstanding this counselor's enthusiasm, the policy met with general resistance at the school-site level and, in part because of this resistance, had only limited success. "We could do a lot better with the racial balance in some of the courses," admitted a secondary school principal. My independent look at the numbers confirmed this assessment. An analysis of information provided by the district showed that African-American students remained under-represented in the most challenging classes. African Americans, who constituted 28% of the high school population, composed only 9.8% of the enrollment in the thirteen high school courses offering weighted grades in the 1995–1996 school year (66/674). This problem centered around the top math and science courses, where African Americans constituted only 5% of the enrollment (10/198).

At the other end of the academic spectrum, African-American enrollment in Home Economics 1 & 2 stood at 55% and 63% of the classroom composition, respectively. Similarly high enrollments existed for art, nutrition, typing, and industrial arts classes.

A large racial divide also continued to exist between ninth-grade low-track Physical Science courses and high-track "Biology with Lab" courses. At East Junior High, African Americans composed 13.8% of the Biology classes and 28.4% of the Physical Science classes (East had a total African-American enrollment of 27%); at West Junior High, they composed 20.2% of the Biology classes and 47.6% of the Physical Science classes (West had a total African-American enrollment of 35%).[2] For a more detailed and sophisticated statistical analysis of Woodland Hills science enrollment, please refer back to Chapter Four.

The registration process for science classes, as described by a counselor, included each school's request that the student's previous-year science teacher provide recommendations "mindful" of the need to "pull kids up and especially the minority kids." However, as noted earlier, some science teachers refused this duty.[3] In addition to the teacher recommendation, the school looks at students' "grades and other [test] scores," according to a secondary school principal. He explained the importance of examining past performance in order to ensure that the student will succeed in the class: "Our goal is to make sure that every student has an opportunity to excel. If you're going to be placed in an environment where you're not going to excel, then you are going to have a problem and we don't want to do that." Therefore, he concluded, sometimes a counselor should advise a child not to take the more challenging course: "I would counsel that parent and I will say, 'do you want your son or daughter to be successful or are we going to plan for them to fail?' " Such reasoning no doubt contributed to continued downward placement of African-American students.

The district, as part of the effort to provide a more challenging curriculum for African Americans, also revised the criteria for admission into AP courses and the gifted program. A point-based calculation, involving composite grades in the subject area, unexcused absences, and teacher and guidance counselor recommendations, determined AP course admissions. Those students who failed to qualify based on this calculation can still provisionally enroll but must then achieve a 70% average in the first grading period.

The re-evaluation designed to get more African Americans into the gifted program also used a revised point system. Unlike the AP system, however, the gifted calculation included factors such as socio-economic status (as evidenced by participation in the free or reduced lunch program), minority ethnicity, and parent education. A top district administrator expressed surprise that this new formula did not produce loud complaints from White parents. Perhaps this relative silence can be attributed to the fact that, as a teacher in the gifted program pointed out, the new method also resulted in the admission of more White students. I did, however, speak to one White parent who charged that the revised criteria had resulted in the admission of unqualified African-American students. She charged that, in the district's zeal to include African-American students, it included "kids who had failed a grade [and] kids who were in remedial programs and in gifted at the same time."

Some teachers shared this negative attitude. According to a school board member, these teachers told her that they reacted to the revision of the AP admissions criteria by upgrading the White students' portfolio scores — essentially trying to balance out the extra points given (they thought) to African-American students. The sad irony, of course, was that African-American students received no "extra points" as part of the AP evaluation; a racial element was only included in the giftedness evaluation. As a science teacher acknowledged, the courts may want more African-American students in the advanced classes, but "the teachers . . . don't believe in that. They really don't. They don't like that at all."

This same teacher insisted that some of the students placed by this effort in the ninth-grade Biology class "have really no business in [there]." "They can't pass," he ventured, "[they] probably couldn't pass [low-track] Physical Science." These students, he concluded, were placed in the advanced classes in order to meet quotas,[4] "and I don't think it's even fair to the students some-times." Agreed his colleague,

> I think we are pushing some kids into these courses that aren't prepared and can't do it. They can't do it. But you're not allowed to tell them they can't do it. I'm sorry, but [not] everybody can do this level of work.

Even given the attitudes expressed by these teachers, it is difficult to argue with the wisdom of the district's emphasis on the role of teachers in promoting more challenging placement decisions. Whether or not district policy gave teachers this formal authority, teacher attitudes would inevitably dictate the success or failure of the process. As an African-American parent commented, the reform's success hinges on the expectations of teachers: "If there were no changes made in teachers' attitude, [in] teachers' caring about students, par-ticularly in the lower grades, . . . encouraging them to progress, to excel, . . . then [the students] don't have an incentive after that to go for advanced courses." Alternatively, as suggested by a board member, detracking might help the district clear the placement hurdle:

> How do you get the guidance counselors to get the students to go into the more challenging courses? Well, I don't see that the students have a choice. The challenging curriculum is across the board for all stu-dents. . . . I don't think that the students have a choice whether they want to take part in the challenging curriculum. There's a certain core program that is demanded now under this challenging curricu-lum and students are no longer allowed to fill up their schedule, es-pecially in the secondary level, with all those elective, ancillary, non-educational programs.

While this board member overstated the degree of detracking by the district, her basic point is correct: if the whole curriculum is challenging, then place-ment decisions become less important.

Alongside the previous discussion of course choice, this examination of the counseling issue accents an interesting way in which normative beliefs im-pacted the detracking zone of mediation. Educators, in part because of their broad-based resistance to the reforms and in part because of their faith in "choice," largely failed to counsel African Americans to take the more chal-lenging courses. Most African Americans thus continued to opt for the lower-track courses. Keeping in mind the faith placed by many White educators and community members in choice mechanisms, this fact reinforced their con-clusion that the source of African-American educational problems was located within their homes and community—not within the schools.

This example also highlights the cyclical nature of the impact of normative forces on the zone. Normative disagreement leads to minimal buy-in and effort, leading in turn to a failed policy. This reinforces the initial normative belief and results in blaming the victim. In turn, educators' resistance to detracking grows stronger, bolstered by further anecdotal evidence that certain (in this case, African-American) students simply do not try.

NEGATIVE BELIEFS ABOUT RACE AND INTELLIGENCE

Since detracking is predicated on having high expectations for all children, successful reform becomes more difficult when teachers do not hold such beliefs. In Woodland Hills, for instance, negative normative beliefs about race and intelligence held by teachers, counselors, and parents strongly acted to shape the detracking zone. Consider the following statement by a junior high science teacher, conflating race with intelligence:

> Since we've now merged with Braddock and North Braddock and Rankin, the percentage now—. . . it may have been 10% [African American] back then. Now it's up to at least 30%, and it's going higher, and it's not getting any easier. It's getting worse. I have a buddy in sixth grade [who tells me that] it's unbelievable . . . the [low] intelligence, the capabilities of the students now.

Another science teacher expressed his resigned belief that "there's nothing we can basically do about the mix of kids we have. I mean, this is the neighborhood that the school is in." A community member agreed. "The demographics are just there," he said, noting that the schools have to expect a "differential level of performance by the children."

Two former principals expanded on this theme. The first complained about students from "a certain area." These students, he opined, observe their mother receiving "food stamps, medical cards, [and] welfare" and, since "that's the life they're used to, . . . they don't feel they have to do anything. It's all given to them" (Miller, 1991, p. 92). Another principal offered his analysis of the disciplinary problems purportedly resulting from African-American child-rearing practices. African-American parents, he professed, teach their children that "if he hits me, I hit him back." "That's their values," he reasoned, concluding:

> We have a lot of fights down there, a lot of drugs down there, a lot of single parent families down there, and a lot of alcoholics down there.

That's where the kids come from. It's hard to convert them to appreciate a better sense of values (Miller, 1991, p. 94).[5]

At least one African-American educator shared some of these negative views. He believed that many African-American parents "do not take and push [academics] like some of the [White parents]." He characterized African-American parents as jobless and not caring about their children's academic success. " 'What do I care about pushing him [academically] because, I'm right here,' " he had such parents saying, " 'You can come back and stay with me.' " This educator also insisted that the court remedies amounted to quotas benefiting unqualified students:

[W]e have to get more Black students in the gifted program, whether they belong there or not, we need to take and get them there for the number. Now I think what we're doing, we're looking at numbers and not looking at whether this kid needs to be there or can be there.

A school board member offered an assessment that was less extreme but just as burdened with negative stereotypes. After explaining that special education children are more likely to come from the economically "suppressed" area of the district than from the White, wealthy area, she described the homes in the poorer area as not having "the appropriate nourishment or [environment] or parents that can help them in school, because [the parents themselves] dropped out of school and started having these babies and have no education of their own."

By approaching the community's African-American culture as an obstacle to be overcome, these school leaders and educators have presumptively doomed that community's children to a subordinate learning status. As Oakes and Lipton (1999) explain, "If we try to teach students by separating what and how they learn from their family's culture or history, these students cannot be smart" (p. 77). The alternative is to build on students' cultural knowledge. "Schools must not accept as a given that a student's existing cultural tools for learning or solving problems are inferior to those of the dominant (or school) culture" (p. 77).

Many African Americans also expressed concerns about students' home lives—and some of these concerns reflected a similarly negative view of aspects of child-rearing in the Black community. An African-American educator noted how some Black students attach a stigma to success, contrasting those students with other Black students who had supportive families:

The youngsters who are doing well have other support systems. They have families who emphasize education and value education, and I think that makes a difference, and the fact that they make honor roll is, for them, an honor. It's not something that they're embarrassed about, because their families value it and they get a lot of encouragement from home.

A mother of two African-American students added her disappointment with the discipline in many of her community's homes:

> There's no discipline. There's no structure in the majority of the homes. So if there's no discipline or structure in the homes, how do you expect [the children to behave] in the school system? [The district has] a lot of discipline problems with the African-American children, because you have to start at home.

Another African-American parent argued that many parents in his community failed to motivate their children sufficiently: "[T]heir parents [must] motivate them and . . . hold the teacher accountable for why [their] child isn't excelling." But, he sighed, "that's the way it is: Certain parents just aren't involved in their child's education."

Notwithstanding such criticisms, these African-American community members differed from their White counterparts in one very important regard: they made no excuses for the schools. Consider the following explanation offered by an African-American educator:

> I think the [home and community] environment has a lot to do with the children coming in—how they react when they come in. But I don't think it has to do with the potential of the child. I think that's the job of that educator. They are the professionals; they have to figure out ways to bring out the best in that child regardless of what that home situation is. . . . I don't agree with [the contention] that it's at home where they are most affected. Because the time we have with them—we can make the most of that time.

She noted, for example, the district's obligation to "present challenging lessons" and "do creative things in the classrooms to hold [the students'] attention."

Similarly, an African-American parent acknowledged the existence of an achievement gap by the time the children entered school: "when our kids first come into kindergarten, there's a gap between what our African-American students know and what the White students know. And that has to be attributed primarily to what is being done at home." He continued, "I do believe that our kids, in the beginning, come in knowing less than what the White students know." He also accepted the need for "African-American parents [to start] reading to our kids at an earlier age, just being academically involved with our children at an earlier age." However, he would not excuse the school district from its obligation "to come up with a way [to teach] all students." "In my mind," he said, the court order recognized that "none of the students, or very few of the students, were unreachable." The order obligated the district "to put in a correction. And, again, this is where I feel that the teachers fail."

Even this deficit view of students' readiness contrasts sharply with the view held by some educators. "We're not miracle workers," said one junior high teacher,

> We try the best we can here, and every teacher knocks himself out. . . . But once [the students] leave this building, there's no reinforcement. [T]here's no reinforcement at the home. There's nobody there to help them with it. [I]t's a losing battle, but yet we're blamed for it.

This teacher continued, describing her perspective of the children's homes: "Parents are not at home. There's no one to take care—a little kid's taking care of [her] little sisters. It's just the way the world is." She concluded by explaining the implications for detracking: "[P]lacing [such students] in regular classrooms and expecting a kid that's reading on a third-grade level to handle an eighth-grade book, that's ludicrous. . . . It's just humanly impossible."

DENIAL

A community member mulling over the role of race in the district concluded that "a lot of people who like neighborhood schools don't give a rat's ass about race." Parents and teachers in Woodland Hills repeatedly expressed a genuine belief that race played only a minimal role in district policies. Focusing on the issue of detracking, a principal noted that, while the district had long been "aware" of segregation between classrooms, "it wasn't an intentional design to do that." He explained that the district had "mixed feelings" about proceeding with detracking because:

> We had a lot of concerns for the young people who were being served by what we called "basic" English at the time as to whether they could survive moving into regular level English. So although it was racially identifiable, of course, it was serving a purpose to be able to get these young people through the educational process. So there was a lot of concern around what would happen if this sort of safety net's pulled out for young people.

Advocates of neighborhood schooling and those worried about the value of their homes also cited the purportedly color-blind nature of their decision-making. Further, educators fervently circled the wagons around the race issue. Very few would acknowledge racial problems or issues. "For the most part," asserted a junior high English teacher, "I believe this staff was racially sensitive before it came together." She continued, "Most of the disagreements over the merger had nothing to do with race or with kids. It had to do with school boards and policies that came over, debts that came over." Similarly, a White community member insisted that any problems in the district should not be framed in terms of race: "There's four hundred and some professional employees, teachers, out there. Some of them are assholes, [and] it's got nothing to do with race."

Others specifically defended course-placement decisions as race-neutral. Perhaps most pointedly, a district representative argued that the results speak for themselves: "You've had people from that minority community successfully get through that school district and go on to bigger and better things, and I don't know that they've had to do it tooth and nail, fighting against institutionalized barriers to their advancement." A junior high English teacher summed up this attitude as follows:

All kids are kids to me. I don't care if they're purple, green, yellow, black, or white. They're all the same to me, and I get so tired of everything being Black versus White. . . . I get tired of everything being a Black versus White issue. . . . I feel like we're in the nineties now. Let's move on. Let's move past this.

Most district teachers shared this desire to eschew further race-conscious remedies or dialogue. Many cited with particular disdain the district's past attempts at "sensitivity training." However, one educator offered a contrasting viewpoint, arguing that race can not and should not be ignored:

I am an African American, and I think that I [perceive things] differently than someone [who] is not an African American. . . . I don't see looking at race as something negative, because I look at race everyday. So . . . when people say to me, "well, I'm color-blind; I don't see the kids as Black or White," personally I have a problem with that because you wouldn't say that [concerning] a bed of flowers. There are colors in a bed of flowers. There's nothing wrong with saying to me, "I do know that so many of my kids are Black or so many of my kids are White." There's nothing wrong with that because they are.

Sonia Nieto extends this point, arguing that "to be color-blind may result in refusing to accept differences and therefore accepting dominant culture as the norm" (Nieto, 1992, p. 109). In Woodland Hills, the attractiveness of a color-blind approach was no doubt partially grounded in such a norm; however, it was also probably grounded in a gut-level fear of racialized discourse. Thinking about her colleagues' reluctance to address race, the above-quoted educator remarked, "I think that people are very sensitive and concerned about maybe saying the wrong thing—that this was a Black kid that did this, or this was a White kid that did that." And, in fact, many teachers did acknowledge to me that they felt "beat up" and unfairly accused of discrimination.

Yet others specifically identified racial issues involving tracking. One African-American parent contested the argument that "properly" done ability grouping necessarily resulted in a fair system. Tracking without discrimination in Woodland Hills, she argued, "is not possible for the African-American children . . . because of the racism." She felt that the two—tracking and racism—were not separable from each other. A White teacher agreed. She noted that English detracking had polarized the community because parents relied on tracking to ensure that "it was safe to send their children here." "As long as [the district] had the advanced classes," she observed, their children would not encounter "the other problems." When asked how much the children's race underlies this parental concern, she declared, "All of it; I think all of it." Parental obstacles were also mentioned by an African-American community member who remarked:

> [D]etracking is a very hard transition. [F]irst of all, in order to detrack children you [must] detrack the parents, and that's a job. Like all those parents who are up there [in the wealthy, White boroughs], they're all for the tracking evidently. [I]n order for Dr. Young to get anywhere with those parents, he has to change their whole thought process. [H]e has to "detrack" them because [for] years and years and years they [have been] programmed for tracking.

RACE AND HOUSING

Some of the community's realtors vocally opposed detracking. More accurately, they opposed desegregation reforms in general, including detracking. One such realtor complained that when she tried to sell houses in the district she got "beat up." Potential buyers, she contended, came to her office already of the opinion that the district "left behind . . . the brighter kids, [in] that they're not going to be allowed to accelerate and move at a faster pace, that they're going to have to wait." "There have been people," she remarked, "that have come in and looked and seen houses that they liked and then they go back to their school, their work or . . . their prospective employer and they [are told], 'don't move to that district. There are too many problems.' "

An administrator dismissed such concerns as excuse-making: "it's real easy to say the school district sucks, [to explain away why you] can't sell a house." And, in fact, other realtors leant support to this critique, telling me that they've had little difficulty selling in the area. When the court issued the desegregation order, one realtor remarked, he and his fellow agents feared disastrous consequences for home prices and sales. But "it didn't have nearly the effect that we thought it would." This realtor, among others, noted the difficulty of disaggregating the various factors that affected home sales. One declared that while many people blamed the court order for any slowdown in real estate, "it's hard to get a cause and effect kind of relationship." These realtors mentioned other contributing factors such as factory closings and the decision by many older residents to sell their homes.

Moreover, when realtors who opposed the court-ordered reforms spoke of its depressing effects on the realty market, yet they omitted the positive reaction of African-American home-buyers. Several people, including two optimistic realtors, noted this phenomenon. "For a lot of the minority people," one asserted, the court order constituted a plus. "I sold a house right up the street here [to an African-American family, and] one of the things they liked about it was the fact that it was in Woodland Hills." African-American families, insisted a district administrator, are "dying to get in here." She related a conversation she had had with an African-American physician who lived in one of the "premier" local school districts. His daughter's school denied her a slot on their cheerleading squad, saying that she came in 13th with only 12 positions available. "His kid," the administrator reported, "just miraculously was thirteenth when they were picking twelve," and the father was convinced that this resulted from racism. "And he wanted to come here because of [the] opportunities" that resulted from the court order.[6] She concluded, "I think in a lot of ways they want their kids to go to a school district that's multicultural, and this is seen as one of the upper-echelon ones that way."

Whatever the degree and impact of White flight, some folks simply refused to concern themselves with the possibility. One of the district's top administrators took this stance: "I have to sit here when people are telling me, you either do it my way or I'm moving out of the district. And I keep hearing, we're gonna move. We're gonna move." Such threats, this administrator said, should not affect district policy. An African-American community member summed up this position: "I just look at [White flight], in all honesty, as part of what you're going to get from the White community when you start integrating."[7]

WOODLAND HILLS' POWERFUL SYMBOLS

Powerful meanings attached to some of the objects and events in the district—meanings that affected community attitudes toward detracking. In their role as symbols, these objects and events acted as additional forces shaping the zone of mediation.[8] The 1981 court-ordered merger of the five school districts provides an easily discernible example. Many people in the district, particularly White parents, used the word "merger" to describe anything that they perceived as connected to the desegregation case, and they usually attached negative connotations to the word. This section examines how such symbols acquired their meanings, and it considers the impact of the symbols on the zone of mediation.

Words and other symbols have no meaning independent of that which we, as a society, give them (Berger and Luckman, 1967; Foucault, 1972).[9] Moreover, these meanings are in a constant process of being born, developed, contested, and redefined. This process, which Foucault calls "discursive formation," takes place within a societal and historical context. To understand how symbols acquire their meaning, we must look to the relationships between existing power structures (such as educational and legal institutions), existing epistemologies, and other existing authorities.[10]

The Merger and Court Order

I will now return to the example of the symbolism of "the merger" in Woodland Hills. The desegregation case and the court's finding that Pennsylvania had violated African-American students' Fourteenth Amendment rights provided the initial context that gave meaning to this concept. Although the court's desegregation orders addressed many aspects of schooling (e.g., busing, remedial programs, and detracking), the merger—the court's first overt act—remains pre-eminent in the minds of many White district residents. The merger caused an immediate and emphatic impact, removing much of their collective identity and undermining their feelings of security. Sixteen years later, those feelings were still wrapped up in the term.

Along the way, the usage of the term evolved in response to the district's changing context and experiences. Programs perceived as having failed, resources perceived as having been diverted, teachers perceived as incompetent, consultants viewed as intruders—all were blamed on court involvement, and all were internalized into "the merger."

The discursive formation of "the merger" was largely, as indicated above, dominated by White parents and teachers. Among African-American parents (and the few African-American teachers), the word did not carry the same meaning or symbolic baggage.[11] The local newspaper, serving an overwhelm-ingly White audience, also participated in giving the term its meaning.

The epistemological context for the production of meaning for "the merger" included the concepts of neighborhood schools and local control, as well as the perceived dichotomy between excellence and equity in schooling. "The merger" acquired its most powerful symbolic meaning when viewed in light of these standards and categories. When White parents spoke of the merger, they conjured up images of unfair disempowerment and of excellence sacrificed for equity. In this context, the word gave White parents a tool to covertly characterize district policies within a racist frame—the racist messages being implicit in the symbol.

Viewed in terms of the zone of mediation, the merger symbolism was a political force. Moreover, it was also a force on an individual level. Consider the following statement made by one district employee to another—both African-American women: "I get so angry, because people still come up to me and say, 'This merger would have never happened if it had not been for you people in Braddock.' I get so angry. We're people, too. We're good people." These speakers (presumably White) used the meaning-laden term "merger" to give this woman the clear message that her community was unwelcome and burdensome.

"Merger" was not the only term loaded with such symbolism. When White parents or teachers spoke of the "court order," "judicial supervision" or the "consent decree," many of these same sentiments and meanings carried over. One principal noted that most White parents view the court order as representing

> something that people have done wrong or it's some kind of negative reflection on what isn't occurring. If someone would say "court order" I think, if you looked in people's minds, they would probably think negative, not all of the positive things that we get because of the court order.

Similarly, an African-American parent observed that White parents packed "court order" with racial meaning. These White parents, she said,

> know the court order is about African-American students, and so it's like something that they don't have to state in terms of race. The court order is there. We know what the court order represents. They don't like what the court order—the results that [are] coming about because of the court order. So, they don't have to say they don't want African-American students in their school district. The court order is there for them to address it in that way.

The consent decree, remarked another African-American parent, is "kind of like a sore that hasn't healed yet." He and others in his community were well aware of the White residents' resentment and bitterness.

In addition, court involvement carried a symbolic meaning related to the district's status and prestige, particularly among White parents. These parents explained that continued judicial supervision gave them and their district a "negative self-image." "It creates a perception," explained one observer, that the district is "not doing things right."

Two different people referred to court involvement as a cloud over their heads. This cloud, explained one, "has to do with the control coming from Washington, as opposed to being self-directed within the district." Removing court supervision, said the other, "would be like blowing [the] cloud away from" the district. Once the court order is gone, suggested a third person, it will be "easier to persuade people that what we're doing [in the district] is good stuff."

Interestingly, several White interviewees stated their feeling that African Americans viewed the court order as a symbol of ongoing racial injustice — but the African-American interviewees did not evidence such an understanding. (When African Americans spoke of racial injustice, it was in a direct sense; they did not use a symbol grounded in past wrongs.) One White interviewee accused the plaintiffs' attorneys of being responsible for giving the local schools a negative racial image — a meaning-producing exercise in its own right: "the plaintiffs' perpetuate [and] reinforce a true or false perception among members of the minority community that we're not doing right by their kids." Acknowledging the importance of symbols, this statement suggests a greater importance placed on the district's image than on the reality of that image.

Another common term in the district was "victim communities," which was used to describe the residents of the boroughs in the old General Braddock school district. On its face, the term characterized these African Americans as victims — which was technically correct, in that the members of the plaintiff class were found to be victims of discrimination. However, the term seemed to be used to reinforce the White belief that African Americans viewed the court order as a symbol of ongoing racial injustice. In this sense, Whites used the term to accuse African Americans of maintaining a culture of victimhood.

Note that meanings of the "court order" co-existed with the meanings of "the merger" discussed above. Since the same contexts and power structures interacted to form these symbols, they acquired similar meanings. At times, the two symbols were synonymous; usually, they were closely related. Only on rare occasions were they used very differently.

Not surprisingly, the court order also had symbolic importance in the realty market. Consider the following case: a woman called the district office in hysterics. She and her husband had just closed on a house in Edgewood, a wealthy, white neighborhood in the district. When her husband told his co-workers about the purchase, they responded, "Oh, my God. You don't want to live there. That's Woodland Hills. They teach you—in the Physical Education curriculum they teach you how to dodge bullets." Such comments scared the couple, resulting in the woman asking the district office if they knew how she could get out of the sale.

The patently exaggerated nature of these messages did not undermine their power. Perceptions of the court order constituted the reality of many White parents and teachers. As one observer explained: "I don't think [people] have a whole clue about what the court order is about. I think, if you asked them, they would like to get rid of it. But they really don't understand it." The "facts" underlying their opposition may have been little more than folklore; yet their opposition was real.

Course Names

Another powerful and prevalent symbol in the district concerned the new name of the detracked English class. The district office designed the detrack-ing, as well as the newly rewritten and upgraded curriculum, so that all stu-dents would receive a course at least as challenging as the old "advanced" class.[12] The central office then informed teachers, parents, students, and com-munity members about the reform, telling them that a single mixed-ability course (entitled, e.g., "English 10" or "English 11") would replace the old sys-tem of "regular" and "advanced" English. Whatever the intent, however, the perception of this change among many—probably most—White parents in the district was, as one parent told me, that their children "were being put into a less rigorous class [and] that everything's going down a level for [their] kids."

"[I]t was an enormous political blunder," one observer commented. "It was stupid. Basically, [the superintendent] told the folks with kids in the upper-track classes that their kids couldn't have academic courses anymore. They were going to have to just take regular English. [It was] the perfect ex-ample of educational reform perceived as dumbing the courses down."[13] In this way, the symbolic meaning of the course name was formed by district his-tory, parental fears, and a carelessly chosen name.

People's perceptions sometimes proved more powerful than their own ob-servations. A district leader said that they would tell people, "come in, take a look at what was in the old curriculum, take a look at what is in the new, and make your own decision." "Well," she continued, "people don't want to do that, or when they do it they see that it's in the curriculum, but where their concerns lie right now is in the delivery of it—making sure what's written is what's taught." A reform supporter conveyed the exasperation that many felt toward this disappointing reaction: "I tell parents all the time, I said, 'You can call this class "Beans and Wieners." I mean, it's still Advanced English.' " But the symbol was intractable. Consider the following excerpt from an interview with a student who had been in the old, advanced class:

Student: [The new course] is not called, like, Advanced English. It's not called Accelerated English. Obviously the expectations are lower in the class.

Q: Is it important what it's called? I mean, I guess they just called it "English," right?

A: Well, they called it English 10. But before, when there was the Advanced [and the regular] English, it [the plain "English 10"] was always associated with dangerous minds—lowest level. [The students seemed to have approached that class] with the attitude that this is gonna be easy, and that just kind of carried through. Now, if they would have left it as "advanced" or "accelerated", I think that might have helped because. . .

Q: There's a lot of symbolic meaning attached to the name of the class?

A: Yeah, when you hear "advanced" you think, work harder. Well, at least I would.

Many of the students used the term "Dangerous Minds English" to refer to the old, lower-track class. The term was probably derived from the movie and television show about a class of disruptive, low-achieving students who respond positively to a caring but authoritative teacher. Although the movie had an upbeat message—the minds were "dangerous" in an almost Freirean sense of unemancipated power—the Woodland Hills students used the term in a derogatory way. "Dangerous," to them, meant "disruptive" and "violent." This provides a hint of the symbolic power embodied in, and generated by, the old two-track labeling of students.

Given the district's inattention to terminology with regard to the English detracking, it is interesting to note the opposite approach it took with regard to science courses. These courses were *not* detracked, but *were* renamed. "Academic Biology," for example, was renamed "Biology with Lab." Corresponding changes were made to Chemistry and Physics. Thus, the new two-tracked biology system consisted of "Biology" and "Biology with Lab," which was a bit misleading, since both courses had a lab component.

The district's primary intention was to use the name change to limit the stigma associated with the lower-track class. But, in this case at least, the symbolic effort made little difference. As one student complained, "It's so dumb to refer to it as, 'we are in Chem with Lab and you guys are just Chem, but you do have a lab.' I mean it makes no sense." Another student agreed:

> Physics with Lab is the advanced one. Now, everyone knows that it's Academic. So why not just keep the name? Oh, yeah. I'm gonna feel stupid 'cuz I'm in regular. Obviously, I knew that was Academic, and I didn't want to take it. I mean, what's the difference?

Old stereotypes quickly adapted to the new labels. Given that the course names were generated by the same contexts and power structures, why wouldn't they?

Race

No discussion of the powerful symbols in Woodland Hills would be complete without mention of race. Whites constructed symbolic meaning around African Americans in general and African-American students in particular. As directly stated by one of the district leaders:

> The perception out there is that this is a horrible place, and it's not. And I think the perception is because we have Black [students]. If we had no Black students in this district, or we had a handful of Black students, there wouldn't be this perception.

Another interviewee observed that the "gifted moms"[14] perceive "that the low-achievers and the poor people are the Blacks."

The district also suffered from perceptions that the schools are "filthy," that "there's graffiti on the walls," that students are constantly fighting, and even—one administrator facetiously remarked—that there are "probably brush fires in the bathrooms." In all these cases, the perceptions were presented in the context of racial concerns. Another person focused her discussion of desegregation's problems on the presence of metal detectors in the district's secondary schools; to her, this meant that the students must be dangerous:

> I mean, obviously the kids every morning are greeted by metal detectors. Every kid's bag is searched. Your personal effects are gone through to come in. Okay. Obviously they're doing it for a reason because it's not goody-two-shoes coming into school, where you wouldn't have to do that.

There was, it should be noted, little truth to any of these perceptions—in fact, the schools were relatively clean, safe, and smoothly run.

These symbols are important to understanding Woodland Hills for two reasons. First, they indicate the district's discursive formation process. Each of these symbols was a tangible creation of the history, politics, beliefs and power relations within the district (as well as outside it, particularly in the case of race, the meaning of which in Woodland Hills was a clear outgrowth of its meaning in larger society). Second, once formed, these symbols acted as forces on the zone of mediation. Just as certainly as college admissions criteria or court orders shaped the zone, so did these symbols.

THE DISTRICT RESPONSE

The negative beliefs (and evasive posturing) of teachers, parents and others in the district about race carried clear implications for their approach to detracking. Educators holding such beliefs, for instance, will not invest time or effort in making detracking work. In fact, as seen in Woodland Hills, many such educators will strive to undermine the reform efforts. This left tracking's defenders free to argue, with considerable success, "that Woodland Hills has such a wide socioeconomic and educational diversity among its students that the elimination of tracking will be very disruptive" (English, 1995).

The district's efforts to address these issues necessarily focused on educators (in the form of racial sensitivity training), since it could do little to address parental and societal racism. Earlier in the district's history, it insisted that its teachers attend "sensitivity training" workshops. A board member proudly recited the list of such workshops: "We've had gender training and race training; we've had different age group training; we've had multiculturalism training. So it's been pretty all-inclusive."

Participants, however, universally described these workshops as unhelpful. One long-time administrator speculated that in fact they "may have stiffened some people's [negative] opinions." Many of the sessions seemed "somewhat degrading," he recalled, "it threw me back to the seventies, [where] you sat in circles and held hands and, oooh, this feels good, and you feel good, and I feel good." A teacher recalled the sessions as being very repetitive: "we were having actually the same people come in and tell us the same stories 2 years later, and that breeds cynicism."

In later years, the district moved away from "sensitivity training" in order to focus their in-services more on curriculum, given the limited number of available in-service days (approximately four days per school year). With the exception of some in-services focusing on multi-cultural issues—still centered on the curriculum—none in the several years preceding this study included anything race-related. A district administrator suggested that, because of the detracking and the revised curriculum, the time had come to bring back training addressing these racial issues:

> Beforehand, it was almost like that sensitivity training was done in isolation. [Now], everyone has come together, and they have developed a product, which is the curriculum. . . . I think that they will begin to see that some of that sensitivity training—if we were to bring it back—would make sense. Because before we were talking about heterogeneous groupings, cooperative learning all of that, [but] we didn't have mixed groups, for the most part.

But others, particularly teachers, did not welcome a return of these trainings. They saw them as punishments—rumors spread among the faculty that if you disciplined too many African Americans, you would be sent off to be "sensitized."

Thus, the limited efforts by the district to improve teachers' racial attitudes and beliefs met with little success. Similar parental attitudes and beliefs also persisted. In considering the shaping of the detracking zone, one cannot separate this enduring normative force from other, previously discussed forces (e.g., teacher and parent resistance). Yet because these beliefs create an oppressively unreceptive context for equity-minded reforms such as detracking, their power merits separate recognition.

12

Compromises and Inducements

Responding to powerful political constituencies, the three school districts subject to detracking orders eventually replaced bold detracking policies with pared-down, less ambitious policies. In Rockford, this scaling-back was precipitated by the introduction of a skeptical appellate court and the election of a more resistant school board. Reading the tea leaves, the Rockford plaintiffs agreed to a limited plan that increased choice and opportunity for minority students within a less-tracked system.

San Jose presented none of Rockford's watershed events—just the steady opposition of a conglomeration of people, events, and goals at odds with the detracking policy. San Jose's district leadership abandoned its commitment to making detracking work educationally, and instead focused its energy on gaining a release from court jurisdiction. The district's pursuit of "unitary status" was confusing to community members with whom I spoke, people who had initially believed that the district was working in good faith toward true racial integration. To achieve the goal of unitary status, the district leadership knew that it must convince the court that the district had remedied its past discrimination—and, as a practical matter, that it had complied with the provisions of the consent decree. Consequently, the leadership's goal became compliance with legalistic provisions rather than the successful implementation of the reforms set forth in those provisions. As one community member explained:

> The provisions of the consent decree are met almost mechanically to the extent that their first priority is cover your ass, write everything up, and try to justify everything on paper. I don't see a spirit of working to try to make this thing work, or a spirit in which the district is

persuaded that these provisions actually make educational sense and are good for the district. . . . [Nor do I see the district willing] to go out and sell them to the community, and defend them, and promote them, and show that this can succeed.

This phenomenon is a form of goal displacement (Wise, 1977). The detracking reform was included in the consent decree to improve the quality of education for the district's Latino students who had previously been discriminatorily placed in lower tracks. While many in the district leadership may have initially empathized with this aim, most eventually tempered their goals and refocused on merely convincing the court that the district was in compliance with the order. Successful detracking requires a serious struggle with pre-existing normative and political beliefs, as well as comprehensive changes in school and classroom practice. Perhaps because confronting such norms and politics is a messy process that exposes racial, ethnic, and class divisions, San Jose's implementors appear to have sought refuge in the letter of the decree to avoid having to grapple with these contentious issues. They made sure that district students were randomly assigned to classrooms at the beginning of each term, but they did not seem to have made any serious attempts to address the more complicated issues that come with heterogeneous grouping.

As in Rockford, the plaintiffs in San Jose took note of the various forces at work, including a district court judge with little enthusiasm for the case, and agreed to a series of modifications to the court order, temporarily staving off an order granting the district its release from court supervision. These compromises, combined with the district's questionable commitment to the goals of detracking, resulted in detracking on a reduced scale and with limited fidelity to the initial intentions.

WOODLAND HILLS

While subject to many of the same forces as were present in Rockford and San Jose, Woodland Hills remained truer to its detracking goals. Yet this district, too, compromised in its pursuit of those goals. In much the same way that court-ordered funding from the Commonwealth had eased the financial burden of the reforms, the district offered its own inducements to ease the normative, political, and pedagogical pain felt by resistant parents. These parents perceived the loss of the advanced English track as a direct blow to their children. Primarily through the creation of more advanced placement classes, and secondarily through its gifted programs, the district assured these parents that the schools would still provide something special for high academic achievers.

Before the English detracking, the high school offered only one AP English class—in the 12th grade. After the detracking, the AP offerings expanded to 10 classes: 5 for the 12th graders and 5 new classes for 11th graders! The high school essentially tranformed the AP courses into an upper track for 11th and 12th graders. As one of the high school English teachers explained, "there was an immediate flight, [with] everyone trying to go into AP." He outlined the numbers:

> At the 11th grade level last year, we okayed I believe 68 students who we felt like could get in there based on their grades and their writing folders and everything else. We ended up with 124 at the beginning of the year. In the 12th grade we okayed only 48; we ended up with 95. . . . I think nationwide, 2% of the kids are involved in the AP programs. At Woodland Hills, we were approaching 20%, and [many of] these kids could not compete on the national exam.

This teacher made no effort to hide the reason for this overwhelming interest in the AP courses. He acknowledged a "perception out there in the community [that] you have to get into the AP to shelter yourself from an inferior English class." A second English teacher concurred that many parents were "afraid of what's in that regular English class and . . . want [their children] in the AP class, even though they technically don't belong there."

Ironically, by accommodating the wishes of students and parents to enroll in the AP classes, the high school may have created the very problem parents feared: inferior heterogeneous classes. The school maintained smaller class sizes for the AP courses, which had the effect of increasing class sizes for the detracked classes. Moreover, the AP courses siphoned many higher-achieving students away from the mixed-ability classes, causing the assortment of students remaining in these detracked classes to resemble the old lower track.

Many English teachers perceived an over-enrollment in AP and argued that the school should maintain only one or two AP classes. Three-fifths of the students taking AP, one such teacher calculated, belonged in the regular class:

> A lot of these students didn't meet the cut off, the criteria. But it just takes parents to say, "well, now, I want my son or daughter in AP," and they're in. . . . Parents will call, raise a fuss, [and] the student's let in. [I]t's frustrating as far as the caliber of the real student who belongs in there because what that does is it affects, then, the regular classes. . . . So that if half of these students belong in regular English, and if they truly were in regular English, then those regular English classes would be much stronger than what they are. But they're not there.

Another English teacher agreed: "What this has done is the bulk of the students who are very high achieving students, who are workers, have gone to AP. And those of us in what we call regular English have been left with in every class maybe four or five students that are really top-notch students." A third teacher complained that her English class amounted to nothing more than "a lower-track class with a couple of higher-track students thrown in." "It's a totally tracked class," she declared.

A related irony resulting from the AP expansion is that the expansion followed an equity-minded change in the AP enrollment criteria, which opened up the classes—at least for a probationary period—to any student desiring to enroll. The district had made this change in order to allow additional African-American students to take the more challenging courses. Although some African Americans did take advantage of this opportunity, the vast majority of the beneficiaries of the new criteria were White students who had formerly attended the advanced classes. Consequently, one reform (opening up AP admissions) undermined a second reform (detracking) by effectively creating a new high track.

Interestingly, AP teachers were among those disenchanted with the new set-up. The expanded AP enrollment, one said, made it difficult to maintain high expectations: "[Y]ou still keep them high, but these kids are struggling to meet them. [M]y worry is that eventually a watering down is going to occur because every year the AP students . . . get weaker and weaker."

The district had seen this ratcheting-up phenomenon before. As a long-time administrator explained, the district had historically used "classic tracking," but, over a period of years, it had eliminated the "basic" (remedial) track, moving those students into the "regular" track. When that happened, noted this administrator, the students in regular moved up to the "advanced" track: "everyone just moved up a notch." Finally, with the elimination of the "regular" track, resulting in those students moving up to the detracked class, the students in advanced began looking for a privileged shelter in the AP classes. This administrator sympathetically described the reaction of many White parents:

> So the parents from the more affluent [boroughs] are saying, "Wait a minute, why are you doing this? You're not giving our students an opportunity to . . . maintain the academic status, so to speak, of having their own gifted [advanced] class. You know, we want our children in with like and same children, rather than the heterogeneous grouping."

A math teacher similarly reported, "the parents feel if you drop the basic track, then your middle track becomes closer to your basic track, and they want their students, their kids, in the upper one and they will basically push them into it."

Many such parents, observed another administrator, enter into a bargain with themselves about sending their children to district schools. He articulated that logic as follows:

> "I will gut out the first 6 years of elementary school, where my child's
> in a classroom with Black kids. I'll gut that out because I know when
> I get to junior high and senior high my kid, through core scheduling
> or whatever, can get away from those kids." Or, "I [will] gut out ele-
> mentary school because my White child is gifted, and I know one day
> a week he will be pulled out."

These parents will not get too upset, this administrator continued, "as long as you're providing the supplemental learning opportunities, [the] small, groupie sort of things." In the high school, the AP courses provided this special inducement. In the elementary grades, the gifted program sufficed.[1] But, this administrator concluded, "at the junior high level, the problem is there's nowhere for these kids to go. There's nowhere for this kid to look a little smarter or look a little more special."

Notwithstanding the questionable rationale given by many students and parents for taking the AP classes, it had one positive result. The AP courses employed a more rigorous curriculum than had the old "advanced" class, so these students presented themselves with a challenge. One student admitted that he had enrolled the previous year in the 11th-grade AP class "pretty much" to avoid the detracked class. He also stated that he should not have been in that class. "But this year," he confirmed, "I'm doing a lot better." Students like this pushed themselves for the wrong reasons, but nonetheless benefited from the effort.[2]

Like the AP program, the gifted program grew from 1994–1997. However, unlike the AP program, this growth did not occur only in response to the detracking. Instead, it appears to have resulted primarily from the district's effort to diversify the program. (Recall that the district revised the criteria for entry into the program, adding factors such as race, ethnicity, and parents' education.) The established gifted parents reacted negatively to the expansion. "[Y]ou had gifted parents who did not want their children in with students who [based on the old standards] did not qualify," observed one administrator, "all of a sudden our gifted parents were saying, 'What is the worth of the program when in fact you have to change it for them to get kids in there?' "

Nonetheless, despite the more recent entry of some African-American students into the gifted program, it remained a refuge for wealthy, White residents. In the Edgewood area, 74% of students joined the program! This astonishingly high percentage compares to a national average of just 6% (Shaver, 1997).[3] Parents of gifted-identified children, according to an administrator, "don't want to hear" about detracking: "They will never listen to it. They believe that their children are the cream of the crop and that they should be exposed to maybe something else that's better."

A student in the gifted program offered the contrasting argument—that benefits received by those in the gifted program should be available to all students. This African American argued that "everybody should have the option" to participate, since it required no "special skill for us to do the stuff that we're doing." An English teacher agreed:

> [W]e've created an elitist situation where certain kids are identified in second grade or wherever [and] get into the special group. And they have money [and] time. [H]ow much more money is spent on that child? [I]t's a great program, but the kids in the middle are not getting that same experience.

Notwithstanding such contentions, superintendent Young showed little willingness to slay or even injure the sacred cows—gifted and AP—of his most powerful constituents. He repeatedly denied rumors that the gifted program would be substantially modified or reduced, and he aggressively expanded the AP program, using this expansion to its fullest public relations potential. As noted above, the detracking efforts both benefited and suffered as a result of these inducements. They made the zone of mediation more receptive to detracking by placating some of the resistance. On the other hand, the AP courses in particular directly undermined the reform itself.

One of the presumptions of the zone model is that the issue (detracking) stays fixed in position, while the zone shifts in response to various forces. However, in some situations, such as that resulting from the addition of AP courses, the reforms shifts in addition to the zone. Interestingly, while the added force (the AP courses) moved the reform further into the heart of the zone—effectively making the zone more receptive to the reform—it simultaneously changed the nature of the effort. The district substituted "Detracking Effort A" with a scaled-down "Detracking Effort B."[4]

Part III

Making Mandates Matter

Making Mandates Matter

Notwithstanding enormous resistance and opposition, the mix of forces described in the previous chapters interacted to create more reform-friendly detracking zones in Rockford, San Jose and Woodland Hills. The dynamic interplay among a wide variety of forces resulted in constantly shifting zones of mediation, with a corresponding influence on the districts' detracking efforts. Although forces had initially combined in each of the districts to create an unreceptive zone, subsequently—with the addition of the court orders' unyielding force—they combined to create tentatively receptive zones. While it was not politically and normatively feasible earlier in the districts' histories, detracking became a viable reform option—even an urgent need. But powerful forces remained poised in each district to reinstate an unreceptive zone. These experiences demonstrate how barriers to equity-minded reform rise and fall and, potentially, rise again.

Part III explores the extent of the districts' detracking reforms, paying particular attention to the ongoing effects of oppositional forces. While these forces were unable to prevent the reforms in the face of court orders, they successfully modified and minimized them, thus hampering the drive toward more equitable instruction. Yet real progress was made. Part III ends with an analysis of the reform process and the resulting changes, including a re-examination of the change literature in light of this study's data and findings.

13

Change and Constancy

Reforms like the ones in Woodland Hills, Rockford, and San Jose do not exist as controlled experiments. In trying to determine the impact of a court mandate to detrack, one cannot compare it to a parallel district with no such mandate. The pre-mandate district, and the trends in place at that time, provides the only available comparison. That is, one can survey the district's changes and can engage in informed speculation as to whether those changes would have occurred in the absence of the mandate.

This chapter examines five types of change that took place in the Woodland Hills School District: the actual extent of detracking and classroom desegregation, expectations for student achievement, instructional methods, the written curriculum, and the supplemental and supportive programs. The role of the district's in-service programs, which fostered some of these changes, will also be discussed.

DETRACKING AND CLASSROOM DESEGREGATION

District leaders offered a variety of explanations for the decision to pursue detracking. Some ascribed it entirely to the court. Some cited the educational benefits of heterogeneous grouping. Some pointed to the segregative problems with tracking. And some alluded to moral considerations: "[Y]ou're playing God with kids and saying, 'I look at you, and I think you can make the cut; and I look at you, and I think you can't make the cut; and we're just not going to deal with you.' " An observer offered the additional speculation that detracking appealed to the administration as a "goodwill gesture, [adding] credibility to

199

the assertion that tracking was not practiced here." But this person also noted the "primary appeal" of detracking—that "it reflected [a] more cutting edge kind of thinking . . . [that] all children should have high standards."

Whatever its rationale, the district definitely reduced its use of tracking. Social studies detracked without incident. In mathematics, while a good deal of stratification remained, several lower-level high school courses, such as "Basic Geometry" and "Introduction to Algebra," were eliminated.[1] Extracurricular activities, such as sports teams and clubs, adopted no-cut policies, resulting in greater desegregation. While Science courses had not yet been detracked, some leaders stated that the district planned to do so in the future. Finally, as discussed earlier, the district detracked Language Arts from 7th through 10th grades.[2]

In addition to this detracking at the secondary level, the district made efforts to group elementary-level children heterogeneously. These elementary school reforms engendered little resistance from parents and teachers; resisters concentrated their energies on the secondary-level English detracking.

English Detracking

English detracking in Woodland Hills met with mixed reactions and mixed success. A secondary school principal remarked that teachers brought "a lot of attitude [and complaints] to the classroom that . . . definitely stood in the way of some student achievement." This principal also maintained that teachers tried to teach the mixed-ability classrooms "in a similar fashion" to the way they taught their classes in the past: "They didn't make an adjustment."[3] Nonetheless, as a board member reasoned, "you don't throw [away reforms] because you have a teacher [who] is not teaching the curriculum as written." And other teachers had greater success. Another secondary principal felt encouraged: "I see a lot of traditionalists admitting that some of these things are really working. [S]o I do see change in that respect." Teachers, too, acknowledged that they "see some real benefits occurring for the regular students, because [they are] expected to do more; I think in many ways they're progressing." Said another, "some of the lower-level students [are] probably getting exposed to things that they would never get exposed to."

One teacher gave the example of "Sally," a junior high African-American student who had formerly struggled in the lower-track English class but began achieving in the mixed-ability classroom. "Somehow," she said, "I'm reaching Sally in that class." Such successes made "everything I'm doing . . . worthwhile," she concluded. An African-American parent offered the example of her own son: "[W]hen my child first went into [the detracked] English course, it was a struggle for him." His old lower-track class had not prepared him for the more challenging work—"the amount of reading, the critical thinking, the analyzing"—in the mixed-ability class. Instead, the lower-track class taught "a lot of grammar—verbs, subjects, run-on sentences."

> I had to get a tutor for him. . . . But it's turned out to be healthy because he has really progressed, better than I thought that he would. [H]e's working more independently. . . . The [detracking] was an asset for my son. [The classes] became more challenging.

As a result, she concluded, her son produced higher quality work, which, in turn, built up his self-esteem. This parent admitted that she had initially thought the superintendent "was setting our children up for failure again." But she expressed pleasure with the reform's progress.

When I concluded my study, the detracking process was still at an early stage, and many district educators focused on such positive signs of things to come. As a top administrator commented, "progress here has been three steps forward, two steps back, but we're making progress." The district expected, and acknowledged the need for, continuing improvement.

Teachers noted some evidence of that improvement by the second year. They began "adapting," observed a high school English teacher. A junior high English teacher similarly noted that the second year proceeded more smoothly "because I'm teaching the same things that I taught last year, [and] I have a mastery [of] the material." As a result, she said, "I don't have to do as much prep work [and] have a little bit more time to maybe think about some creative ways [to] meet everybody's needs."

Another junior high teacher declared that she saw a change in the students, compared to the reform's first year:

> Last year, the kids who had come from the basic [classes] were still acting out and pretty disruptive in the class. [They still wanted] to be spoon-fed everything, expecting everything to be done in one period—which [is the way it] had been in the past—and that's why it took so long. But this year, with the two groups together, now in their second year of being together, [they are all doing much better].

This teacher also pointed to the adjustment made by the former high-track students to their new classmates: "As the year progressed, they began to recognize that these other students were in fact human beings, and we worked through projects and portfolios. By the end of the year, we were working much better together."

Other teachers reported less progress. "I don't see much success with my slower kids. I don't see them pushing themselves any harder [outside the classroom]," lamented one. Another volunteered, "I don't know if detracking is good because a kid knows [when] he doesn't know [something]," and he knows that the other students are aware of his ignorance, "[s]o they'll turn around and call each other dumb; that's what they do."

Detracking's success largely depends on teacher attitudes, expectations and effort, so these judgments can become self-fulfilling. A junior high educator noted the importance of teacher support:

> Some of . . . the lower-functioning kids . . . who have not traditionally had to do a lot of the challenging material [and] are not used to doing a lot of writing and a lot of critical thinking, have said this is really hard, and some of them kind of give up unless they're really pushed.

An African-American community member also mentioned the need for that extra push. He protested that detracking would not work without teachers' active assistance, and some teachers, he cautioned, "are just not going to put out to help a [struggling] student." Without that help, he continued, "you've got some students who are just totally lost and trying to achieve, but, yet, at the same time it destroys their urge to achieve."

Like the teachers, the district's students provided a mixed perspective. For example, a White high school student, who had formerly attended the advanced classes and now attended the AP English class, strongly opposed detracking. "You can't force that on a kid," she said, "If that kid doesn't want to learn, you can't say, 'You're gonna learn.' You cannot make someone learn." She continued:

> [With] the three-track system, you can kind of fit everybody's needs better, because not all students are up here, but they're not all down here, either. And, like, if you get below a "C", you have to go from way up here to down here. What good does that do? If there was a middle ground, [then a] student who couldn't make the "C" in the AP class . . . could probably get a "B" or an "A" in the advanced, [but if she is] down in the lower class, [she's] gonna probably [receive] straight hundreds.

In contrast, an African-American high school student, who had formerly attended the advanced classes and had then been placed in the detracked class, took the change in stride. Comparing Advanced with detracked English, she remarked, "It wasn't really different for me. I think for . . . people that were in regular English, it was probably a little bit harder. But for [those of us who came from the Advanced classes,] it was basically the same. It was just the same kind of English that we were doing before; [there] wasn't a big difference." She insisted that "[b]asically, [none of the students] really cared about how there was only going to be one [class]."[4]

Many teachers suggested that detracking had a detrimental impact on the so-called "advanced students." One such teacher identified "advanced kids who literally say, 'Why should I do anything extra if nobody else has to?' They just want to do what they have to do to get their 'A' and that's it." Agreed another, "what has happened here in the last 2 years is our better students now realize that they have to do very little to get that 'A'."

A third teacher explained that many students who had taken the advanced class "did not like being put back in a regular class [and] were not happy campers." They feared that "these other students were going to hold them back." The teacher also mentioned the desire of some "advanced" students to associate with their "cliques."

Integrated English

The third English track for 11th and 12th graders (along with AP and "de-tracked" English) was "Integrated English."[5] Supporters described this class as "dedicated to students . . . going out into the business world." Said a top administrator:

> We took our regular language arts course (11th and 12th grade) and we infused some job skills kinds of things with the literature that we already have. . . . And we told the counselors, now, some of your vo-cational kids . . . really should be in this course.

"It's career-oriented English—vocational and technical English—and it doesn't ignore literature, by the way, because they still do some of that as well," extolled a teacher. It provided "a separate, . . . very practical, . . . curriculum," said another, for "the kids who are going straight into the workplace or straight to a technical school—who are not particularly interested in college."

Students in Integrated English, according to this second teacher, com-prised "not as diverse" a group as the regular English classes. A third English teacher noted that Integrated English "is offered as the 'other' English course and, . . . when you read the description of it, it sounds like a good course." It was intended, she continued, for students interested in vocational education, and the students were "supposed to [read] the regular 11th-grade literature."

But in many ways the focus became remedial. Instead of simply reading the literature, for example, the students first listened to it on tape and then read it. "You have to do [that]," explained a teacher, "because they are poor readers—which [is] essentially the bottom line of that class—the thing that they have in common is they cannot read." Whatever the designers' intent, the classes contained "pretty much the lowest achievers" at each grade level; the students in the class had all done very poorly in their previous year's English class, according to an educator at the high school. "They say they don't have a dumping ground here, but they do," he concluded.

The rapid conversion of this apparently well-intentioned effort, ostensibly an opportunity for vocational students, into a low-track "dumping ground," offers some important lessons about curriculum differentiation. In some ways, the intended vocational emphasis did take hold. Most of the students viewed themselves as vocationally bound, and some had already begun pursuing vocational goals. Moreover, the teachers infused the curriculum with more technical and business writing than was found in the mainstream course. However, the classes' enrollment lacked academic diversity. The teachers, confronted with classrooms filled with low academic achievers, faced the same hurdles as the teachers of the former low-track English classes. Instead of maintaining high expectations focused on preparing students for success in a vocational or technical career, these teachers offered their students a less-challenging English curriculum.

Even one of the course's strongest supporters acknowledged a problem with achieving a larger and more diverse enrollment. "We have not been able to get students to involve themselves," he said regretfully, "we only have one class in the junior and one at the senior level, [and] we should have [many more than that enrolled]." "[S]omewhere along the line," he continued, "we did not sell it to the students, we didn't sell it to guidance, we didn't sell it to the community, and I'd like to see a renewed effort there. Because, originally, our plans were to take [the course] clear down to the ninth grade."

Another educator also pointed to a breakdown at the guidance counselor level, but he offered a less positive critique. He accused the school of "shoveling" the course's true low-track nature "under the carpet." "The counselors," he said,

> don't understand the course, [and] they don't really push the course. They only offer it if they think a student has difficulty in English and it might be for them an easier course. They even say this is an easier course, so again [everyone's] expectations are lower.

Consequently, the course's composition determined its essence. When the district and school conceived of it, they envisioned a broad cross-section of business- and vocation-minded students learning the same core material as their college-bound colleagues, but with a practical emphasis. But counselors and others came to view it merely as an easier course—a substitute for the former "regular" English. The enrollment reflected those perceptions, and low expectations and a less challenging curriculum followed.

Science Tracking

Secondary science courses presented the most obvious example of on-going tracking.[6] Recall from the earlier discussion of the district's symbols that the leadership renamed the science courses but retained their stratification. (Please refer to Appendix 6 for a rough outline of the district's science offerings.) A principal defended a degree of sorting students, explaining that the schools must sometimes "segregate [children] on secondary levels academically because we plan for children to succeed, not for children to fail." He reasoned that the schools should not allow a child to take courses that are too difficult: "[D]oes it make sense for [an unprepared] child to be placed in an environment where he's not going to succeed? . . . I think that's a legitimate question."

About half the ninth-grade students enrolled in Physical Science, the other half in Biology with Lab. Notwithstanding this even division, teachers called Biology with Lab the "premier class" while remarking that the "general population" enrolled in Physical Science. At the same time, commented a principal at one of the junior highs, "for some reason, we have some pretty good students in Physical Science."

Most educators acknowledged the basic stratification between the two courses. A Physical Science teacher declared that many ninth graders selected Physical Science as an "easy way through." The "higher achievers," he said, took the Biology with Lab class, leaving the ones with limited "mental capabilities upstairs" in the Physical Science course. He described the latter students as not having the ability to "hold on to [a lesson] even if they were taught it, and then—if they were taught it—they have a hard time understanding it. . . . They just can't put all that together."

Students' placements in science classes depended on previous grades and teacher recommendations. The school put a recommended class on each student's tentative schedule, but the student and the student's parent could opt to reject the placement. An eighth-grade science teacher explained the process as follows:

> I go through the whole list myself. [S]ome are [easy: the] straight 'A' students. That's who should go in there. [T]hen you go to the 'B' students. And then you have some 'C' students who have worked real hard and [are] doing the best they can and they; they're also selected. [T]he last decision, [however,] is made by the Biology teacher. I just give him my list, and he may ask me about a certain student, and I [will say whether I] feel they can make it or not.

In addition, although the schools did not strictly enforce them, the science classes had mathematics prerequisites. Students' math placements varied

206 MAKING MANDATES MATTER

tremendously, with some taking Algebra in the seventh grade while others waited until ninth grade. This variation mirrored the students' "intellectual capacity," explained a principal. A counselor described the math prerequisites as an "expectation" that, for example, students taking Biology with Lab in the ninth grade will also take Geometry, "even though there's no geometry in Biology." This Geometry expectation, she explained, looked "ahead to the Academic Chem, where there is Algebra II, which is the subsequent math course."[7] A science teacher, however, disputed the necessity of this requirement. Even students in the more advanced Chemistry class need not have any particular math background—just "algebra percentages," he asserted.

Whatever the argument's legitimacy, educators repeatedly offered varying mathematics abilities as a rationale for maintaining the two-track science system. For instance, one explained, the regular Chemistry course provided "a solid Chem course to a kid who may not be able to succeed with his math skills" in the advanced course. "This way," continued this science teacher, "we can really broad-base him, and every single student at Woodland Hills could pass a Chemistry course." As with the "Integrated English" course, the school designed the lower-level Science courses' curricula to be more "practical:"

In a regular Chemistry course, we balance equations, but it's not hit as hard, because, let's face it, [that kind of information] is not something that you would probably need in everyday life. But you should know . . . a lot more about the chemistry of the food, and . . . photography, that kind of thing. So, the information and the priorities of the information [are] a little bit different.

One can draw another comparison to the Integrated English experience: the sorting of students undermined the intention of maintaining high expectations for all courses. The Physical Science teachers acknowledged having lower expectations for those classes. The "bad students," one such teacher explained, made the Physical Science classes "more of a challenge to teach." He explained that he used more demonstrations and participatory (yet superficial), eye-catching activities to hold students' attention, while cutting back on the substantive material. Again, whatever the district's original intentions towards these courses, the classrooms' composition determined their essence.

A single appraisal cannot comprehensively and fairly characterize the progress of detracking in Woodland Hills. Much changed, and many students benefited. At the same time, compromises and shortcomings subverted the reform's ultimate success. Consequently, students in courses such as Integrated English and Physical Science continued to receive a less-challenging curriculum, while students in the nominally "detracked" 11th and 12th grade English found themselves back in an environment closely resembling the former "regular" English.[8] Other students, particularly those in the detracked 7th–10th grade English who had formerly been low-tracked, generally found higher expectations and more challenging instruction.

Moreover, classroom segregation decreased substantially. Under the old system, the advanced classes consisted almost entirely of White students, while African-American students languished in the low-track classes. While similar problems continued in the expanded AP program and in some of the higher-level electives, the situation nonetheless was greatly improved. As a district administrator justifiably boasted, the reforms provided "opportunities [to] a lot of African-American students [who] would have never thought that there was life for them beyond high school."

TEACHERS' EXPECTATIONS FOR STUDENTS

Along with the structural detracking reform came a degree of normative reform. Some teachers, witnessing success from formerly low-tracked students, began to raise their expectations. Discussing a girl who had previously attended the lower-level reading course, one teacher observed that while she might receive a lower grade in the mixed-ability class, "I think really she'll come out of this one better . . . because she's being exposed to some higher-level things and with a little more difficulty." Another teacher explained that she tried to keep her expectations high for her heterogeneous 12th-grade English class: "My attitude toward [detracked English is] I ask them on day one, 'how many of you are going to college?' Eighty percent of those hands go up, [so] I'm teaching a college-preparatory course." Many of these students might delay entering college for a couple of years, she said, but that does not justify watering down the curriculum. She added that with patience and support, the students "can get Shakespeare [and] Canterbury Tales. . . . They can get through it."

Her colleague agreed, stressing the importance of not compromising, even if she felt sympathy for the student:

> I've seen kids who came to me, for example, with low grades, and they say they are not very good in English, and I say that doesn't mean you can't become better. And I push and I push, and I've said, "Do you need help? I'll meet you on my prep break. You need help, I'll give you my lunch period, I'll stay after school, I'll come early. But what I won't do is I won't give you a break. But I will help you."

A principal praised this type of approach, pointing to scholarly research concerning the importance of high expectations. She explained that children who have a low academic self-image can nevertheless achieve "[i]f you believe a child can do it, and you provide the type of support that a child needs." The children often did not expect challenges and high expectations, she concluded, but they could rise to the occasion.

Unfortunately, most Woodland Hills teachers did not appear to share these sentiments. They never accepted the normative tenets underlying detracking and reserved their high academic expectations for only some of their students. Said one:

> These kids won't do the work that I could have got out of kids 10 years ago. I think it's just the society. They don't push themselves. You still have kids that can do it, but there are fewer of them per class when you have just as many kids.

Because successful detracking hinges on these normative beliefs, the reform, at least in its initial stages, fell short of its goals.

CHANGED INSTRUCTIONAL METHODS

Instructional methods largely followed expectations. As a secondary school principal observed, some of the teachers with lower expectations "need to look at different strategies versus standing in front of the room and just talking." Another secondary school principal noted that his faculty "needs to [spend] some time on learning how to challenge." He remarked that they failed to pose questions "that will require thought or to gather data to formulate an answer." Instead, he said, their questions seek "short . . . one word answers that don't generate discussion . . . or challenge a student to think."

On the other hand, those teachers who maintained high expectations for all students designed lessons intended to challenge all students. For example, I observed a teacher in a seventh-grade heterogeneous English class who seemed constantly aware of each student's needs. She had assigned the students to write descriptive paragraphs, emphasizing "action verbs." When a high-achieving student finished early, the teacher approached her, read through the paragraph, and asked the student, "Can I challenge you?" The teacher then pointed out areas where the student could improve, and set her back to work.

Similarly, I observed a primary school teacher who immediately found demanding lessons for her "top student" once she had completed the basic coursework. This teacher described how she kept expectations high for this student, teaching skills and knowledge additional, but tangential, to the organized class activities. Another elementary school teacher described a district science program called "Assets." She stressed the program's "multi-abilities" and individualized design. One Asset module called for students to grow a flower and keep a journal about the experience. During this part of the project, some students wrote detailed accounts while others simply wrote, "the flower's growing." However, as part of that same module, students used frozen bees to pollinate the flowers. Even the "low learners," she reflected, will "write and write and write about pollinating: 'the bee was frozen, and I did this and then'—and they learn more in that four weeks [the module's duration]." At the same time,

> The brighter students [do] graphing. They write everything down. I have them make rulers with centimeters. . . . It frustrates the lower ones. But the brighter ones do it, and when the lower ones see it they learn it from them. They'll say, "Oh, that's a centimeter."

These types of assignments challenged every student. They did not—as some detractors of the reform alleged—treat all students in the mixed-ability classes as if they were identical. Instead, through creative lessons, everyone in the classroom could thrive. Carol Tomlinson (1995) explains that heterogeneous classes can challenge advanced learners if the curriculum is appropriately differentiated, utilizing techniques that allow students to make sense of information and ideas, to explore curriculum content, and to demonstrate what they have learned.

A junior high English teacher explained how she changed her teaching in the wake of detracking. For students who are "a little bit above," she said, "you give them either something critical or creative to do above and beyond, and they'll get graded accordingly." This approach does not quite meet Tomlinson's standards for an appropriately differentiated curriculum, but it does demonstrate movement toward those standards. This teacher went on to tell me that, for those students who experience difficulty, "you need to get them into small group[s] and maybe show them examples and spend some time with them." The classroom's mixed-ability nature demands these new techniques: "Those were things that I never did before. I mean I had them lined up like ducks [before]."

A high school science teacher, who earlier in her career had taught only high-track classes, explained that the district laid her off and, when it recalled her, she found herself confronted with "what they referred to as 'sleaze bally' courses—courses that had the roughest kids." She found that her former teaching methods no longer worked. "You can not stand up there and lecture to these kids," she explained, "because they weren't going to listen:"

> I suddenly realized—all these years I thought I was a helluva teacher—and I just realized I really had just great students, and the

real teachers are the ones that are down in the trenches. To [involve] a class of twenty-four kids [who] are not slightly interested in what you're doing is really what teaching is about.

So she re-tooled and changed her instructional methods, focusing on maintaining several consecutive, ongoing activities. Other secondary science teachers, she said, need to begin "decreasing the emphasis on lecture and increasing the emphasis on science as a process, not as a collection of facts." "[S]ome of them, [but] not all of them," she reflected, "are actually doing it."[9]

The more successful English teachers described a variety of methods that they found useful for teaching heterogeneous classes. They mentioned cooperative learning most often, also citing such techniques as portfolio-based assessment and oral expression (class participation). The following comment, from a high school teacher, represented most:

Class participation helps the lesser-able students. . . . A lot of group work, call it cooperative learning if you want, a lot of group work, oral presentations and group presentations. . . . Many, many times they love to get up in front of classes and give presentations. . . . Portfolio work, I think, helps the weaker student. My weakest student will put together a portfolio for me.

Another high school teacher noted the need to vary activities between such exercises as writing, art, and oral expression "to have enough activities so that everyone can get some success. [T]hat's just very important."

Consistent with such goals, the English department committed itself to using portfolio-based assessment, and most teachers appeared supportive. The district's portfolio structure included four different categories: a reflective essay, reading, writing, and listening. One teacher explained that portfolio assessment challenges all students and allows low-achievers to succeed:

There's an ownership in a portfolio that doesn't always exist in other types of assignments that you give. [T]hey have to talk about themselves, their strengths and weaknesses as a speaker, a listener, a writer and a reader, and they've never, ever done that before, and it's amazing to read them and . . . how honest they will be. [Some] will do well on a portfolio [who] I know . . . would have failed a department midterm and final exam.

These teachers also emphasized, however, that portfolios constituted a "much more demanding" means of assessment than tests. "[S]tudents here do not take mid-terms and final exams seriously," stated one, but they "have to care [about] this portfolio because there's so many steps, so many things they have to do to put it all together. There's no fluffing it off." (For a discussion of a less earnest student response to project-based learning, see McQuillan, 1998).

The transition to cooperative learning, as discussed earlier, was also a struggle for many teachers. While some teachers and classes thrived, others toiled unsuccessfully to find an effective formula. Teachers experienced a similar mixture of success and struggle with each of these new instructional methods. Some had little or no difficulty, some struggled, and some never tried. Accordingly, the instructional methods used by district teachers did evolve to become more appropriate for heterogeneously grouped classrooms. But much room for continued improvement remained.

CURRICULAR REFORM

In 1993, the American Association of School Administrators conducted a court-ordered audit of the district's curriculum (AASA, 1993a, 1993b). The audit concluded, among other things, that the district lacked alignment between its written, taught, and tested curriculum. It declared most courses' curricula inadequate and recommended a systematic revision. The district therefore began a 6-year process of curriculum revision, undertaken as a cooperative effort of faculty, staff, parents, community members, and administrators. By the time of my study (1996–1997), they had completed work on the elementary curriculum as well as some courses at the secondary level, totaling 61 published curriculum guides.

The district's detracking efforts, while not the primary focus of the curriculum revisions, were reflected in some of the suggested activities for extensions, second efforts, and multiculturalism. A curriculum coordinator reported:

> There are a lot of support materials that help the teachers implement the strategies that they want to use, [such as] good ideas for oral activities, good ideas for cooperative learning activities, good ideas for different types of writing. . . . I think the materials have gone a long way to help the teachers implement whatever strategies they want to use.

Because teachers were integrally involved in the writing of the new guides, they by and large welcomed the finished product. An intermediate school teacher stressed the curriculum's noticeable improvement: "It's 100% better than it was when I started here."

A mid-course post-audit conducted by the International Curriculum Management Audit Center (ICMAC), the successor to the AASA audit department, declared that the district had "energetically undertaken the ongoing process of reviewing curriculum and rewriting curriculum guides" (ICMAC, 1997, p. 41), and declared that the revised curriculum improved upon the old curriculum. Thus, as with the issues of detracking, expectations of students, and instructional methods, the written curriculum improved substantially as a result of the district's reform efforts.

PROGRAMS

The COIP budget funded a variety of programs designed to provide students with academic support. The district offered some of these programs to all students, while others were targeted at students with specific needs.

The most extensive of these programs, in terms of both expense and number of students reached, was called "HOTS" (Higher Order Thinking Skills). Every fourth, fifth, or sixth grader who scored less than 50% on either the math or reading sections of the Iowa Test of Basic Skills (and could show potential for working at or above grade level[10]) could participate in HOTS. Each of the district's three intermediate schools maintained a HOTS classroom—essentially a computer room divided into three sections. In each section, students could work on a separate project. The lab had software focusing on math, logic, geography, and reading. Teachers helped students with writing and the use of word processors, and also coordinated open-ended small group discussions. Through a focus on thinking and social interaction, rather than drill, practice, and memorization, the program aimed to develop the higher-order thinking skills needed to succeed in heterogeneous secondary-school classes.

When I observed the HOTS classrooms, the students, temporarily pulled out of their regular classrooms, displayed a great deal of interest in their tasks. Some wrote stories and some worked on educational puzzles and games, but all were cultivating meaningful skills. The intermediate school principals wholeheartedly endorsed the program, using such accolades as "tremendous," "very worthwhile," and "top-notch." But other people were less supportive of the program, pointing to the cost: it served about 600 students per year for approximately $900,000. One such skeptic reasoned, "this is great, but if we had to do this with our own money [rather than COIP money] there's no way we could do this." Even a HOTS defender acknowledged that "it's hard to say" if the program could survive the ending of COIP funding. He speculated that the program "probably would change [and] be condensed." He concluded that HOTS "would go slowly, but it would go."

Members of the "Citizens for Quality Education" (CQE) parent group (discussed earlier) also opposed HOTS. According to an African-American parent who had met with the CQE group, these White parents opposed the idea of teaching study skills: "It seems like anything that's added extra, they're against that. But like I always tell them, our children need those programs to bring them up to speed."

Another such program, Reading Recovery, targeted first through third graders identified by their teachers as needing substantial reading assistance. Also funded through COIP, Reading Recovery provided a select group of at-risk youngsters with an intense learning experience. Every school day, the teachers gave each student a one-on-one 30-minute lesson. They read a new book every day.[11] At the end of 16–20 weeks, the student exits the program, hopefully reading at grade level.

Like HOTS, Reading Recovery drew considerable praise for its success with students. Its 1996–1997 budget expanded from $39,000 to $113,000, and the program moved from just one primary school to all three. However, skeptics again questioned its cost. Each Reading Recovery teacher served only 8–12 students per year, making it three times as expensive as HOTS. The result, explained one observer, was that teachers viewed Reading Recovery as "a nice thing. It's great. [It] costs too goddam much, [and] it's too intense, [but it's] a great idea." This observer continued:

> I think [the district policy-makers] look at Reading Recovery and say, "what the hell's this got to do with desegregation? What the hell's this got to do with White versus Black?" [Do] you think these kids in the second or third grade that are getting Reading Recovery need it or are benefiting from it because of . . . the way they drew those lines 20 years ago?

In any case, according to a top district administrator, the cost of Reading Recovery made it "one that . . . would go quickly [following the end of court supervision]. Or it would [become] part of our Title I program."

Off-campus tutorial assistance constituted another sizable item in the COIP budget. While the program was available to students of all ages, abilities and backgrounds, it was housed at sites located primarily in the district's African-American neighborhoods. For the peer-tutorial program, the district hired secondary students (under the supervision of district teachers) to tutor younger students. The district also maintained a related after-school tutorial program at each of the three intermediate school sites.

Like HOTS and Reading Recovery, the tutorial programs drew praise from teachers and parents. An African-American parent, however, did complain that the district inadequately promoted the tutorials to parents and students. He felt that the district should work more closely with the African-American community to get the word out and identify students in need of help. A junior high counselor agreed that most struggling students never used after-school resources. Some White parents raised a different concern about the tutorials, arguing that the sites should be evenly dispersed throughout all communities, rather than concentrated in African-American neighborhoods.

Finally, the COIP budget funded Language Arts and Math Labs. Again, all students had access to these labs, but teachers and counselors identified specific students to use the labs during the school day (as a "study hall" course). At the high school, for example, teachers sent to the Math Lab those students who had received a "D" or "F" in math the previous year. Educators worked with these students to set and achieve designated goals. The students attended the Lab for a minimum of two periods a week.

In addition to the COIP programs, the district boasted a small Headstart program, serving 30 four-year-olds,[12] and a Title I program.[13] At the end of each school year, the elementary school educators identified those students not operating at their grade level and recommended them for Title I assistance the following year.

All these programs combined to form an impressive support system, particularly for students in the lower grades. According to top officials, the district planned to focus efforts on the younger students, thereby heading off problems in later years. In the meantime, they hoped that limited support for older students would provide an adequate safety net. In legal terms, this plan makes a great deal of sense: once the district has remedied the vestiges of discrimination for one age cohort, a court will be unreceptive to arguments that vestiges reappeared to hurt a later cohort. However, whether or not "vestiges" do reappear, the educational problems most likely will after the supportive programs described above are eliminated or reduced.

As a top district administrator confirmed, no political constituency ever developed for these programs other than their teachers, who never organized to protect them. Parental support never materialized because of the turnover rate among the children served by the programs. These programs, therefore, certainly resulted in change, but these changes—perhaps more than any others in the district—existed in monetary limbo.[14] When the court-ordered funding disappears, the programs may turn out to have made little lasting impact.

STAFF DEVELOPMENT

The Woodland Hills School District has been continually changing since its inception, and its leadership has looked to staff development to assist with these changes. In the 10 years preceding my study, the district furnished more than 30 in-services and more than 25 after-school or summer staff development opportunities (MESA Associates, 1997b). Yet, as was briefly discussed in Chapter Eleven, the teacher response was not positive. When asked about staff development, most teachers rolled their eyes (some literally, some figuratively) and protested, "We've been in-serviced to death!"

The COIP budget funded approximately four days of in-service training annually per teacher. According to a recent study by the district Evaluator, most of this training did not relate in any way to classroom instructional strategies or to teaching a diverse classroom. More importantly, after reviewing the records of these in-services and conducting some supplemental interviews, the Evaluator concluded, "The evidence reviewed suggests that many teachers did not receive (or accept) effective levels of District-sponsored training and support in the implementation of cooperative learning, heterogeneous instruction, and the use of multicultural curricula."

Amplifying this problem, the teachers who avoided the in-services may well have needed them more than those who attended. One educator noted that these absent teachers "are not strong [and] have been around a long time." He surmised, however, that in-servicing would not help them anyway. A long-time principal in the district confirmed this dilemma:

> I'm workshopped and in-serviced out, and in-service programs are not the answer. It looks good on paper, and it pleases the courts, but that's not the answer. We can have all the speakers we want. But if you look in the audience at an in-service program, you see people reading newspapers, knitting and complaining. Teachers are getting paid $250 to sit there and listen to someone and complain. So workshops aren't the answer (Miller, 1991, p. 85–6).

The district's most extensive staff-development effort aimed at detracking brought several teachers to Woodland Hills from a neighboring district, Fox Chapel, that had recently voluntarily detracked.[15] The visitors presented a 3-day workshop in the summer of 1995, principally focused on effective strategies for heterogeneous classrooms. But, pointing to Fox Chapel's wealthy, White, non-diverse student body, Woodland Hills teachers gave their suggestions little credibility. Moreover, Woodland Hills did not follow-up on the Fox Chapel training by continuing to offer in-services about instruction in a heterogeneous class. Instead, most subsequent staff development focused on "classroom management" issues.

Several teachers I spoke with contended that part of the problem was a resentment of outsider in-service trainers. One cynically explained this resentment as follows: "The reason that the people on the hill [the district administrators] are bringing these people in [to conduct in-services] is because to keep their jobs they have to justify that the staff here is incompetent." This teacher contended that each year the administrators "pick some topic — say, oh, our faculty just can't make tests [or] our faculty can't deal with

minorities" — and force teachers to sit through the workshops. These outsiders have "been told that the teachers are terrible," he asserted, "That's why
they're brought in, right? The assumption [behind our need for] professional
development is that we're no good, right? I mean, why else would you bring
people in?" While most teachers did not join this one in perceiving staff development as an insult or an attack, neither did they perceive it as helpful.
They began each new staff development with a presumption (perhaps re-
buttable) that it will waste their time.

In any case, Woodland Hills' staff-development activities were not designed to help educators think critically about their normative beliefs concerning race, intelligence, and behavior. Addressing these normative areas
presents a real challenge for this and other districts. The level of success for
their detracking efforts largely hinges on such a critical examination.

CONCLUSION

In the wake of the Woodland Hills court order, the district's schools experienced substantial change in at least five areas: detracking and classroom desegregation, expectations for student achievement, instructional methods, the
written curriculum, and supplemental and supportive programs. But the
change in all these areas was less than that intended or desired by the court
and by others pushing for reform. The following two chapters attempt to make
sense, from the perspective of the policy-maker, of this tension between
change and constancy.

14

Reform and Opposition
in Perspective

The schools in Woodland Hills, Rockford, and San Jose changed. They changed as a result of a court order. And they changed to the general advantage of the districts' African-American and Latino students.

Undoubtedly, they could have changed more, producing more benefits for these minority students. But the fact remains that dedicated people in these districts spent years struggling to improve the schools and, as a result, they became better places for low-income students and students of color.

WOODLAND HILLS

For Woodland Hills' more advantaged students, who had formerly enrolled in the higher-tracked classes, detracking brought mixed blessings. On the one hand, some teachers responded to the challenge presented by heterogeneous classes by reforming their instructional methods. All students in their classrooms saw a greater use of authentic instruction (and assessment) and more lessons designed to develop higher-order thinking. On the other hand, some teachers made insufficient changes, or none at all, to adapt to the new classes. Although the quantitative results reported in Chapter Four indicated that detracking did not present a significant overall disadvantage to the formerly high-track students, such educational harm may have been experienced by these students if they were placed in detracked classrooms with lesser-skilled or resistant teachers.

Interestingly, only one opponent of detracking with whom I spoke acknowledged that many, probably most, of these unsuccessful teachers had also experienced little success under the former, tracked system. This opponent, a White parent, described these teachers as "set in a rut, back in whatever year they started. . . . They use the same dittos that they used then."[1]

Detracking exposed such weaknesses in two ways. First, while the unsuccessful teachers had never taught much in the way of higher-order thinking skills, they did pace their drill and memorization lessons at a rate appropriate to the tracked student body.[2] The switch to heterogeneous classes pulled that rug out from under them, leaving them pondering whether to "teach to the top" or water down the lessons and target them to the "middle" or the "bottom."

Second, and most importantly, detracking exposed more of the privileged students to these weaker teachers. Before detracking, these teachers had primarily taught the low tracks, and this system was effectively enforced by powerful parents. A secondary school principal noted that wealthy, White parents knew who the good teachers were and "scream[ed]" if the school placed their children with the weaker teachers. This principal noted that the most knowledgeable parents, who "have the highest socioeconomic level . . . will get the better teachers. [Yet the district will] allow those [weaker] teachers to stay there and . . . let the kids fall where they may . . . It is unfair." Another principal contended that this disparity arises because the "general kids" and their parents demand much less of their teachers:

> They don't go home and tell their parents, . . . "Yeah, all we did today was a worksheet. Yep. All we did today, again, was a worksheet." They're thrilled to do that. Their parents are thrilled that they're not in trouble. Their parents are thrilled that someone's keeping them there for 40 minutes. . . . If your child was in the college prep or academic, you would say to the child, "what did you do today?" Child might say, "I did a worksheet." That's okay. That'd be okay. If you came home the second day, "What did you do?" "I did a worksheet." Third day, "I did a worksheet." Now you're going to start to be concerned. "Do you read?" You will start asking him to tell things like that. Doesn't that make sense?

A high school teacher agreed. Less successful teachers had also accomplished little before detracking, he said, but "in the regular English classes, they were dealing with kids whose parents wouldn't complain that there were no standards. Now they are dealing with kids whose parents will complain when there are no standards."

The former situation was equally difficult from the perspective of those teachers saddled with the old low-track English classes. One called them "nightmare classes." Another recalled, "You could hardly get through anything because [the students] just wanted to come and fool around." One younger teacher, who clearly had difficulty managing disruptive students, said:

> The first 2 years I was in this Junior High I had the lower-track kids, and it was pure hell. . . . I was in tears twice a week. I mean it was absolutely horrendous. [Detracked classes are] better for me to do my job, because I only have maybe five or six discipline problems in a class, rather than a class of all discipline problems. [T]his is better than what I had before. This is definitely better.

What makes this last statement particularly interesting is that it came from a struggling teacher. Unlike many of her counterparts, however, this teacher showed a commitment to improving. Even when teaching a lower-tracked class, she refused to lower her expectations, and she became tremendously frustrated when unable to teach due to disruptions.

Other educators described the low-track classes' poor academic instruction. A top district administrator characterized the old regular English course as "mindless—synonyms, antonyms, drill, sentence structure." A principal admitted that teachers generally made "no attempt to teach the lower group." A teacher acknowledged, "we weren't doing what was right by [the low-tracked students]. I don't think we met their needs." And a school board member declared that she "could point out any number of pitfalls with the old system. The old system labeled children. The old system did not challenge."

An African-American parent recalled that teachers had miserably low expectations for students in the low-track English class. When students misbehaved or ignored their work, the teachers did nothing, since the students "act[ed] just the way they [expected], anyway." Detracking, she said, "put [these teachers] to the challenge." And some teachers began to meet that challenge; said one, "I see some real benefits occurring for the regular student because he's expected to do more. I think . . . in many ways they're progressing."

Thus most of the criticisms of detracked education were equally applicable, if not more so, to the prior, tracked system. Yet those involved in school change often find the limitations of a traditional system such as tracking to be less noticeable than the limitations of the revised system (mixed-ability classes). The best attempts to measure the effects of tracking conclude that tracked students (and this holds true for those in the high, medium, or low track) gain no achievement advantage over comparable non-tracked students—even without accounting for changes in instructional methods or curriculum (Slavin, 1990). The quantitative data from Woodland Hills, discussed in Chapter Four, support these conclusions.

Under either system, a district like Woodland Hills would contain inferior teachers. But the poor teaching became much more apparent to powerful constituencies when it was highlighted by detracking. The most vocal opponents of reform in the district campaigned for a return to tracking. They did not aim to improve instructional methods, but sought instead a return to the previously flawed system, their only concession being to call on the district to ensure non-discriminatory class placements. While these parents complained loudly about the poor instruction their own children purportedly received in detracked classes, they remained willing to foist similar instruction onto other children. The same can be said about classroom disruptions. Most teachers contended disruptions underwent an overall decrease following detracking, yet resistant White parents focused exclusively on a supposed increase compared to the old advanced classes.

Of course, some students who had previously enrolled in the advanced English track did receive inferior instruction (with more disruptions) in their new detracked classes. These students undoubtedly lost a privileged position. To the extent that their parents were upset about the decrease in the quality of their children's school experience, one might argue that their complaints were justified. But the resistance was also propelled by other, less legitimate issues. Parents objected to the withdrawal of status, the removal of a symbolic gold star of high-track ranking from their children's foreheads. These parents saw their own children as special, and they demanded something extra (see Wells & Serna, 1996). Other parents simply preferred the old advanced courses' racial and class make-up. They wanted their children to continue to associate with the wealthier, Whiter group.

Most, if not all, districts contain parents with similar attitudes (recall the earlier discussion of resistant parents in San Jose). In many such districts, these parents hold political sway as they did, for a long time, in Woodland Hills and its predecessor districts. And despite the court mandate, these parents maintained considerable influence. Nevertheless, the force of the mandate, superimposed upon many other forces in the district, shifted the zone dramatically, and real change ensued.

This change did not resolve all the district's problems—uneven teaching quality, for instance, continued to hamper many students' educational experiences. However, when compared with the district's former inequities, the change resulted in a general improvement for the entire student body as well as a targeted improvement for African Americans, the group of students who had most suffered in the past.

SAN JOSE AND ROCKFORD

This perspective also yields insight into the reforms implemented in San Jose and Rockford. The study of the San Jose Unified School District presented ample evidence to support the maxim that we cannot mandate what matters.

After all, the district leadership—after an initial period of enthusiasm for the Consent Decree described by one observer as a "love fest"—steadily reduced its commitment to the reforms' success, focusing instead on merely obtaining a grant of unitary status. However, since the issuance of the initial court order in 1985, the district participated in a variety of innovative reforms, including Henry Levin's Accelerated Schools and the College Board's Equity 2000. Even acknowledging their shortcomings, the district's schools and classrooms have indeed become more integrated, and remedial classes have been eliminated. The lawsuit and the resulting court order have empowered the formation of community groups with equity-minded missions. The awareness of many in the community has been raised concerning issues of equity and racial justice in the schools.

I had an interesting conversation with one San Jose teacher who—early in our discussion—indicated that her impression was that the court order had failed. As we talked, she mentioned a variety of programs and advances she had witnessed over the years. Near the end of the conversation, I asked her whether she thought those changes would have occurred without the lawsuit, and—seemingly surprised at her own answer—she said, "no." Most educators in the district, she explained, are not otherwise inclined to embark on these types of equity-minded activities. The court order, it turns out, did not fail. Rather, it failed to accomplish all that it theoretically could have done were it not for the many other forces pushing the zone in the opposite direction.

Reformers in Rockford began their efforts facing greater hurdles than those in either San Jose or Woodland Hills. The segregation there was more overt and the racial divisions more pronounced. From this perspective, in particular, Rockford has accomplished a great deal. While the district retains tracking, the lowest tracks are gone and the highest tracks are no longer reserved for White children. The tracks are also less rigid, allowing some upward movement. Thus, even in the environment of hostility to these reforms at the highest district levels in Rockford, the court forced real change.

15

Third-Order Change:
Modifying the Change Literature
as Applied to Equity-Minded Reform

THE BATTLE OVER CONTEXTUAL TURF

Every reform proceeds within a unique context. This context, represented in this book by the notion of the zone of mediation, is shaped by a myriad of forces. When forces are added, subtracted, strengthened or weakened, the zone shifts. With each shift, the zone becomes more receptive or more hostile to the reform. From this perspective, the reform process is a battle over contextual turf.

In contrast, change literature generally presents the school change process in terms of the technical aspects of schools' internal domains. The focus of this literature is on structural and resource needs and issues within the schools. When this literature addresses equity-minded reforms, it usually assumes that school systems will move on their own toward more equitable and efficacious pedagogies. Taking the optimistic if naive view that school systems are overwhelmingly composed of educators, school leaders, and parents who are committed to social justice, this literature recommends centralized assistance and/or prompting to help these people out with their bottom-up efforts. Such a view presupposes that, because racist beliefs are ostensibly at odds with basic American values, Americans will, if given the opportunity, naturally move away from their past racist practices. The naïveté of this view was argued by Hochschild (1984) 17 years ago and reconfirmed by the stories in this book, which call attention to the exceptional socio-political barriers that change agents encounter as they attempt to initiate and implement equity-minded school reforms. These stories highlight the need for research and theory to take better account of such barriers.

Some change literature does acknowledge the socio-political nature of the change process as well as the need to alter past assumptions and beliefs. This literature also points out that community support or resistance can play an important role in the initiation of an innovation (Fullan, 1991, 1999; Lipman, 1998; Sarason, 1982, 1990). Rarely, however, does this discussion move beyond a neutral analysis and into a discussion of the assumptions and beliefs that underlie community support or resistance and that serve to create and sustain inequitable practices. (The work of Pauline Lipman and Amy Wells offer two exceptions, and descriptive publications such as Wheelock (1992) are also helpful in laying the groundwork for advances in change theory.) Most literature has instead advocated that schools become learning organizations where teachers and administrators serve as "change agents," expert at dealing with change as a normal part of their work life (Fullan, 1994, 2000; Louis & Miles, 1990). This neutral focus overlooks more controversial aspects of schools and reform. The potential implications of such issues as race, class, and gender are not meaningfully discussed.

Consequently, the lessons educators learn from the change literature are overwhelmingly in the form of neutral—albeit essential—advice, for example that educators must see themselves as in the business of making improvements. As Fullan (1994) explains, to "make improvements in an ever changing world is to contend with and manage the forces of change on an ongoing basis" (p. 4). The neutrality of this advice is not particularly troubling when it is applied to such reforms as portfolio-based assessment or the introduction of new technology, reforms designed to benefit all students equally. However, equity-minded reforms are intended to benefit most directly those in less powerful positions within schools and communities; they almost always implicate issues of race and/or class. Accordingly, a neutral reform paradigm fails to adequately describe the equity-minded reform process.

Vincent Roscigno has raised similar concerns with what he calls the "structural" education literature. He accuses the literature of neglecting "the fact that what goes on in a given school or in a given classroom is embedded within a local social context that may itself vary with regard to the degree of racial antagonism and the level of political-economic opportunity available to whites and blacks" (Roscigno, 1995, pp. 144–145). Focusing on the process whereby teachers' expectations are formed, he asserts that "teacher attitudes and behaviors are shaped and often reinforced . . . by local race relations and racial ideologies embedded in the social organization of localities" (Roscigno, 1995, p. 145).

In earlier chapters, I explained that reformers face enormous challenges when seeking to achieve parity of opportunity across diverse groups of students. I identified a variety of social, political, historic, and economic forces that shape the process of introducing and implementing equity-minded change efforts. These forces play a huge role in the battle over contextual turf that determines the fate of a reform. Yet the scope of the existing change literature's consideration of that turf battle has been largely limited to technical and cultural issues. In this chapter, I offer a critique of the change literature, a critique grounded in a more comprehensive analysis of relevant forces. This expanded scope of included forces leads to a very different set of models and recommendations.

RECONCEPTUALIZING THE ROLE OF NORMS AND POLITICS

Part II of this book identifies forces as we tend to perceive them in our daily lives. Chapter Nine, for instance, identifies "resistant teachers" as a force. But such straightforward labels highlight only part of the story. To shed light on other important themes, the same forces can be broken down into the four dimensions discussed at the outset of Chapter Six: inertial, technical, political, and normative. This perspective is particularly useful given the dominant role played by norms and politics in the equity-minded change process. It also illustrates less straightforward forces, such as the normative and political forces identified in Chapters Ten and Eleven.

For reforms to be most successful, each of these four dimensions must be addressed. Reformers commonly begin by focusing on the technical dimension—which is fine. Detracking reformers, for instance, may devote considerable efforts to helping teachers develop knowledge and skills (e.g., cooperative learning) useful for teaching a heterogeneous class. Many detracking schools also adopt related reforms such as team teaching, common planning periods, or revised curricula. These reforms may very well shift the zone of mediation for the technical dimension (the "Technical Zone") to become favorable to detracking. But this is only one aspect of the school district's overall zone of mediation.

For example, when I spoke with teachers in Woodland Hills about their needs, they overwhelmingly focused on the technical dimension, particularly the need for planning time. And when I spoke with district leaders about steps taken in the past and planned for the future in order to make detracking successful, they too identified items in the technical realm. As is predicted by the change literature, resources became an important need. While the district could certainly have done more to increase the favorable nature of the technical context for the reform, the Technical Zone was nonetheless substantially transformed by the district's efforts, becoming receptive to detracking.

The district had less success in transforming inertial forces. By their nature, these forces are largely dependent on the passage of time. Shifts in the

other three zones (technical, normative, and political) that produce meaningful changes in daily practices will, over time, lead to a shift in the Inertial
Zone. In the meantime, however, inertial forces increase the difficulty of making progress in the technical, normative and political realms.

The court order, the COIP funding, and the district leadership all added
powerful reform-friendly political forces. Yet the district failed to develop
strong grass-roots support for detracking. The resulting Political Zone was
therefore only tentatively receptive to the reform. Moreover, this dynamic
highlights the difficulty that Woodland Hills' leadership will have should it
wish to continue the reform after the court order ends—when the order and
the COIP funding disappear as forces.

Similarly, the district failed to address the normative dimension. Beliefs
and values—both historical and ongoing—drove educators and others to dismiss detracking's premise that all students should be academically challenged.
Substantially shifting this Normative Zone would require a great deal of effort
and time, yet it is crucial to sustaining a detracking reform and to making heterogeneous classes most successful.

This zone framework highlights the parallels between the focus of the
change literature and the focus of the change agents in Woodland Hills. Both
largely ignore the most vexing issues. Recall the discussion in Chapter Seven
of the broad array of historical and external forces that shaped the detracking
zone of mediation preceding the court mandate. The "White flight" and the
"Save our Schools" campaign arose out of normative and political resistance
to desegregation. Similarly, the uneven distribution of political power between
African-American and White residents acted to shape a hostile pre-mandate
zone. The local press, informal parental/teacher networks, pressure exerted by
college admissions standards, AP tests, and court decisions—all of these factors
influenced the situation, yet the traditional change paradigm does not account
for them. The uneven distribution of political power between various constituencies presented a particularly daunting problem for the future of detracking in Woodland Hills, San Jose, and Rockford.

The change literature also fails to predict or explain the role of the forces
presented in Chapter Eight. As discussed in greater detail below, the literature
cautions against the initiation of reforms through top-down mandates. Yet the
detracking reforms discussed in this book would not have existed without court
mandates. Those mandates prompted a variety of positive changes, including
funding, data collection and use, oversight, and curriculum revision.

The change literature's most profound weakness, however, lies in its failure to account adequately for the normative resistance discussed in Chapters
Nine through Eleven. Teachers' low expectations for particular groups of students and negative beliefs about race explained so much of the detracking stories. Yet these crucial elements do not fit into the existing change model. Nor

does this change model satisfactorily account for the compromises and inducements discussed in Chapter Twelve. As discussed below, the change literature presents mutual adaptation as non-problematic and even desirable. It gives little warning of the detrimental consequences of yielding to the pressure of local elites.

In sum, the extant change literature, as applied to equity-minded reforms, neglects two primary areas: (a) the political battle, including the need for change agents to mobilize a political constituency and other powerful pro-change forces; and (b) the normative battle, including the need for change agents to address teachers' negative normative beliefs about race and intelligence. These are recurring themes in this book's reform stories. The fate of the change processes depended on the results of ongoing normative and political battles over contextual turf. Normative and political forces dominated the shaping and reshaping of the detracking zones.

The zone portrayal also calls attention to the multi-dimensional role played by court orders. In addition to providing money and direction necessary to meet technical needs, the orders put in place an indispensable political bulwark and make significant contributions in the normative and inertial realms. However, the zone framework simultaneously highlights the reality that a court order is a temporary, stopgap measure. In the long term, if the detracking zone is to remain receptive to the new policy, reformers must build a normative, political and technical foundation that will outlast court involvement.

The neutral, technical focus of much traditional change literature must, therefore, be supplemented in order to explain this change process. While change does frequently depend on increased resources, "[i]nitiatives that primarily reallocate ideological stakes—where losers fear giving up 'rights' as well as interests . . . are not going to be much affected by revenue availability" (Mazzoni, 1991, pp. 118–119). Accordingly, the following sections consider the actual impact of ideology on the equity-minded change process.

DOWNWARD MUTUAL ADAPTATION

As a general rule, the fact that an equity-minded reform has been initiated in a given school or community provides a good indication that the zone of mediation in that school or community was, at one point at least, relatively receptive to the reform. However, this hospitality tends to be extraordinarily tenuous and susceptible to being revoked at almost any time (Wells & Serna, 1996). The reform can be thought of as being located at the zone's margin; with only a slight shift in the zone the reform will no longer be tolerated. Understanding such potential complications at the implementation stage of equity-minded reforms requires movement beyond a neutral perspective.

As an example of the potential difficulties encountered when applying neutral change theory to the implementation of equity-minded reforms, consider Berman and McLaughlin's (1978) well-known advice about mutual adaptation. Variability, they say, is both inevitable and desirable. They tell us that the most successful reforms come about when both the project (reform) and the setting (school) are changed. Following this logic, Tyack and Cuban (1995) advise policy-makers not to design reforms to be implemented precisely as planned. Instead, they suggest, policy-makers should view their plans as "hypotheses" that will be transformed as they are implemented.

However, if the project is an equity-minded reform, the changes that arise as a result of interaction with the pre-existing school context will almost always be in the direction of less equity. That is, the pressures from the school and the community will likely favor the dominant societal actors (the local elites) at the expense of the reform's intended beneficiaries (Apple, 1993; Popkewitz, 1991; Wells & Oakes, 1996; Wells & Serna, 1996). Seen from this perspective, variability and mutual adaptation are the enemies of successful reform. For those in the greatest need, greater variability and greater adaptation result in less positive change (see Huberman & Miles, 1984).

Berman and McLaughlin (1975) themselves distinguish between mutual adaptation and "co-optation," which they define as the loss of a reform's fundamental features due to extreme accommodation to the local context. However, adaptation of an equity-minded reform is invariably in the direction of co-optation, the only question is one of degree. That is, while such a reform may contain elements that are enhanced due to mutual adaptation (e.g., modifying a detracking reform to take advantage of a school's pre-existing math lab), the equity aspect of the reform (reduced stratification of opportunities) will likely be watered-down. Touching on this point, Elmore and McLaughlin (1988, p. 36) contend that "adaptation is not simply a matter of policy-makers acquiescing to local and regional differences in tastes and competencies. It is, more fundamentally, active problem-solving." These authors do not, however, move beyond a neutral description of this concern and into a discussion of the need for problem-solving around equity-minded reforms to tackle normative and political issues.

At the most basic level of implementation, techno-structural reforms (and the technical and structural aspects of equity-minded reforms) do often implicate some difficult issues of culture and power (see McQuillan, 1998). However, in comparison to equity-minded reforms, techno-structural reforms usually benefit from a higher comfort level among educators and other implementors. In San Jose and Woodland Hills, I noted that a greater portion of educators seemed to "believe in" these reforms. These educators gravitated toward those reforms and activities that were most consistent with their pre-existing practices and beliefs. I term this phenomenon "selective implementation," although it also exists (very powerfully) at reforms' initiation stage. Moreover, it occurs at both the macro- and the micro-levels—in the state legislature as well as in the classroom.[1] In terms of the change literature, there is nothing new in this latter observation. The value lies in exploring its implications and in modifying recommendations and models to comport with the reality.

Mutual adaptation can be thought of as a bottom-up component to a reform initiated at the top. Consider Woodland Hills' mutual adaptation. Resistance and opposition from bottom-up forces caused compromises, inducements, and ineffective implementation. Unfortunately, all of this adaptation resulted in less equity. The changes pressed by these detracking opponents all favored the local elites who had benefited from the tracked system. Similar processes played out in Rockford and San Jose.

Contrast this lesson with the advice of Berman and McLaughlin (1978) and of Tyack and Cuban (1995), urging policy-makers to welcome the transformation of reforms at the local level. Such mutual adaptation between the original reform and the community, these scholars advise, brings the most successful reform. But, from the perspective of Woodland Hills' African-American students, the mutual adaptation sabotaged successful reform. I call this process "downward mutual adaptation." While much change literature assumes that mutual adaptation will simply make a reform responsive to local needs, the concept of downward mutual adaptation recognizes that those local "needs" may be in conflict with the reform's most important goals.

The Woodland Hills and San Jose experiences did, however, demonstrate a different way in which bottom-up elements can join top-down reforms. Some of the teachers and administrators in these districts favored detracking. If, prior to the court order, one of these teachers had proposed that her school detrack, her efforts would have met with overwhelming resistance. The detracking zone, at that time, made detracking unfeasible. The zone changed, however, in the wake of the detracking mandate. After the court issued its mandate, this hypothetical teacher and others at the school site (and community) level, who previously could not mount an effective reform effort, could now confidently move forward with their bottom-up ideas.

On this point, the change literature misses half the picture. It accurately predicts that, because of site-level resistance to external pressure for change— attempting to marginalize the reform by reducing it to a superficial add-on to the existing school ethos and structures—the mandates would not be implemented as planned. However, this literature does little to predict that these mandates would change the reform context so that the efforts of reform supporters would become more effective.

In this way, top-down and bottom-up forces combined to form what can be called a systemic reform—a distant cousin of the systemic reform advocated by Smith and O'Day (1991). Smith and O'Day's systemic reform called upon the central government to set voluntary standards (with associated assessments and assistance) while giving local policy-makers the freedom to devise locally appropriate means of meeting those standards. In contrast, the systemic reforms prompted by the centralized authority (the court) in Woodland Hills, San Jose and Rockford began with a mandate specifying the means of accomplishing an equity-minded goal, but implementation relied on local initiative (see McDermott, 1999).[2] While both types of systemic reform hope for the top-down element to stimulate a bottom-up element, mandated reform addresses the problem identified by McDermott (1999) and by Wells and Oakes (1996) of local micro-politics subverting the creation of equal opportunities to learn.[3]

Accordingly, while some bottom-up involvement can indeed strengthen an equity-minded reform, the change literature naively welcomes any and all such contributions. This is a mistake. Forces acting to reshape the zone should not be welcomed simply because they arise from the local level. Each force, whether it comes from the bottom up or from more remote levels, should be considered with regard to its potential impact on the zone. In this way, the mutual adaptation process for a reform should be informed, at every step, by an understanding of the reform's normative and political context.

Downward mutual adaptation preys on the politically and normatively impaired in much the same way that an opportunistic virus preys on the immunologically impaired. Consequently, as a person would build up her biological defense systems to fight off a viral attack, schools and districts undergoing equity-minded reform efforts must build up their political and normative "defense systems" to fight off these adaptation attacks. The following subsections explore three steps that change agents can take in order to make mutual adaptation equity-mindful: (a) develop a political constituency for the reform, (b) ground the efforts in democratic values and irreproachable educational principles, and (c) focus staff development on critical inquiry.[4]

Political Mobilization

Political mobilization provides one powerful way for proponents of equity-minded change to avoid downward mutual adaptation. Consider Woodland Hills' political dynamic, as described in Chapter Seven. In the past, the district's African-American community had remained relatively silent and uninvolved, allowing powerful White parents to dominate political debate. Similarly, in San Jose Latino parents had considerably less political power than their White counterparts. The latent political power of both minority communities went largely untapped. Continuation of this trend would result in these districts' zones slowly but inevitably shifting (mutually adapting) in response to building oppositional forces to become more and more unreceptive to detracking. In the short term, this would cause ineffective implementation; in the long term, it would cause a return to tracking.

Community groups and even plaintiffs' attorneys can play an important role in stimulating greater involvement. But the schools and districts should also view such constituency-building as a core part of their detracking reform efforts. Historically, awakening political power in these communities has not been easy, but more must be done in the future. The alternative is untenable:

> It is ultimately neither respectful nor effective for educators to pit themselves as advocates for children who are disadvantaged by the status quo against the parents of the children who benefit from the current system. The full participation of all segments of the community is required to eliminate the gap between the educational opportunity expressed in the American Creed and the reality of educational failure for so many students. (Oakes, Wells, Yonezawa, & Ray, 1997, p. 69.)

To assist in his analysis of several specific cases of political empowerment, Joel Handler (1996) surveyed the development of scholarly definitions of "power"—including those of Lukes (1974) and Gaventa (1980). These scholars explain that powerlessness can result from feelings of fatalism, self-deprecation, apathy, and the internalization of dominant values and beliefs. "Political consciousness and participation are reciprocal and reinforcing; those who are denied participation will not develop political consciousness" (Handler, 1996, p. 119). Handler quotes Gaventa's (1980, p. 23) conclusion that "power relations can be understood only with reference to their prior development and their impact comprehended only in light of their own momentum."[5]

Of course, if power is defined merely as the accomplishment of political goals, then the minority communities in Rockford, Woodland Hills, and San Jose did have considerable power. Through the courts, these communities trumped the ordinary political influence of the powerful White communities. However, that trump card will disappear when court supervision ends, and raw political influence over school board politics will once again hold sway. If the leadership of these districts and schools hope to continue their present policies, they must consider ways to enhance the democratic political power of the districts' minority communities.

"In the final analysis," Handler observes, "empowerment rests on a basic contradiction—it envisages a democratic process of equality between participants who are unequal in terms of power and resources" (Handler, 1996, p. 240). He, therefore, stresses the importance of outside resources to assist in the empowerment. In Rockford, San Jose, and Woodland Hills, court orders provided such outside resources—both power and money. But additional applications of power and resources will be needed in the future to overcome this contradiction.

The development of strategies to ensure that all constituent voices are heard seems a perfectly legitimate school district activity. True democratic deliberation requires responsiveness to all people, not just those with the loudest voices (Fraser, 1992; Young, 1990). Equity-minded change agents must make a concerted effort to catalyze the assembly of a strong, supportive political constituency for their reforms, or those reforms will simply be mutually adapted into oblivion. The present change literature discusses the need for the "institutionalization" of reforms, but its focus is technical and cultural—not political. Accordingly, it largely neglects important lessons about both creating and sustaining a receptive context (zone) for equity-minded reforms.

Reforms Expressly Grounded in Values and Principles

Reporting on their experience with schools undergoing voluntary detracking reforms, Oakes et al. (1997) offer several additional recommendations that would assist in making mutual adaptation more equity-mindful. They suggest that change agents avoid harmful compromises with local elites by maintaining a focus on the ideals underlying detracked schools. This focus, they contend, assists change agents in eschewing new forms of stratification and grouping. The leaders in Woodland Hills, San Jose, and Rockford did not do this, which partially explains the dilution of their reform efforts (recall the compromises and inducements discussed in Chapter Twelve).

Oakes et al. (1997) also advise that change agents ground their reforms primarily and openly in democratic values and only secondarily in empirical evidence. While not as effective an argument-ender as "the court says we have to," this principled position avoids constant arguments about whether detracking "works" to improve student performance. These authors suggest that change agents emphasize the "educational high ground" upon which detracking rests: all children can learn, and all children should receive a high-quality education. They note that the teaching strategies recommended for detracked classes—active engagement in solving interesting and relevant problems—are also recommended in gifted programs (and are often used in gifted classes but very rarely used in low-track classes).

Detracking's supporters in Woodland Hills occasionally made this latter argument. It often fell on deaf ears, however, in part because many teachers of detracked classes failed to employ such advanced instructional methods and in part because a considerable amount of the opposition to detracking was grounded in normative beliefs resistant to evidence about the benefits of actual classroom instruction.

Critical Inquiry

The final suggestion offered by Oakes et al. (1997) asks change agents to consider "cultivat[ing] a climate of continuous learning and inquiry among faculty and parents [including the use of some] professional development time around detracking to examine the relationship between common-sense conceptions of intelligence, student ability, and valued knowledge, and social factors—including race, class, and gender" (p. 69). Nothing in the traditional change literature addresses the need for such a direct confrontation of normative beliefs. But the experiences of the school districts discussed in this book demonstrate why such a critical inquiry is necessary to forestall downward mutual adaptation (see also Lipman, 1998, and the earlier discussion of critical inquiry, in Chapter Nine).

In Woodland Hills, instead of preparing teachers to confront important normative issues, the district overwhelmingly focused its staff development efforts on technical issues. These techno-structural efforts lacked the ability to confront the district's most pressing problems, which were normative. Nor could they realistically be relied upon to create a bulwark against downward mutual adaptation. In the absence of such a strong, normative bulwark, forces opposed to detracking can be expected to continue chipping away at the reform.

This different emphasis (normative as opposed to technical) presents a major implication of an equity-minded rethinking of the school change literature. Shifting to a stress on normative issues propels a staff development shift from methods to inquiry. The need for technical learning remains, but it is dwarfed by the need to engage in a serious questioning of beliefs and values. Because the change literature neglects mutual adaptation's harmful potential, as well as the normative forces that can turn that potential into reality, the need for critical inquiry does not fit into the traditional reform model. Yet without such an inquiry, downward mutual adaptation remains free to run amok. Similarly, the necessity of each of the above recommendations only becomes apparent when one informs the mutual adaptation process with an understanding of equity-minded reform's normative and political contexts.

MANDATES MATTER

Few axioms are as well accepted in the educational change literature as Milbrey McLaughlin's, "We cannot mandate what matters" (see Elmore & McLaughlin, 1988; Fullan, 1993). Moreover, the relative lack of success of many attempts to mandate change from above would seem to provide strong support this axiom. However, equity-driven, top-down mandates should be viewed not so much as attempts to mandate what matters as attempts to *change* the pre-existing mandates of what matters. These pre-existing mandates include cultural imperatives—articulated and unarticulated—to act, react, or perceive in particular ways.

If we define a top-down mandate as a force external to a school or a community that shapes policy in that school or community, then we can appreciate that top-down mandates are being issued perpetually and inevitably. For instance, before the court order mandated Woodland Hills' detracking policy, other forces, such as pressures from external institutions, teachers, parents and the local press, effectively issued such mandates by shaping the zone of mediation. The new mandate simply added to the mix. From this perspective, we *can* mandate what matters, we just must understand that a single, top-down mandate is unlikely to be effective in substantially altering the overall impact of a myriad of influences on a school or community. The zone framework illustrates the reality that an untold number of forces constantly shape and reshape a reform's context. When a reform idea first enters a site, it takes its place on top of layers and layers of history.

Moreover, mandates can alter beliefs as well as behavior. Consider the impact of the *Brown v. Board of Education* mandate: in the decision's wake, intentional segregation became morally as well as legally unacceptable for a majority of Americans. Likewise, exposure to heterogeneous classes gave some Woodland Hills teachers the opportunity to observe quality work from students who they had formerly thought of as low achievers—leading to a greater support for detracking. If combined with a critical inquiry process, even further progress could have been made.

Viewed from the zone perspective, one can easily understand how court mandates succeed in prompting change and how, simultaneously, a wide assortment of resistant forces succeeds in making the zone less receptive to reform. These opposing phenomena co-exist; they are not mutually exclusive. Not surprisingly, then, the detracking efforts in Woodland Hills, as well as in Rockford and San Jose, demonstrated the combined impact of these forces. Bold changes became more cautious, tempered by compromises, inducements, shortcomings, and resistance. Unquestionably, the top-down mandates resulted in greater detracking than would have otherwise occurred, yet they could not eliminate oppositional forces. Each court order simply became another force interacting with all the others.

The bottom-up focus of school change literature casts local educators and community members as the primary actors in the promotion of reform. Policy-makers are urged to establish the conditions for effective administration, to charge local practitioners with the development of solutions, and to refrain from pre-determining decisions (Elmore & McLaughlin, 1988; Firestone & Corbett, 1989). This advice contributed to the wave of decentralization that began in the early 1980s. However, as documented in the case studies set forth in this book, equity issues are frequently not among the concerns of the political majority at more local levels of governance. As a result, decentralization of policy making authority to these local communities may lead to neglect of the equity concerns of the politically less powerful (Elmore, 1993). Under normal circumstances, "local elites" can (and often do) block reforms that they perceive as grounded in values different from their own (Fullan, 1991; Lipman, 1998; McDermott, 1999; Wells & Serna, 1996).

Historically, more central authorities have been able to advance equity policy goals to a much greater extent than have local authorities (Peterson, 1981). Even Arthur Wise, a strong critic of centrally-mandated reform, acknowledges that some local schools are unwilling or unable to solve some equity-minded problems, and that, in such cases, more central authorities are more likely to be successful (Wise, 1982). Fullan (1991) also notes that reforms favoring the least advantaged are the least likely to be proposed at the local level. Further, bottom-up strategies diminish the opportunity for, and responsibility of, non-local leaders with status and power to inspire and advocate on behalf of non-neutral reforms.

Consequently, community resistance to practices perceived by politically powerful local residents as harmful to their personal interests (i.e., those practices perceived as substantively redistributive) usually will require top-down mandates and monitoring. Policy-makers must recognize that in a highly decentralized system local political resistance to reforms aimed at giving low-income and non-white students access to high-status knowledge will be difficult to overcome (Wells and Oakes, 1996).

The researchers cited above seem to be describing what can be termed an "equity exception" to the general recommendations against strong reliance on top-down mandates requiring specific changes. This exception arises out of the local-level normative and political resistance generated by equity-minded reforms and resulting in a fundamentally different reform process. From initiation forward, this resistance alters the way that schools react to change, so it must also alter the way that change agents and scholars approach change.

A central policy-making body wishing to promote an equity reform might, for example, be ill-advised merely to propound a set of general equity principles, because resistance and political opposition by local elites may undermine any anticipated bottom-up aspect to the reform. Instead, the central body should craft a more specific mandate, sufficient to substantially shift the zone of mediation, thereby overcoming such local resistance. As Boyd (1989) has explained, we need a balanced approach to educational improvement using elements of top-down and bottom-up reform judiciously, "according to the characteristics and needs of the given policy problem" (Boyd, 1989, p. 517; see also Fullan, 1991, 1994, 1999; Huberman & Miles, 1984).

The concept of the zone of mediation also explains why top-down and bottom-up reforms need not be viewed as antithetical. Consider a hypothetical teacher who would like to move her school toward detracking. In 1999, she brings up the idea with some of her colleagues and is told, in no uncertain terms, that they like the present tracked system and have no interest in change. In 2000, a court issues an order requiring the district to detrack its schools. We know from the change literature that a top-down mandate to detrack is unlikely to be implemented as planned. Site-level forces will most likely resist the external pressure for change and will try to marginalize the reform by making it a superficial add-on to the existing school culture and school structures (Cuban, 1992). However, this mandate might also help to shift the zone of mediation at this school so that a detracking reform would now be more acceptable and less marginalized. Accordingly, this teacher and others at the school site (and community) level, who were previously unable to mount an effective reform effort, can now, in 2001, more confidently move forward with their *bottom up* ideas.

The adversaries of detracking at this school may persist in their opposition, but the court has eroded their strategic position. The zone has shifted to move the fringe closer to the center. By analogy, the boundaries of the playing field have shifted to include some who were previously on the sidelines. It is, perhaps, unlikely that they will overwhelm the more established players, but they are now in the fray (see Thompson, 1984, for an elaborate discussion of this point). Thus, while the ultimate impact of a detracking mandate may be unascertainable in advance, such a mandate might nonetheless—even given imperfect implementation—be a positive force in the direction of greater equity (Welner & Oakes, 1996).

REDEFINING SUCCESSFUL REFORM

Fullan (1991) posits that school reform can be broken down into four stages: initiation, implementation, continuation, and outcome. But, as Hargreaves (1994) observes, most change literature has focused primarily on the implementation stage of school reforms. As we have seen, this focus has resulted in an emphasis on the need for a strong bottom-up component to the initiation of these reform efforts. The literature accurately explains why, when reform is initiated by teachers and others at the site level, the implementation stage experiences greater success. However, a reform cannot be successfully implemented if it is never initiated. Moreover, if equity-minded reforms are to be initiated, the zone of mediation must first be (or become) receptive. If a zone is unreceptive to such change, thus presenting a daunting barrier to initiation, then a top-down mandate emerges as an attractive option.[6]

Nonetheless, scholars writing about the role of courts in initiating school change tend to take the same approach as is generally taken with other forms of top-down mandates: focusing on the implementation stage and therefore dismissing the judicial role as inefficient and unproductive (see, e.g., Wise, 1977). They generally define success in terms of the degree to which agreed-upon goals are achieved. For example, if the educators in a school district decide to embark on a detracking effort, they may state one of their goals as follows: "We will implement heterogeneous grouping within 2 years." The degree of success of this particular reform would typically be assessed based on a determination of how much heterogeneous grouping the district in fact achieved after 2 years.

The following formula conceptually demonstrates this type of analysis:

Goals (G): the complete set of the desired goals of the reform;

Subset (S): the subset of the desired goals successfully implemented.[7]

Successful reforms are measured by how closely Subset/Goals (S/G) approaches 1. The analysis focuses on the specific reform, and the results of the analysis would be expressed, "This implementation of Reform X was (or was not) successful in achieving Goal Y." As a general rule, the change literature focuses on implementation issues and then works backwards to consider issues of initiation. Consequently, this literature advocates those forms of initiation (bottom-up) that best promote successful implementation.

In contrast, in order to evaluate the overall, global efficacy of different approaches to reforming schools, the analysis should begin *before* the school, district, state, or federal government has already inaugurated the reform. An initial decision to embark upon a reform is, after all, a major hurdle, and bottom-up change arises neither in a random fashion nor necessarily in line with best practices. By focusing only on how much of what was originally initiated or adopted is ultimately implemented, the analyst overlooks the issue of the likelihood of the reform actually being adopted in the first place. This omission can be remedied by broadening the analysis to include the universal (i.e., societal or nationwide) change likely to result from the reform proposal.

For example, if a foundation publishes a recommendation that all school districts equalize intra-district funding among district schools, the amount of change likely to result from the reform proposal will depend, in part, on the number of districts sufficiently convinced by the foundation's arguments to initiate a voluntary reform. The "universal change" may involve as few as zero, one or two districts or as many as thousands throughout the nation.

Therefore, a more comprehensive formula for such an analysis might look like:

Goals (G):   the reform's complete set of desired goals;

Breadth (B):   the breadth of the targeted community;

Likelihood (L):   the likelihood that any given jurisdiction within the targeted community will initiate the reform;[8]

Portion (P):   once initiated, the successfully implemented portion of the desired goals; and

Change (C):   the absolute, global change likely to result from the reform.

A reform idea's potential for success is then expressed using the product of Goals, Likelihood, Portion, and Breadth: $G*B*L*P = C$.[9] (As with the earlier formulation, success should be considered to include successful continuance or durability.) Unlike the traditional conceptualization, this expanded framework appraises initiation as well as implementation.

My intention in setting forth this alternative perspective on school reform is to address the problematic nature of top-down strategies for pursuing equity-minded reforms. If one considers such reforms with the first formula in mind, then top-down mandates seem ill-conceived for all of the persuasive reasons presented in the school change literature. Clearly, a strong bottom-up component to the reform should result in a greater value of Portion/Goals (P/G). If, however, one applies the second formula, then the value of top-down mandates as potentially the best *practical* policy available in many situations becomes clear. At some point, the smaller value of "P" (the Portion of the goals successfully implemented) is overcome by the larger value of "L" (the Likelihood of the reform being initiated).[10]

The Woodland Hills, San Jose, and Rockford reforms, for example, yield unimpressive quotients of P/G. Detracking in these districts encountered huge obstacles and widespread resistance. The implemented reforms differed substantially from the ideal. By traditional standards, then, they did not constitute particularly successful reforms. According to the change literature, one would expect that bottom-up initiation in these districts would have resulted in much greater success.

However, contrary expectations emerge when one considers the likelihood of initiation, the reform's breadth, and the actual resulting change ("L," "B" and "C," respectively). Little chance existed that any of these districts would have initiated detracking without legal pressure. Moreover, any detracking so initiated might have been on a smaller, single-school scale (see Oakes et al., 2000). Consequently, the greater values for "L" and "S" generated by the top-down mandates more than offset the smaller values for "P," and the resulting change was enhanced.

These conceptual formulas illustrate a straightforward idea. In ideal circumstances, bottom-up reforms are preferable, but in the real world, such reforms will accomplish nothing unless they arise. In contrast, top-down reforms, while imperfect, can bring about real change, but change that will probably not be as originally designed.

THIRD-ORDER CHANGE

The experiences of Woodland Hills, San Jose, and Rockford point to the need for reformers and scholars of reform to treat equity-minded change as different in kind, not just in degree, from more technical school changes. The need to change normative beliefs and tame political opposition substantially transforms the change process. Yet, because of its neutral focus, most change literature neglects this transformation. Larry Cuban (1992), for instance, distinguishes only between changes of different magnitudes in his two-part typology for educational change. He categorizes changes that simply improve the effectiveness of current practices as "first-order" or "incremental" changes, and those that seek to alter the basic ways that organizations function as "second-order" or "fundamental" changes (Cuban 1992).

Building on Cuban's model, I consider equity-minded reforms such as detracking to be "third-order changes," defined as fundamental changes that also seek to reform educators' and community members' core normative beliefs about such matters as race, class, intelligence, and educability. Such an extension of Cuban's model highlights the need to think about equity-minded reforms as different in kind from their less factious cousins.

I find the zone of mediation framework to be helpful in explaining how these third-order changes are most distinguishable from the other two categories. Cuban's first-order as well as some of his second-order reforms can be viewed as efforts to improve how schools carry out their work in areas that do not challenge larger, external forces. Other reforms, however, constitute efforts to fundamentally renegotiate the terms of mediation with those external forces. These reforms attempt to alter the impact of larger forces on particular groups of individuals and families; they challenge those larger forces. They are third-order changes—they directly oppose and confront prevailing external forces and, therefore, are most likely to fall outside the zone of mediation.

This revised approach recognizes that the scope (or success) of a change effort is often less dependent upon the reform itself than upon the magnitude and direction of exogenous forces (i.e., forces other than the reform effort itself). It directly addresses the quantity and quality of supportive and oppositional forces. It accounts for the reality that reform efforts take place within a dynamic context, shaped in part by powerful oppositional forces. While some reforms are quickly accepted by a school or a district, others face these obstacles.

Each reform takes place within its own unique context; each reform is one new force, layered upon the existing mish-mash of forces. For the most fortunate reforms, these existing forces create a welcoming zone of mediation, but third-order changes are rarely so blessed. Differential contexts may be tied to the value, worth, or merit of the reform; that is, some reforms may justifiably face an unreceptive zone because of recognized inadequacies. But an unreceptive zone can also be formed by the sorts of normative and political forces discussed in this book. Many reforms confronting such hostile contexts promote important democratic values. As Lipman (1998) notes, "A measure of the relevance of educational reforms is the extent to which new initiatives address the challenges posed by structural change and growing inequality and by the extent to which they confront central issues of race and class inequality, racism, and the need to teach to racial and ethnic diversity" (p. 10).

Reformers and reform scholars are thus presented with a choice. A third-order change idea can be abandoned because normative and political opposition will present huge obstacles to initiation and implementation, which will probably result in a compromised policy. Alternatively, the idea can be pursued with an awareness of those obstacles and a determination to overcome them. In the latter case, the ideal policy might nonetheless be substantially compromised as the reform process moves forward. But, given a worthwhile goal, more good will likely come from this compromised effort than from a premature abandonment. In fact, a compromised effort may fairly be considered a tremendous success. The contextual realities illustrated by the zone of mediation model highlight the fact that "compromises," while not to be welcomed, are inevitable consequences of exogenous forces. The (desirable) changes, on the other hand, which are subjected to these compromises, should be praised as fruits of the reform effort.

THE ROLE OF COURTS

What does this reframing of the change literature mean for the role of court orders in educational change? Clearly, court orders can substantially shift the zone of mediation. Equally clearly, they are not a panacea. But, just as democracy has been described as "the worst form of government except all those other forms that have been tried from time to time" (Churchill, 1947), court-mandated school reforms which address equity issues may be the worst type of such reform except all the other types that have been tried (or, more accurately, aborted or passed over) from time to time. Simply put, court-mandated reforms, while flawed, are sometimes the only *realistic* reform option available.

In reaching this conclusion, I am mindful of the research discussed earlier which recommended that policy-makers set the conditions for effective administration but refrain from predetermining decisions (Elmore and McLaughlin, 1988). Successful policy-makers, according to this research, must charge local practitioners with the development of solutions. Elmore (1983) terms this "delegated control," as opposed to "hierarchical control." When it comes to equity issues, however, the impetus for change, whether delegated or hierarchical, becomes problematic. This holds true with regard to local as well as central authorities. At the local level, community "elites" frequently obstruct equity-minded policies. While more central authorities are sometimes better placed to advance these goals, they too are not immune from the political pressures opposed to equity-promoting policy initiatives. Consequently, equity reform is often not forthcoming from either the community level or more central levels.

In such cases, any reform would have to be initiated by an anti-majoritarian source, and the courts become the best and indeed the only realistic option. As Kenneth Clark explained in discussing the importance of the judicial role in the *Brown* decision:

> If the issue of desegregation of the public schools were put to a referendum now, twenty years after that historic decision, the chances are that it would be defeated. But this should not be surprising. If this were not so, there would have been no need to take these cases before the federal courts. The present controversies centering around the implementation of the *Brown* decision in northern cities make even more clear . . . that a critical function of the federal courts is to protect the constitutional rights of American minorities, particularly when those rights are being opposed or in any way qualified or threatened by the majority (Clark, 1977, p. 8).

This anti-majoritarian role of the courts (i.e., forcing change against the wishes of a political majority demanding stability) is a well-established principle of our governmental system (Bickel, 1962; Hamilton, 1788; *Marbury v. Madison*, 1803). We live in a *constitutional* democracy, and the protections of the Constitution place limits on our democratic preferences (see Tribe, 1988).

Court mandates share many attributes with legislative and administrative mandates, so many of this study's findings about top-down mandates might well be generalized. Most importantly, all these mandates remove some decision-making authority from local elites. However, courts (particularly federal courts) maintain a freer reign to make anti-majoritarian decisions. Looked at through the zone lens, these courts feel substantially less pressure to replicate decisions previously mandated by the pre-existing forces that shaped a zone unreceptive to the reform. In contrast, district, state and federal officials are all subject, directly or indirectly, to pressure from voters and constituents that could reach the level of threatening their jobs.

These lessons about top-down mandates exist on a continuum. They apply most strongly to the federal courts, less strongly to state courts and to federal officials, and still less strongly as centralized officials become subject to more direct voter pressure. Yet even those in the latter category might use mandates to overcome local resistance to equity-minded reforms. A separate analysis would apply to each unique school and district.

Evans, Murray and Schwab (1997) analyzed the impact of court-mandated school finance reforms, comparing them with school finance reforms initiated by state legislatures in the absence of a court mandate. In each of the eleven states where courts overturned school funding plans, state governments responded by adopting legislation reforming education finance. The authors found that these states reduced spending inequality between rich and poor schools by anywhere from 16% to 38%. Moreover, these states accomplished this equalization by raising state revenues and leaving local revenues unchanged. That is, total revenues rose significantly in districts with the smallest local revenues (through additional state funding), while spending in the wealthiest districts remained unchanged. However, legislative reforms not made in response to successful litigation had no perceptible impact on the overall level of education revenues or the distribution of those revenues. The study's authors conclude that this type of reform "is politically difficult and any reforms the states adopt on their own are unlikely to alter the distribution of educational resources" (Evans, Murray, & Schwab, 1997, p. 29). While acknowledging the long and difficult legal battles necessary to compel the finance reforms, they assert that courts appear to be a more effective means of obtaining this type of change than legislatures alone.

Keep in mind, however, that a court mandate to equalize funding, followed by a legislative mandate carrying out the court's order, does not implicate many of the ground-level normative and political issues discussed in this book. The sorts of parental and teacher resistance seen in Rockford, San Jose, and Woodland Hills are largely inapplicable to a state-level reformulation of school finance.[11]

COURT-ORDERED DETRACKING

Tracking systems show extraordinary resilience and resistance to change, and court-ordered detracking reforms must overcome significant barriers. Organizationally, tracking receives support from, and provides support to, schools' other practices. Politically, detracking efforts generally must overcome local opposition and build supportive communities both within and outside of the schools. Normatively, tracking is grounded in widespread negative beliefs about race and intelligence (Oakes, 1992). These technical, normative *and* political forces help to explain both the necessity of court-ordered reforms and the hurdles that these reforms will have to clear. For example, judicial involvement is often necessitated by political forces that prevent the reforms from otherwise occurring. These same political forces often undermine court-mandated detracking efforts.

Overcoming these barriers is never an easy task, but I would offer the contention, grounded in the above theoretical discussion, that a court order can play an important and positive role. In particular, such an order assists in overcoming political barriers blocking a reform's initiation. Further, courts can serve district administrators and board members as political bogeymen, shouldering the burden of blame for politically unpopular measures. The court order may make opponents of detracking more inclined to resign themselves to the inevitability of the reform. Court orders shift the hypothetical zone of mediation within which communities will allow professional administrators and educators to act.

The "$G*B*L*P = C$" formula highlights the potential importance of using a court order to overcome political barriers to detracking. Without a court order, one can expect an extremely small value of "L" (Likelihood of the reform being undertaken) in districts with a history of segregation; given the court order, however, the value may become quite large.[12] A court order can also assist in overcoming organizational barriers. Courts invariably direct such orders at districts rather than schools. Therefore, site-level efforts generally find district-level support (e.g., staff development and curricular reform) for the implementation of mandated detracking. Such support becomes particularly important in light of the district-level opposition to reform encountered by many detracking schools (see Oakes, Wells & Associates, 1996; Oakes et al., 2000).

Top-down mandates, however, may encounter greater difficulty in overcoming normative barriers. Wise (1977) discusses a hyperrationalization called "wishful thinking," which he defines as policy-makers incorrectly believing that they can accomplish change simply by decreeing it (p. 45). A corollary to this is that policy-makers sometimes incorrectly believe that educators will accept the importance of a change simply because it has been decreed. As explained above, however, I question Wise and others when they contend that we cannot mandate what matters. I believe that court orders can potentially shift the zone of mediation and, consequently, change "what matters" in a district. Such a mandate will not result in full acceptance of a policy, just greater acceptance (Welner & Oakes, 1996).

REFORM AFTER COURT INVOLVEMENT

The earlier discussion of downward mutual adaptation included several ideas concerning the need for change agents to work actively to sustain a receptive zone of mediation. This section now considers that same need in relation to one particular phenomenon: the motion for unitary status.

Woodland Hills' superintendent had repeatedly stated his desire to bring court supervision to "as swift an end as possible." In October 1999, the Woodland Hills School District and the Commonwealth of Pennsylvania made a legal motion seeking a determination that they had achieved "unitary status" and a consequent end to court supervision. (Recall that the court, if it is to grant such a motion, must find that the defendants have remedied both the past discrimination and the vestiges of that discrimination.) The Rockford School District, too, filed such a motion in 2000, although it had only recently begun implementing changes. District leaders were clearly heartened by the Seventh Circuit Court of Appeals' indication in 1997 that it would welcome a unitary status motion once some reforms were in place.[13] The San Jose Unified School District has also filed several such motions in the past, each time resulting in a compromise that modified the consent decree and scaled back the reforms.

Using Woodland Hills as an example, consider what will happen when the court supervision ends. In the optimistic opinion of Woodland Hills' superintendent, "very little would change within the district." While acknowledging the loss of substantial resources and some "political cover," he contended that "as long as I am here, and I think I could speak for the board, the district would never go back to segregating the schools." But without the powerful force of the court mandate, is this optimism naive? When asked, most other district educators agreed with the superintendent's general perspective. A school counselor, for instance, commented that she did not know whether the district would be "better off" without the court order, but, because of the order, "people have begun to focus on multiculturalism and reaching all students." She concluded, after some thought, that the progress had "moved along far enough so that the gains would continue."

Siding with this counselor, a White observer rejected the idea that "there's a bunch of evil, racist people out there waiting for [a release from court supervision] so that they can work their horror against those minority people." He continued:

I don't think that in 2 years, with unitary status [granted], that all of a sudden the district is going to stratify everything grossly and end up with all the Black kids in some class[es] and these other classes that are all lily-White. . . . I think a lot of things would keep going the way they're going, to tell you the truth, except they're going to go that way with fewer people [and] less money.

A board member I spoke with agreed that the detracking policy would remain, although she grounded her belief in an incorrect notion that the court mandate would somehow persist after the court supervision ended. An English teacher, however, disagreed. "If the community was vocal enough, they might reinstate [the tracked system]," she speculated, "[a]nd then the regular [classes] would become a zoo again."

Regarding busing and building assignment, the vast majority of administrators, board members, and community members confirmed that the basic system would remain, with some periodic adjustments prompted by demographic shifts. Busing costs the district about $5.5 million annually,[14] and this item has raised complaints every budget cycle. Generally speaking, idealism and integrationist sentiments probably cannot outweigh the community's desire to cut expenditures. However, as one administrator explained, the district really has no choice because it long ago sold off many of the buildings from the predecessor districts. This left some areas without neighborhood schools at certain grade levels. Even if the district wished to entertain the idea of resegregation, she ventured, they could not do it. "I don't think this district would ever go back to neighborhood schools," confirmed a district leader, "That's not an option." A long-time observer agreed, "unitary status or otherwise, they're gonna be hell-pressed to get away from the building pattern they have right now. [The district will have] to live with this long after unitary status." Thus, by adopting the integrated building pattern, the district essentially institutionalized between-school desegregation. Other aspects of the district's reform effort, however, have not been so fortunate.

Most people cited academic support programs as the area likely to take the biggest blow when court supervision ends. "Money," declared a top administrator, "is going to have an impact:"

I don't know how many of the programs can be sustained just on district funds. That's why even at this point we're beginning to look at outside funders. And we are looking for ways to sustain what's going on now, because [the superintendent] has always talked to us about the fact that this will not be going on forever. And when we believe that we have done a good job and we feel like we are ready to move toward unitary status, . . . he wants to take the proactive stance to be the first one to recommend that we begin to cut back.

The superintendent, according to a local newspaper article, "said that if and when the district is freed from the court order, the level of the tax increase will depend on whether the district can cut some of the court-ordered programs" (Verrilla, 1994).

Expecting a decreased need for those programs, a board member told me: "[In] 5 or 6 years, when the court order goes away, we're probably not going to have a need for as many of those programs because we're going to have remedied most of the problems." This optimism may be born of necessity, since unitary status will almost definitely bring program cutbacks, particularly since the programs had no significant political constituency. Accordingly, the motion for unitary status presents a real challenge to those who desire to sustain a receptive detracking zone. The district must recognize the court order's current powerful impact on the detracking zone and the corresponding impact of its eventual elimination. In order to sustain the receptive zone following the court supervision's end, the district must focus enormous energies on bolstering additional supportive forces and reducing the power of oppositional forces. Again, political mobilization efforts and critical inquiry efforts stand as two important and representative examples of this need.

SUMMARY

We are still so new in this process. We're just starting. And I think it's going to take years to get this district where it needs to be. It will outlive me; I know that.

The Woodland Hills administrator who made this comment believed strongly in the detracking reform. She wanted desperately to see it succeed. Yet she also possessed the wisdom to perceive and understand the tremendous obstacles to its success. She appreciated the extended process that begins with numerical, technical detracking but which continues until normative and political barriers have been cleared. "What a lot of people don't understand," she observed, "is that this is a long-term commitment, and that you won't see change, positive change, immediately."

Perhaps, however, this last comment voiced too much pessimism. Consider the high school teacher in this same district who, after just one year, noted "some real success stories . . . with detracking." He enthusiastically pointed out "some teachers who are adapting, and we'll see more success stories to come." Similarly, another of Woodland Hills' administrators applauded the district's progress: "We've made more strides since Superintendent Young has been here, and I'm so proud of . . . where we're going. Before, I felt like I was making excuses. Now, I know that I'm not making excuses, that the boat is moving in the right direction."

"[I]t would have been unrealistic to expect [detracking] to succeed in one year," remarked a Woodland Hills English teacher in detracking's second Fall. "It may get better this year." He later confirmed seeing real improvement in the second year. One of his colleagues agreed. She, too, saw improvement, but she wondered whether the district would be willing to see the reform through. "Historically," she said, "this school district comes up with all these wonderful new innovative ideas and they never, ever back us with the money to support it. And I think that's what frustrates a lot of us."

Finally, consider the comments of a long-time observer in Woodland Hills. "I don't envision wholesale success," she said, but "I think that it ultimately will present much more improvement than we have to date." She concluded:

[T]here are a lot of fine people in that school district—a lot of good employees with expertise and with dedication and commitment. It's just that we tend to talk about the others because they are in the way. But I do think it's a fine school district. It would be awfully nice if many of the African-American students could participate in the richness that exists out there and benefit from it.

Epilogue

On July 25, 2000, U.S. District Judge Maurice B. Cohill ruled that the Woodland Hills School District had met nearly all of its court-mandated remedial obligations. In response to the district's unitary status motion filed the previous October, the court released the district from court supervision over student assignment, faculty and staff assignment, facilities, transportation and activities. Judge Cohill concluded that the vestiges of past discrimination had been remedied in those areas. He also removed court oversight on guidance and counseling on condition that the district follow a transition plan on guidance positions.

The district's remaining requirements center on the elimination of tracking in mathematics. Cohill wrote that "tracking has a strong impact on minority students, who generally make up a higher percentage of students in lower-level courses" (*Hoots*, 2000, pp. 27–28). The transition plan calls for eliminating pre-algebra (which was formerly offered in seventh through eleventh grades) and offering all students algebra in the eighth grade. The plan also includes a phasing-in of Connected Math for sixth- and seventh-graders. The superintendent said that the district was already planning a transition to Connected Math, which he lauded for its flexibility and usefulness in challenging diverse students in heterogeneous environments.

Primarily because of his concerns about math tracking, Cohill refused to remove court supervision of curriculum, assessment, instruction and staff development. The district was also ordered to continue in-school math tutoring labs in the high school and both junior highs. With these exceptions, however, the court accepted the school district's three-year transition plan toward permanent removal of all court supervision. The judge ordered the state to pay 90% of the transition plan costs.

In his opinion, Judge Cohill spoke of the district's progress in glowing terms. "Woodland Hills has been transformed in the past 29 years," he said, "from a new district created by court order in a climate of much anger and bitterness, to a school district whose motto, appropriately, is 'All Children Can Learn' " (*Hoots*, 2000, p. 77). Describing Woodland Hills as "an excellent

249

school district striving to get better," he continued, "The evidence shows that the district—with funding and assistance from the commonwealth—has developed an educational program designed to improve the academic performance of all students, including African-American students" (*Hoots*, 2000, p. 71). Cohill added, "Even the most disheartening testimony presented at the hearing, which documented the continuing racial disparity in achievement and in incidents leading to student discipline, does not affect our conclusion that the district itself is doing a fine job of educating all of its children" *(Hoots,* 2000, p. 77). "The court," he concluded, "is confident that, with the exception of its failure to eliminate tracking in mathematics, the district now provides an equal educational opportunity to all of its students, regardless of race" (*Hoots*, 2000, p. 71).

Judge Cohill's praise of the progress made by Woodland Hills while it operated under the court mandate supports this book's conclusion that such mandates can drive positive change. However, the school district will now face some of the challenges discussed at the end of Chapter Fifteen. As several interviewees had surmised, important programs expired upon the court's finding that past problems had been remedied. During the 3-year transition plan, state funding for costs associated with court-ordered activities—about $4.5 million a year—will be phased out. The Higher Order Thinking Skills (HOTS) program was immediately eliminated, along with an SAT preparation course and pre-kindergarten programs. The widely-lauded Reading Recovery program fared only a little better; its funding will run out at the end of the 2000–2001 school year. Also given a single-year reprieve was K–6 summer school, while after-school and community-based tutorials were targeted for elimination after 2 years. Similarly, COIP-associated staff positions, such as guidance counselors and clinical supervisors, were due to be phased out within 1 or 2 years.

Whether Woodland Hills' detracking itself survives is, of course, an open question. At a district public meeting subsequent to Judge Cohill's decision, several parents showed up to request reinstatement of accelerated English, arguing that the district "is obligated to provide challenges for students who want them" (Brodbeck, 2000). In response to such pressure, I anticipate that the district will continue to negotiate incremental increases in stratification.

On August 11, 2000, the Rockford court announced that it, too, would partially grant unitary status. However this opinion, by Magistrate Judge P. Michael Mahoney, was very different from that handed down by Judge Cohill. Judge Mahoney's opinion lambastes the school board for its failure to implement the court's mandates in good faith. The first section of the opinion relates, in devastating detail, the board's recalcitrance and bad faith. Accordingly, and notwithstanding the 1997 Seventh Circuit opinion urging a quick resolution of the case, Mahoney denied most of the school district's requests.

On the issue of good/bad faith, the language of the two opinions provides a stark contrast. Commenting on the good faith of the Woodland Hills school board, Judge Cohill wrote, "The Board, although often opposed to judicial supervision and to many of our remedial programs, nevertheless supported [the superintendent] on the issue of detracking the Language Arts curriculum in the face of strong opposition by some white parents as well as by many of the teachers who taught the upper level courses" (*Hoots*, 2000, p. 71). Judge Mahoney, commenting on the bad faith of the Rockford school board, wrote that board members' "actions have demonstrated a refusal to participate meaningfully in the litigation, an outright abdication of their legal function, and efforts to derail the remedial process" (*People Who Care*, 2000, p. 15). This course of conduct, concluded Mahoney, "has left this court without any rational basis for finding good-faith support of the remedial process. . . . The court's experience in this case and the evidence admitted at trial make one proposition exceedingly clear: This Board, at this time, cannot be fully trusted with the constitutional welfare of the minority students committed to its care" (*People Who Care*, 2000, p. 23).

While the Rockford court restored local control over student discipline and co-curricular programs, the district's unitary status motion was denied in relation to between- and within-school integration. The court also ordered that the district continue various remedial programs, including Success For All, Reading Recovery and All-Day Kindergarten, through at least the 2006 school year. Judge Mahoney decided to stay the course with regard to in-school desegregation — keeping the $+/-12\%$ standard and attributing implementation problems to lack of effort, rather than to the goal itself. At the high school level, the judge wrote, compliance with classroom desegregation objectives was "in a shambles." (He included in his opinion the slice analysis presented in Appendix 1 of this book, showing on-going racial discrimination in the district's track placements.) The Rockford School Board voted to appeal this ruling, one member going so far as to call the opinion a "perpetuation of evil" (Wiser, 2000).

On April 18, 2001, the Seventh Circuit panel, again headed by Chief Judge Richard Posner, issued a terse opinion completely reversing Mahoney's judgment. This opinion offers a stark reminder of the cautions set forth in Chapter Five. The success of education-rights litigation ultimately depends on the underlying values of judges. As discussed earlier, Judge Posner values governance by the school's local community and believes that the interference of federal courts in such local control is an egregious wrong. He has little tolerance for charges of official discrimination in the absence of a smoking gun. Rockford's unequal educational attainment, he reasoned, is attributable to factors beyond the control of the school board, such as poverty, family size, "parental attitudes and behavior . . . and ethnic culture" (*People Who Care v. Rockford*, 2001, p. 1076).

An attorney for the People Who Care plaintiffs responded strongly to this part of Posner's opinion: "Ethnic culture—that is one step away from genetic inferiority. . . . I felt that was the most blatantly racist statement I've heard a judge say in a long time" (Associated Press, 2001). But the opinion should also be criticized for following the same disingenuous path as the 1997 opinion. Again, Posner played fast and loose with the lower court's factual findings, distorting some and ignoring others.

From one perspective, the appellate reversal in Rockford must be understood as a huge setback to the equity-minded efforts of that community's minority parents. But even Rockford has a silver lining. Certainly the leadership in Rockford—in particular, the school board majority—has been extraordinarily obstinate, moving forward only while kicking and screaming. Yet, while this resistance has squandered resources and opportunities, it has not prevented all progress. Judge Mahoney noted the successful integration of elementary school classrooms as well as the vast majority of junior high classrooms. Moreover, the mandate managed to eliminate the most blatant discrimination at the high school level. And two of the most hostile members of the school board majority lost their re-election bids on April 3, 2001, just two weeks before Posner reversed the desegregation judgment (Bonne, 2001). Resistance will continue, but progress can still be made.

Judge Cohill concluded his Woodland Hills unitary status opinion with thoughts that put this resistance in further perspective:

> Much has been made of the fact that the schools in the Woodland Hills School District have been the subject of litigation for nearly thirty years and under judicial supervision for twenty of those years, the implication being that this timeframe has been excessive and unnecessarily prolonged. School desegregation cases, however, are not susceptible to speedy adjudication. Most follow a trajectory similar to what we have seen in this case: a finding of liability; a fairly lengthy phase during which the parties which have been on opposite sides of a very heated litigation have difficulty agreeing on proposals to remedy the constitutional violation; strong opposition from many parents, teachers, and members of the community; and then a long stretch where the voluminous components of the desegregation remedy are not only implemented, but gradually take root, and the school district itself becomes an altered place. Only then can the question of whether the school district has achieved unitary status even be considered. Changes must occur not only in the routines of transporting, assigning, teaching, and evaluating students in a newly multicultural, heterogeneous educational environment, but also in the individuals—children, teachers, administrators, parents, and the commu-

nity—who truly *are* the school district. (*Hoots*, 2000, pp. 76–77; emphasis in original).

Given sufficient time, patience, and effort, positive change in Rockford may also persist and take root. The difficulty of this change process is undeniable, but it is commensurate with the importance of the change.

Appendix 1

Rockford Placement of Majority and Minority High School Students at Each "Slice" of
Math/Reading Achievement in Regular and Advanced Classes—1999–2000

Math/Reading Achievement— (Deciles)	Majority Students	Minority Students
First (Lowest)	633 Percent Advanced: 3%	1212 Percent Advanced: 2%
Second	941 Percent Advanced: 5%	1207 Percent Advanced: 4%
Third	1166 Percent Advanced: 7%	1103 Percent Advanced: 7%
Fourth	1492 Percent Advanced: 15%	1109 Percent Advanced: 13%
Fifth	1367 Percent Advanced: 20%	667 Percent Advanced: 15%
Sixth	1819 Percent Advanced: 31%	650 Percent Advanced: 24%
Seventh	1788 Percent Advanced: 46%	446 Percent Advanced: 37%
Eighth	2346 Percent Advanced: 61%	377 Percent Advanced: 59%
Ninth	2271 Percent Advanced: 74%	227 Percent Advanced: 70%
Tenth (Highest)	2124 Percent Advanced: 86%	98 Percent Advanced: 81%

Appendix 2

Factors Driving Science Achievement in Woodland Hills

GRADE 9		
Cohort 1	*Value**	*Std. Error*
Race	5.05	1.43
Track Placement (H to L), 9th Grade	−4.37	1.44
Sex	−4.68	1.17
Gifted Status	6.37	1.80
ITBS Science	0.23	0.04
Multiple R-Squared: 0.350		
Cohort 2	*Value*	*Std. Error*
Race	6.57	1.68
Track Placement (H to L), 9th Grade	−4.02	1.62
Sex	−5.42	1.29
Gifted Status	7.88	1.80
ITBS Science	0.10	0.04
Multiple R-Squared: 0.284		
Cohort 3	*Value*	*Std. Error*
Race	4.26	1.38
Track Placement (H to L), 9th Grade	−3.69	1.24
Sex	−4.17	1.07
Gifted Status	5.57	1.45
ITBS Science	0.23	0.04
Multiple R-Squared: 0.292		

*Because all of the analyses presented in Appendix 2 are "treatment" contrast analyses, the regression coefficients represent the effect size of a given contrast. The direction of each transition (contrast) is as follows:

    Race: From African American to White;
    Sex: From Female to Male;
    Course: From High- to Low-Track;
    Gifted Status: From not gifted-identified to gifted-identified.

(*continued*)

Factors Driving Science Achievement in Woodland Hills
(*continued*)

GRADE 10

Cohort 1	Value	Std. Error
Race	5.58	1.28
Track Placement (H to L), 10th Grade	9.84	2.03
Track Placement (H to M), 10th Grade	15.26	2.80
Sex	−0.28	1.03
Gifted Status	2.23	1.55
Track Placement (H to L), 9th Grade	−9.04	1.91
Average, 9th Grade	0.68	0.05
Multiple R-Squared: 0.403		

Cohort 2	Value	Std. Error
Race	3.48	1.40
Track Placement (H to L), 10th Grade	3.38	1.74
Track Placement (H to M), 10th Grade	9.81	2.45
Sex	−3.85	1.11
Gifted Status	4.73	1.46
Track Placement (H to L), 9th Grade	−6.34	1.77
Average, 9th Grade	0.41	0.06
Multiple R-Squared: 0.259		

Cohort 3	Value	Std. Error
Race	4.75	1.13
Track Placement (H to L), 10th Grade	5.42	1.48
Track Placement (H to M), 10th Grade	12.10	2.20
Sex	−0.14	0.88
Gifted Status	6.79	1.14
Track Placement, 9th Grade	−6.35	1.61
Average, 9th Grade	0.60	0.04
Multiple R-Squared: 0.453		

(*continued*)

Factors Driving Science Achievement in Woodland Hills
(*continued*)

GRADE 11

Cohort 1	Value	Std. Error
Race	2.31	1.13
Track Placement (H to L), 11th Grade	1.22	1.83
Track Placement (H to M), 11th Grade	5.94	2.00
Sex	−1.67	0.88
Gifted Status	−1.21	1.25
Track Placement (H to L), 10th Grade	−8.19	1.63
Track Placement (H to M), 10th Grade	−16.33	1.80
Average, 10th Grade	0.44	0.05
Multiple R-Squared: 0.449		

Cohort 2	Value	Std. Error
Race	−0.70	1.02
Track Placement (H to L), 11th Grade	−0.62	1.30
Track Placement (H to M), 11th Grade	11.39	1.51
Sex	−0.89	0.81
Gifted Status	1.08	1.07
Track Placement (H to L), 10th Grade	−5.80	1.25
Track Placement (H to M), 10th Grade	−18.08	1.61
Average, 10th Grade	0.59	0.04
Multiple R-Squared: 0.517		

Cohort 3	Value	Std. Error
Race	0.67	1.13
Track Placement (H to L), 11th Grade	6.35	1.67
Track Placement (H to M), 11th Grade	15.35	1.66
Sex	−0.70	0.87
Gifted Status	1.25	1.07
Track Placement (H to L), 10th Grade	−8.57	1.39
Track Placement (H to M), 10th Grade	−19.12	1.59
Average, 10th Grade	0.57	0.04
Multiple R-Squared: 0.435		

Appendix 3

Factors Driving English Achievement in Woodland Hills

MAIN EFFECTS ONLY

Low-Track to High-Track Transition

	Value*	Std. Error
6th Grade ITBS	0.76	0.03
Sex	−0.09	0.41
Race	1.50	0.56
Lunch Status	0.11	0.50
Gifted Status	1.86	0.55
Junior High	−0.63	0.45
Track Placement	2.39	0.52

Multiple R-Squared: 0.771

Untracked to Low-Track Transition

	Value	Std. Error
6th Grade ITBS	0.79	0.02
Sex	−0.95	0.30
Race	1.54	0.39
Lunch Status	−0.26	0.34
Gifted Status	2.11	0.41
Junior High	−0.31	0.32
Track Placement	−0.57	0.42
Track Placement(2)**	0.95	0.25

Multiple R-Squared: 0.768

(continued)

Factors Driving English Achievement in Woodland Hills
(*continued*)

High- to Untracked Transition		
	Value	Std. Error
6th Grade ITBS	0.79	0.02
Sex	−0.95	0.30
Race	1.54	0.39
Lunch Status	−0.26	0.34
Gifted Status	2.11	0.41
Junior High	−0.31	0.32
Track Placement	−1.13	0.38
Track Placement(2)	−0.76	0.27
Multiple R-Squared: 0.768		

*Because these are "Helmert" contrast analyses, the regression coefficients should be doubled in order to arrive at the effect size of a given contrast. The direction of each transition (contrast) is as follows:

Lunch: From no lunch to free/reduced lunch;

Race: From African American to White;

Sex: From Female to Male;

School: From West JH to East JH;

Course: From Low- to High-Track (each table identifies a different transition);

Gifted: From not gifted-identified to gifted-identified.

Note also that the multiple r-squared listed for each analysis corresponds to the simple linear model.

**Owing to the peculiarities of Helmert contrast analysis, the term labeled "track placement(2)" represents the impact of the transition of the arithmetic average of high track and untracked students contrasted with low track students. For the purposes of this study, this contrast is meaningless, yet this term is a necessary byproduct of the analysis.

(*continued*)

Factors Driving English Achievement in Woodland Hills
(*continued*)

WITH TWO-WAY INTERACTIONS		
Low- to High-Transition		
	Value	Std. Error
6th Grade ITBS	0.84	0.05
Sex	−0.89	1.88
Race	5.96	2.28
Lunch Status	−2.17	2.32
Gifted Status	−2.67	2.66
Junior High	−2.08	2.14
Track Placement	1.80	2.27
ITBS:Sex	0.03	0.04
ITBS:Race	−0.10	0.04
ITBS:Lunch	0.04	0.05
ITBS:Gifted	0.08	0.04
ITBS:School	0.02	0.04
ITBS:Track	0.01	0.04
Race:Sex	−0.52	0.61
Race:Lunch	−0.13	0.68
Race:Gifted	0.35	0.88
Race:School	0.09	0.66
Race:Track	0.83	0.77
Sex:Lunch	0.52	0.54
Sex:Gifted	−0.13	0.62
Sex:School	−0.02	0.50
Sex:Track	0.01	0.57
Lunch:Gifted	−0.66	0.84
Lunch:School	0.42	0.57
Lunch:Track	0.67	0.70
Gifted:School	−0.77	0.71
Gifted:Track	−0.38	1.05
School:Track	0.98	0.63
Multiple R-Squared: 0.788		

(*continued*)

Factors Driving English Achievement in Woodland Hills
(*continued*)

Untracked to Low-Tracked Transition		
	Value	*Std. Error*
6th Grade ITBS	1.13	0.05
Sex	−2.00	1.06
Race	1.02	1.27
Lunch Status	−1.02	1.17
Gifted Status	−2.77	1.68
Junior High	−1.10	1.13
Track Placement	1.23	1.54
Track Placement(2)	1.32	0.95
ITBS:Race	−0.01	0.04
ITBS:Sex	0.05	0.03
ITBS:Lunch	0.04	0.04
ITBS:Gifted	0.14	0.04
ITBS:School	0.03	0.03
ITBS:Track	−0.09	0.04
ITBS:Track(2)	−0.01	0.03
Race:Sex	−0.50	0.40
Race:Lunch	−0.19	0.41
Race:Gifted	−1.14	0.60
Race:School	−0.65	0.42
Race:Track	−0.54	0.51
Race:Track(2)	0.75	0.36
Sex:Lunch	0.25	0.35
Sex:Gifted	−0.28	0.42
Sex:School	0.30	0.33
Sex:Track	1.08	0.44
Sex:Track(2)	0.23	0.26
Lunch:Gifted	0.22	0.51
Lunch:School	−0.11	0.36
Lunch:Track	−0.18	0.47
Lunch:Track(2)	0.26	0.31
Gifted:School	−0.14	0.47
Gifted:Track	−0.63	1.01
Gifted:Track(2)	0.06	0.40
School:Track	−0.88	0.45
School:Track(2)	0.18	0.28

Multiple R-Squared: 0.784

(*continued*)

Factors Driving English Achievement in Woodland Hills
(*continued*)

	High- to Untracked Transition	
	Value	*Std. Error*
6th Grade ITBS	0.81	0.03
Sex	−2.45	1.30
Race	2.68	1.55
Lunch Status	−1.72	1.49
Gifted Status	−0.04	1.85
Junior High	−1.63	1.40
Track Placement	−2.97	1.75
Track Placement(2)	−0.07	1.20
ITBS:Race	−0.03	0.03
ITBS:Sex	0.04	0.02
ITBS:Lunch	0.04	0.03
ITBS:Gifted	0.04	0.03
ITBS:School	0.03	0.03
ITBS:Track	0.04	0.03
ITBS:Track(2)	−0.02	0.02
Race:Sex	−0.48	0.40
Race:Lunch	−0.22	0.42
Race:Gifted	−0.54	0.58
Race:School	−0.71	0.42
Race:Track	−0.81	0.56
Race:Track(2)	−0.70	0.34
Sex:Lunch	0.24	0.35
Sex:Gifted	−0.39	0.43
Sex:School	0.33	0.33
Sex:Track	−0.87	0.39
Sex:Track(2)	0.44	0.29
Lunch:Gifted	0.13	0.52
Lunch:School	−0.14	0.37
Lunch:Track	−0.37	0.46
Lunch:Track(2)	−0.24	0.32
Gifted:School	−0.37	0.48
Gifted:Track	0.19	0.50
Gifted:Track(2)	−0.40	0.66
School:Track	0.16	0.41
School:Track(2)	−0.49	0.31
Multiple R-Squared: 0.781		

Appendix 4

The Zone of Mediation for Oakville (First Approach)

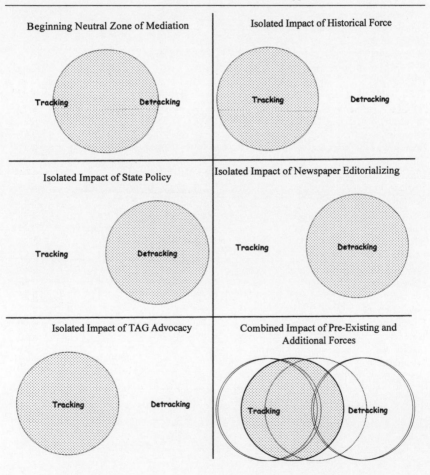

Appendix 5

Beginning Zone of Mediation

Addition/Layering of New Forces

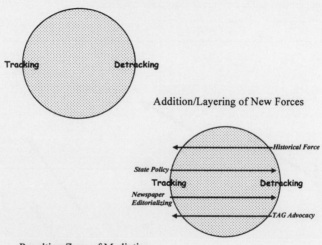

Resulting Zone of Mediation

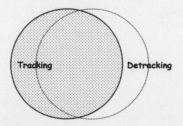

Appendix 6

Science Stratification in Woodland Hills

Beginning in the ninth grade, science courses in Woodland Hills show a division between high- and low-track classes. The following presents a rough outline of those courses. The thickness of the arrows corresponds to the approximate student breakdown:

9th Grade	10th Grade	11th Grade[1]	12th Grade

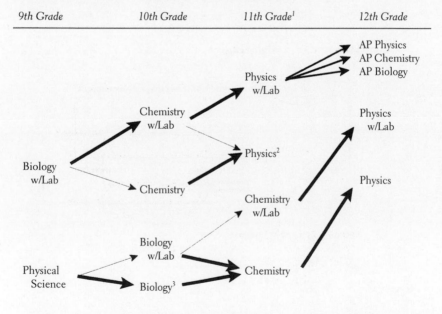

[1]Beginning in the 11th grade, a large number of students begin taking elective courses. Interestingly, the students attach a hierarchy to these electives, also. Thus, they perceive Zoology and Anatomy as challenging, high-status courses that prepare the students for college, while they perceive Ecology and Geology as low-status courses, taken by lower-achievers. The above chart omits these elective courses for two reasons: (1) I did not confirm the validity of these perceptions, and (2) the Biology, Chemistry, Physics series constitutes the main college preparatory curriculum.

[2]A few students who complete the lower-level Physics class in the 11th grade may take one or more of the AP courses—the Physics with Lab class in not a pre-requisite—however, most of these students will either take a 12th grade elective or no science course.

[3]Not shown on the chart are those students who do not continue in the series or who take only electives. This happens mostly with students in the lower track.

Notes

NOTES TO CHAPTER ONE

1. The original defendant school district in Wilmington was divided by the federal court into four successor districts. For the sake of simplicity, however, I will refer to the Wilmington case as still involving a single school district.

2. The detracking orders were obtained in *Hoots v. Commonwealth of Pennsylvania*, 1992; *People Who Care v. Rockford Board of Education School District No. 205*, 1994; and *Vasquez v. San Jose Unified School District*, 1994. A detracking order was not obtained in *Coalition to Save our Children v. State Board of Education, et al.*, 1995.

3. I joined Dr. Oakes in investigating the tracking in Wilmington's schools. I was not involved in her initial investigations in either Rockford or San Jose.

4. Race is unquestionably the most prominent "suspect classification" recognized under Fourteenth Amendment jurisprudence. Gender classifications, however, are also subject to heightened scrutiny from the courts, and various other characteristics (e.g., age, national origin, and "illegitimacy") have raised occasional judicial eyebrows.

5. This ideal of the policy-making process is somewhat akin to the "participatory" educational opportunity advocated and developed by Kenneth Howe (1997).

6. As discussed later in the book, not all "equity" concerns are equally justifiable. Some parents advocating a horizontal form of equity believe that their children's "merit" deserves to be rewarded with various forms of symbolic status. Such parents view as inequitable the removal of this status, which is attached to placement of their children in a high-track class. School leaders who attempt to bring this concern under the reconciliation umbrella, however, usually end up frustrated since detracking inevitably redistributes such status.

7. Tracking has additional historical roots in the efficiency-oriented reform proposals of so-called "administrative progressives" (e.g., Ellwood Cubberley) who dominated the educational landscape during the three decades preceding World War II (Tyack, 1974; see also Ravitch, 2000, who correctly notes that these efforts were also tinged with racism).

NOTES TO CHAPTER TWO

1. In the case of *Larry P. v. Riles* (1984), the federal court ruled that the use of IQ tests for track placement could be unconstitutional.

2. A high-level administrator in one of the districts offered the following analogy to explain the trepidation felt toward Dr. Oakes and me when we began studying the district:

> [T]he perception that I think a lot of staff members have for the two of you, and I share to some extent myself, is [analogous to when we're] watching those National Geographic Explorers [television programs]. I used to watch them with my daughter. [T]he documentarian [would] say, and here's the baby zebra, . . . and the lions are sort of stalking through the grass, and this zebra's going to be eaten alive, and my daughter keeps saying, "Run, run. Daddy, why don't they tell it to run. Why don't they scare it away?" And sure enough, the lion pounces on the zebra. . . . You're the lions.

3. The district covers less than 14 square miles and serves 12 suburban municipalities. It has approximately 60,000 residents and 29,000 residences.

4. The low-income figures are based on Chapter 1 (Title I) applications as reported to the Pennsylvania Department of Education.

5. In addition to General Braddock, the merged districts were Churchill, Edgewood, Swissvale, and Turtle Creek.

6. The secondary schools were desegregated in the first year, the elementary schools in the second.

7. The parties never agreed on the precise extent of that legal effect, and the court has never had a need to resolve the uncertainty.

8. I made four, week-long visits to the district during the 1996–1997 school year. I conducted semi-structured interviews with educators, policy-makers, students, and community members; I observed classrooms and school board meetings; and I collected school-specific documents. In addition, I collected data about formal district policies and conducted interviews with district administrators. Written protocols guided the interviews and observations, and these protocols also evolved in response to the developing theory and changing boundaries. Other interviewees included attorneys and others connected to the desegregation case. All told, I completed more than 90 interviews, spanning a wide variety of perspectives and viewpoints. I also analyzed the non-numerical documentary data using "content analysis" techniques, in order to classify courses into various track levels, determine placement criteria and processes, and identify curricular goals and course content.

9. These figures are as of 1995–1996. The proportion of African Americans increased slightly at both schools during the following year.

10. This ranking improved to 299th in 1997, beating out Davenport, Iowa. In 1998, the magazine changed its presentation format, only comparing cities of similar

sizes in the same region. Rockford was listed in the category, "midsized cities in the midwest," and it ranked 24th out of 24. The magazine again changed its format in 1999. The on-line rankings now allow readers the flexibility to select the weights given to various rating factors. Using this on-line "quick search" engine and rating all factors as equally important, Rockford moved up to 278th.

11. The other three cases arose out of districts in Kansas, South Carolina, and Virginia.

12. The provision requiring the racial segregation of schools was finally removed formally from the constitution in July of 1994.

NOTES TO CHAPTER THREE

1. For example, the federal (Fourteenth Amendment) Due Process Clause may support some tracking challenges (grounded in such decisions as *Goss v. Lopez*, 1975; *Hobson v. Hansen*, 1967; and *Wisconsin v. Constantineau*, 1971), as might Title I of the Elementary and Secondary Education Act (see Weckstein, 1999, pp. 327–330; Losen, 1999, pp. 535–536). The educational rights granted in various state constitutions should also not be overlooked. (See, e.g., California Constitution, Art. IX, Sections 1 & 5, which impose an affirmative duty on the State to provide all California students with a basic public education. Other states' courts have relied on similar education clauses to issue watershed rulings, primarily invalidating inequitable school funding laws and procedures. See, e.g., *Edgewood Independent School Dist. v. Kirby* (Texas), 1989; *McDuffy v. Secretary of Educ.* (Mass.), 1993.) The Connecticut Supreme Court applied that state's education clause, in combination with its segregation clause, to order educational improvements, as well as desegregation, in Hartford schools (*Sheff v. O'Neill*, 1995).

State constitutions' equal protection clauses can also provide a useful legal basis for tracking challenges. (See, e.g., *Serrano v. Priest*, 1976, and *Butt v. State of California*, 1992, which together maintain that education is a fundamental interest in California and that denial of education provides an independent basis on which to make an equal protection claim. Strict scrutiny is triggered under the California equal protection guarantee if the state discriminates on the basis of race or wealth or if the fundamental interest in education is denied or infringed.)

2. Section 601 of Title VI provides, "No person in the United States shall, on the ground of race, color or national origin, be excluded from participation in, be denied benefits of, or be subjected to discrimination under any program or activity receiving Federal financial assistance." Title VI, section 602, "authorizes and directs" federal departments and agencies that extend federal financial assistance to particular programs or activities "to effectuate the provisions of section 2000d [section 601] . . . by issuing rules, regulations, or orders of general applicability." 42 U.S.C. § 2000d-1. The Department of Education, in exercising its statutory authority under section 602, promulgated such a regulation, codified as 34 C.F.R. §100.3(b)(2), which prohibits a funding

recipient from "utilizing criteria or methods of administration which have the effect of subjecting individuals to discrimination because of their race, color, or national origin, or have the effect of defeating or substantially impairing accomplishment of the program as respects individuals of a particular race, color, or national origin." That is, the regulation does not include an intent requirement. It is section 602 that may provide the basis for post-*Alexander* disparate impact lawsuits under 42 U.S.C. §1983 (see *Powell v. Ridge*, 1999, p. 403; Mank, 2001). Mank (2001) outlines this approach and makes a strong case for its advisability.

3. It should be noted, however, that *Brown* and its progeny have been criticized for their basic premise that desegregation should be the remedy for such discrimination. Professor Derrick Bell (1977) has argued that "societal racism can disadvantage African-American children as effectively (although more subtly) in integrated as in segregated schools" (p. 373). He contends that African-American leaders should not be wedded to any particular goal or remedy. Instead, they should listen to what African-American parents want from schools and then design strategies that utilize constitutional rights and political leverage to achieve those educational goals. If separate but equal schooling is what the African-American parents want, then that should be the goal.

Most African-American leaders, however, remain committed to desegregation. For example, Julius Chambers (1977), then-President of the NAACP Legal Defense Fund, rejected Professor Bell's suggestion that African Americans may want to use the *Plessy* "separate but equal" doctrine, rather than the *Brown* case, in order to achieve equal educational opportunity. "[W]e are not told how equal educational opportunities will be accomplished under present-day societal racism even with new emphasis on separate but equal or representation on or control of local school boards" (p. 42).

This debate has intensified in recent years, with some younger African-American leaders advocating abandoning desegregation in favor of a focus on improving neighborhood schools. Some polls show most African Americans in agreement with this policy.

4. Craven (1977), a Judge on the U.S. Court of Appeals for the Fourth Circuit, stated this idea (of the relative inability of social scientists to sway courts) rather eloquently: "judges seem to have seldom allowed sociology to interfere with a good theory" (p. 156). I return to the question of judicial values in Chapter Five.

5. This discussion of desegregation has focused on between-school, rather than within-school, issues. However, segregated educational facilities at the classroom level can replace, and even intensify, harmful segregation at the school level. Several studies have focused on the role of tracking and racially segregated classrooms in subverting gains that might otherwise come about from desegregation (see Cohen, 1984; Hallinan & Williams, 1989; Koslin, Koslin, & Pargament, 1972; Mickelson, 2000; Schofield & Sagar, 1977).

6. Similarly, Wells & Crain (1994) point out the damage done by the overemphasis on test score comparisons and measurements of short-term outcomes, Coons (1977) seems to believe that any social science evidence is just window-dressing, and Brown (1992) argues that goals focused only on the benefits of desegregation for African Americans perpetuate the stigmatization of African Americans as inferior.

NOTES TO CHAPTER FOUR

1. In lieu of presenting the details of the initial Rockford data, I refer the reader to relevant pages of the detailed opinion published by the federal district court. *People Who Care v. Rockford School District* (1994). I have, however, included analyses of more recent Rockford data, gathered in connection with the district's motion for unitary status filed in late-1999.

2. In each case, the quantitative data came directly from the school district. When school districts operate under the supervision of a federal court, they are often required to keep detailed records concerning each student's courses, achievement, race and other characteristics.

3. Tables 4.2 and 4.3 divide students into 10 groups, or slices, according to their achievement score. Students in the first slice were those who scored between 0 and 9 normal curve equivalent points (NCEs), inclusive, on the ITBS. These 10-point slices continue through the 90–99 slice. NCEs are not percentiles. Each 10-point range in a normal distribution differs in the percentage of the population it includes depending upon its particular position in the normal distribution. The slices closer to the center of the distribution include a much larger proportion of the population than the slices closer to the tails.

4. I examined three cohorts of students: the classes of 1995, 1996 and 1997. Each cohort included two transitions: from 9th to 10th grade and from 10th to 11th grade. Figures 4.5 and 4.6 present only the first transition for the first cohort. The phenomenon, however, remained consistent for each cohort and each transition.

5. The three slices between 10 and 39 do show an incremental preference for high-track placement of African Americans over Whites. However, these preferences involve small numbers of students, small numerical differences, and percentage differences of 1% or less.

6. Both logistic regression and the more common linear regression are useful tools for developing prediction models. As demonstrated in the following section (concerning the prediction model for students' achievement), linear regression is best used when the dependent variable can take on many different values (e.g., scores along a scale of 1–100). By contrast, logistic regression is used where, as here, the dependent variable can have only two values (e.g., high-track or low-track); the model estimates the probability of either of the two events occurring. More technically, linear regression estimates the parameters of the model using the method of least squares; regression coefficients are selected that result in the smallest sum of squares between the observed and the predicted values of the dependent variable. In logistic regression, the parameters of the model are estimated using the maximum-likelihood method; the selected coefficients make the observed results most likely.

7. The designation of a student as, for instance, "gifted" is probably based upon a variety of factors, such as the student's grades, test scores, race, free/reduced lunch status, and sex. Including exceptional ability as a variable, therefore, can hide the strength

of these other factors. For instance, assume a simplified case where Mary is designated as gifted for two reasons: she scored in the 95th percentile on the ITBS and she is female. If we run an analysis using these three independent variables (exceptional ability, ITBS, and sex), the latter two variables will be washed out by the first. Put another way, the first "captures" the second and third.

8. As explained in the following discussion of the factors driving students' achievement (GPA), the relationship described by these logistic regression models is self-perpetuating. ITBS score and GPA drive course placement, but they also drive higher GPA—*and* course placement drives higher GPA.

9. Crosstabs allow for direct, two-way comparisons. Assume, for example, a data set with 20 people, 10 of whom are male. Among those males, 4 were placed in the high-track and 6 were placed in the low-track. Among those same males, 3 were African American and 7 were White. To investigate the racial breakdown of track placement among male students, we would run a cross tab of the 10 male students, which would give us the percentages of White high-track students, White low-track students, African-American high-track students, and African-American low-track students.

10. I first divided the students into five relatively comparable sub-sections, based on their SAT9 scores (the scores used are national percentiles). The first subsection consisted of students scoring in the bottom 20% of all students. The second was the next highest-scoring quintile, up through the top 20%. I then divided the students in these quintiles into students placed in the higher-level classes and those placed in lower-level classes. I did this for both math and English. The RSD students take the SAT9 only through the 10th grade, so I focused on the earliest grades possible: 8th grade for math; 9th grade for English. Next I plotted these students' progress over time. About 10% of students each year moved between ability-levels, generally in a downward direction (recall the earlier discussion of rigidity). In order accurately to demonstrate the impact of remaining in a given track, students who moved are not represented.

The most dramatic example of the impact of ability grouping is the contrast between the higher-grouped math students from the 2nd quintile and the lower-grouped students from the 3rd quintile: the group means actually cross. That is, after three years of ability grouping, the low-tracked group with an initial mean of 39 had a mean of 41, while the high-tracked group with an initial mean of 25 had a mean of 42.

11. This model uses treatment contrasts; the regression coefficients state the actual effect size for each independent variable. Also, please note that, while I focus in this section on Cohort 1, the other two cohorts show similar results, as set forth in Appendix 2.

12. This result can be explained, in whole or in part, by the fact that the distribution and mean of grade distribution were elevated in the higher-tracked classes.

13. In fact, the strongest interactions are between the course placement and achievement variables.

14. Note that the regression models, which show "contrasts" between students placed in different tracks, do not determine whether these differences should be expressed as benefits or as detriments. As felt by real students, they are no doubt expressed

as both. However, I have decided to express all the differences as detriments. That is, I assume that each student begins with a score of 80, and any differences between the most-advantaged student and the less-advantaged students are then subtracted from that base score.

15. To account for the non-orthogonality (i.e., the fact that the untracked Cohort B has many more students than the Cohort A high- and low-track subgroups), these analyses used so-called "Helmert contrasts." One of the quirks of such contrasts is that the resulting regression coefficients must be doubled in order to arrive at the effect size. (Note that continuous variables, such as ITBS scores and averages, are not coded using such contrasts, and their coefficients should not be doubled.)

16. Appendix 3 includes these analyses with two-way interactions.

17. Due to the use of "helmert contrast coding," the coefficient representing the transition from high track to untracked (-2.97) must be doubled.

NOTES TO CHAPTER FIVE

1. The complete published opinion in *People Who Care v. Rockford Board of Education School District No. 205* is found at 851 F.Supp. 905 (N.D. Ill. 1994). The opinion is over 300-pages long, but the tracking analysis is, for the most part, limited to pages 940–999.

2. The district's "system-wide attempt to separate the races" was summarized by the district court as including, but not limited to, the following:

1. The tracking of students by race into various educational programs offered by the [district];
2. The drawing and alteration of school attendance area boundaries in such a way as to create, maintain or increase racial or ethnic segregation of students;
3. The maintenance of racially and ethnically segregated branches of schools;
4. The failure to design and implement an effective desegregation plan even when ordered to do so by a Federal Court and by the [Illinois State Board of Education];
5. The provision of inequitable transportation and access to transportation to students based upon their race and ethnic origin;
6. The disproportionate placing of the burdens of desegregation on minority students;
7. The disparate placement of facilities and equipment so as to burden minority students and not provide them with an equal educational opportunity;
8. The perpetuation of discriminatory conditions in the make-up of the Rockford Board of Education; and,
9. The disproportionate burdens placed on minorities in the assignment of special education students. (*Rockford*, 1994, p. 933.)

3. The term "finding" is used in law to refer to an evidentiary conclusion reached by a jury or a judge. The court's findings are usually expressly set forth in one section of the court's opinion.

4. The alternative programs were found by the court to have "created isolated classrooms of white students in predominantly black schools in which children were in the same buildings, but had no interaction" (*Rockford*, 1994, p. 915).

5. Juries and judges invariably rely upon such foreseeable segregative results of decisions, and other forms of "circumstantial" evidence, to determine intent. As this court explained, "where proof of intent is involved, it is a rare circumstance indeed where a defendant admits that there was an intention to violate the law" (*Rockford*, 1994, p. 932).

6. Judge Posner, an appointee of President Reagan, is one of the most prominent judges in the nation. He is popularly known for his recent role as "mediator" in the Microsoft antitrust litigation. In legal circles he is probably best known as a foremost advocate and architect of the economic analysis of legal issues, which focuses attention on the economic consequences of judicial decisions, but he has written extensively on a wide variety of subjects. In general, he advocates that laws should be interpreted pursuant to a rigorous investigation of how the law is actually applied and how it alters people's behavior.

7. Interestingly, this standard was applied by the Eleventh Circuit Court of Appeals in *Georgia State Conference of Branches of NAACP v. Georgia* (1985) to a situation that was the inverse of the Rockford case. The trial court had determined that the school district's tracking system in that case was educationally beneficial and an appropriate educational practice (basically Judge Posner's viewpoint). The appellate court refused to second-guess this determination, citing *Swint* and *Anderson*.

8. This highlights an important point, particularly for attorneys reading this chapter: the school district did not make detracking a significant issue during the hearings for the remedial order. The detracking provisions had been proposed by the court-appointed Special Master and were adopted by the court with little opposition (and much stipulation) from the school district. Therefore, since the parties did not extensively contest this issue, the record that was presented to the court of appeals—while containing the earlier-presented evidence of the *discriminatory use* of tracking by the district—contained little evidence concerning the *educational detriments* of tracking and the educational benefits of detracking. A more extensive record might have provided the evidence necessary to support a detracking order—even before this same appellate panel. Perhaps more importantly, the *Rockford* appellate decision has little applicability for future cases if a stronger record, setting out tracking's educational disadvantages, is developed at the trial level in those cases.

9. The unworkability of the Posner model was conceded by the school district in later proceedings: "It is almost impossible to provide totally objective criteria for ability grouping. Such a requirement is not consistent with providing students the best educational opportunities available" (*Rockford*, Case no. 89 C 20168 (W.D. Ill.), Order of Magistrate, May 7, 1998, p. 3).

10. The appellate opinion also expresses indignation at the perceived "reverse discrimination" resulting from the remedial order, providing a startling contrast to the panel's apparent lack of anger concerning the school district's discrimination against African Americans.

11. This appellate reasoning hinges on the absence from the trial court record of documentation of a discriminatory intent by the district at the time of tracking's initial adoption. But, as noted in footnote 8, these issues were never placed at issue (i.e., there was never an active controversy between the parties), so there was no reason to develop an adequate record.

12. Moreover, Posner's legal positivism and minimalism are themselves such principles.

13. The Supreme Court, in *Milliken v. Bradley*, 418 U.S. 717 (1974), and *Missouri v. Jenkins*, 515 U.S. 1139 (1995), evidenced a similar value preference for local control over equity.

14. Surprisingly similar judicial dynamics played out in two of the other districts in this study. The desegregation cases in both San Jose and Wilmington passed from one judge to another, and in both cases the succeeding judges voiced values different from their predecessors. In San Jose, the judge who initially heard the case died soon before the consent decree was signed. He was relatively "hands-on" and involved in ensuring that the school reforms were effectively implemented. Upon his passing, the case was assigned to a judge who, while very competent and not hostile to the plaintiffs, viewed the litigation in a much more technical and distant way. The lesson that the school district (and the plaintiffs) seemed to take from this shift in judges was that a lesser degree of reform would suffice in order to obtain a grant of unitary status.

The contrast in judges was considerably more stark in Wilmington. Recall that the court had ordered busing in 1978. This desegregation was remarkably peaceful and, by most accounts, successful (Orfield, 1999), yet it became a heated political issue in 1992 during Delaware's gubernatorial campaign. Gary Scott, the Republican candidate, who was running behind Thomas Carper, the Democrat, erected a number of billboards demanding an end to busing, and this apparently struck a chord among the electorate. Carper responded by agreeing to ask the federal court to declare that the Wilmington area had ended discrimination (achieved unitary status) and should, therefore, be released from court control. Carper, now a U.S. Senator, subsequently won the election and began his pursuit of the unitary status motion.

In response to the renewed controversy, the business community and several other community leaders brokered a fragile agreement among the four school boards and the plaintiff. They agreed to a 4-year phase-out of court control in return for programs to benefit minority students within the schools, including efforts to reduce the disproportionate number of African Americans suspended from school and placed in special education. At the end of the 4 years, local school officials would be given the authority and discretion to decide whether to continue efforts towards desegregation. Further, the school boards agreed to replace the at-large system of electing board members with a district system intended to boost minority representation.

Before going into effect, the settlement needed the approval of both the court and the state legislature. Murray Schwartz, the judge who had overseen the litigation for the past decade and a half, recused himself from further deliberations concerning the case because he had become too involved in the negotiations. He was replaced with Sue Robinson, an appointee of the elder President Bush who—by all indications— wished to limit court involvement as much as possible. On the eve of the vote in the state legislature to provide the funding necessary for the settlement agreement, she issued a memorandum suggesting that she was reluctant to get involved in quality-of-education issues. The compromise was already under attack by conservative legislators as a "quota plan," and the Judge's comments—signaling that she would withdraw the court from involvement in desegregation activities—served to kill the deal. A few years later, notwithstanding the evidence reproduced on Chapter Four, she granted the districts' motions for unitary status.

15. Two years later, in March of 1999, the same appellate panel issued an interesting opinion in which Judge Posner chastised the RSD school board for failing to take the right message away of the 1997 opinion. The desired message was apparently, *Now, go back to Rockford, cooperate a bit, make a some progress, and you will then be entitled to a grant of unitary status*. Instead, the opinion empowered those vehemently resisting desegregation. They elected a new majority to the school board, and this new board majority voted to withhold funding from the remedial order. Judge Posner's exasperation is palpable: "We hoped that our 1997 decision, in cutting back the scope of the comprehensive remedial decree, would set the stage for an early termination. We had thought it would be followed by the school board's submitting a plan for winding up the litigation within a definite and short period of time. Instead we are being inundated by groundless appeals [by the school board and its members] challenging peripheral and for the most part unexceptionable facets of the magistrate judge's administration of the remedial decree" (*People Who Care v. Rockford*, 1999, p. 1090–91).

NOTES TO CHAPTER SIX

1. In American school literature, the use of the term "school ethos" is most commonly associated with Rutter (1979), who focused on high expectations, a positive interpersonal environment, and an emphasis on academics. In the United Kingdom, "school ethos" is the term generally used to refer to a school's philosophy and environment. Similarly, an Irish Department of Education circular describes what is meant by a positive school ethos: "the quality of relationships, both the professional relationships between teachers and the ways in which pupils and teachers treat each other. This positive ethos permeates the school and helps in forming a strong sense of social cohesion within the school" (Ireland, Dept. of Ed. and Science, 1990; see also Martin, 1997).

2. In addition, pioneering social psychologist Kurt Lewin (1951) developed "Field Theory," explaining how environmental forces shape human behavior. He saw human behavior as existing within a context formed by "driving" and "restraining"

forces, resulting in a "quasi-stationary" equilibrium. He developed a basic change model of unfreezing, changing, and then refreezing. For change to occur, he argued that existing forces must first be altered. Simply adding a new change (driving) force, he observed, often produced an immediate counterforce, resulting in the equilibrium being maintained.

This theory of resistance to change might initially seem at odds with my recommendations in this book. After all, Lewin ultimately recommends focusing on removing restraining forces, arguing that driving forces are usually already present. In contrast, I assert that equity-minded school change may benefit most from new driving forces (in the form of mandates). However, Lewin's theorizing was about psychological change—akin to the normative changes that I discuss in this book. Lewin was concerned with prejudice and the changing of normative beliefs. Within that psychological/normative frame, we are in agreement. Restraining forces standing in the way of psychological change do need to be removed, an idea discussed in greater detail in Chapter Nine. I do not agree, however, that Lewin's observations and recommendations can be transferred to the broader context of political change.

3. Boyd touches on this idea when he acknowledges that "persuasive and skillful [educators can use] public relations techniques [to] modify the community zone of tolerance to some degree to reduce the extent to which it constrains them" (Boyd, 1976, p. 552).

NOTES TO CHAPTER SEVEN

1. Many of the persons interviewed for this study stressed the importance of confidentiality, and such confidentiality was promised in writing to everyone interviewed. Toward this end, all names of interviewees and district figures are pseudonyms. However, because of this assurance of confidentiality, because of the strong concerns of many interviewees, and because the districts themselves could not be (and have not been) kept confidential, I judged the use of pseudonyms to be, for most interviewees, insufficient to maintain anonymity. Instead, I sometimes identify informants using such terms as "an interviewee" or "an observer" or, as in this case, a "long-time community member." At other times, more specific terms, such as "a teacher" or "an English teacher" or even "a secondary school English teacher" seemed appropriate. In deciding how much specificity to use, I considered a variety of factors, including: (a) the quotation's degree of controversy; (b) the uniqueness of the speaker's status (i.e., "an English teacher" is less unique than "an assistant superintendent"); and (c) the importance of standpoint and context for the understanding the particular statement.

Certain people, such as a district superintendent, are identified (using pseudonyms) and attributed only for statements previously published. That is, quotations in the newspapers and official reports from the Office of Evaluation are properly attributed to the speaker or writer. However, any statements that such people made in confidence to the author remain confidential.

2. The use of an initial capital letter in brackets to begin a sentence within a quotation indicates that material has been omitted, including, but not necessarily limited to, the beginning of the next sentence. For the sake of visual clarity, I have chosen not to use an ellipse in some of these situations. For example, part of this quotation might have originally read: "It's a great American tradition: hate your neighbor. You know. It's like that, so if he lives just far enough away, you can hate him."

3. Teachers told of tracking in reading, science, math, and English, some beginning as early as the fourth grade. For example, a high school math teacher recalled:

> When we first went into the merger we had two [lower-level] courses, . . . one was a Basic Algebra and one was a Basic Geometry. [S]everal years into the merger, they questioned those [courses] because of the word Basic. [So we] changed the title to "Introduction to Algebra" and "Introduction to Geometry," [which continued] for another couple of years and then they were dropped.

4. Some of the remedial classes were eliminated as early as 1983. In connection with the consent decree negotiation and agreement, almost all of the remaining remedial classes were eliminated by 1988.

5. The qualitative aspects of this study are descriptive and explorative; they are not designed to quantify. Nonetheless, in deciding which ideas, viewpoints, and phenomena to present and to emphasize, some implicit quantification was necessary. If 3 people held viewpoint X about a subject, and 20 other people held viewpoint Y, the discussion of this matter would present viewpoint Y as the dominant viewpoint. An obvious example of this phenomenon is the viewpoint of Woodland Hills' secondary English teachers about the detracking reform: a substantial majority favored tracking. To give the reader an idea about how much weight to place on any given statement, I use descriptive terms such as "a few," "some," "many," "most," or "a substantial majority." These terms lack precise quantifiable definitions, but are intended to be understood as they would be in everyday use (i.e., the above list is in increasing numerical order).

6. The curriculum audit team investigated the board in terms of its influence on curriculum reform, and it was not in a position to issue a conclusive statement about these matters of Board demeanor, nor did it purport to do so. Instead, the team simply reported the evaluations offered by the people they spoke with.

7. This purported recommendation, if true, would be at odds with The College Board's "Equity 2000" program, which advises against ability grouping (The College Board, 1989). This teacher's statement, however, is not offered for its validity; rather, it is offered to show one instance of the support that college admissions pressures can offer for continuing a stratified system.

8. Among the cases discussed in the articles were *Board of Education v. Dowell* (1991) (Associated Press, 1991), *Freeman v. Pitts* (1992) (Associated Press, 1992), and *Missouri v. Jenkins* (1995) (Epstein, 1995).

NOTES TO CHAPTER EIGHT

1. The 1985 desegregation order focused on achieving between-school desegregation using magnet schools and a "controlled choice" plan that allowed for parental choice of schools, so long as the resulting ethnic balance at each school remained within a predetermined range.

2. In general, the monitor's report seemed to fall on deaf ears. District officials saw her as being aligned with the interests of the plaintiffs. They seemingly mistrusted her and put considerable effort into limiting her ability to investigate the schools effectively (e.g., by arguing that her budget should be decreased).

3. Indeed, the African-American principal of one of the district's southern high schools had moved to phase out tracking (Watson, 1991b).

4. The College Board is a membership-based, nonprofit educational organization that oversees the tests taken by high school students applying for college. Through its Equity 2000 project it has worked with school systems around the country for the past decade to eliminate tracking in mathematics programs in middle and high schools, with the goal of having all students successfully complete college-preparatory algebra and geometry.

5. These statements were made on September 30, 1994, at a conference, "Grant Writing and Designing Schools for Equity and Excellence: Increasing Within-School Integration," Culver City, California.

6. The earned income tax is a 0.5% tax on income earned by district residents.

7. A lawsuit challenging the funding system was filed in the early 1990s. However, the dismissal of this action was affirmed in October 1999, by the Pennsylvania Supreme Court (*Pennsylvania Association of Rural and Small Schools v. Association of School Districts in Support of Excellence and Equity*, 558 Pa. 374, 737 A.2d 246 (1999)). A separate lawsuit, based on the Department of Education regulations enforcing Title VI of the 1964 Civil Rights Act, has been filed by City of Philadelphia and its school district, calling attention to the disparate impact of the state's funding formula on minority students. This second action has met with greater legal success (see *Powell v. Ridge*, 189 F.3d 387 (3d Cir. 1999)). After the U.S. Supreme Court refused to review the Third Circuit decision (in *Ryan* v. *Powell* and *Ridge* v. *Powell* (Case Nos. 99-527 and 99-574)), the parties agreed to a funding package for the City schools. The agreement's term lasts only one year, but the *Powell* plaintiffs agreed to suspend prosecution of the lawsuit for that year (Snyder, Mezzacappa, & Sanchez, 2000).

8. The other parties invited the Commonwealth to join in this process, but the invitation was not accepted. The Commonwealth, they charged, has instead made a practice of resisting payment until a court order mandating payment.

9. Consider Pennsylvania House Bill No. 1689, passed in 1996, which stated, "It is the finding of the general assembly that the neighborhood school is the cornerstone of Pennsylvania's education policy on the assignment of pupils to public school." The

bill withdrew authority from the state human relations commission (and all other state agencies) to mandate busing for desegregation purposes. (Wakefield, 1996a.)

10. The formula funded special education based on the approximation that each district had a population with 15% moderately impaired students and 1% severely impaired students. Specifically, the funding (as of the 1996–1997 school year) was determined as follows: (a) by multiplying the district's actual Average Daily Membership by 15% times $1,040; plus (b) multiplying the district's actual Average Daily Membership by 1% times $13,000.

In addition, the state provided a small aid supplement to districts with special education costs in excess of 150% of the state average. This supplement, however, did not cover all additional costs, and it decreased substantially following the 1995–1996 school year.

11. The approximate numbers for the 1996–1997 school year proved even more startling. The district budgeted about $7.8 million for special education, and the state may reimburse only $1.3 million (see Estadt, 1997d).

12. On a related note, Pennsylvania is one of eight states that include gifted children within the Individualized Education Program (IEP) requirement. That is, gifted students are entitled to an IEP similar to that provided for special education students. However, this state mandate comes with no funding. As a top district administrator put it, "they're not considered in the equation. You get nothing extra for gifted [identified children] except the fun of delivering IEPs to all these parents."

13. The vote for this 3-mill increase came just 5 days after the board had deadlocked 4–4 on a budget that included a 4-mill increase. During the intervening weekend, an unofficial board committee worked to cut $1.1 million from the budget. These cuts included, among other things, a decision to delay a new $150,000 elementary Spanish program for at least one year. (Dudiak, 1997b.) Recall that a 1-mill increase is the equivalent of a $1 increase on each $4,000 of assessed property value.

14. It is worth noting, as evidence of parental resistance to desegregation efforts, that when Judge Weber died in 1990, parents flooded the district office with calls anxiously asking if his death legally brought about the end of the merger (Brody, 1995).

15. Young and other administrators also cited as a major accomplishment their ability to establish a firm and court-approved COIP budget in a timely fashion. Prior to Young's tenure, the district and the Commonwealth disputed the amount and contents of the COIP budget until well after the district spent the money. As discussed earlier, this resulted in a tremendous amount of insecurity and murkiness concerning programs. It also resulted in the district having to settle, after the fact, for incomplete reimbursement. No doubt, this accomplishment did help to shape a more hospitable zone of mediation for detracking. Court-mandated funding acted as a positive force on that zone; and Young increased the security and reliability of that funding.

16. In part, the memorandum reads:

> I have been consistent in telling you, and any parents who are willing to listen, that the research indicates and my experience shows that heteroge-

neous grouping is the only way that we can expect and receive high standards of achievement from all children. The research also indicates that teachers who are properly trained to teach heterogeneously grouped classes are able to challenge all students by diversifying their instruction.

One thing is clear, however, many teachers who have been assigned highly motivated children in homogeneous groupings find it disturbing when they are given heterogeneously groupings of students. There is no doubt, teaching heterogeneously grouped children is difficult. It requires planning and skill, but I expect it from all of our teachers.

17. Ultimately, as discussed in the Epilogue, Young succeeded in gaining a release of the district from most court supervision, and he then retired.

NOTES TO CHAPTER NINE

The title quotation is from Samuel Johnson (1755, preface): "If the changes that we fear be thus irresistible, what remains but to acquiesce with silence, as in the other insurmountable distresses of humanity? It remains that we retard what we cannot repel, that we palliate what we cannot cure."

1. A principal explained that the teachers had only themselves to blame for the increased course load, saying that they "did it to themselves" when their union negotiated and approved the most recent contract. He stated that the union vote split "right down the line" between elementary teachers and secondary teachers, "and there were more elementary teachers." The elementary teachers perceived the secondary teachers as getting off easy with only five courses a day.

2. After this study was completed, a high-level administrator told me that the secondary schools had begun, in the 1997–1998 school year, assigning one less section (from six down to five) for their English teachers. This was negotiated with the teachers' union and was done to accommodate both detracking and the extra time needed for portfolio-based assessment. For the same reasons, these English teachers, according to the administrator, are also now provided a substitute teacher for one day per month.

3. As mentioned earlier, other teachers had a very positive attitude about the detracking. These teachers are discussed in greater detail at the end of the following discussion of teacher resistance.

CHAPTER TEN NOTES

1. Of those public secondary schools that reported offering core curriculum courses differentiated in terms of content, quality (or intensity) of work, or expectations regarding independent work (86% of all schools), the vast majority (83% of that 86%) indicated that they gave students open access to any course—provided that the students had taken the prerequisite course(s) (NCES, 1994).

NOTES TO CHAPTER ELEVEN

1. One high school teacher devised a "theory," explaining as follows:

There's sort of like a critical mass. If you've got [a majority of] kids on the willing-to-work side, if you have two-thirds of your class, they'll pull the other third along. But what happens when the pendulum swings two-thirds of the way the other way? When you have one-third of the class that is doing great, but you have to spend your time with all the discipline problems, getting activities for the other two-thirds of the class, these advanced kids start saying, hey, you're neglecting us. You're spending all your time with these kids. So they start acting out, and at some point, if you have a bell shaped curve in your class that's tipped one way or the other so you have a critical mass of either want-to-learns or critical mass [of] don't want to learns, it can throw you either way.

2. Again recall the district's position that its science courses were not tracked. District leaders explained the apparent tracking, and at least some of the racial disparities, in these courses by pointing to the fact that the "with lab" courses have separate lab periods, while the regular courses just try to fit labs into their daily instruction. Since vo-tech students simply do not have sufficient time in their schedules to accommodate the extra lab periods, they enroll in the regular course and the "tracking" becomes an unfortunate artifact. The district later offered this same rationale to the court, in connection with a motion for unitary status, and the court accepted the argument (*Hoots*, 2000, p. 36; see discussion in the epilogue to this book).

3. Recall the teacher quoted earlier as saying, "I think it's a matter of choice for the student[s] to take whatever they'd like to take." Another teacher insisted that he, too, "would leave the decision to the guidance counselor, the student and the parents." Other teachers demonstrated a questionable capacity to administer the task. For instance, a science teacher, commenting on an outwardly-bright African-American girl in his class, dismissively opined, "she's not bad, [but] she doesn't have the tools to be an 'A' student at this level of Chemistry."

4. The "quota" allegation was incorrect—the district did not have a racial quota for these classes. However, such false beliefs were nonetheless present among the faculty and powerfully impacted the detracking zone. Consider the junior high school language arts teacher who mistakenly insisted that her school offered an AP Biology class to ninth graders. She then argued that some students, who had "barely passed Reading" were placed in this imaginary AP Biology class "because first of all, they're minority and secondly they have to be put in there because guidance counselors have to put so many minority [students] in every class."

5. A White community member offered a very similar critique: "a lot of times, the schools are being called upon to teach kids things that . . . are contrary to what they're being taught in their communities. [T]hat's a big rock to move."

6. As one of the reforms, the court ordered a "no-cut" policy for extra-curricular activities such as athletics and cheerleading. This provision was included to avoid discrimination similar to that alleged by this father.

7. In addition to White flight, the district had to contend with generic housing discrimination. For example, a realtor related an incident that, she said, had occurred in 1996. She thought she had sold a house on an all-White street to an African-American family. She drew up the agreement of sale, but the seller's realtor then told her that the house had already sold. "That house," she said, "is still on the market. [But] he absolutely refused to sell us property on that street."

8. These symbolic meanings can be thought of either as separate forces acting on the detracking zone or as an aspect of the individual forces otherwise exerted by the symbolic object. For example, the symbolic meanings attached to the merger and the court order—meanings that I address below as separate, distinct forces—can be thought of as an additional facet of the force exerted by the court order (along with such other facets as funding and mandated data collection).

9. The conceptual framework applied in this chapter is loosely based on the ideas of Michel Foucault (1972) and Berger and Luckman (1967). These scholars agree that objects are not real in and of themselves; the perceptions of them are, in fact, reality. Commonly accepted meanings, then, are merely socially-constructed realities, and these perceptions drive behavior, values and policies. An organization's "culture," along with the people in the organization, generates meanings. People in organizations accordingly perceive symbols according to their culturally-determined values.

10. This is not just a simplification of Foucault's analysis; it is also a presentation of a narrow slice of a broad theory. Briefly, and using a significant dose of Foucault's terminology, he discusses the formation of objects—the relation between words, things, and context. Signs (signifiers), he notes, may compose discourses, but discourses should be thought of as more than assemblies of signs. Foucault maintains that relationships within history and society actively create discourses.

Objects of discourse, including the objects that we commonly call symbols, are created or formed by "surfaces of emergence" (1972, p. 41). These surfaces, the social and historical contexts underlying the symbol, make the object "manifest, nameable, and describable" (p. 41).

Powerful institutions, which Foucault calls "authorities of delimitation," take on the primary role of naming and describing objects of discourse (pp. 41–42). Discursive formation results from the relations between these various authorities (p. 43–44). Foucault also offers the idea of "grids of specification." These compose the categorized backdrop against which authorities place objects to give them meaning in discourse (p. 42).

Symbols, then, exist only "under the positive conditions of complex groups of relations" that are present in the context of the object rather than in the object itself (p. 45). The mediation between the object and its context results from such discursive relations.

11. In fact, very few potent symbols (using the term in a narrower sense than would Foucault) arose in the interviews with African Americans. The most notable exception concerns the district's allegedly inequitable use of discipline. For many African-American parents, the schools' disciplining of their children imparted meaning about racial misunderstanding, fear, and even hatred on the part of White teachers and administrators.

This paucity of symbols arising out of conversations with African Americans is not very surprising if we think about symbols as tools of power. Among teachers and parents, the power in the district rested overwhelmingly with Whites.

12. The old written English curriculum was actually the same for both the lower track and the upper track; it was the taught curriculum that evidenced the stratification.

13. This same symbolic issue is no doubt why Hank Levin uses the term "Accelerated Schools" for his reform model. These schools use mixed-ability classes, and the message that Levin tries to send to the community is that all students will receive an accelerated curriculum. It should be noted, however, that White parents do not always accept this characterization (see Oakes, Welner, and Yonezawa, 1998).

14. The terms "gifted moms" and "Edgewood parents"—which were both frequently used to label those White parents who opposed detracking—also had significant symbolic meaning in the district. "Gifted moms" is a term used in many districts across the nation and usually is intended to construct an elitist façade on the labeled parents. This was, indeed, how the term was used in Woodland Hills. "Edgewood parents" carried the same connotations but is unique to Woodland Hills. Edgewood was the most politically conservative and one of the wealthiest neighborhoods in the district.

NOTES TO CHAPTER TWELVE

1. The gifted program actually extended all the way through high school, but at the secondary school level the vast majority of its activities took place outside of regular school hours.

2. The number of students taking English AP classes increased substantially again in the 1997–1998 school year. However, the district continued to view this in a very positive light, reporting that the expanded group of students has been achieving well on the AP tests.

3. These are U.S. Department of Education Statistics. In Pennsylvania, gifted programs, like special education, are required by the state's regulations and standards. Each state sets its own definition of giftedness, including the test cut-offs. Some states, for instance, identify only the top 2% of students as gifted (Oakes & Lipton, 1999, p. 291).

4. Similarly, as discussed in Chapter Thirteen, the district placed "vocational" 11th and 12th grade students in a class called "Integrated English." These classes served as a third track for those two grades, further undermining the detracking.

NOTES TO CHAPTER THIRTEEN

1. When the district eliminated these two courses in 1988–1989, several math teachers submitted a letter of complaint to the school board, arguing that the cuts hurt the students enrolled in a non-academic curriculum. "The courses meet the needs of a

portion of the student population," the letter contended (Staff, 1989). Teachers continued to put forward similar arguments about remaining courses such as "Applied Math" and "Consumer Math." As discussed in the Epilogue, the district court in 2000 demanded that the district address this remaining tracking in math.

2. Recall that the district effectively added an AP track and, as discussed later, a vocational track for the 11th and 12th grades.

3. See also MESA Associates (1997b), discussing teacher resistance, as well as Chapter Nine, which discussed resistance by teachers and parents.

4. The racial distinction between these perspectives reflected the district's general division. However, this portrayal should not be understood as absolute; some White students supported the detracking, and some African-American students opposed it.

5. An eighth grade reading course provided an example of residual tracking within the language arts. A reading teacher reported: "There is a separate eighth grade reading class . . . for the kids who don't function too well—that aren't functioning well in the regular reading and also in English, so that they do channel them in there."

6. Recall that central office leaders readily acknowledged that some tracking remained in the district. Said one, "I didn't need somebody coming into the district to verify where tracking was going on. In about a half an hour, I could probably write down instance by instance where that is occurring." However, some of these same leaders denied that the science courses were tracked.

7. To clarify: starting in seventh grade, a student can take one of three different math courses: General Math, Pre-Algebra or Algebra I. If a student took Pre-Algebra in seventh grade, she would usually take Algebra I in eighth grade and then Geometry in ninth. So a student taking either Pre-Algebra or Algebra in the seventh grade would be on a track preparing her for Biology with Lab in the ninth grade. But a student taking General Math in the seventh grade would usually not be prepared for that science class.

8. As discussed earlier, the character of these courses depended heavily upon the teacher. Some teachers did succeed in making them quite challenging. Further, the rewritten and improved curriculum contributed to these successes.

9. Two reports from the district Evaluator contain similar data. The first report, based on a student survey, includes the following statement from a White high school student in a heterogeneous English class:

I feel that this year my English teacher gives each one of us a chance to prove what type of English student we are. She knows some students are better than others and encourages us to do our best and that's how she grades. (MESA Associates, 1997a.)

The second report, based on a teacher survey, includes the following statement from a secondary English teacher:

I have found working with such a diverse group requires me to rethink constantly how my lesson is prepared and delivered. I use comparisons to encourage inferential thinking. I give specific parameters to each subject to encourage a certain level of success. I model each written assignment with a paper of my own. Peer editing, "study buddies," and alternative assignments are also part of my plan. . . . I work hard to gain the students' respect by being fair and enthusiastic. (MESA Associates, 1997b.)

However, both reports also strongly suggest that the majority of teachers have struggled in their attempts to reform their instructional methods to meet the needs of a heterogeneous classroom.

10. According to one of the program's administrators, the district considered students who scored in the 0%–10% range to lack such potential.

11. According to a Reading Recovery administrator, the students "read a book that they've all read before, very successfully. . . . They tell a story, and the teacher writes the story, and they cut it up, and then they put words together to form a story. They put it in an envelope and take it home and there's activities at home, and so forth. . . . [There is] a complete reversal in terms of focus; they don't focus on what they're not able to do, they focus on what they can do."

The district's official description of the program states, "In the theoretical model, reading is viewed as a psycholinguistic process in which the reader constructs meaning from print. Components of the [Reading Recovery] program include perceptual analysis, knowledge of print conventions, decoding, oral language, prior knowledge, reading strategies, and metacognition, as well as error detection and error correction strategies."

12. Headstart, rather than the district, selected these students. Income, rather than academic need, constituted the selection criteria.

13. Since none of the district schools had more than half its students receiving free and reduced lunches, they did not qualify under the rules at the time for "schoolwide" Title I assistance. The district, therefore, targeted Title I assistance through a preschool program, an extended-day kindergarten, and specialist assistance for grades 1–5.

14. The local newspaper quoted a district spokesperson as saying, "It has always been the district's position that if something is court ordered and the court no longer funds it, we discontinue the program. There is nothing we can do" (Wakefield, 1996b).

15. Fox Chapel's detracking effort was initiated by a reform-minded superintendent. However, that superintendent has since left the district, and the high school principal is reportedly struggling to keep the reform in place. Similar scenarios have unfolded in districts across the nation (see Oakes, Wells & Associates, 1996; Oakes, Quartz, Ryan, & Lipton, 2000) and should serve as a further caution to those in Woodland Hills, San Jose, and similar districts who are contemplating how to preserve their reform after the court order is lifted and/or a supporter leaves the superintendency.

NOTES TO CHAPTER FOURTEEN

1. This discussion of the district's weaker teachers necessarily generalizes. However, these teachers do not constitute a monolithic group. Some of the weaker teachers

continually strove for self-improvement and probably developed into much better teachers in the period following my study. Others made no such effort.

2. Or, at least, they thought so. Considerable research, including that presented in this book, demonstrates that "homogeneous" classes actually contain quite diverse ability levels. Said one African-American student: "Advanced English wasn't Advanced English. When we had Advanced English, there were kids in there who just behaved well and whose parents requested it. So it wasn't as if it was [an] advanced class." District teachers also acknowledged that placements depended on behavior as well as perceived ability.

NOTES TO CHAPTER FIFTEEN

1. As one example of a macro-level reform that benefited from selective implementation, consider the growth of IQ testing. Paula Fass (1989) notes the rapid acceptance and expansion of IQ testing in the 1920s, attributing the phenomenon to the consistency between this reform and the prevailing values of scientism and preoccupation with quantification (pp. 49–50).

2. McDermott (1999) contends that Americans' championing of local educational control is somewhat misguided. "Local school politics," she writes, "is characterized by low levels of participation, and more critically by decision-making processes largely closed to ordinary citizens. Democratic local control of public education is a potent ideal; it should also be regarded as a myth" (p. 7). She asserts,

> Existing institutions of local control are both too local and not local enough. Because of the way in which they segment the population, they are too local to produce equality of educational opportunity. At the same time, they are too centralized and dominated by professionals to maximize citizens' capacity to influence decisions about their children's education (p. 122, footnote omitted).

Accordingly, she proposes state-level allocation of resources and other equity-related matters, and school-level control of most decisions about curriculum and pedagogy (p. 122).

3. Wells and Oakes (1996) use detracking research to argue that such local-control dynamics would be likely to undermine systemic reform, as outlined by Smith and O'Day (1991, 1993). Specifically, the goal of equality for students within schools will, they argue, probably be fought and defeated by local elites.

4. For a more detailed discussion of normative and political steps upon which to ground a successful detracking reform, see Welner and Oakes (2000).

5. Handler also presents differing views, including those of post-structuralists, who would reject the above explanations and definitions as too structured and top-down (Handler, 1996). The constructs of Lukes and Gaventa, however, offer useful explanations of the power issues identified in the four districts I studied.

6. Huberman and Miles (1984) found that in nearly two-thirds of the implementation cases they studied, not all of which were equity-minded reforms, the prime

motive for the adoption of the innovation was administrative pressure, which varied from strong encouragement to raw power.

7. Successful implementation should be considered, for the purposes of this conceptual formula, to include successful continuance or durability. The focus is on fidelity: the extent to which the implemented policy matches the intended, planned policy. Successful implementation does *not* include, for purposes of this discussion, the success of the policy in achieving ultimate educational or societal goals, such as increased test scores or improved racial relations.

8. The targeted community could be as small as a single school or classroom or as large as the nation or world.

9. Again, these formulas are offered only as a conceptual device; quanitification of these factors would be difficult if not impossible.

10. Berman and McLaughlin (1978) recognize a related phenomenon: "ambitious projects were less successful in . . . terms of the percentage of the project goals achieved, but they typically stimulated more teacher change than projects attempting less" (p. 88). Expressed in terms of the $G^*B^*L^*P = C$ formula, Berman and McLaughlin are noting that a larger value of G and/or B can compensate for a smaller value of P.

11. But see McDermott's (1999) discussion of resistance to the combined finance reform plus desegregation in Connecticut in the wake of *Sheff v. O'Neill* (1995), and Douglas Reed's (2001) discussion of "the primacy of local control and local resources" and "the interlocking ties of property wealth, home rule, and governmental fragmentation . . . that courts have not been able to alter, let alone erase" (chapter 7, page not available). Consider also the resistance of wealthy Vermont residents to the finance reform (called "Act 60") in the wake of *Brigham v. State* (1997), discussed in Sack (1998).

12. In contrast, one can expect a small value for "P" (the successfully implemented portion of the desired goals) if a defendant district fails to engage its educators in a process of confronting and addressing the variety of serious and challenging issues raised by detracking. Particularly germane to the present discussion is Cuban's comment that "[d]istricts, schools and classrooms as organizations absorb external pressures for change and convert them into routine add-ons compatible with existing practices" (Cuban, 1992, p. 217).

13. As discussed in the Epilogue, these recent motions for unitary status in Rockford and Woodland Hills were decided as this book was going to press. Both motions were granted in part and denied in part, with the Woodland Hills court going much further in releasing the school district from court supervision.

14. Pennsylvania law requires public school districts to provide private (and parochial) school students with transportation to and from school, as long as the destination school is located within 10 miles of the district. Woodland Hills must bus about 2,000 non-public students, in addition to the approximately 5,200 bused public school students. Accordingly, the court-ordered school assignment plan accounts for only part of the busing budget (probably a little more than half).

Bibliography

Alexander v. Sandoval (2001)., 121 S. Ct. 1511.

American Association of School Administrators (AASA). (1993a). *A curriculum management audit of the Woodland Hills School District.* March, 1993. Arlington Virginia: Authors.

American Association of School Administrators (AASA). (1993b). *Plan for the implementation of the curriculum and testing redesign.* Submitted September 15, 1993. Arlington Virginia: Authors.

Anderson v. City of Bessemer City, 470 U.S. 564 (1985).

Anyon, J. (1997). *Ghetto schooling: A political economy of urban educational reform.* New York: Teachers College Press.

Apple, M. W. (1993). *Official knowledge: Democratic education in a conservative age.* New York: Routledge.

Associated Press. (1984, December 7). Justice Dept.: Cities may end busing. *Post Gazette.*

Associated Press. (1991, January 16). Court says some schools may halt forced busing. *Tribune Review.*

Associated Press. (1992, March 31). Top court relaxes integration supervision; Ruling affects school districts. *Pittsburgh Press.*

Associated Press. (2001, April 19). School desegregation ruling spawns mixed reaction.

Bankston, C. & Caldas, S. J. (1997). Majority African American schools and social justice: The influence of de facto segregation on academic achievement. *Social Forces,* 75, 535–555.

Barnard, C. (1938). *The functions of the executive.* Cambridge, MA: Harvard University Press.

Barr, R. & Dreeben, R. (1983). *How schools work.* Chicago: University of Chicago Press.

Bell, D. A., Jr. (1977). Waiting on the promise of *Brown.* In B. Levin & W. D. Hawley (Eds.), *The courts, social science, and school desegregation* (pp. 341–373). New Brunswick, New Jersey: Transaction Books.

Berger, P. L., & Luckman, T. (1967). *The social construction of reality*. Garden City, NY: Doubleday Anchor.

Berman, P. & McLaughlin, M. W. (1978). *Federal programs supporting educational change, vol. VIII: Implementing and sustaining innovations*. Santa Monica, California: RAND Corporation.

Bickel, A. M. (1962). *The least dangerous branch: The Supreme Court at the bar of politics*. Indianapolis, Indiana: Bobbs-Merrill.

Board of Education v. Dowell, 498 U.S. 237 (1991).

Bolman, L. G. & Deal, T. E. (1984). *Modern approaches to understanding and managing organizations*. San Francisco: Jossey-Bass.

Bonne, M. (2001, April 19). What will the incumbent school board do? *Rockford Register Star*.

Bourdieu, P. (1985). The forms of capital. In J. Richardson (ed.), *Handbook of theory and research for the sociology of education*. Westport, CN: Greenwood.

Bowles, S. & Gintis, H. (1976). *Schooling in capitalist America*. New York: Basic Books.

Boyd, W. L. (1976). The public, the professionals, and educational policy making: Who governs? *Teachers College Record*, 77, 539–577.

Boyd, W. L. (1989). Policy analysis, educational policy, and management: Through a glass darkly? In N. Boyan (Ed.), *Handbook of research on educational administration* (pp. 510–522). New York: Macmillan.

Braddock, J. H. (1980). The perpetuation of segregation across levels of education: A behavior assessment of the contact-hypothesis. *Sociology of Education*, 53(3), 178–186.

Braddock, J. & Dawkins (1993). "Ability Grouping, Aspirations, and Attainments: Evidence from the National Educational Longitudinal Study of 1988," *Journal of Negro Education*, 62(3), 1–13.

Bridges, E. (1967). A model for shared decision making in the school principalship. *Educational Administration Quarterly*, 3(1), 49–61.

Brigham v. State, 166 Vt. 246, 692, A.2d. 384 (1997).

Brodbeck, D. (2000, August 23). Officials, residents discuss ruling's ramifications. *Woodland Hills Progress-Star*.

Brody, L. (1995, December 17). An education in fighting bias: Voluntary solution seen as best choice. *The Sunday Record*.

Brown v. Board of Education, 347 U.S. 483 (1954).

Brown, K. (1992). Has the Supreme Court allowed the cure for *de jure* segregation to replicate the disease? *Cornell Law Review*, 78(1), 1–83.

Brown, S. (1999). "High school racial composition: Balancing excellence and equity." Paper presented at the annual meeting of the American Sociological Association.

Bryson, J. & Bentley, C. (1980). *Ability grouping of public school students: Legal aspects of classification and tracking methods.* Charlottesville, Virginia: The Michie Company.

Burbules, N. C., Lord, B, & Sherman, A. (1982). Equity, equal opportunity, and education. *Educational Evaluation and Policy Analysis, 4*(2), 169–187.

Burger, K. (1996, June 9). Opposition to 'scattered housing' plan lingers in Pittsburgh's eastern suburbs. *Tribune Review.*

Butt v. State of California et al., 4 Cal.4th 668 (1992).

Callahan, R. E. (1962). *Education and the cult of efficiency.* Chicago: University of Chicago Press.

California Department of Education (1992a). *It's elementary.* Sacramento: CDE.

California Department of Education (1992b). *Second to none: A vision of the new California high school.* Sacramento: CDE.

California Department of Education (1987). *Caught in the middle: Educational reform for young adolescents in California public schools.* Sacramento: CDE.

Carnegie Council for Adolescent Development (1989). *Turning points: Preparing American youth for the 21st Century.* Washington DC: The Carnegie Corporation of New York.

Chambers, J. L. (1977). Implementing the promise of *Brown:* Social science and the courts in future school litigation. In R. C. Rist & R. J. Anson (Eds.), *Education, social science, and the judicial process* (pp. 32–49). New York, New York: Teachers College Press.

Charters, W. W., Jr. (1953). Social class analysis and the control of public education. *Harvard Educational Review, 24*(4), 268–283.

Churchill, W. (1947, November 11). Address to House of Commons.

Clark, K. B. (1977). Social science, constitutional rights, and the courts. In R. C. Rist & R. J. Anson (Eds.), *Education, social science, and the judicial process* (pp. 1–9). New York: Teachers College Press.

Coalition to Save our Children v. State Board of Education, et al., 901 F.Supp. 784 (D. Del. 1995).

Cohen, E. G. (1984). The desegregated school: Problems in status, power and interethnic climate. *Groups in contact: The psychology of desegregation,* 77–95.

Coleman, J. S., Campbell, E. Q., Hobson, C., McPartland, J., Mood, A., Weinfeld, F., & York, R. (1966). *Equality of educational opportunity.* Washington DC: U.S. Government Printing Office.

Consent Decree (1988, June). *Hoots v. Commonwealth of Pennsylvania* (Case No. 71-538).

Cook, T. (1984). School desegregation and black achievement. National Institute of Education. Washington DC: U. S. Department of Education.

Coons, J. L. (1977). Recent trends in science fiction: *Serrano* among the people of number. In R. C. Rist & R. J. Anson (Eds.), *Education, social science, and the judicial process* (pp. 50–71). New York, New York: Teachers College Press.

Cowie, R. (1995, March 15). New curriculum appears to cut advanced study. *The Woodland Hills Progress.*

Crain R. L. & Mahard, R. E. (1978). Desegregation and black achievement: A review of the research. *Law and Contemporary Problems, 42*(3), 17–56.

Crain R. L. & Mahard, R. E. (1982). Desegregation plans that raise black achievement: A review of the research. Santa Monica, CA: RAND.

Crain R. L. & Mahard, R. E. (1983). The effect of research methodology on desegregation achievement studies: A meta-analysis. *American Journal of Sociology, 88*(5), 839–854.

Craven, J. B., Jr. (1977). Further judicial commentary: The impact of social science evidence on the judge: A personal comment. In B. Levin & W. D. Hawley (Eds.), *The courts, social science, and school desegregation* (pp. 150–156). New Brunswick, New Jersey: Transaction Books.

Cuban, L. (1992). Curriculum stability and change. In P. Jackson (Ed.), *Handbook of research on curriculum* (pp. 216–247). New York: Macmillan.

Darling-Hammond, L. (1995). "Inequality and access to knowledge," in James A. Banks & Cherry A. McGee Banks (Eds.), *Handbook of research on multicultural education,* (p. 465). New York: Macmillan.

Dawkins, M. P. (1983). Black students' occupational expectations: A national study of the impact of school desegregation. *Urban Education, 18,* 98–113.

Dawson, D. (1985, December 5). Untitled [Letter to the editor]. *San Jose Mercury News,* p. 10B.

Diaz v. San Jose Unified School District (N.D.Cal. 1985), 633 F.Supp. 809.

Dickens, A. (1996). Revisiting Brown v. Board of Education: How tracking has resegregated America's public schools. *Columbia Journal of Law and Social Problems, 29,* Summer, p. 469.

Dornbush, S. (1994). *Off the track.* Paper presented as the 1994 Presidential Address to the Society for Research on Adolescence, San Diego, CA.

Dudiak, Z. (1995, April 19). Class sizes too large, parents say. *The Woodland Hills Progress.*

Dudiak, Z. (1996, March 6). Possible tax loss in school district close to $50,000. *The Woodland Hills Progress.*

Dudiak, Z. (1997a, February 12). Detracking not backed. *The Woodland Hills Progress.*

Dudiak, Z. (1997b, June 24). Taxes rise by 3 mills. *The Woodland Hills Progress.*

Dworkin, R. (1977). *Taking rights seriously.* Cambridge, MA: Harvard University Press.

Edgewood Independent School Dist. v. Kirby, 777 S.W.2d 391 (Tex. 1989).

Edmonds, R., & Frederiksen, J. (1979). *Search for effective schools: The identification and analysis of city schools that are instructionally effective for poor children*. Cambridge, MA: Harvard Center for Urban Studies. (ERIC Document Reproduction Service No. ED 170-396).

Elmore, R. F. (1983). Complexity and control: What legislators and administrators can do about implementing public decisions. *Political Science Quarterly, 94*(4), 601–616.

Elmore, R. F. (1993). School decentralization: Who gains? Who loses? In J. Hannaway and M. Carnoy (Eds.) *Decentralization and school improvement: Can we fulfill the promise?* (pp. 33–54). San Francisco: Jossey-Bass Publishers.

Elmore, R. F., & McLaughlin, M. W. (1988). *Steady work: Policy, practice, and the reform of American education*. Santa Monica: RAND.

English, E. (1995, April 5). Exploring the debate over curriculum. *The Woodland Hills Progress*.

Epps, E. G. (1977). Impact of school desegregation on aspirations, self-concepts and other aspects of personality. In B. Levin & W. D. Hawley (Eds.), *The courts, social science, and school desegregation* (pp. 300–313). New Brunswick, New Jersey: Transaction Books.

Epstein, A. (1995, June 14). Kansas City desegregation plan rejected as too costly. *Post Gazette*.

Estadt, B. (1997a, December 31). Year in review; Part 2. *The Woodland Hills Progress*.

Estadt, B. (1997b, December 31). State special education funds could jump. *The Woodland Hills Progress*.

Evans v. Buchanan. 447 F.Supp. 982 (D.Del. 1978).

Evans v. Buchanan. 512 F.Supp. 839 (D.Del. 1981).

Evans, W. N., Murray, S. E., & Schwab, R. M. (1997). Schoolhouses, courthouses, and statehouses after *Serrano. Journal of Policy Analysis and Management, 16*(1), 10–31.

Fatla, M. (1990a, August 20). "Report and recommendation regarding desegregation remedies." In *Hoots v. Commonwealth of Pennsylvania* (Case No. 71-538).

Falta, M. (1990b, September 25). "Supplement to report and recommendation of August 20, 1990: Comments on objections." In *Hoots v. Commonwealth of Pennsylvania* (Case No. 71-538).

Fass, P. S. (1989). *Outside in: Minorities and the transformation of American education*. New York: Oxford University Press.

Finley, M. (1984). Teachers and tracking in a comprehensive high school. *Sociology of Education, 57*, 233–243.

Firestone, W. & Corbett, H. D. (1989). Planned organizational change. In N. Boyan (Ed.), *Handbook of research on educational administration* (pp. 321–340). New York: Macmillan.

Fordham, S. & Ogbu, J. U. (1986). Black students' school success: Coping with the burden of "acting White." *Urban Review, 18,* 176–206.

Foucault, M. (1972). *The archeology of knowledge.* Translated by Rupert Swyer. New York: Dorset Press.

Fraser, N. (1992). Rethinking the public sphere: A contribution to the critique of actually existing democracy. In C. Calhoun (Ed.), *Habermas and the public sphere* (pp. 109–142). Cambridge, MA: MIT Press.

Freeman v. Pitts, 503 U.S. 467 (1992).

Fullan, M. (1991). *The new meaning of educational change.* New York: Teachers College Press.

Fullan, M. (1993). *Change forces: Probing the depths of educational reform.* London: Falmer Press.

Fullan, M. (1994). Coordinating top-down and bottom-up strategies for educational reform. In R. Elmore & S. Fuhrman (Eds.), *The governance of curriculum. The 1994 ASCD Yearbook* (pp. 186–202). Alexandria, Virginia: Association for Supervision and Curriculum Development.

Fullan, M. (1999). *Change forces: The sequel.* London: Falmer Press.

Fullan, M. (2000). The three stories of education reform. *Phi Delta Kappan, 81*(8), 581–584.

Gamoran, A. & Berends, M. (1987). The effects of stratification in secondary schools: Synthesis of survey and ethnographic research. *Review of Educational Research, 57,* 415–436.

Gardner, H. (1983). *Frames of mind: The theory of multiple intelligences.* New York: Basic Books.

Gaugler, T. (1997, March 5). "No excuses for detracking now." Letter to the editor. *The Woodland Hills Progress.*

Gaventa, J. (1980). *Power and powerlessness: Quiescence and rebellion in an Appalachian valley.* Urbana: University of Illinois Press.

Georgia State Conference of Branches of NAACP v. Georgia, 775 F.2d 1403 (11th Cir. 1985).

Goss v. Lopez, 419 U.S. 565 (1975).

Gould, S. J. (1981). *The mismeasure of man.* New York: Norton.

Greene, J. (2000). "Challenges in practicing deliberative democratic evaluation." In K. Ryan and L. DeStefano (eds.), *Evaluation as a democratic process: Promoting inclusion, dialogue, and deliberation.* New Directions for Evaluation, 85, Spring, 13–26. San Francisco: Jossey-Bass Publishers.

Guardians Association v. Civil Service Commission of New York, 463 U.S. 582 (1983).

Guido, M. (1994, January 15). S.J. Unified settlement would reduce forced busing. *San Jose Mercury News,* p. 1A.

Hallinan, M. T. (1994). Tracking: From theory to practice. *Sociology of Education*, 67(2), 79–91.

Hallinan, M. T. & Williams, R. A. (1989). Interracial friendship choices in secondary schools, *American Psychological Review*, 54, 67–78.

Hamilton, A. (1788). "Federalist no. 78." New York: *Independent Journal*.

Handler, J. F. (1996). *Down from bureaucracy: The ambiguity of privatization and empowerment*. Princeton, NJ: Princeton University Press.

Haney López, I. F. (1994). "The social construction of race: Some observations on illusion, fabrication, and choice." *Harvard Civil Rights - Civil Liberties Law Review*, 29(1), 1–62.

Hargreaves, A. (1994). *Changing teachers, changing times: Teachers' work and culture in the postmodern age*. New York: Teachers College Press.

Hawley, W. D., & Rist, R. C. (1977). On the future implementation of school desegregation: Some considerations. In B. Levin & W. D. Hawley (Eds.), *The courts, social science, and school desegregation* (pp. 412–426). New Brunswick, New Jersey: Transaction Books.

Hehir, T. & Gamm, S. (1999). Special education: From legalism to collaboration. In J. P. Heubert (Ed.), *Law and school reform: Six strategies for promoting educational equity*, pp. 205–243. New Haven: Yale University Press.

Hobson v. Hansen, 269 F.Supp. 401 (D.D.C. 1967), *aff'd sub nom. Smuck v. Hobson*, 408 F.2d 175 (D.C. Cir. 1969).

Hochschild, J. L. (1984). *The new American dilemma: Liberal democracy and school desegregation*. New Haven: Yale University Press.

Hoelter, J. W. (1982). Segregation and rationality in black status aspiration status. *Sociology of Education*, 55, 31–39.

Hoots v. Commonwealth of Pennsylvania, (3rd Cir. 1992). Unpublished opinion, September 21.

Hoots v. Commonwealth of Pennsylvania, 359 F.Supp. 807 (W.D. Pa. 1973).

Hoots v. Commonwealth of Pennsylvania, 545 F.Supp. 1 (W.D. Pa. 1981).

Hoots v. Commonwealth of Pennsylvania, 559 F.Supp. 335 (W.D. Pa. 1982).

Hoots v. Commonwealth of Pennsylvania, (W.D. Pa. 2000). Unpublished opinion, July 25.

Hosek, J. (1987, June 11). Woodland Hills' tax hike denounced. *Post Gazette East*.

House, E. R., and Howe, K. R. (1999). *Values in evaluation and social research*. Thousand Oaks, California: Sage.

Howe, K. R. (1997). *Understanding equal educational opportunity: Social justice, democracy, and schooling*. New York: Teachers College Press.

Huberman, M. & Miles, M. (1984). *Innovation up close: How school improvement works*. New York: Plenum.

Iknoian, T. (1986, January 22). Almaden parents meet with Cortines. *San Jose Mercury News*, section Extra 4, p. 1.

Ingersoll, R. (1999). The problem of underqualified teachers in American secondary schools. *Educational Researcher, 28*, 26–37.

International Curriculum Management Audit Center, Inc. (ICMAC). (1997). *A curriculum management post-audit of the Woodland Hills School District*. Huxley, Iowa: Authors.

Johnson, S. (1755). *A dictionary of the English language* (4th ed.). London: W. Strahan, J. & F. Rivington.

Keyes v. School District No. 1, 413 U.S. 189 (1973).

Koslin, S., Koslin, B., & Pargament, R. (1972). Classroom racial balance and students' interracial attitudes. *Sociology of Education, 45*, 386–407.

Kulik, J. (1992). *An analysis of the research on ability grouping: Historical and contemporary perspectives*. Storrs, CT: National Research Center on the Gifted and Talented.

Kunz, D. W. & Hoy, W. K. (1976). Leadership style of principals and the professional zone of acceptance of teachers. *Educational Administration Quarterly, 12*(3), 49–64.

Kurlaender, M., & Yun, J. T. (2000). *Is diversity a compelling educational interest? Evidence from metropolitan Louisville*. Report of the Harvard Civil Rights Project. Cambridge, MA: Civil Rights Project.

Lamphere, L. (1992). Introduction: The shaping of diversity. In L. Lamphere (Ed.) *Structuring diversity: Ethnographic perspectives on the new immigration* (pp. 1–34). Chicago: University of Chicago Press.

Larry P. v. Riles, 793 F.2d 969 (9th Cir. 1984).

Lau v. Nichols, 414 U.S. 563 (1982).

Levin, H. M. (1977). Education, life chances, and the courts: The role of social science evidence. In B. Levin & W. D. Hawley (Eds.), *The courts, social science, and school desegregation* (pp. 217–240). New Brunswick, New Jersey: Transaction Books.

Levine, E. & Wexler, E. (1981). *P.L. 94-142: An act of Congress*. New York: Macmillan Publishing Company.

Levine, R. (1972). *San Jose, the urban crisis, and the feds*. Santa Monica, California: RAND Corporation.

Lewin, K. (1951). *Field theory in social science: Selected theoretical papers*. Republished in *Resolving social conflicts & Field theory in social science* (1997). Washington DC: American Psychological Association.

Little, J. W., & McLaughlin, M. W. (1993). Introduction: Perspectives on cultures and contexts of teaching. In J. W. Little & M. W. McLaughlin (Eds.), *Teachers' work: Individuals, colleagues, and contexts* (pp. 137–163). New York: Teachers College Press.

Lipman, P. (1998). *Race, class and power in school restructuring*. New York: SUNY Press.

Lipsky, M. (1980). *Street-level bureaucracy*. New York: Russell Sage Foundation.

Londen, J. (1995). Has the Supreme Court allowed the cure for *de jure* segregation to replicate the disease? *University of San Francisco Law Review, 29*, 705.

Losen, D. J. (1999). Silent segregation in our nation's schools. *Harvard Civil Rights - Civil Liberties Law Review, 134,* 517.

Louis, K. S. & Miles, M. B. (1990). *Improving the urban high school*. New York: Teachers College Press.

Loveless, T. (1999). *The tracking wars: State reform meets school policy*. Washington D.C.: Brookings Institution Press.

Lubman, S. (1995, December 5). Few details on program for gifted. *San Jose Mercury News*, p. 1B.

Lucas, S. R. (1999). *Tracking inequality: Stratification and mobility in American high schools*. New York: Teachers College Press.

Lukes, S. (1974). *Power: A radical view*. London: Macmillan.

MacIver, D., Plank, S., & Balfanz, R. (1998). *Working together to become proficient readers: Early impact of the Talent Development Middle School's student team literature program*, Report of the Center for the Education of Students Placed at Risk. Baltimore: Johns Hopkins University.

Mackler, B. (1969). Grouping in the ghetto. *Education and Urban Society, 2*(1), 80–96.

Mank, B. C. (2001). Using § 1983 to enforce Title VI's section 602 regulations. *Kansas Law Review, 49*, 321.

Marbury v. Madison, 1 Cranch 137, 2 L.Ed. 60 (1803).

Martin, M. (1997). *Report on discipline in schools*. Dublin, Ireland: Government Publications. Report commissioned by Minister for Education Niamh Breathnach on disruption in schools.

Mazzoni, T. L. (1991). Analyzing state school policymaking: An arena model. *Educational Evaluation and Policy Analysis, 13*(2), 115–138.

McDermott, K. A. (1999). *Controlling public education: Localism versus equity*. Lawrence, Kansas: University Press of Kansas.

McDuffy v. Secretary of the Executive Office of Education, 415 Mass. 545, 615 N.E.2d 516 (1993).

McGivney, J. H. & Moynihan, W. (1972). School and community. *Teachers College Record, 74*(2), 317–356.

McLaughlin, M. W. (1976). Implementing a mutual adaptation: Change in classroom organization. *Teachers College Record, 77*(3), 339–351.

McPartland, J. M. & Braddock, J. H. (1981). Going to college and getting a good job: The impact of desegregation. In W.D. Hawley (Ed.), *Effective school desegregation: Equality, quality, and feasibility.*

McQuillan, P. J. (1998). *Educational opportunity in an urban American high school.* New York: SUNY Press.

McNeal v. Tate County School District, 508 F.2d 1017 (5th Cir. 1975).

Means, T. (1994, June 9). Change urged in TAI math, language arts. *Post Gazette East.*

Means, T. (1995a, January 12). U.S. court to resolve dispute over funds. *Post Gazette East.*

Means, T. (1995b, April 20). District in dark on state share of costs. *Post Gazette East.*

Means, T. (1995c, June 14). Woodland Hills gets less money than sought. *Post Gazette East.*

Means, T. (1996, June 9). No tax increase proposed. *Post Gazette East.*

Mehan, H., Villanueva, I., Hubbard, L., & Lintz, A. (1996). *Constructing school success: The consequences of untracking low achieving students.* New York: Cambridge University Press.

Meier, K. J., Stewart, J. J., & England, R. E. (1989). *Race, class, and education: The politics of second-generation discrimination.* Madison: University of Wisconsin Press.

Merriam, S. B. (1988). *Case study research in education: A qualitative approach.* San Francisco: Jossey Bass.

MESA Associates (1997a, February). *1996 English class survey report.* Prepared for the WHSD Office of Evaluation. Pittsburgh, PA: MESA Associates.

MESA Associates (1997b, May). *Analysis of teacher responses: English class survey study.* Prepared for the WHSD Office of Evaluation. Pittsburgh, PA: MESA Associates.

Mickelson, R. A. (2000). "Subverting *Swann*: Tracking and second generation segregation in the Charlotte-Mecklenburg schools." Paper presented at the annual meeting of the American Educational Research Association in New Orleans, Louisiana, April 24–28, 2000.

Miller, J. D. (1991). *Oral histories of elementary principals in relation to the implementation of a court-ordered school desegregation plan.* Ed.D. dissertation, University of Pittsburgh.

Milliken v. Bradley, 418 U.S. 717 (1974).

Mills v. Board of Education, 348 F.Supp. 866 (D.D.C. 1972).

Missouri v. Jenkins, 515 U.S. 1139 (1995).

Montgomery v. Starkville Mun. Separate School Dist., 665 F.Supp. 487 (N.D. Miss. 1987).

Moses v. Washington Parish School Board, 456 F.2d 1285 (5th Cir. 1972).

National Center for Educational Statistics. (1994). *Curricular differentiation in public high schools.* Washington DC: U.S. Government Printing Office.

National Governors Association. (1993). *Ability grouping and tracking: Current issues and concerns*. Washington, DC: National Governors Association.

Nieto, S. (1992). *Affirming diversity: The sociopolitical context of multicultural education*. White Plains, NY: Longman.

Nikolai, G. (2001, April 19). No going back to the "good old days." *Rockford Register Star*.

Note. (1989). "Teaching inequality: The problem of public school tracking," 102 *Harvard Law Review* 1318.

Oakes, J. (1985). *Keeping track: How schools structure inequality*. New Haven, CT: Yale University Press.

Oakes, J. (1990). *Multiplying inequalities: The effects of race, class, and tracking on opportunities to learn math and science*. Santa Monica: RAND.

Oakes, J. (1991). Grouping students for instruction. In M. Alkin (Ed.), *Encyclopedia of educational research, vol. 4* (6th ed.) (pp. 562–568). New York: Macmillan.

Oakes, J. (1992). Can tracking research inform practice? Technical, normative, and political considerations. *Educational Researcher. 21*(4), 12–22.

Oakes, J. (1993). Report prepared for the court in *Vasquez v. San Jose Unified School District, et al.* (N.D.Cal.).

Oakes, J. (1995). Two cities: Tracking and within-school segregation," in L. Miller (ed.), *Brown plus forty: The promise*. New York: Teachers College Press.

Oakes, J. (2000). Report prepared for the court in *People Who Care v. Rockford Board of Education School District No. 205* (N.D. Ill.).

Oakes, J., Gamoran, A., and Page, R. (1992). Curriculum differentiation: Opportunities, outcomes, and meanings. In P. Jackson (Ed.), *Handbook of research on curriculum* (pp. 570–608). New York: Macmillan.

Oakes J. & Guiton, G. (1995). Matchmaking: Tracking decisions in comprehensive high schools. *American Educational Research Journal, 32*(1), 3–33.

Oakes, J. & Lipton, M. (1999). *Teaching to change the world*. San Francisco: McGraw Hill College.

Oakes, J., Quartz, K. H., Ryan, S. & Lipton, M. (2000). *Becoming good American schools: The struggle for civic virtue in school reform*. San Francisco: Jossey-Bass.

Oakes, J. & Wells, A. S. & Associates (1996). *Beyond the technicalities of school reform: Policy lessons from detracking schools*. Los Angeles: Authors.

Oakes, J., Wells, A. S., Yonezawa, S., and Ray, K. (1997). Equity lessons from detracking schools. In A. Hargreaves (Ed.), *1997 ASCD yearbook: Rethinking educational change with heart and mind*, (pp. 43–72). Alexandria, VA: ASCD.

Oakes, J., Welner, K., & Yonezawa, S. (1998). *Mandating equity: A case study of court-ordered detracking in San Jose schools*. Berkeley, CA: CPS Publications.

Oakes, J., Welner, K., Yonezawa, S., & Allen, R. (1998). Norms and politics of equity-minded change: Researching the "zone of mediation." In M. Fullan (Ed.), *International handbook of educational change* (pp. 952–975). Norwell, MA: Kluwer Academic Publishers.

O'Day, J., & Smith, M. (1993). Systemic reform and educational opportunity. In S. Fuhrman (Ed.), *Designing coherent educational policy*, pp. 250–312. San Francisco: Jossey-Bass.

Orfield, G. (1999). Conservatives and the rush toward resegregation. In J. P. Heubert (Ed.), *Law and school reform: Six strategies for promoting educational equity*, pp. 39–87. New Haven: Yale University Press.

Pennsylvania Association of Retarded Citizens (PARC) v. Commonwealth, 343 F.Supp. 279 (E.D. Pa. 1972).

People Who Care v. Rockford Board of Education School District No. 205, 851 F.Supp. 905 (N.D. Ill. 1994).

People Who Care v. Rockford Board of Education School District No. 205, 111 F.3d 528 (7th Cir. 1997).

People Who Care v. Rockford Board of Education School District No. 205, 171 F.3d 1083 (7th Cir. 1999).

People Who Care v. Rockford Board of Education School District No. 205, (N.D.Ill. 2000), slip opinion. [Online] Available at: http://www.nysd.uscourts.gov/courtweb/pdf/D07ILNC/00-07995.PDF.

People Who Care v. Rockford Board of Education School District No. 205, 246 F.3d 1073 (7th Cir. 2001).

Peterson, P. E. (1981). *City limits*. Chicago: Univ. of Chicago Press.

Plyler v. Doe, 457 U.S. 202 (1982).

Popkewitz, T. S. (1991). *A political sociology of educational reform: Power/knowledge in teaching, teacher education, and research*. New York: Teachers College Press.

Posner, R. A. (1999). *The problematics of moral and legal theory*. Cambridge, MA: Harvard University Press.

Powell v. Ridge, 189 F.3d 387 (3d Cir. 1999).

Pullman-Standard v. Swint, 456 U.S. 273 (1982).

Quarles v. Oxford Mun. Separate School Dist., 868 F.2d 750 (5th Cir. 1989).

Raudenbush, S. W., Rowan, B., & Cheong, Y. F. (1993). Higher order instructional goals in secondary schools: Class, teacher, and school influences. *American Educational Research Journal*, 30(3), 523–553.

Ravitch, D. (1983). *The troubled crusade: American education, 1945–1980*. New York: Basic Books.

Ravitch, D. (2000). *Left back: A century of failed school reforms*. New York: Simon & Schuster.

Reed, D. (2001). *On equal terms: The constitutional politics of educational opportunity.* Princeton, N.J.: Princeton University Press.

Rees, D. I., Argys L., & Brewer, D. (1996). Tracking in the United States: Descriptive statistics from NELS. *Economics of Education Review, 15*(1): 83–89.

Republic of Ireland, Department of Education and Science. (1990). *R.R. 144329, Circular 20/90.* Dublin, Ireland: Department of Education and Science. [Online] Available at: http://www.irlgov.ie/educ/generalpolicy/discipline.htm.

Robinson v. Cahill, 62 N.J. 473, 303 A.2d 273 (1973).

Rodgers, H. R., and Bullock, C. S. III (1972). *Law and social change: Civil rights laws and their consequences.* New York: McGraw-Hill.

Roscigno, V. J. (1995). The social embeddedness of racial educational inequality: The black-white gap and the impact of racial and local political-economic contexts. In M. Wallace (Ed.) *Research in social stratification and mobility,* Vol. 14: 135–165. Greenwich, Conn.: JAI Press.

Rose v. The Council for Better Education, Inc., 790 S.W.2d 186 (Ky. 1989).

Rouvalis, C. (1984, June 14). Judge Weber scolds state in Woodland Hills case. *Post Gazette East.*

Rutter, M. (1979). *Fifteen thousand hours: Secondary schools and their effects on children.* Cambridge, MA: Harvard University Press.

Sack, J. L. (1998, October 28). In Vermont's funding shakeup, a bitter pill for the "gold towns." *Education Week.*

Sapon-Shevin, M. (1994). *Playing favorites: Gifted education and the disruption of community.* New York: SUNY Press.

Sarason, S. (1982). *The culture of the school and the problem of change* (2nd ed.). Boston: Allyn & Bacon.

Sarason, S. (1990). *The predictable failure of educational reform.* San Francisco: Jossey-Bass.

Schiff, J., Firestone, W. & Young, J. (1999). "Organizational context for student achievement: The case of student racial compositions." Paper presented at the annual meeting of the American Educational Research Association in Montreal, Canada, April 19–23, 1999.

Schofield, J. W. (1995). Review of research on school desegregation's impact on elementary and secondary school students. In J.A. Banks & C.A. McGee Banks (eds.) *Handbook of research on multicultural education.* (pp. 597–616). New York: Simon & Schuster Macmillan.

Schofield, J. W. (2000). Maximizing the benefits of a diverse student body: Lessons from school desegregation research. In G. Orfield (ed.) *Diversity challenged.* Cambridge: Harvard Education Publishing Group.

Schofield, J. W. & Sagar, H. A. (1977). Peer interaction patterns in an integrated middle school. *Sociometry, 40*(2), 130–38.

Serrano v. Priest, 18 Cal.3d 728 (1976).

Sheff v. O'Neill, 238 Conn. 1, 678A.2d 1267 (1995).

Simmons on Behalf of Simmons v. Hooks, 843 F.Supp. 1296 (E.D. Ark. 1994).

Simon, H. A. (1947). *Administrative behavior*. New York: Macmillan.

Singleton v. Jackson Municipal Separate School District, 419 F.2d 1211 (5th Cir.), *vacated in part and reversed in part sub nom. Carter v. West Feliciana Parish School Board*, 396 U.S. 290 (1970).

Sirotnik, K. & Oakes, J. (1986). Critical inquiry for school renewal: Liberating theory and practice. In K. A. Sirotnik & J. Oakes (Eds.), *Critical perspectives on the organization and improvement of schooling* (pp. 3–94). Hingham, MA: Kluwer-Nijhoff Publishing.

Sirotnik, K. & Oakes, J. (1990). Evaluation as critical inquiry: School improvement as a case in point. In *New Directions for Program Evaluation, 45*, (Spring).

SJUSD (1994). *School accountability report card*. San Jose: Author.

Slavin, R. (1986). *Using student team learning*. Baltimore, MD: Center for Research on Elementary & Middle Schools, Johns Hopkins University.

Slavin, R. E. (1987). Ability grouping and student achievement in elementary schools: A best-evidence synthesis. *Review of Educational Research, 57*(3), 293–336.

Slavin, R. (1990). *Achievement effects of ability grouping in secondary schools: A best-evidence synthesis. Review of Educational Research, 60*(3), 471–500.

Slavin, R. (1993). Ability grouping in the middle grades: Achievement effects and alternatives. *The Elementary School Journal*, May.

Smith, M., & O'Day, J. (1991). Systemic school reform. In S. Fuhrman & B. Malen (Eds.), *The politics of curriculum and testing*. Bristol, UK: Falmer Press.

Snyder, S., Mezzacappa, D., & Sanchez, R. (2000, June 1). City, Pa. reach school accord. *Philadelphia Inquirer*.

Solow, B. (1990, August 22). U.S. puts Woodland Hills burden on state. *Pittsburgh Press*.

Spence, L. (1984, December 29). "Resisting tyranny." Letter to the editor. *Post Gazette*.

Staff (1984, August 15). Opinions offered of forced busing. *The Woodland Hills Progress*.

Staff (1988, February 19). No news is good news. Numbers are encouraging on the desegregation of San Jose Unified schools [Editorial]. *San Jose Mercury News*, p. 10B.

Staff (1989, January 25). Math courses to stay. *The Woodland Hills Progress*.

Staff (1993, January 20). TAI math program examined. *The Woodland Hills Progress*.

Sternberg, R. (1988). *The triarchic mind*. New York: Viking.

Stipulated Modified Remedial Order (1994, February 18). Filed with the Court in *Vasquez v. San Jose Unified School District*, Case No. C-71-2130 (N.D. Cal.).

Tanaka, V. G. (1999). "Comment: People Who Care v. Rockford Board of Education and the spectrum of race-conscious remedies," 1999 *Wisconsin Law Review* 347.

The College Board. (1989). *Access to knowledge*, edited by J. I. Goodlad. New York: College Entrance Exam Board.

Tomlinson, C. (1995). *How to differentiate instruction in mixed-ability classrooms*. Alexandria, VA: Association for Supervision and Curriculum Development.

Torriero, E. A. (1990, May 20). Hidden segregation? Report challenges success story. *San Jose Mercury News*, p. 1B.

Tribe, L. H. (1988). *American constitutional law* (2nd ed.). Mineola, NY: Foundation Press.

Tropea, J. (1993). Structuring risks: The making of urban school order. In R. Wollons (Ed.) *Children at risk in America: History, concepts and public policy*. Albany, NY: SUNY Press.

Tweedie, J. (1983). The politics of legalization in special education reform. In *Special education policies: Their histories, implementation, and finance* (Chambers, J. & Hartman, W., Eds.). Philadelphia: Temple Univ. Press.

Tyack, D. (1974). *The one best system*. Cambridge, MA: Harvard Univ. Press.

Tyack, D. & Cuban, L. (1995). *Tinkering toward utopia*. Cambridge, Massachusetts: Harvard University Press.

Tyack, D., James, T., & Benavot, A. (1991). *Law and the shaping of public education, 1785–1954*. Madison, WI: University of Wisconsin Press.

United States v. Board of Education of Lincoln County, 301 F.Supp. 1024 (S.D. Ga. 1969).

United States v. Tunica County School Dist., 421 F.2d 1236 (5th Cir. 1970), *cert. denied*, 398 U.S. 951 (1970).

United States v. Yonkers Board of Education, 123 F. Supp. 2d 694 (S.D.N.Y. 2000).

Vasquez v. San Jose Unified School District (N.D. Cal. 1994), unpublished stipulation, case no. C-71-2130.

Verrilla, M. (1994, March 16). District aims for freedom from courts. *The Woodland Hills Progress*.

Wakefield, K. (1996a, February 7). Forced busing demise mulled. *The Woodland Hills Progress*.

Wakefield, K. (1996b, June 26). Court cited for summer class cuts. *The Woodland Hills Progress*.

Washington v. Davis, 426 U.S. 229 (1976).

Watson, A. (1985a, June 16). This integration plan won't ride on a bus. S.J. Unified opts for magnet school plan. *San Jose Mercury News*, p. 1A.

Watson, A. (1985b, June 17). 5 years, $5 million fail to integrate S.J. schools. *San Jose Mercury News*, p. 1A.

Watson, A. (1985c, October 13). Why board decided it had to close S.J. High. *San Jose Mercury News*, p. 1A.

Watson, A. (1985d, October 30). S.J. school busing opposed. *San Jose Mercury News*, p. 1B.

Watson, A. (1985e, November 28). Almaden parents file own desegregation plan. *San Jose Mercury News*, p. 1B.

Watson, A. (1985f, December 13). Judge scolds S.J. Unified officials. *San Jose Mercury News*, p. 1B.

Watson, A. (1986, March 27). Desegregation order to force reassignment of S.J. teachers. *San Jose Mercury News*, p. 8B.

Watson, A. (1988a, April 7). Judge rejects Hispanic petition on desegregation. *San Jose Mercury News*, p. 2B.

Watson, A. (1988b, April 18). 'Whiz Kid' programs include few gifted Hispanic pupils. Hispanic 'Whiz Kids' often left out. *San Jose Mercury News*, p. 1A.

Watson, A. (1989, December 4). Desegregation's aftermath. S.J. schools now seek integration, academic parity. *San Jose Mercury News*, p. 1B.

Watson, A. (1991a, May 30). Hispanic kids benefit little from S.J. Unified integration. *San Jose Mercury News*, p. 1A.

Watson, A. (1991b, June 2). Equal, but separate. Five years of busing have mixed kids in the classroom, but they have done little to bring their worlds together. *San Jose Mercury News*, p. 1L.

Weckstein, P. (1999). School reform and enforceable rights to quality education. In J. P. Heubert (Ed.), *Law and school reform: Six strategies for promoting educational equity*, pp. 306–389. New Haven: Yale University Press.

Weinberg, M. (1977). The relationship between school desegregation and academic achievement: A review of the research. In B. Levin & W. D. Hawley (Eds.), *The courts, social science, and school desegregation* (pp. 241–270). New Brunswick, New Jersey: Transaction Books.

Weinstein, R. S. (1976). Reading group membership in first grade: Teacher behaviors and pupil experience over time. *Journal of Educational Psychology, 68*(1), 103–116.

Wells, A. S., & Crain, R. L. (1994). Perpetuation theory and the long-term effects of school desegregation. *Review of Educational Research, 64*, 531.

Wells, A. S. & Oakes, J. (1996). Potential pitfalls of systemic reform: Early lessons from research on detracking. *Sociology of Education*, extra issue, p. 135–143.

Wells, A. S., & Oakes, J. (1998). Tracking, detracking, and the politics of educational reform: A sociological perspective. In C. A. Torres & T. Mitchell (Eds.), *Emerging issues in the sociology of education: Comparative perspectives* (pp. 155–180). Albany, NY: SUNY Press.

Wells, A. S. & Serna, I. (1996). The politics of culture: Understanding local political resistance to detracking in racially mixed schools. *Harvard Educational Review*, 66(1), 93–118.

Welner, K. & Oakes, J. (1996). (Li)Ability grouping: The new susceptibility of school tracking systems to legal challenges. *Harvard Educational Review*, 66(3), 451–470.

Welner, K., & Oakes, J. (2000). *Navigating the politics of detracking*. Arlington Heights, Illinois: Skylight Publishing.

West, K. C. (1994). A desegregation tool that backfired: Magnet schools and classroom segregation. *Yale Law Journal*, 103, p. 2567.

Wheelock, A. (1992). *Crossing the tracks: How "untracking" can save America's schools*. New York: New Press.

White, E. (1985, October 6). Shutting down San Jose High is unfair and racist [Opinion article]. *San Jose Mercury News*, p. 7F.

Wiehe, C. (1985, October 4). District plan punishes San Jose High hardest [Opinion article]. *San Jose Mercury News*, p. 7B.

Wilson, J. M. (1985, November 12). Desegregation protest isn't justified [Letter to the editor]. *San Jose Mercury News*, p. 6B.

Wisconsin v. Constantineau, 400 U.S. 433 (1971).

Wise, A. (1977). Why educational policies often fail: The hyperrationalization hypothesis. *Curriculum Studies*, 9, 43–57.

Wise, A. (1982). *Legislated learning: The bureaucratization of the American classroom* (2nd ed.). Berkeley, CA: University of California Press.

Wiser, M. (2000, August 15). School board split over ruling. *Rockford Register Star*, p. 1A.

Yonezawa, S. (1997). *Making decisions about students' lives: An interactive study of secondary school students' academic program selection*. Ph.D. dissertation, UCLA.

Young, I. M. (1990). *Justice and the politics of difference*. Princeton: Princeton University Press.

Index

309